Edited by
**BRIAN V. MARTINDALE, ANTHONY BATEMAN,
M   AEL CROWE and FRANK MARGISON**

P ychosis:
P ychological Approaches
a d their Effectiveness

Putting Psychotherapies at the Centre
of Treatment

GASKELL
for the International Society for the Psychological
Treatments of the Schizophrenias and other Psychoses
(ISPS)

British Library Cataloguing-in-Publication Data
A catalogue record for this book is available from
the British Library.
ISBN 1–901242–49–8

Distributed in North America
by Balogh International Inc.

The views presented in this book do not necessarily reflect those
of the Royal College of Psychiatrists, and the publishers are not
responsible for any error of omission or fact.

Gaskell is a registered trademark of the Royal College of Psychiatrists.

The Royal College of Psychiatrists is a registered charity (no. 228636).

Produced by Bell & Bain Limited, Thornliebank, Glasgow.

Contents

iii

About the editors

Dr Brian V. Martindale is a Member of the Board of the International Society for the Psychological Treatments of the Schizophrenias and Other Psychoses (ISPS) and Chairman of the UK Network of ISPS. Together with colleagues he organised the 12th International Symposium of the ISPS in London in 1997. He was a Founding Member and first Chairman (1991–97) of the European Federation of Psychoanalytic Psychotherapy in the Public Sector and is currently Western European Zone representative for psychiatry to the World Psychiatric Association. He is a psychoanalyst and Consultant Psychiatrist in Psychotherapy for the Ealing, Hammersmith and Fulham Mental Health NHS Trust in West London.

Dr Anthony Bateman is Consultant Psychiatrist in Psychotherapy at St Ann's Hospital, Haringey Healthcare, London and Honorary Senior Lecturer at Royal Free and University College Hospitals, London. He has been involved in psychotherapy research for a number of years and has a special interest in the treatment and outcome of borderline personality disorder as well as the integration of psychotherapy into psychiatric practice.

Dr Michael Crowe is Consultant Psychiatrist at the South London and Maudsley Trust and Honorary Senior Lecturer at the Institute of Psychiatry. He currently chairs the Joint Psychotherapy Department at the Maudsley, where he practises and teaches behavioural and cognitive therapy, couple relationship and sexual therapy. He also specialises in the treatment of patients with borderline disorders who repeatedly harm themselves.

Dr Frank Margison is Consultant Psychiatrist in Psychotherapy at Manchester Royal Infirmary. He has been involved in the development of the psychodynamic–interpersonal (Conversational) model of therapy for about 20 years, and more recently in outcome research and measures for psychotherapy.

Contributors

Jukka Aaltonen, Professor of Family Therapy, Jyväskylä University, PO Box 35, FIN-40351 Jyväskylä, Finland

Sonja Åbb (died 1998) formerly of South Stockholm Psychiatry, Sköntorpsvägen 29, 12038 Årsta, Sweden

Yrjö Alanen, Professor of Psychiatry (Emeritus), Vähämeenkatu 3C, FIN-20500 Turku, Finland

Ian Baguley, Programme Director, School of Nursing; Coupland III, University of Manchester, Oxford Road, Manchester M13 9PL, UK

Anthony Bateman, Consultant Psychiatrist in Psychotherapy, Halliwick Psychotherapy Unit, Haringey Healthcare, St Ann's Hospital, St Ann's Road, London N15 3TH, UK

Antony Butterworth, Pro-Vice Chancellor, Coupland III, University of Manchester, Oxford Road, Manchester M13 9PL, UK

Matthew J. Chinman, Instructor of Psychology, Department of Psychiatry, Yale University School of Medicine, 389 Whitney Avenue, New Haven, CT 06511, USA

Michael Crowe, Consultant Psychiatrist, South London and Maudsley Trust and Honorary Senior Lecturer, Institute of Psychiatry, Denmark Hill, London SE5 8AZ, UK

Johan Cullberg, Professor of Psychiatry, Department for Community Medicine, Parachute Project, PO Box 17533, S–11891 Stockholm, Sweden

Anthony S. David, Professor of Cognitive Neuropsychiatry, Institute of Psychiatry and GKT School of Medicine, Denmark Hill, London SE5 8AF, UK

Larry Davidson, Associate Professor of Psychiatry, Yale University School of Medicine, #160 CMHC, 34 Park Street, New Haven, Connecticut 06519, USA

Kieran Fahy, EDTA, Coupland III, University of Manchester, Oxford Road, Manchester M13 9PL, UK

Wayne S. Fenton, Director of Research, Chestnut Lodge Hospital, 500 West Montgomery Avenue, Rockville, Maryland 20850, USA

David Fowler, Consultant Clinical Psychologist, Senior Lecturer in Clinical Psychology School of Health, University of East Anglia, Norwich NR4 7TJ, UK

Philippa Garety, Professor of Clinical Psychology, Guy's, King's and St Thomas' School of Medicine, King's College, London, Department of Academic Clinical Psychology, 3rd Floor, Adamson Centre for Mental Health, St Thomas' Hospital, Lambeth Palace Road, London SE1 7EH, UK

Gillian Haddock, Senior Lecturer, Research and Teaching Building Department of Clinical Psychology, Withington Hospital, Nell Lane, Withington, Manchester, M20 8LR, UK

Peter Hayward, Clinical Psychologist, Institute of Psychiatry, London SE5 8AF, UK

Jan O. Johannessen, Chief Psychiatrist, Rogaland Psychiatric Services, P.O. Box 1163, Hillevåg, 4095 Stavanger, Norway

Nick Kanas, Professor of Psychiatry, University of California, San Francisco; and Associate Chief, Mental Health Service (116A), Department of Veterans Affairs Medical Center, 4150 Clement Street, San Francisco, California 94121, USA

Roisin Kemp, Senior Lecturer and Consultant Psychiatrist, Royal Free School of Medicine, Pond Street, London NW3 2QG, UK

Elizabeth Kuipers, Professor of Clinical Psychology, Institute of Psychiatry, King's College London; Department of Psychology, Institute of Psychiatry, De Crespigny Park, London SE5 8AF, UK

Stacey Lambert, Associate Research Scientist, Department of Psychiatry, Yale University School of Medicine, 34 Park Street, New Haven, Connecticut 06519, USA

Stuart Lancashire, Research Fellow, Section of Psychiatric Nursing, Institute of Psychiatry, 12 Windsor Walk, Denmark Hill, London SE5 8AF, UK

Tor K. Larsen, Research Fellow, Rogaland Psychiatric Services and University of Oslo, P.O. Box 1163, Hillevåg, 4095 Stavanger, Norway

Klaus Lehtinen, Senior Lecturer, Tampere University Medical School, P.O.Box 607, FIN-33101 Tampere, Finland

Ville Lehtinen, Research Professor, National Research and Development Centre for Welfare and Health, P.O.Box 220, FIN-00531 Helsinki, Finland

Frank Margison, Consultant Psychiatrist in Psychotherapy, Gaskell Psychotherapy Centre, Manchester Royal Infirmary, Swinton Grove, Manchester M13 0EU, UK

Brian V. Martindale, Consultant Psychiatrist in Psychotherapy & Honorary Clinical Senior Lecturer, Imperial College School of Medicine; John Connolly Unit, Ealing Hammersmith and Fulham NHS Mental Health Trust, Uxbridge Road, Southall, Middlesex, UB1 3EU, UK

William R. McFarlane, Chairman, Department of Psychiatry, Maine Medical Center, 22 Bramhall Street, Portland, Maine 04102, USA
Thomas H. McGlashan, Yale Psychiatric Institute, Yale University, 184 Liberty Street, New Haven, Connecticut 06510, USA
Patrick McGorry, University of Melbourne Department of Psychiatry, Early Psychosis Prevention and Intervention Centre (EPPIC), Locked Bag 10, Parkville 3052, Australia
Loren R. Mosher, Director, Soteria Associates, Clinical Professor of Psychiatry, UCSD Adjunct Professor of Psychiatry, USUHS, Bethesda, MD 2616 Angell Ave, San Diego, California 92122, USA
Viljo Räkköläinen, Medical Director, Kupittaa Hospital, Kunnallissairaalantie 20, FIN-27000 Turku, Finland
Roberta Siani, Clinical Psychologist, Department of Medicine and Public Health, Section of Psychiatry, Psychotherapy Service, University of Verona, Ospedale Policlinico, 37134 Verona, Italy
Orazio Siciliani, Professor of Psychotherapy, Department of Medicine and Public Health, Section of Psychiatry, Psychotherapy Service, University of Verona, Ospedale Policlinico, 37134 Verona, Italy
William H. Sledge, Professor of Psychiatry, Yale University School of Medicine, 34 Park Street, New Haven, Connecticut 06519, USA
David A. Stayner, Assistant Professor of Psychiatry, Yale University School of Medicine, 34 Park Street, New Haven, Connecticut 06519, USA
Nick Tarrier, Professor of Clinical Psychology, Research and Teaching Building, Department of Clinical Psychology, Withington Hospital, Nell Lane, Withington, Manchester M20 8LR, UK
Greta Thorén, Psychologist, South Stockholm Psychiatry, Sköntorpsvägen 29, 12038 Årsta, Sweden
Per Vaglum, Faculty of Medicine, University of Oslo, PO Box 1111, Blindern 0317, Oslo, Norway

Acknowledgements

I would like to give credit to my fellow editors, Anthony Bateman, Michael Crowe and Frank Margison, who have been a great help throughout the preparation of this book. The Board Members of ISPS gave firm support to me for the idea of publishing an evidence-oriented book. I would also like to thank all the authors who have been so cooperative in the preparation of their chapters and revisions, and for being patient during the final phases. Philippa Martindale has been most helpful in the early phases of the editing before the book was passed to Gaskell for the final editing. Thanks are due to David Jago, Head of Publications at the Royal College of Psychiatrists, for his advice and support as well as to his staff, especially Zoë Stagg, Assistant Scientific Editor. Anonymous Gaskell reviewers made helpful suggestions after the first proposal and again in the final stages. Finally, the greatest thanks are due to my wife and children for tolerating the inevitable and considerable inroads into family life that are inevitable when preparing a book and when one does not have an academic post.

Brian V. Martindale
Senior Editor

Preface

The purpose of this book is to describe and discuss a range of psychological therapies for people with psychotic disorders. It is based on the thinking that lay behind the 'Building Bridges' International Conference, London, October 1997, in which many of the authors of this book participated. As was the aim of the conference, this book highlights information about psychologically based interventions in psychosis in order to 'build bridges' between professionals from different mental health disciplines who use different models of treatment. Hopefully it will also build bridges with planners, politicians, administrators and user organisations concerned with the provision of services for persons vulnerable to psychosis.

By focusing on the psychological treatments of psychosis, this book intends to play a part in promoting a better balance and integration between psychological and pharmacological treatments than has often been the case (Clinical Standards Advisory Group, 1995; Jones et al, 1996; Lehman et al, 1998). This integration is particularly lacking in much of contemporary psychiatry.

With authors contributing from several countries, we hope that it will motivate both clinicians and researchers working with people with psychotic disorders in diverse settings. We also hope that it will be of value to professionals involved with developing policies or managing mental health and social services who have responsibility for providing interventions aimed not only at symptom reduction and (re)admission rates, but also at quality of life and social function.

Our goals are:
- (a) to bring to wider attention a range of psychologically-based approaches;
- (b) to give an outline of the rationale for each therapy;
- (c) to summarise how each therapy is conducted;
- (d) to give some research evidence of effectiveness.

The authors have provided extensive references to fuller descriptions of the therapies and relevant research. We do not claim to have been comprehensive in terms of describing all the psychological approaches that may have a part to play in services for patients with psychosis. We think that the chapters will serve as evidence that a number of psychological treatments and interventions have an important part to play in psychotic disorders, that these treatment approaches should be made more widely available, and that investment in clinical training programmes and support for further research in the psychological treatments should have rich rewards.

The International Society for the Psychological Treatments of the Schizophrenias and Other Psychoses

The International Society for the Psychological Treatments of the Schizophrenias and Other Psychoses (ISPS) is led by distinguished clinicians and researchers and has been promoting international conferences in different parts of the Western World since 1956. The ISPS provides active international support for interested clinicians and researchers. The ISPS is particularly well represented in Scandinavian countries. In the latter, the implementation and integration of psychological therapies in mainstream mental health provision is generally more advanced than in many other Western countries. The ISPS will be supporting the development of national and local ISPS groups. In turn, these will be active in sharing information, training, supporting research and organising conferences, etc., with the primary task of making more professionals available who have skills in implementing effective psychologically based interventions and integrating these, where appropriate, with other therapies.

For further information about the ISPS contact:
The International Society for the Psychological Treatments of the Schizophrenias and other Psychoses (ISPS)
c/o Seprep
Jernbanetorget 4A
N–0154 Oslo, Norway
Tel +47 2310 3777
Fax +47 2310 3779
E-mail: isps@isps.org   Web site: www.isps.org

References

CLINICAL STANDARDS ADVISORY GROUP (1995) *Schizophrenia, Vol. 1.* London: The Stationery Office.
JONES, E., ALEXANDER, J. & HOWORTH, P. (1966) Out of hospital: after-care for people with schizophrenia. *Health Trends,* **28,** 128–131.
LEHMAN, A. F., STEINWACHS, D. M. & THE SCHIZOPHRENIA PORT CO-INVESTIGATORS OF THE PROJECT (1998) Patterns of usual care for schizophrenia: intial results from the Schizophrenia Patient Outcomes Research Team (PORT) client survey. *Schizophrenia Bulletin,* **24,** 11–20.

Foreword

This book lies at the heart of psychiatry as a modern 21st century discipline and will challenge those who wish that psychiatry could be confined to a neuroscience perspective only. It will also challenge those who remain outside what they characterise (often without conceptual knowledge) as the medical 'diagnostic' model.

Schizophrenia, or the group of schizophrenias, is not only a universal disorder, but has been shown to have a better prognosis in non-Western countries. Nature and nurture, biology and sociology mutually interact. The expression of genes is, therefore, determined in a substantial measure by the environment – disability is linked to family expectation, stigma and employment prospects.

The 'brain part' of psychiatry can, unless tempered by the mind, lead to a distancing from the interpersonal dimensions, an excessive preoccupation with medication issues may overlook the social consequences of weight gain, sexual underperformance and dyskinesia and the effects they have on self-esteem and personal image in an autonomous individualistic competitive world.

As this pioneer book makes clear, psychological therapies require well-trained therapists who are required not only to handle their own fears of proximity to disturbed and occasionally dangerous thinking, but also to retain their familiarity with biological processes and the evidence base for the effectiveness of antipsychotic medications.

Psychiatry is based firmly within both the biological and social sciences and draws similarly on developmental and cognitive psychology. As Barrett (1996) discovered in his participant observation study in a mental hospital in Australia, a complete team should contain within it the necessary expertise to manage the group of patients who suffer from psychosis – but only in exceptional cases will a single member of the team, including the psychotherapy enthusiast, possess all those skills.

The psychotherapy skills described in this book (ranging from cognitive to dynamic, humanistic to educational) are linked by a deep sense of humanity and an understanding that an interpersonal approach may reduce the stigmatisation of the individual and that people with these disorders remain people – and are less likely to be socially excluded. The evidence summarised in these chapters would suggest that these therapies may not only prevent relapse and reduce disability, but are also an important component of a curative approach.

This multi-author book should be thoroughly read, by trainees and consultant psychiatrists and also by others working in the mental health field. The complex psychological skills described should become a core competence for consultant psychiatrists irrespective of sub-speciality; the impact of the schizophrenias and related psychoses span all ages of man.

Symbolically, Shakespeare does indeed need to come again to 'Broadmoor', and psychological metaphors can touch the depths. This interpersonal approach to the psychoses now needs to be appropriately prioritised. The necessary training and supervision needs to be costed into mental health service budgets. The methods should be core competencies for psychiatrists and should not be left for others to undertake alone.

It was sad that my late brother, Murray, could not speak at the conference that provided the energy for this wide-ranging book. Nevertheless (and not for the first time), he has indirectly influenced a therapeutic approach that will continue to inspire others. Brian Martindale and his co-editors and contributors have aptly summarised the science and the practice of psychological treatments for severe psychoses that older generations of psychiatrists were never taught. Life-long learning is just that.

This is a 'state of the art' book.

References

BARRETT, R. (1996) *The Psychiatric Team and the Social Definition of Schizophrenia: An Anthropological Study of Person and Illness.* Cambridge: Cambridge University Press.

John Cox
President, Royal College of Psychiatrists

1 Introduction

BRIAN V. MARTINDALE, ANTONY BATEMAN, MICHAEL CROWE and FRANK MARGISON

Biological and psychological approaches – a rapprochement is needed

In recent decades, much of the research emphasis in schizophrenia has been focused on brain sciences. The 1990s were described as 'the decade of the brain' – in view of the rapid development of knowledge in neurosciences. There have been promising developments in psychoses stemming from these approaches. Important parallel research has taken place in the fields of genetics, neuroanatomy, neuropsychology and pharmacology. However, there has been considerable concern that this emphasis has not been matched by comparable investment into psychological perspectives, let alone attempts to investigate the relationships between these multiple domains (Strauss, 1992; Robbins, 1993).

This book represents an attempt to redress the balance and emphasises a considerable range of theoretical frameworks, therapies and settings that are clinically useful for the individual, family and even community affected by psychosis.

The ongoing work of Tienari may be one favourable illustration of the otherwise relatively untapped potential of looking at the interrelationship of biology and psychology in schizophrenia research (Tienari *et al*, 1994). Tienari researches the relationship between heredity and family environment in schizophrenia. In this ongoing, painstaking work conducted over decades, adopted children whose biological parents have schizophrenia are followed up and compared with adopted children whose biological parents have no evidence of schizophrenia. Sophisticated blind measurements are made of the functioning of the adopting family. The likelihood of schizophrenia, other psychoses and severe mental illness is greater in those whose biological parents had schizophrenia, confirming previous studies that have indicated a genetic contribution to some cases

1

of schizophrenia. However, the increased incidence was found only in those where family functioning had been rated as disturbed. The psychological status of each parent functioned independently and cumulatively as a predictor. These research findings open and re-open many doors. They invite questions about the specific nature of those aspects of the well-functioning family that are protective to a genetically vulnerable child (the latter fact probably being unknown to the adopting parents). The identification of these protective psychological factors may be one area that perhaps should now be given research priority. Otherwise, it will not be possible to make full use of the preventive possibilities that will surely soon come from neurobiological research which will lead to even narrower identification of the markers and traits predisposing some people to schizophrenia. The phenomena described by Tienari can be understood from several psychosocial perspectives. The psychodynamic model of "holding" (Winnicott, 1961) or "containment" (Bion, 1959, 1962) may be relevant to conceptualising these protective functions, as may Vgotsky's (1966) theories. The family system's concept of 'low expressed emotion' relevant to relapse may have identified a similar mode of interaction between the growing child at risk and the primary care-takers. Further research is needed to clarify the possibility that such 'protective' families may induce wide-ranging and flexible coping strategies.

While exhorting those pursuing the biology and genetics of schizophrenia to pay close attention to their interaction with environmental and psychological factors, those interested in the psychological origins of psychosis and psychological therapies also need to be aware of neuropsychological findings such as difficulties of cognition, attention and memory in a percentage of people who go on to develop schizophrenia (Dawson & Nuechterlein, 1984; Nuechterlein & Dawson, 1984; Sharma & Harvey, 1999). This is vital if misunderstandings are not to be repeated, when, for example, earlier generations of psychotherapists made assumptions of cerebral integrity in schizophrenia. We would draw attention particularly to the work of Hogarty *et al* (1995) and Grotstein (1996), who have made significant contributions to modifying psychotherapies to take account of neurobiological differences such as those of attention capacity and working memory in some cases of schizophrenia.

Rise of drug treatments for schizophrenia and neglect of psychological and psychosocial approaches

When something new is discovered there is often a tendency to exaggerate its implications and to neglect the value of what has gone before. There is no doubt that the introduction of neuroleptics was of considerable benefit to many patients (Dixon & Lehman, 1995). However, their arrival also seems to have spurred a reductionistic belief in the possibility of physical explanations and treatments being not only necessary, but also sufficient in schizophrenia. Monistic and reductionistic thinking in many approaches to schizophrenia have been well discussed by Robbins (1993). Treatment has recently reflected an unbalanced focus – tending towards the medically defined symptoms of schizophrenia rather than the psychosocial contexts of the disorder (Strauss, 1992). This has had the destructive consequence of relegating to the periphery of care skilled psychological support and treatment (Clinical Standards Advisory Group, 1995; Jones *et al*, 1996; Lehman *et al*, 1998). This is also referred to in Chapter 13, where McGorry refers to the serious consequences of the reductionistic approach following the introduction of neuroleptics. To understand patients and to respond with skill to their human and developmental needs, professionals need to rediscover the personal and psychological perspective.

The lack is particularly reflected in the impoverished nature of contemporary training for many psychiatrists who often do not gain any experience of extended therapeutic relationships with patients. Psychiatric nursing for patients with psychoses can easily become just an extension of the medical approach with the relatively narrow, albeit important, focus on symptom monitoring and checking for adherence with medication, often administered by injections (Woof *et al*, 1988). In the UK, there has also been a radical change in the practice and philosophy of mental health social work. It is now the exception to find a social worker with either the skills or the remit to carry out casework with service users with psychoses that is centred on a therapeutic relationship. These changes in role were noted in the published review *NHS Psychotherapy Services in England* (Department of Health, 1996). Fleck (1995), who has witnessed similar changes over many decades in the USA, has written eloquently on the wide-ranging retrogressions in the provision of mental health services and psychological care in the face of some progression. The situation is such that Garety (Chapter 2) reports that those involved in some cognitive therapy trials were not expecting significant beneficial effects from those control groups who were offered supportive counselling and befriending "delivered by skilled therapists. The latter set out to establish a therapeutic relationship, to use empathic counselling techniques and to talk reflectively about the lives and experiences of the service users". This statement indicates the extent to which the importance of good interpersonal counselling skills seems to have become disregarded as being of therapeutic importance in routine

4 Martindale et al

psychiatric practice with people with psychotic disorders. Chapter 2 outlines the relative benefits of cognitive therapies, supportive counselling and 'treatment as usual'.

We hope that this book will play a significant role in the rehabilitation of psychotherapeutic skills as a necessary foundation in any treatment with people with psychotic vulnerabilities. Chapter 7 by Davidson *et al* illustrates the profound differences in outcome between an approach that took careful note of what the patients had to say and one that assumed that the professionals 'knew best'.

In spite of the advances stemming from neuroleptic medication, their limitations and potential side-effects are insufficiently stressed (Karon, 1989). Roth (1986) estimates that, for 35% of people with schizophrenia, drugs made "little or no lasting impression" and Kane's review of more recent literature puts the figure at closer to 50% (Kane, 1996). It is not widely known that the majority of pharmaceutical trials in psychosis are of short-term duration (6–8 weeks) (Geddes on behalf of the RCP/BPS Guideline Development Group, 2000). In many cases, medication leads to a reduction in symptoms rather than complete removal. Positive symptoms tend to respond to a greater degree than negative ones. There had been a tendency to continue to raise the dosage of drug when clinical response was inadequate (Bollini *et al*, 1994). Patients may be maintained for long periods of time on dosages many times in excess of that recently recognised as needed for dopaminergic blockade, and relapse may still occur. It has now been shown that even 2 mg of haloperidol (which is associated with a mean dopamine receptor (D_2) occupancy of 67%) can produce an effective clinical response (Remington *et al*, 1998). The side-effects of larger doses are often physically, emotionally and socially disabling and tardive dyskinesia is often irreversible. The newer atypical antipsychotic drugs are being carefully evaluated. A recent and careful review of the evidence indicates that there is not yet proof that these newer medications are superior to the older neuroleptics in efficacy or side-effect profile if the latter are used in lower dosages. Longer term trials are needed comparing lower doses of typical with atypical neuroleptics (Geddes on behalf of the RCP/BPS Guideline Development Group, 2000). Several chapters in this book go some way to beginning to gather evidence for the effectiveness of an alternative approach of low dosage neuroleptics combined with good psychological care and therapies. It does need emphasising that, for the majority, optimal medication helps with only some aspects of the struggles that persons with psychotic disorders have in living fulfilling lives with good quality relationships (Lehman, 1998).

Clinicians have observed that in recent years more patients with psychotic vulnerabilities seem to be actively seeking psychological help.

It is suggested that this might partly correspond to the fact that the newer medications, besides their benefits on positive symptoms and lower rate of obvious side-effects, do not have the profound enervating effects on patients on too large doses of the typical neuroleptics. It also needs to be remembered that something like 30% is the usual rate of spontaneous recovery in placebo controls of trials evaluating neuroleptic drugs (Karon, 1989) and that there are reports of some groups of patients who have a better prognosis without medication than with (Hamilton *et al*, 1963; Paul *et al*, 1972; Mosher *et al*, 1976; Paul & Lentz, 1977; Rappaport *et al*, 1978; also see Chapter 12.)

It is clear that further research is needed into the subgroups of patients with schizophrenia in which neuroleptic medication is more likely to be helpful and those in which it may be less so or even unhelpful to be given on a routine basis. Vaughn & Leff's work on expressed emotion in families leads them to state "it is clear ... that drugs make no difference for patients living in low expressed emotion homes" (Vaughn & Leff, 1976). The Kupittaa study from Finland, outlined in Chapter 12, points to one direction for further research: in the subgroup of patients with schizophrenia who were identified as having broken down in the context of an identity crisis, more than half were effectively treated without neuroleptics at any time and 90% without neuroleptics during follow-up. None of them were psychotic at follow-up 4–8 years later.

Structure of the book

The recent striking advances in cognitive–behavioural approaches are highlighted in the early chapters covering cognitive therapy for psychosis and adherence therapy. Family interventions also have a well-established role. McFarlane (Chapter 4) reviews some of the modern integrative approaches to work with families including his own work with 'family groups'. Baguley *et al* (Chapter 5) show the importance of integrating training in these methods with evaluation of both adherence to the model and of clinical outcomes and also the need for changes in service delivery to use the newly trained professionals most effectively.

Kanas (Chapter 6) describes the development of integrated group approaches particularly suited to patients with schizophrenia. When considering hospital versus community settings for treatment, Davidson *et al* (Chapter 7) show that the implementation of treatment programmes needs to pay much closer attention to the users' views and needs and the social function of the hospital if community treatments are to be effective. Fenton & Mosher (Chapter 8) examine evidence of effectiveness of a community residential unit as an alternative to hospital admission in a randomised sudy.

Individual psychoanalytical approaches have suffered from the relative lack of formal research evaluation, although we argue that there has been more research than is commonly realised. In Chapter 9, by Siani & Siciliani, there is an attempt to integrate the underlying theory of the approach (derived from Kohut's work on the self) with relevant measurement strategies.

In the next section of the book, the emphasis is on early interventions and the need-adapted psychotherapeutic approaches pioneered in Finland – but now increasingly implemented in other Scandinavian countries and further afield. We have invited authors from Norway, Sweden and Finland to contribute to this book. Johannessen (Chapter 11) discusses various forms of prevention in psychosis and shows that it was possible to radically reduce the duration of untreated psychosis in a Norwegian community. Cullberg (Chapter 10) demonstrates, in a Swedish pilot study, the effectiveness of the need-adapted psychosocial approach as an alternative to an in-patient hospital focus. The penultimate chapter is an account of a number of projects developing in Finland – the home country of the need-adapted approach. It is striking in the simplicity of the underlying humane and patient-centred principles of care at the level of the individual patient but also highlights the daunting complexity of changing the organisation of care at a national level. In these chapters, it is most important to note the emphasis on the consistency and quality of the primary therapeutic relationship with the patient and also his or her family. This could be a factor of the greatest significance that distinguishes the Scandinavian approaches from much of contemporary psychiatry with its emphasis on throughput and where it is often the least trained psychiatrists who are on rotating training schemes who are directly involved with the person with psychosis.

Finally, McGorry (Chapter 13) draws together many of the themes from elsewhere in the book in giving an account of the integrated approach to treatment in his Australian service. Essentially, he argues for comprehensive holistic services adequate to deal with the complexity of schizophrenia. However, his approach is a model of pragmatism (while keeping in mind fundamental principles) in the thorough evaluation of community and individual needs and outcomes.

Approaches to research

Several of the chapters remind us of some basic principles of research on complex disorders. For example, with disorders characterised by a typically long, often relapsing and complex course it is essential to have long-term follow-up. This is difficult to achieve, but the cohort method is used to good effect in the need-adapted study.

The second principle is in the use of measures that are not only psychometrically robust, but also meaningful to users, families, commissioners and clinicians. Outcome measures for studies in schizophrenia have tended to focus on either positive symptoms or functional deficit. Several of the studies reported here attempt to use a wider approach, including health economic measures and assessment of social function from a positive as well as a negative viewpoint. Nevertheless, we lack widely used instruments that allow comparisons across the diverse treatment settings described here. Ideally, such instruments will balance generalisations with theoretical coherence, but often these goals are found to be incompatible.

Developing treatments go through an initial stage of single case studies, open trials and randomised controlled trials to achieve formal testing (to assess efficacy), and into the dissemination stage where clinical effectiveness in service settings and with less selected patient groups is undertaken. This somewhat simplified model is the orthodox approach to assessing the usefulness of any new treatment. This view of evidence-based practice is implied in some chapters, whereas others emphasise what might be summarised as 'practice-based evidence', in that the focus is on service delivery, and how it can be improved.

Without going into detailed debate about the advantages and limitations of the randomised controlled trial as the 'gold standard' of research (see Margison *et al*, 2000, for a fuller discussion), there are some specific issues raised by the research reported in this book. First, there is the difficulty in defining the nature of the intervention being tested when the treatments are complex and multi-modal, as, for example, in different in-patient settings. The difficulty in defining precisely the intervention being tested leads to subsequent problems in defining an appropriate 'no treatment' or 'comparison' control group. This difficulty is not unique to this field; similar problems of research design influence research in, for example, therapeutic communities. A further difficulty arises in the problem of independence of measurement. Most inferential tests are based on the assumption that each subject is, effectively, independent of all other subjects. It is hard to sustain this assumption if the intervention itself incorporates common elements (such as groups, community meetings and community living experiences) involving several subjects together.

Cognitive therapy for psychosis

It is only in the last decade that this approach has been considered to be potentially useful in psychosis. Garety *et al* review the impressive developments that have been made (Chapter 2) in cognitive therapy for psychosis. Successful trials were initially reported with people who had persistent/resistant positive symptoms of hallucinations and delusions in the face of adequate medication. In more recent years trials have been undertaken for cognitive approaches in acute episodes. These trials have been successful in showing significant advantages over the interventions offered in control groups. Readers will be impressed by the extent to which the approach described in this chapter involves a focus on achieving and maintaining a therapeutic relationship and the extent to which the patient and his or her individual life experiences and experience of psychosis are placed at the centre of the approach. Garety underlines the importance of these less specific factors as well as the specificity of cognitive–behavioural techniques for a range of symptoms that the person with psychosis may experience.

Garety's summary of the theoretical basis on which cognitive therapy of psychosis is built, gives weight to abnormalities in cognitive or information processing. Although a debate cannot be the main focus of Chapter 2, one possible explanation for the cognitive distortion is the 'unmanageable' quantity and quality of certain affects that characterise psychosis. Her cases suggest that a model of psychotic breakdown might be developed that deals with cognitive distortion as a pragmatic way of getting at psychotic thinking. However, other models may be developed that integrate the cognitive distortion with the view from psychodynamic theory of 'unmanageable affects'. A testable theory of disturbance of affective–cognitive regulation is needed to move the research field into a new integrative approach to psychopathology.

It is clear from Garety's description that cognitive therapy has considerable potential with a range of symptoms in schizophrenia. In contrast to the need-adapted or integrated approaches it is particularly suited to evaluation by randomised controlled trials that have already demonstrated its effectiveness in skilled hands. It seems distinctly possible that future research may well show that its role could be considerably extended in influencing the overall quality of life of the person vulnerable to psychosis if it were to pay even greater attention to the premorbid vulnerabilities of the person prone to psychosis (Martindale, 1998). In that case it may be necessary to offer much longer term interventions than in the research carried out to date. It is possible that it has the potential to do this as the cognitive approaches described include forming a personal relationship with the patient with psychosis and showing interest in his or her personal experiences. To this extent cognitive therapy is an approach that has recovered something very important in the treatment of patients with schizophrenia that had been lost in previous decades.

Chapter 3 is on 'compliance therapy', which is centred around the view that most people will benefit considerably if they take regular antipsychotic medication and that, once taking medication regularly, they will be much more amenable to rational discussion about their problems – including those of medication. Therefore, measures that lead to greater adherence to medication will generally be in the patient's interest. It is important to note in Chapter 3, as in Chapter 2, just how much emphasis is placed on establishing a collaborative non-judgemental therapeutic relationship, along with an empathic reflective attitude and related features. These components form the bedrock upon which the issues of medication are worked through, using additional techniques that combine features of motivational interviewing and cognitive–behavioural techniques with respect to medication. The evidence points to this being an effective approach requiring a relatively small amount of time from a trained person. As the authors themselves state, the term 'compliance therapy' may be misunderstood to be a form of authoritarian coercion with respect to medication. In fact, the authors point out that success with this approach leads to "the maximum of consensus between patients, carers and professionals".

Family interventions

The confirmation of genetic contributions, of neuropsychological and neuroanatomical differences and the positive contributions of neuroleptics have all contributed to a turning away from work with families. Tienari's research, referred to earlier, is a notable exception (Tienari *et al*, 1994). Family therapy interventions, validated more than two decades ago, demonstrated that substantial reductions in relapse and admission rates can be achieved (Vaughn & Leff, 1976), but they are still rarely implemented (Dare, 1996; Lehman, 1998) and very few psychiatrists have trained in these approaches. It is likely that there are two major reasons.

First, there is a widespread resistance to the idea that the quality of family life may have a role in altering the risk of the disorder or its relapse – probably a fear that professionals will be seen as blaming families. This area has been well discussed by Johnstone (1993). There is a great risk that, in this emotionally laden atmosphere, the evidence for the role of families in protecting children with genetic vulnerabilities, may be ignored (Tienari *et al*, 1994). If professionals have 'blamed' families in the past, greater skill and training of clinicians is now needed to gain positive help from families rather than an avoidance of family work.

A second and related reason to minimise psychological contact with individuals and families may be the psychological stress for the professional (Searles, 1959; Kuipers, 1998; Martindale, 2000). Professionals may not always be conscious of the nature of their involvement or disengagement and there is again a risk that professionals may feel criticised when they experience stress. Leaders of mental health services need to create settings that are emotionally secure enough for staff to be able to look at psychological factors within the professional system that may interfere with best practice. It is usually only the maturest of organisations that have the capacity to do this. In recent years there has been much greater field research into such organisational factors favouring or hindering the work of mental health professionals (see, for example, Obholzer & Roberts, 1994).

McFarlane's work in Chapter 4 describes the re-establishment of family work in schizophrenia growing out of and beyond the psycho-educational model. This approach breaks with the earlier family therapy models that focused on family malfunction with all the attendant risks of 'fault or blame finding'. One way that McFarlane's model tries to avoid this is to refer explicitly in family meetings to schizophrenia as a "medical illness". Making a good alliance with the family is essential from the beginning as it helps patients and families to identify their own therapeutic goals. Compared with earlier psychological approaches, McFarlane, like other contemporary psychosocial researchers (Hogarty *et al*, 1995), advocates a 'slowly, slowly' approach, stabilising each phase before moving to the next. There is a conscious effort from the beginning to identify strengths within the family. McFarlane's chapter describes the principles of the family education model and then moves on to the multiple family method in which therapeutic work takes place involving several families treated together, each with a member who has had psychotic breakdowns. McFarlane reports a series of impressive outcome research findings into multiple family groups for the rehabilitation of the patient with psychosis. It will be clear how much the multiple family approach is a further practical extension of an ideology that puts at its heart the utilisation of the family as a positive resource of support, ideas and creativity. The multiple family approach, which includes active encouragement of socialisation between families, contributes greatly to the reversal of the tendency to social isolation of the patient with schizophrenia and his or her family. McFarlane's clinical research extends multiple family work to the vocational field. The outcomes are promising for multiple family groups, with reductions in relapse and readmission rates compared with single family therapies and improved success rates in vocational rehabilitation – let alone the likely considerable cost benefits. There is also a high rate of cooperation from patients and their families. However, there needs to be appropriate caution, and there is a need to examine issues such as generalisability. There is a need for further replication under tightly controlled conditions with detailed examination of health economic information. Nevertheless, the approach seems promising, and very worthy of further research.

McFarlane makes reference to the basic training and ongoing supervision requirements for family approaches. Research is now needed into the training requirements for mental health professionals to implement into routine practice a range of effective methods from research conditions so as to be able to sustain such good results. Support from clinical and administrative hierarchies is clearly essential and this is substantiated in Chapter 5 by Baguley *et al*. They discuss a university-based training for mental health staff aimed at bringing into clinical practice skills shown to be clinically effective in research settings. Though the particular training has three main modules (problem-centred case management; family work; and psychological management of psychosis) the research evaluation described in Chapter 5 focuses on cognitive–behavioural family management skills. The main findings confirm that, though the course does give trainees the clinical skills intended, there are problems related to the dynamics of the institutions and the organisation of casework in the teams to which the trainees return. These militate against significant amounts of family work actually being undertaken by many of the trainees. This is compounded by the lack of ongoing supervision and clinical peer support for that work. Baguley *et al* state that these sobering findings are found in similar training programmes that have been evaluated, such as those of Corrigan *et al* (1992), Kavanagh *et al* (1993) and Fadden (1997). A strategic approach involving a 'cascade' approach to training with sound institutional support may be pre-requisites for the generalisability of these hard-won skills. This has been taking place in Western Lapland (as described in Chapter 12) and also in the West Midlands area of the UK (Fadden, 1999).

Groups and social functioning

It is now well established (Alanen, 1997; Olin *et al*, 1998) that there has often been a deterioration in social relationships and social involvement for some time prior to a schizophrenic illness. Certainly, a psychotic episode and its aftermath is often characterised by severe disruptions in such relationships with multiple implications for quality of life. It would, therefore, seem logical that cautious exposure to therapeutic group situations might be an appropriate setting for clarification of social difficulties and therapeutic endeavours towards improvement of interpersonal relating. Previous hesitation about this approach may have been linked to the theory that patients with schizophrenia had reduced ability to 'screen out' environmental stresses, and, hence, group approaches may expose the patient to 'toxic' confrontations with other group members.

Chapter 6 by Kanas starts by reflecting on the outcome research literature into group therapies over two decades, looking at different theoretical approaches. Though the review was not fully systematic, and nearly all the outcome studies had some flaws in their design, all groups tended to be more effective than no group controls, but there was considerable variation according to the main theoretical approach. As a consequence, Kanas has developed a new model that combines the most useful aspects of previous approaches – the integrative approach. Depending on the phase of illness, the aims are to use group settings to enable the members: (a) to work together on better managment of psychotic symptoms; and (b) to work on difficulties in interpersonal relationships. Kanas describes the ways in which, based on his review of the literature, he thinks groups are best organised and conducted, how topics are selected and how these aspects differ from groups for people with non-psychotic disorders. In Kanas's view, groups should be one of a range of therapies for people with psychotic vulnerabilities; issues such as medication dosage are considered in a different setting, except where there are interpersonal consequences. The results of this integrative model, with the focus modified according to whether the groups were of in-patients or out-patients, seem to indicate that groups are very acceptable to patients and are experienced as helpful, with few drop-outs.

Kanas reports out-patient group research, carried out four months after termination, demonstrating marked differences between group-treated patients and controls in how well patients felt that they were relating to others and how well they were coping with psychotic symptoms. Preliminary research indicates that the methods can be taught to other therapists. Clearly the group approach has considerable potential for further development. An important question for further research is to evaluate the potential value of a longer term group setting as an effective and economic way for some persons with psychotic vulnerabilities. It is worth noting in this respect that Kanas observes that in 'repeater' groups, more 'sophisticated' topics are addressed including long-standing maladaptive patterns of behaviour.

The chapter by Davidson *et al* (Chapter 7) is an interesting extension of group work into the community. It focuses on the problem of multiple and costly readmissions (nearly 40% of patients). They found a medical approach focusing on objective and external criteria and offering education about relapse and readmission prevention to be ineffective. In contrast to this medical approach, therefore, they actively undertook research work to listen closely to the patients' own subjective accounts of their experience of their lives both in hospital and in the community. They found that there were three central types of issue that had not been taken into account sufficiently but played a significant role in readmission and had made the relapse prevention programme ineffective. These central themes related to the experience in the community to which patients were discharged: social isolation, demoralisation and disconnection from services. In contrast to professional beliefs, hospital was experienced as a positive experience for the patients, on account of both material provision and receipt of human care. Research efforts were directed towards those patients who were readmitted within three months of a previous admission. The intervention that was put into place was a modified assertive outreach programme with a high degree of support for consumer-led outreach and support, group community and recreational activities as well as clinical coordination. It was aimed at meeting the basic needs of patients who had had difficulty meeting these themselves while living in the community. Patients were provided with transport to a range of group activities the patients played a major part in organising.

The initial findings reported in Chapter 7 and are promising. Patients with a psychotic diagnosis seem to benefit most with a fourfold decrease in hospital admissions and a reduction by a factor of 32 in the number of hospital days compared with the (non-randomised) controls. A much larger randomised control study is now in progress looking at many additional measurements.

Fenton & Mosher's study (described in Chapter 8) has some features that overlap with those of Cullberg's paper (Chapter 10). Fenton & Mosher emphasise the relatively fixed nature of the budgetary climate within which most mental health services operate. As has already been stated, hospital care for patients with schizophrenia consumes a very large percentage of most budgets. If savings can be made from this expense, it may be the most effective way of releasing funds for improved psychosocial and pharmacological treatments and preventive services. In their randomised study, voluntary patients were allocated to traditional hospital care or to a local residential crisis home taking up to eight residents. They found that costs were reduced by 37% in the residential crisis home, that it was more acceptable to residents, that there was no difference in clinical effectiveness at discharge or six-month follow-up and that 87% of admissions could be contained in the residential setting (the residential setting provides a supportive, normalising environment, but does not offer formal treatments in the way that the study by Cullberg in Chapter 10 does). This study by Fenton & Mosher is important in providing more rigorous evaluation than in other studies of the comparative effectiveness of crisis residential care compared with hospital, and suggests an important way in which funds could be released for community treatments by reducing hospital costs.

Psychodynamic psychotherapy

An important issue that needs to be readdressed is the belief that research in the past has shown psychodynamic psychotherapy to be ineffective. This is not the case. The serious deficiencies in the early trials of psychodynamic psychotherapy and medication have repeatedly been overlooked when judgements have been made (Karon, 1989; Alanen, 1997). Karon's thorough and readable review is an important contribution to this topic. The following paragraphs are a summary of some points made in Karon's review of the six major early American controlled studies on psychotherapy and medication.

The first study to compare psychoanalytical psychotherapy with medication was from Pennsylvania (Bookhammer *et al*, 1966) and the patient groups compared were all young, first-admission patients. Tentative conclusions were that the particular form of intensive psychotherapy technique was about equal in effectiveness with medication. Karon, although praising the study as being among the first attempts at rigorous evaluation of psychotherapy, highlights the likelihood that the research psychotherapy technique was highly questionable in its practice in that it differed considerably from that of the institution described in earlier accounts. The research therapy was carried out in the presence of an audience and may well have had quite an intimidating element to it.

The Wisconsin study (Rogers *et al*, 1967) was mainly a service user-centred approach with small numbers of patients seen twice a week for up to 2.5 years compared with two (non-randomised) control groups treated with medication. Although many findings were not impressive, after termination the psychotherapy patients had nearly a 100% reduction in bed usage in the following year (117 *v.* 219 days significant only to $P=0.1$). This suggests that the study may have been under-powered to test the hypothesis that length of stay was altered by the treatment intervention. Other statistically significant findings were a tendency to deny illness less and greater appropriateness on the Thematic Apperception Test. There were a number of important findings that related increased warmth, empathy and genuineness in the therapeutic relationship with other positive outcomes. Karon emphasises the value of this study in demonstrating the quality of the therapeutic relationship impacting on outcome. This study was also very useful in that it demonstrated the complexity of doing meaningful research in this field and the necessity to study and control for the quality of the psychotherapy.

The California project, from Camarillo State Hospital, is most often quoted as showing definitively that medication is the indispensable treatment of choice and that psychotherapy is ineffective (May, 1968). The same psychiatrists treated a total of 228 different patients by five different methods (psychotherapy without medication, psychotherapy with medication, medication alone, electroconvulsive therapy and milieu therapy). The idea of this was to control for therapist personality variables, rather than to clarify which were important in predicting outcome. This is an important gap as they are likely to be a crucial aspect of therapeutic effectiveness. The selection criteria eliminated the very sick and the not very sick. Karon points out the many unconsidered problems in treatment by the same inexperienced therapists in five approaches. He also considers evidence for the possible authority conditions in which the therapists functioned. Though it seems as if the trial was rigorous in many features of the design, a crucial fact is that the therapists were particularly inexperienced in using psychotherapy to treat patients with schizophrenia, as were the supervisors. He therefore highlights the very doubtful quality control of the psychotherapy. In addition, the ending of therapy and the final evaluations both took place on the very day of discharge from hospital! This is hardly a neutral time for a patient with schizophrenia in psychotherapy. It is likely that most reviewers of this study would be appropriately convinced that psychotherapy of patients with schizophrenia by inexperienced therapists in a hospital setting is not beneficial, but few other conclusions could safely be drawn.

In Karon's review of the Massachusetts study (Grinspoon *et al*, 1972) he again highlights the poor quality control of the therapy in that, though the therapists were experienced psychotherapists, they were mostly not experienced with either patients with chronic schizophrenia or with the economic and ethnic culture of the patients they were treating. More than half the patients had received electroconvulsive therapy or insulin comas, and all had been in a state hospital for more than three years. Behavioural measures did not improve for the psychotherapy patients, but 68% were able to live outside hospital compared with 37% of the (non-randomised) control group. Anecdotal evidence indicated that only one patient could be said to have developed a positive therapeutic alliance.

The Illinois project (Paul & Lentz, 1977) of patients with chronic treatment-resistant schizophrenia compares two forms of intensive psychosocial interventions (rather than individual psychotherapy) with routine treatment. The former was found to be considerably more effective in leading to discharge and also considerably more cost effective. In a controlled trial of placebo and medication on wards with the active psychosocial therapies, it was found that medication was associated with less improvement in both short- and longer term measurements. However, this observation may have been an artefact, as patients already doing well may not have been given medication in a non-randomised study.

The trial of treatment of schizophrenia in which quality control of the psychotherapy itself was most carefully protected is that by Karon & Vandenbos (1981) in Michigan. Although numbers were small ($n=36$), the patients tended to be severe cases from seriously socially disadvantaged backgrounds. The main problem with this study is that the patients in the control group were moved from the admitting hospital, if they did not improve sufficiently for discharge, to a state hospital – albeit with better auxiliary facilities than the admitting hospital. This was in contrast to the two groups involved in psychotherapy that remained in the admitting hospital in order to be able to receive the psychotherapy. With this important proviso, blind evaluations at six months showed that the results of the inexperienced therapists could be accounted for solely by medication effects as in the California study above (May, 1968). However, at this stage the quality-controlled experienced psychotherapists had significantly better results in terms of reduction in hospitalisation days and measures of thought disorder, whether or not medication was administered. By 12 months the patients of the inexperienced but supervised therapists were functioning better than the control group on medication. At the end of 20 months, psychotherapy (average 70 sessions) was more effective than medication, with the patients of the experienced therapists showing a balanced improvement across all measures. One interesting finding was that those in therapy with the most experienced therapist showed superior improvement in thought disorder when not on medication. For inexperienced therapists, the improvements were less balanced. Karon makes some most interesting points about the possible reasons for the variation in thought disorder findings between different therapists with respect to their attitudes to medication and to the affective control that results.

Two years after termination, psychotherapy patients had had half the number of hospitalisation days compared with the medication control group, and patients of experienced therapists did better than those of the inexperienced. Changes in thought disorder seem to be a better predictor of longer term ability to function outside hospital than short-term behavioural criteria, supporting other researchers' findings.

Karon's own interpretation of his earlier study is more positive than is usually reported, but there is a danger in multiple retrospective comparisons, particularly in a non-randomised trial where the treatment condition (psychotherapy or non-pychotherapy) was confounded with location (state hospital versus private hospital). However, the review from Karon puts a very different perspective on the frequently misquoted studies from two or more decades ago.

There is a consistency in all the studies quoted above that psychotherapy patients spend less time in hospital than those in medication-only group controls. The Michigan study had a number of cost evaluations that were positive in the long term for the psychotherapy group. In addition, only 33% of the latter needed welfare payments compared with 75% of those of the medication-only controls. Karon stresses that the cost benefit findings would have been completely the opposite if the evaluations were only done at six months of treatment.

Reviewing these early studies gives a number of pointers towards variables of therapeutic technique and timing that have been looked at in later studies and these will be considered both in this introduction and in some of the chapters that follow.

Therapeutic alliance

One important point is the question of therapeutic alliance. In a psychotherapy research project that is often quoted as unfavourable to psychotherapy (Gunderson *et al*, 1984), the drop-out rate was very large (69%) and only 76% of those completing the treatment study allowed themselves to be evaluated. Karon (1989) notices in that study that the therapists insisted that the patients were maintained on medication. He wonders what effect this had on the therapeutic alliance when the literature he quotes indicates that more than half of patients discontinue medication because of its unpleasantness. It seems most important that we try to develop more sophisticated measures of this crucial, but complex, factor of therapeutic alliance that involves both patient and therapist variables. In particular, a good measure is needed to evaluate whether the patient is generally and genuinely cooperating in the therapy (in the same way that a trial of medication would need to have some accurate means of knowing that the patient was taking it). This is not intended to imply that it is a static, simple or easily dichotomised concept. The everyday recognition of the human capacity to be in two minds towards some aspect of life is of particular relevance when working with patients with psychotic vulnerabilities (Richards, 1993; Sinason, 1993). Cognitive therapists also partly base their approach on being able to engage one reflective part of their patient's mind with another part of their mind. The crucial issue for research purposes is to have tools that can give some useful evaluation as to whether a particular therapist and patient dyad has developed a capacity to engage in the therapeutic task, whatever that might be and what factors may be getting in the way of it.

Length of treatment availability

Gunderson *et al* (1984) himself has speculated that psychotherapy may be the treatment of choice for the longer term goals. For many people, schizophrenia is a very lengthy disturbance with a considerable number of internal and external obstacles and risks to be overcome if there is to be a recovery. Ever changing professional relationships cannot inspire confidence in patients of supportive help being available in trying to face challenges again. Everyday clinical experience in psychiatry is informative of the frequency of relapse and distress seen during the time of rotations of competent junior psychiatric or nursing staff.

> For example, Jill, a girl of 20 with a long premorbid history of unstable self-esteem as a girl/woman (always contrasting herself unfavourably with her brother), had a prolonged schizophrenic breakdown after her first boyfriend rejected her for another girl in a cruel fashion. It took two years of patient therapeutic work aided by medication to help her regain her mental state such that she could start to study again, regain a peer group for ordinary social relationships, then gain a menial job.
> After a further six months she was promoted into a trainee job more in keeping with her interests and college studies. At this point she remains very anxious about her psychological safety if she should try to form a relationship again with a boy, yet is very sad at the thought of not trying. Clearly, this patient would be likely to be hindered rather than helped if she should have a constantly changing primary therapist during the next two or three years when she herself wished to form a stable relationship.

In most public mental health services, the most junior staff member often has the most contact with such patients. Concern about this state of affairs has led some mental health services in Norway to adopt '10 commandments' for schizophrenia treatment (Thorsen *et al*, 1999). These include:

(a) a guarantee of two hours a week of psychotherapy for five years with an experienced psychotherapist if needed/wanted;
(b) the primary nurse or other key worker must not be expecting to move on within a year;

(c) family contact is made on at least a monthly basis and often more frequently, especially at the beginning.

Aspects of the need to build on the potential for patients to have long-term therapeutic relationships are referred to in Chapters 9, 11 and 12.

Personal therapy

Hogarty has been researching the psychotherapy of schizophrenia for many years. Out of his own team's research experience and that of others, he has developed a personal therapy for people with schizophrenia. Hogarty clearly regards schizophrenic recovery as having a number of delicate phases, each of which has its own particular therapeutic needs. His therapeutic approach could be said to be an integrative one, in that he carefully combines aspects of various models into a new model that has the following features (among others):

(a) acknowledges the likelihood of an underlying pathophysiology;
(b) minimises iatrogenicity, especially with respect to medication;
(c) identifies and controls family and other environmental provocations;
(d) extends therapy beyond the crisis in careful stages and in a directed fashion;
(e) learns and teaches the affective cues of personal vulnerability (e.g. the often escalating and dysfunctional responses to certain affects, whatever the stressor);
(f) increases foresight (rather than insight) of emotional states in self and their expression and those of others;
(g) is designed explicitly to forestall late relapse.

Hogarty *et al* (1995) further delineates both the therapeutic stages in tabular form and the essential features of personal therapy, contrasting it with traditional psychodynamic therapy and with family psychoeducation. He has now published outcome studies of two trials of personal therapy for people with schizophrenia:

(a) those living in families who were randomly allocated to:
   (i)   supportive therapy;
   (ii) family psychoeducation/management;
   (iii) personal therapy;
   (iv) a combination of (ii) and (iii);
(b) those living independently of family who were randomly allocated to either:
   (i) personal therapy;
   (ii) supportive therapy.

All patients were offered therapy lasting three years by very experienced clinicians. The main findings were:

(a) In spite of extensive psychiatric histories, only 29% relapsed. Most patients entered the trial in only partially remitted conditions after very brief hospitalisations. The drop-out rate was very low for such studies (18%) and most of these were not in the personal therapy allocation.

(b) Personal therapy was more effective in both trials than the other therapies in areas of social adjustment but more so in those living with families.

(c) Personal therapy was associated with more relapses than supportive therapy in those living independent of families. Most relapses were in those who had not yet achieved basic symptom and residential stability.

(d) In those who did not receive personal therapy social adjustment improvement was confined to the first 12 months only.

(e) By contrast in personal therapy, social adjustment increased with time and did not seem to have peaked at the end of the trial at three years. Persistent symptoms led to more than 40% of patients not having moved into the advanced form of personal therapy by the end of the three-year trial.

(f) Personal therapy was experienced as more helpful (67%) than family (37%) and supportive (51%) therapies.

Hogarty's approach is integrative at the level of an individual therapy. As described in the work of Arieti (1974) and Margison & Mace (1997) there are features that are compatible with several underlying models, fused into an integrated approach. When considering integration in this context, it is worth distinguishing the integration of therapeutic approaches at the level of an individual treatment plan as described by Hogarty, from the wider implications for integration of treatment approaches in the service as a whole, as discussed in later chapters of the book.

Psychoanalysis and psychoanalytical psychotherapy now have a plurality of theoretical models. There are also many different emphases within the techniques that relate to the theoretical model, the nature of the clinical problem and the style, experience and personality of the psychoanalyst. It is, therefore, most important to differentiate the vast amount of knowledge and clinical experience that has accumulated from working psychoanalytically with people suffering from psychosis from the many different techniques used by therapists with these disorders. It is the different techniques and styles of work that need to be evaluated and compared and not all lumped together as if psychoanalysis was a single variable like a medicine given in a single dose.

There are not many contemporary psychoanalytical studies of treatment of patients with psychosis in which empirical outcome research data are used that have some coherence with the theoretical model. A measure should be theoretically coherent with the therapy, but there is also a view that the research, at worse, becomes tautological: patients are trained to give responses that they can tell will please their therapist, whatever the model of therapy under study. We are fortunate with the contribution in Chapter 9 of Siani & Siciliani in that they have attempted to reconcile this difficulty with a careful choice of outcome measures. Whatever the theoretical framework used, most would agree that, descriptively, the self of a person with psychosis is, by definition, highly disturbed. Adapting a psychoanalytical model that has been particularly developed to treat narcissistic disorders of the self (pioneered by Kohut), Siani has treated a number of people with psychosis in a way that has some close parallels with the personal therapy of Hogarty, though there are clearly many differences too. Both Hogarty and Siani emphasise the great care they take in monitoring the timing and staging of their interventions, the slow careful building up of trust and dependency. Both approaches are very different from that of earlier psychoanalytical work with patients with psychosis. It is said that the earlier approach was often quite active in style and that interpretations or reconstructions were given too early, leading to patients feeling overwhelmed and tending to relapse. Siani allows the relationship with the therapist to be central as the site of healing, reorganisation and gradual strengthening of the self. Hogarty uses the therapist relationship in a much more cognitive style, working with the patients to monitor their affects and reshape dysfunctional responses to their own affects by focusing 'out there' in his or her environment.

Siani uses 'the Karolinska Psychodynamic Profile' to measure the structural and psychodynamic aspects of the self and personality that psychoanalysts think underpin mental health and disturbance of all kinds. In this pilot study striking improvements towards normality are achieved in the two-year period of the therapy compared with the control group. This work needs to be replicated and extended to larger numbers. It would, however, be helpful if external measurements of change could also be carried out that would allow some comparison with outcomes from other approaches.

Timing and integration of treatment interventions

In Chapter 11, Johannessen *et al* report research of an area of great importance from many perspectives. Those who organise mental health services, epidemiologists, public health physicians, mental health economists and all concerned with the quality of life of people with schizophrenia and with stigma will be interested in the findings. An intensive publicity campaign was conducted in Rogaland, Norway to educate the public and a range of professionals about schizophrenia. The primary intention is to bring all those with psychosis into good quality professional treatment as soon as possible after onset. Other reviews have indicated that intervention at the earliest stages of illness development may reduce the extent, and morbidity of psychotic disorders (Wyatt & Green, 1995; McGlashan, 1998). This hopeful conclusion is based on correlations between duration of psychosis (DUP) prior to treatment and long-term morbidity following treatment. Wyatt (1991) reviewed studies suggesting that the long-term outcome of schizophrenia is better for patients treated earlier with neuroleptics. Few professionals are aware of several studies that have found a very long average duration of illness (DUI) and DUP before adequate treatment is instigated. Loebel *et al*'s (1992) findings are similar to those of other studies. He found a DUI of 151 weeks and a DUP of 52 weeks.

Johannessen's research addresses two vital questions:

(a) Is it possible to reduce the length of time that people with psychosis are untreated in a community?
(b) If this is possible, does earlier treatment of high quality improve the longer term prognosis?

Johannessen's research answer to the first question is undoubtedly yes – and dramatically so. Time and ongoing research will tell if it is possible to maintain the marked reduction in the DUP over a period of years. We only have tentative answers to the second aspect of the question: whether the prognosis is beneficial when DUP is substantially reduced. The importance of this question hardly merits spelling out, whether in terms of the human benefits to persons vulnerable to psychosis and their families or in economic terms. Schizophrenia accounts for a huge percentage of health budgets – some 60% of the total psychiatric budget in Norway (Rund, 1994). In the UK, schizophrenia is the third largest consumer of in-patient hospital costs in terms of all medical diagnostic categories (following learning disability and stroke) (Knapp & Healey, 1998).

In Chapter 10 by Cullberg *et al*, the focus is more on the usual approach to patients presenting with psychosis using hospital beds being compared with a predominantly psychosocial community treatment approach combined with only low doses of neuroleptic medication intended to minimise the risk of sedation and other side-effects. This approach to medication contrasts with a different approach commonly seen in recent decades in Western countries in which the dosage is sometimes radically increased when it has failed at low doses. When the patient needed to be cared for away from home, instead of hospital, priority was given to using a small apartment dwelling with one or two nurses only where relatives can also stay. The principles of the experimental approach are to give psychosocial support and intervention at the earliest opportunity – actually in the home if possible – concentrating on reducing the crisis situation and acute stress. Only when the psychosis has abated is dynamic or cognitive psychotherapy offered if requested for ongoing difficulties, including working with their premorbid origins. Family help is offered for as long as needed. Easily available continuity of support will be given for five years (because in other studies it seems to have been ended too early). Benzodiazepine medication is used initially if psychosocial help is insufficient for containment and to give time to see if the psychosis will settle without neuroleptics. When neuroleptics are used, the dosage prescribed is very modest by most standards.

This is a very promising 'first episode' pilot study and augurs well for the much larger Parachute Project study in Sweden that is now under way with some 200 patients experiencing a first episode in 18 centres. In the pilot study, Cullberg found that patients needed far less use of hospital beds and needed neuroleptics less often and in much lower doses. By the end of the study fewer of the patients participating in the experiment were on permanent disability benefits.

In Chapter 12, Alanen *et al* descibe the development of the need-adapted model of the treatment of psychotic illnesses that is now widely implemented in Finland and increasingly implemented in other Scandinavian countries (see also Chapters 10 and 11). In Finland, services for whole geographical sectors of the population are organised around the key principles of the need-adapted model adapted to local situations. Persons with schizophrenia are regarded as very heterogeneous in their antecedent characteristics, the precipitating factors, and so on. Hence interventions are based on a very careful assessment of the individual and his or her family and life situation and the model being named need-adapted. This assessment is ongoing, so that the focus or type of intervention is modified as the needs change. Medication is used to support the interventions, which are psychotherapeutic or psychosocial in their emphasis. In the need-adapted model, it is particularly important to engage people presenting with their first episode of psychosis as early as possible and to engage their families too. Alanen *et al*'s experience has shown that it is most important to maintain long-term contact with most patients, which does not mean that intensive therapeutic regimes are needed in the long term.

Results are presented by comparison of cohorts of patients. One of the most important conclusions is that it is possible to organise services of a high quality to a whole population that are predominantly psychotherapeutic in orientation. The results seem very favourable for the patients and it seems possible to train all staff in a geographical area (as in Western Lapland). The finding in the Kupittaa and Acute Psychosis – Integrated Treatment (API) studies that successful outcomes can be accomplished in large numbers of patients without the need for any neuroleptics at all, if sound psychotherapeutic resources are available, will challenge the basic approach of clinicians in most Western countries. Some similarities will be noted with the personal therapy model.

It was a deliberate choice to place McGorry's chapter at the end of the book. We decided that it would be best to start with chapters that focused on particular approaches and provided evidence for their effectiveness. It was thought appropriate to end the book with a chapter that gives a clear and optimistic overview from a very experienced clinician and researcher of the principles on which a comprehensive psychotherapeutic service should be conducted within a biopsycho-social model.

McGorry's way of thinking about comprehensive holistic services has much in common with that of Hogarty *et al* (1995), the need-adapted approach of Alanen *et al* (1997), and that of integrative pluralism espoused by Margison & Mace (1997). These approaches have in common the careful staging and flexibility of the therapeutic approach, moving only gradually to more advanced goals once the patient is clearly stabilised after the earlier goal and is also ready, willing and able to move on. All these approaches have in mind the enormous variability between one person and another with schizophrenia without minimising what they have in common in terms of aspects of their psychotic breakdown and continuing vulnerability to further psychotic episodes.

To make the point more clearly through clinical vignettes, the longer term work would need to be very different in the following patients experiencing first episodes both aged 18:

> Patient A had shown no previous signs of disturbance and comes from a stable, loving and emotionally open background and has coped well with adolescence. She breaks down after the unexpected successive deaths of both parents, the second dying just a few weeks before she is due to leave home for university for the first time.

> Patient B comes from a chaotic family, has an extensive history of abuse both physically and sexually and has a five-year history of difficulties in coping academically and socially at school. The patient left school at 16 and has not coped with employment for more than a few weeks at a time, has used a lot of illicit drugs but not for some months. After experiencing psychotic symptoms she takes 18 months to get professional help.

McGorry argues powerfully that even if the eruptions of psychosis were to be proven to have a biological explanation, the effect of psychosis is to wreak havoc on the often already compromised and delicate psychological developmental tasks of adolescence and early adulthood. The very fact of having had a psychosis leads to additional problems that disrupt these tasks often for a long time. In addition, they bring stigma and shame and the ongoing terror of experiencing psychosis again in the face of being rechallenged with important life issues (to return to an example from earlier in this introduction, the wish and fear of Jill of forming a relationship with a boy again). Hence the importance of an empathic and trusted psychotherapeutic relationship to accompany the patient as he or she faces personal vulnerabilities and tries to master life's challenges or seek fulfilling compensations for those personal vulnerabilities. It is quite striking by how much many of these contemporary approaches revive some of the central pillars of the psychotherapeutic approaches from some decades earlier, for example, the integrated approach described by Arieti (1974).

McGorry summarises the practical application of these principles in the Early Psychosis Prevention and Intervention Centre (EPPIC) project in Melbourne, Australia and shows that an active psychosocial approach to first-episode psychosis in young people brings a much improved psychosocial functioning, a reduction in neuroleptic use and a very marked reduction in suicide rate. McGorry ends by stressing the enormity of the task ahead in mobilising the support and resources for the training required to implement a comprehensive biopsychosocial approach. This contrasts with the more obvious potential commercial benefits from investment in pharmaceutical advances. We share his view that such an integration is timely.

Conclusion

The clinical methods and the outcome research described in the chapters of this book are an indication of the progress being made in the psychological treatments of schizophrenia and other psychoses. These are not alternative treatments but complement the important advances in pharmacological treatments of these conditions. We hope to facilitate the urgent need to counter the often-prevailing view that medication is the only worthwhile approach to treatment. Several of the therapies described benefit not only some of the specific symptoms of schizophrenia, but also the other important problems that may have preceded the psychosis or that follow in its wake. There is an emphasis in several chapters on the first breakdown, the importance of accurate clarification of underlying psychological vulnerabilities and then the choosing of effective and relevant interventions to reduce the chances of chronicity. Chapter 11 demonstrates that it is possible to reduce the amount of untreated psychosis in the community.

Nearly all chapters emphasise the centrality of forming a good relationship with the patient (and with his or her family) with continuity and stability of staff involved. The need for this and the skills required to achieve it are too often neglected. Our evidence points to the need for the care of the relationship between the person with psychosis and the key professional(s) to be put back at the heart of the therapeutic endeavour. It is only once this has been achieved that there is the possibility of a range of interventions actually being used therapeutically by the patient. All in all, we think we have clearly demonstrated that there now exists a range of psychological approaches and attitudes that show considerable promise. If these were more widely available through the appropriate training of clinicians there would be significant reduction in illness and improved chances of a productive life. In addition the wider utilisation of psychological approaches and better therapeutic relationships should assist in the reduction of stigma and fear attached to such disturbances, with the consequent seeking of help at an earlier stage and the easier reintegration of patients and their families into society.

References

ALANEN, Y. O. (1997) *Schizophrenia. Its Origins and Need-Adapted Treatment.* London: Karnac Books.

ARIETI, S. (1974) *Interpretation of Schizophrenia.* New York: Basic Books.

BION, W. (1959) Attacks on linking. *International Journal of Psychoanalysis,* **30**, 308–315.

—— (1962) A theory of thinking. *International Journal of Psychoanalysis,* **33**, 306–310.

BOLLINI, P., PAMPALLONA, S., ORZA, M. A., ET AL (1994) Antipsychotic drugs: is more worse? A meta-analysis of the published randomized control trials. *Psychological Medicine,* **24**, 307–316.

BOOKHAMMER, R. S., MYERS, R. W., SCHOBER, C. C., ET AL (1966) A five-year clinical follow-up study of schizophrenics treated by Rosen's 'direct analysis' compared with controls. *American Journal of Psychiatry,* **123**, 602–604.

CLINICAL STANDARDS ADVISORY GROUP (1995) *Schizophrenia. Vol 1.* London: HMSO.

CORRIGAN. P. W., KWARTMAN. W. Y., & PRAMANA, W. (1992) Staff perception of barriers to behaviour therapy at a psychiatric hospital. *Behaviour Modification,* **64**, 132–144.

DARE, C. (1996) Evidence: fact or fiction. Future directions of psychotherapy in the NHS: adaptation or extinction? *Psychoanalytic Psychotherapy,* **10** (suppl.), 32–45.

DAWSON M. E. & NUECHTERLEIN, K. H. (1984) Psychophysiological dysfunction in the developmental course of schizophrenic disorders. *Schizophrenia Bulletin,* **10**, 204–232.

DEPARTMENT OF HEALTH (1966) *NHS Psychotherapy Services in England: Review of Strategic Policy.* London: HMSO.

DIXON, L. & LEHMAN, A. (1995) Family interventions for schizophrenia. *Schizophrenia Bulletin,* **21**, 631–643.

FADDEN, G. (1997) Implementation of family interventions in routine clinical practice following staff training programme: a major course for concern. *Journal of Mental Health,* **6,** 599–612.

—— (1999) Psychoeducation. A West Midlands initiative to train mental health professionals to work in effective partnership with users and their families. *OpenMind* **96,** March/April, 16.

FLECK, S. (1995) Dehumanising developments in American psychiatry in recent decades. *Journal of Nervous and Mental Diseases,* **183,** 195–203.

GEDDES, J. R. ON BEHALF OF THE RCP/BPS GUIDELINE DEVELOPMENT GROUP (2000) Atypical antipsychotics in the treatment of schizophrenia: systematic review, meta-regression and evidence-based treatment recommendations. *Schizophrenia Research,* **41,** 40.

GRINSPOON, L., EWALT, J. R., & SHADER, R. I. (1972) *Schizophrenia, Pharmacotherapy, and Psychotherapy.* Baltimore: Williams & Wilkins.

GROTSTEIN, J. S. (1996) Orphans of the 'real': 1. Some modern and postmodern perspectives on the neurobiological and psychosocial dimensions of psychosis and other primitive mental disorders. In *Contemporary Treatment of Psychosis* (eds J. G. Allen & D. T. Collins). Narthral, NJ: Jason Aronson.

GUNDERSON, J. G., FRANK, A. F., KATZ, H. M., *ET AL* (1984) Effects of psychotherapy in schizophrenia: II. Comparative outcome of two forms of treatment. *Schizophrenia Bulletin,* **10,** 564–598.

HAMILTON, M., HORDERN, A., WALDROP, F. N., *ET AL* (1963) A controlled trial on the value of prochlorperazine, trifluoperazine, and intensive group treatment. *British Journal of Psychiatry,* **109,** 510–522.

HOGARTY, G. E., KORNBLITH, S. J., GREENWALD, D., *ET AL* (1995) Personal Therapy: a disorder-relevant psychotherapy for schizophrenia. *Schizophrenia Bulletin,* **21,** 379–393.

JOHNSTONE, L. (1993) Family management in "schizophrenia": its assumptions and contradictions. *Journal of Mental Health,* **2,** 255–269.

JONES, E, ALEXANDER, J & HOWORTH, P. (1996) Out of hospital: after-care for people with schizophrenia. *Health Trends,* **28,** 128–131.

KANE, J. M. (1996) Factors which can make patients difficult to treat. *British Journal of Psychiatry,* **169** (suppl. 31), 10–14.

KARON, B. P. (1989) Psychotherapy versus medication for schizophrenia: empirical comparisons. In *The limits of Biological Treatments for Psychological Distress. Comparisons with Placebo* (eds S. Fisher & R. P. Greenberg), pp.105–150. Hillsdale, NJ. Lawrence Erlbaum Associates.

—— & VANDENBOS, G. R. (1981) *Psychotherapy of Schizophrenia: the Treatment of Choice.* New York: Aronson.

KAVANAGH, D. J., CLARK, D., PIATKOWSKA, O., *ET AL* (1993) Application of congnitive–behavioural family interventions in multidisciplinary terms: what can the matter be? *Australian Psychologist,* **28,** 1–8.

KNAPP, M. & HEALEY, A. (1998) Economic evaluation of psychological treatments for schizophrenia. In *Outcome and Innovation in Psychological Treatment of Schizophrenia (eds* T. Wykes, N. Tarrier & Shôn Lewis), pp. 259–282. Chichester: John Wiley and Sons.

KUIPERS, E. (1998) Working with carers: interventions for relative and staff carers of those who have psychosis. In *Outcome and Innovation in Psychological Treatment of Schizophrenia* (eds T. Wykes, N. Tarrier & S. Lewis), pp. 201–214. Chichester: John Wiley & Sons.

LEHMAN, A. F. (1998) The role of mental health research in promoting effective treatment for adults with schizophrenia. *Journal of Mental Health Policy and Economics,* **1,** 161–172.

——, STEINWACHS, D. M. & THE SCHIZOPHRENIA PORT CO-INVESTIGATORS OF THE PROJECT (1998) Patterns of usual care for schizophrenia: initial results from the Schizophrenia Patient Outcomes Research Team (PORT) client survey. *Schizophrenia Bulletin,* **24,** 11–20.

28   *Martindale et al*

LOEBEL A. D., LIEBERMAN J. A., ALVIR, J. M. J., *ET AL* (1992) Duration of psychosis and outcome in first-episode schizophrenia. *American Journal of Psychiatry*, **50**, 369–376.

MARGISON, F. & MACE, C. (1997) *Psychotherapy of Psychosis*. London: Gaskell.

——, BARKHAM, M., EVANS, C., *ET AL* (2000) Measurement in psychotherapy: evidence-based practice and practice-based evidence. *British Journal of Pychiatry*, in press.

MARTINDALE, B. V. (1998) Commentary. *Advances in Psychiatric Treatment*, **4**, 241–242.

—— (2000) New discoveries concerning psychosis and their organisational fate. In *A Language for Psychosis: the Psychoanalysis of Psychotic States* (ed. Paul Williams). London: Whurr Books.

MAY, P. R. A. (1968) *Treatment of Schizophrenia: a Comparative Study of Five Treatment Methods*. New York: Science House.

McGLASHAN, T. H. (1998) Early detection and interaction of schizophrenia: rationale and research. *British Journal of Psychiatry*, **172**, 3–6.

MOSHER, L. R. & MENN A. Z. (1976) Dinosaur or astronaut? One-year follow-up from the Soteria project. *American Journal of Psychiatry*, **133**, 919–920.

NUECHTERLEIN, K. H. & DAWSON, M. E. (1984) Information processing and attentional functioning in the developmental course of schizophrenia. *Schizophrenia Bulletin*, **10**, 160–203.

OBHOLZER, A. & ROBERTS, V. Z. (1994) *The Unconscious at Work*. London: Routledge.

OLIN, S. S., MEDNICK, S. A., CANNON, T., *ET AL* (1998) School teacher ratings predictive of psychiatric outcome 25 years later. *British Journal of Psychiatry*, **172** (suppl. 33), 7–13.

PAUL, G. L., TOBIAS. L. L. & HOLLY, B. L. (1972) Maintenance psychotropic drugs in the presence of active treatment programs. *Archives of General Psychiatry*, **27**, 106–115.

—— & LENTZ, R. J. (1977) *Psychosocial Treatment of Chronic Mental Patients. Milieu Versus Social Learning Programs*. Cambridge, MA: Harvard University Press.

RAPPAPORT, M., HOPKINS, H. K., HALL, K., *ET AL* (1978) Are there schizophrenics for whom phenothiazines may be unnecessary or contra-indicated? *International Pharmaco-Psychiatry*, **13**, 100–109.

REMINGTON, R., KAPUR, S. & ZIPURSKY, R. (1998) Pharmacotherapy of first-episode schizophrenia. *British Journal of Psychiatry*, **172**, 66–70.

RICHARDS, J. (1993) Cohabitation and the negative therapeutic reaction. *Psychoanalytic Psychotherapy*, **7**, 222–239.

ROBBINS, M. (1993) *Experiences of Schizophrenia*. New York: Guilford Press.

ROGERS, C. R., GENDLIN, E. T., KIESLER, D. J., *ET AL* (1967) *The Therapeutic Relationship and its Impact: a Study of Psychotherapy with Schizophrenics*. Madison, WI: University of Wisconsin.

ROTH, M. (1986) Diagnosis and prognosis of schizophrenia. In *Handbook of Studies of Schizophrenia. Part 1: Epidemiology, Aetiology and Clinical Features* (eds G. D. Burrows, T. R. Norman & G. Rubinstein), pp. 169–182. Amsterdam: Elsevier.

RUND, B. R. (1994) Schizophrenia, how much do we use on treatment and research? *Journal for the Norwegian Medical Association*, **21**, 2682–2683.

SEARLES, H. F. (1959) The effort to drive the other person crazy – an element in the aetiology and psychotherapy of schizophrenia. *British Journal of Medical Psychology*, **32**, 1–18.

SHARMA, T. & HARVEY, P. (1999) *Cognition in Schizophrenia*. Oxford: Oxford University Press.

SINASON, M. (1993) Who is the mad voice inside? *Psychoanalytic Psychotherapy*, **7**, 207–221.

STRAUSS, J. S. (1992) The person with schizophrenia as a person. In *Psychotherapy of Schizophrenia: Facilitating and Obstructive Factors* (eds A. Werbart & J. Cullberg). Oslo: Scandinavian University Press.

THORSEN, G. R. B. T., HAALAND, T. & JOHANNESSEN, J. O. (1999). Treatment of schizophrenia; patients needs and rights. In *The Psychosocial Treatment of Psychosis* (eds T. S. Borchgrevink, A. Fjell & B. R. Rund), pp. 193–204. Oslo: TanoAschehoug.

TIENARI, P., WYNNE, L. C., MORING, J., *ET AL* (1994) The Finnish adoptive family study of schizophrenia. Implications for family research. *British Journal of Psychiatry,* **164**, 20–26.

VAUGHN, C. & LEFF, J. P. (1976) Influence of family and social factors on the course of psychiatric illness. *British Journal of Psychiatry,* **129**, 125–137.

WINNICOTT, D. W. (1961) The theory of parent–infant relationships. In *The Maturational Process and the Facilitating Environment,* pp. 37–55. London: Hogarth Press.

WOOF, K., GOLDBERG, D. P. & FRYERS, T. (1988) The practice of community psychiatric nursing and mental health social work in Salford: some implications for community care. *British Journal of Psychiatry,* **152**, 83–92.

WYATT, R. J. (1991) Neuroleptics and the natural course of schizophrenia. *Schizophrenia Bulletin,* **17**, 325–351.

—— & GREEN, M. F. (1995) *Early Treatment Improves the Outcome of Schizophrenia. Abstract Symposium No 98D.* Washington, DC: American Psychiatric Association.

VGOTSKY, L. S. (1966) *Development of the Higher Mental Functions.* Cambridge, MA: MIT Press.

2 Cognitive–behavioural therapy for people with psychosis

PHILIPPA A. GARETY, DAVID FOWLER and ELIZABETH KUIPERS

The complexity and severity of the problems presented by people with psychosis present a considerable challenge to therapists. As we have previously discussed, a striking characteristic of people with schizophrenia-spectrum psychoses is the diversity of their problems (Fowler *et al*, 1995). These can include almost every possible mix of delusions, hallucinations, perceptual anomalies and subjective experiences of disorders of thinking and the will. People also differ to the degree to which the associated problems of anxiety, depression, risk of suicide, social disability and risk of relapse are present. Attempting to understand why different problems occur, interact and covary, over time and in response to the environment and to different interventions, is an important aspect of cognitive therapy. A key skill of cognitive–behavioural therapy for people with psychosis is the ability to apply psychological theory to the attempt to make sense of the problems of the individual case.

Cognitive–behavioural therapy (CBT) for psychosis is undergoing rapid development. First, it is shifting its focus from the treatment of individual positive symptoms, especially delusions and hallucinations, to therapy with people who present with complex and diverse difficulties, which include these symptoms among an array of other problems (Fowler *et al*, 1995; Chadwick *et al*, 1996). Second, the previous applicability of cognitive approaches had been restricted to people with relatively stable positive symptoms that had not responded to antipsychotic medication, but more recently therapy has been developed for people in acute episodes (Drury *et al*, 1996) and for young people experiencing their first episode of psychosis (McGorry, 1998). Finally, the research evaluations of the effectiveness of this approach have become more sophisticated, as we have moved from reports of single cases and small case series to more rigorous randomised controlled trials (e.g. Kuipers *et al*, 1997). There is now convincing evidence from controlled trials for the effectiveness of CBT at reducing symptoms and associated distress in people with medication-resistant psychosis. The more recent developments of acute episode and early psychosis work show encouraging benefits and are currently the focus of active research efforts.

In this chapter, we will describe contemporary practice in CBT for psychosis, discuss its theoretical underpinnings, aims and methods and review the outcome research. Although Beck (1952) wrote a case report describing an early application of cognitive ideas, much of the published work that we will review has been developed and conducted in the UK, where more recently there have been active research groups refining the therapeutic processes and evaluating outcome. However, workers in Sweden (Perris, 1989) and Australia (Jackson *et al*, 1998) have also developed cognitively oriented approaches, the latter group specifically for early psychosis, which we will discuss. Three UK groups have published books that provide detailed descriptions of their therapy approach: Kingdon & Turkington (1994), Chadwick *et al* (1996) and Fowler *et al* (1995). Tarrier, Haddock and colleagues have also contributed therapy descriptions in chapters and edited volumes (e.g. Haddock & Slade, 1996; Tarrier *et al*, 1997). It is apparent from comparing these publications that the approaches described share much in common, and that, over the past decade, there has been a fruitful cross-fertilisation of ideas and a resulting convergence in methods. For example, there is a consensus that the earlier more behavioural approaches that emphasised stress management and coping strategies for positive symptoms, while still considered useful, have yielded primacy to cognitive methods that identify thoughts and interpretations of experiences and explore alternative less distressing meanings (see Fowler *et al*, 1995; Chadwick *et al*, 1996; Tarrier *et al*, 1997). Nonetheless, we are still in a period of rapid development and we can anticipate further changes as the research provides us with evidence as to the most effective elements of therapy for different individuals and for different stages of illness.

CBT: theoretical basis

There are a number of theoretical models and hypotheses that provide a theoretical underpinning to CBT for psychosis and the therapist should have a thorough grounding in this literature (see Fowler *et al*,

1995, for a fuller discussion). In general, psychoses are viewed as heterogeneous and multi-factorial, and as best understood within a biopsychosocial framework. It is assumed that there are different degrees to which biological vulnerability, psychological processes and the social environment have contributed in the individual case to the expression of psychosis (Garety *et al*, 1994; Fowler *et al*, 1995). This is consistent with widely accepted 'stress–vulnerability' models (Zubin & Spring, 1977; Strauss & Carpenter, 1981). These posit that the individual has an enduring vulnerability to psychosis, possibly, but not necessarily, of genetic or neurodevelopmental origin, which may be increased by childhood experiences, whether social, biological or psychological. The psychosis becomes manifest on subsequent exposure to a range of additional stresses, which again may be social, biological or psychological, such as adverse environments, drug misuse or major life transitions. A further set of factors may be important in maintaining the illness in the longer term (such as the meaning attributed to psychotic experiences, loss of social roles or the use of medication). In applying the stress–vulnerability framework in the context of CBT, the key implication is that there are different factors exerting their influence in different cases and at different times. The therapist aims to try to develop an individual account of a person's vulnerabilities, stresses and responses (Fowler *et al*, 1998).

Cognitive models of psychosis add further detail to the stress–vulnerability framework. The core symptoms and experiences of psychosis are manifest as disturbances of cognition: both basic cognitive processes concerned with information processing, resulting in anomalies of perception and experience of the self, and conscious appraisals and judgements leading to unusual beliefs. Cognitive psychology, drawing on an understanding of cognitive processes in the general population, has found evidence of disruptions and biases in these processes, which are thought to contribute to the development and persistence of the symptoms of psychosis (e.g. Frith, 1992; Bentall, 1994; Hemsley, 1994; Garety & Freeman, 1999). To give just one example, Frith (1992) has proposed that it is a deficit in the self-monitoring of thoughts and intentions to act (a cognitive process occurring outside conscious awareness) that gives rise to the symptoms of thought insertion and alien control. Cognitive accounts have also considered how psychotic experiences are appraised by individuals resulting in emotional disturbance, such as depression and anxiety, and in negative evaluations of the self, which jointly contribute to the development and maintenance of symptoms and distress (e.g. Chadwick & Birchwood, 1994; Close & Garety, 1998). CBT draws on these accounts of cognitive and emotional processes, in psychosis, in people with emotional problems and in the general population. The central assumption of the cognitive approach to psychosis is that people with psychosis, like all of us, are attempting to make sense of the world and their experiences. The meanings attributed to their experiences, together with their earlier development, will influence the expression and development of symptoms, emotional responses and behaviour. Helping people to become aware of the processes that influence their thoughts and emotions and to re-evaluate their views of themselves and the psychosis is, therefore, central to therapy.

However, in placing these cognitive accounts of psychosis within broader stress–vulnerability models, it is clear that there is a role for a range of different interventions with people with psychosis. We therefore see individual therapy as only one approach in a wide array of potentially beneficial methods of treatment and support. These include medication and approaches that change the social environment, including family work, the provision of opportunities for social and vocational activity and user-led groups (Roth & Fonagy, 1996).

Therapy in practice

The general aims of CBT for people with psychosis are three-fold (Fowler *et al*, 1995). They are: to reduce the distress and disability caused by psychotic symptoms; to reduce emotional disturbance; and to help the person to arrive at an understanding of psychosis in order to promote the active participation of the individual in the regulation of risk of relapse and social disability. The general approach is concerned with understanding and making sense, working to achieve collaboration between the person with psychosis and the therapist, rather than didactic, interpretative or confrontational styles.

CBT is a structured and time-limited therapy, although the duration and frequency of therapy sessions will vary according to the nature and severity of the person's problems. In working with people with relatively stable medication-resistant symptoms we have generally offered nine months of therapy, on a weekly or fortnightly basis, averaging about 20 sessions. However, this may range from 12 to 30 sessions, over six months to more than a year, as negotiated. Booster sessions may also be offered over a longer period, or a brief period of more intense work if problems re-emerge. Two recent therapy trials, discussed below (Kuipers *et al*, 1997, 1998; Sensky *et al*, 2000), were conducted on the basis of nine months' therapy. However, Tarrier and colleagues have typically offered therapy over a shorter period (less than three months), at a higher frequency (twice weekly) (Tarrier *et al*, 1993, 1998). Work focused on acute episodes may also be of shorter duration, although it is more intense (Drury *et al*, 1996; Haddock *et al*, 1998). It should be noted that CBT is normally offered alongside a range of other treatments and services, as discussed above. Some studies have investigated the effects of combined psychological interventions, such as individual cognitive–behaviourally oriented therapy with family intervention (e.g. Buchkremer *et al*, 1997). Although valuable and relevant to service provision, such studies do not provide definitive evidence on the specific effectiveness of CBT, which is needed before it can be recommended for widespread implementation. Furthermore, the extent to which people engage in a range of interventions, including medication, is variable. CBT can be offered to people who do not engage in other services.

We have conceptualised therapy as a series of six stages, although this should be seen as a guiding framework to be applied flexibly (Fowler *et al*, 1998).

Building and maintaining a therapeutic relationship: engagement and assessment

CBT begins with a period of building and establishing a collaborative therapeutic relationship in which helping the service user feel that he or she is understood is of paramount importance. This can be a challenge with people with psychosis who may be suspicious, angry with mental health services or deny the relevance of therapy for their problems. If attention is not paid to these issues, early drop-out is likely. Our solution is a flexible approach to therapy that is sensitive to the service user's beliefs and emotions and starts by working from the service user's own perspective. Particularly at this stage, we emphasise checking and discussing with service users how they experience the sessions and their thoughts about the therapist's role. If the service user finds sessions arousing or disturbing, we recommend shortening sessions or changing the topic to a less distressing subject. The occurrence of psychotic symptoms during the session, such as hallucinations or paranoid ideas, is acknowledged and very gently discussed. The primary aim is always to ensure that the sessions are tolerable. Gradually the therapist moves from empathic listening to more structured assessment interviewing, in which the therapist attempts to clarify the particular life circumstances, events and experiences that provided the context for the onset of psychosis and makes a detailed analysis of specific distressing symptoms and other problems. As well as establishing a trusting relationship, the therapist aims to arrive at a preliminary set of shared goals for therapy, that are relevant to the service user and expressed in their own terms. For example, goals might be: 'to feel less paranoid while out of the house' or 'to cope better with the voices when at the day centre' or 'to feel less upset and angry with myself if the day goes badly'. Quite limited goals such as these can be elaborated or changed as therapy progresses.

Cognitive–behavioural coping strategies

Work on coping strategies develops directly from the assessment in which current distressing symptoms and experiences have been identified, such as episodes of hearing voices or feeling anxious and suspicious when out. A range of cognitive and behavioural strategies has been shown to reduce the occurrence or duration of such problems, such as activity scheduling, anxiety reduction and attention control techniques (Fowler & Morley, 1989; Tarrier, 1992). These methods are essentially pragmatic, and can bring particular relief in cases where symptoms are experienced as overwhelming and uncontrollable, resulting, for example, in self-harm or disturbed behaviour. The aim is to foster feelings of control and hope and to provide practical help in the early stages of therapy. For example, one service user always developed paranoid ideas when in town, walking past strangers in crowds. Therefore he often avoided these situations. On assessment, it emerged that the paranoid ideas were triggered by the anomalous experience of his attention becoming fixed on 'the blacks of people's eyes'. He found himself staring at people's eyes and faces and then worried that the objects of his attention would be hostile. Although, at a later date in therapy, the nature and interpretation of these experiences and ideas were explored more fully, a coping strategy was developed that involved stopping regularly to direct his attention to shop windows for a short time. By using this strategy, this service user became able to manage trips to the town centre without becoming overwhelmed by delusional ideas. Such strategies can be reviewed and updated in the course of therapy.

Developing a new understanding of the experience of psychosis

Discussion of the experience and meaning of psychosis is a central and crucial element of CBT. This involves exploring the service user's understanding of their predicament (Are they ill, 'mad', 'schizophrenic', stressed? What caused the problems? What helps? How do they view the future? What does this mean about them?), and tentatively offering an individualised formulation based upon the assessment and the theoretical framework outlined above. The therapist may make links between the nature of the delusions presented, the person's life history, the specific context in which the symptoms were first formed and the processes that seem to be maintaining them. Here, the therapist aims also to normalise and destigmatise psychotic experiences and unusual beliefs, discussing how they can occur in the general population, particularly under conditions of stress, such as sensory and sleep deprivation (Kingdon & Turkington, 1994). Depending on the ability and interest of the service user, we discuss biopsychosocial theories of psychosis and cognitive models of symptoms. The possible mechanisms of anti-psychotic medication are often usefully discussed and set within the broader stress–vulnerability framework. In fostering a new or fuller understanding of the experience of psychosis, the therapist aims to reduce the guilt or denial associated with it and to provide a rationale for engaging in behaviours that will promote recovery.

Addressing delusions and hallucinations

It is not assumed that simply discussing a formulation will lead to belief change. Where delusions and belief about voices are well-established, they are typically maintained by repeated misinterpretations of specific events, by ongoing anomalous experiences and by cognitive and behavioural patterns that preferentially seek out confirmation and prevent disconfirmation of existing beliefs (Garety & Hemsley, 1994). For example, there is strong evidence that some people with delusions 'jump to conclusions' on the basis of little evidence and that they have a biased attributional style in which other people are blamed for negative events (Bentall, 1994; Garety & Freeman, 1999). The beliefs may also be functional and, at the least, will have made subjective sense of puzzling or distressing experiences. Therefore, the emotional consequences of changing strongly held beliefs need to be explored. After discussing in general terms how events may be misinterpreted and how inner experiences (thoughts or images) may be mis-attributed to external sources, it is helpful to make a detailed analysis of day-to-day experiences and judgements. In each session, over a number of weeks or months, these are reviewed and alternatives generated. Chadwick *et al* (1996) have provided a detailed account of this work with delusional beliefs, while Chadwick & Birchwood (1994) have developed approaches to auditory hallucinations that emphasise that changing the beliefs held about the voices (e.g. about their identity or powerfulness) will reduce distress.

This central work of identifying and changing the distressing and disabling delusions and hallucinations, by a systematic process of reviewing the evidence and generating alternatives, draws on standard cognitive approaches. However, there are some differences of method. First, as will have been noted, we only undertake this work once the therapeutic relationship is firmly established. It may often be that this detailed discussion of delusions and hallucinations will take place in the second half of therapy. Second, the approach is gentle and non-confrontative; the therapist must carefully judge whether and how far to challenge the service user's interpretations. Also, perhaps more commonly than in standard cognitive therapy, the therapist may supply alternative interpretations rather than always seek to ensure that the user generates them. This helps to compensate for the cognitive inflexibility or impairment of some service users. Third, despite our best efforts, some service users firmly resist re-evaluating their beliefs; in these cases, we aim to 'work within' the delusions, identifying possible ways of reducing distress and disability despite the continuance of the belief. For example, one person believed that the voice of God commanded her to jump out of the window; she had in fact, more than once jumped out of an upstairs window, causing herself serious harm. However, she was not willing or able to re-evaluate the evidence for the belief that she had a special relationship with God and heard his voice. Instead, it was possible to retain the belief that God talked to her in this way, but to discuss whether a benevolent God would wish her to do herself harm. The consequences of acting and not acting on such commands were explored, together with anxiety reduction strategies to manage the high levels of arousal experienced at such times.

Addressing negative self-evaluations, anxiety and depression

Low self-esteem is common in people with psychosis (Freeman *et al*, 1998). Furthermore, links between the content of delusions and hallucinations and the characteristics of threatening and traumatic events in a person's earlier life may have been identified in the assessment and formulation stages. These may indicate that there are long-standing unresolved difficulties and associated negative self-evaluations (e.g. believing the self to be evil or worthless). Such self-evaluations are likely to be involved in the processes maintaining delusions and voices, for example, by being congruent with and thereby confirming the accuracy of abusive voices (Close & Garety, 1998). Having identified negative evaluations, standard cognitive therapy approaches are often applicable, reviewing the history of the development of these ideas over the life-span and re-evaluating the evidence. Many people with psychosis have experienced very adverse life events and circumstances, including the psychosis itself and its consequences. In such cases, re-appraisal may take the form of assisting the service user to view him- or herself as not, for example, 'a total failure' or 'a worthless person', but as someone who has struggled heroically with adversity.

The impact of the experience of psychosis is also relevant not only to specific evaluations, but also more generally to depression and anxiety. Birchwood *et al* (1993) have documented how people can experience demoralisation and feelings of loss of control as a result of the onset of psychosis, while McGorry *et al* (1991) have identified traumatic reactions to onset. Anxiety is often severe in people with psychosis, and frequently precedes the acute onset, but is often overlooked (Freeman, 1998). Again, standard cognitive approaches of identifying automatic thoughts and exploring alternative appraisals of these experiences are recommended.

Managing risk of relapse and social disability

The final stage involves reviewing the work done in therapy and looking to the future. The understanding that service users have of the psychosis will influence their engagement with services and supports and their attitudes to medication. This is reviewed and discussed as appropriate. The approach is not didactic, but will aim to help the person to weigh up the advantages and disadvantages of different strategies and plans. Although aspects of social functioning will have been discussed throughout therapy (e.g. social relationship issues, work or other activities), short-term and medium-term plans are discussed further, in the light of what has been learned in therapy. At this stage, it may also be helpful to review what has been learned about the specific individual precursors of relapse and to discuss strategies to reduce the risk of relapse (Birchwood, 1996).

Outcome research

Most of the research literature concerns CBT with people with medication-resistant psychosis, while more recently work with people during acute episodes and with early psychosis has been developed. A new area of work is the introduction of cognitive–behavioural groups. A selective review of the outcome research follows. Since the aims and methods of CBT with different service user groups vary to some extent, we will briefly outline them.

Work with people with medication-resistant psychosis

The aims and methods of CBT for people with relatively stable psychoses, who continue to experience symptoms despite adequate antipsychotic medication, are as described in the preceding sections. The methods described are from our own work, which has attempted to provide a comprehensive but individualised treatment approach. It should be noted, in contrast, that some published reports focus on working with a particular symptom, such as delusions (e.g. Chadwick & Lowe, 1994; Sharp *et al*, 1996; Kinderman & Bentall, 1997) or hallucinations (Morrison, 1994; Haddock *et al*, 1996). Some also use a more restrictive range of therapeutic techniques than described above, such as the earlier coping strategy enhancement work of Tarrier *et al* (1993) or work focused on belief about voices by Chadwick & Birchwood (1994). In general, these more specific approaches are increasingly being integrated into a more comprehensive therapeutic approach and the focus has shifted from symptoms to the person with a range of needs and problems, as we discussed in the opening paragraphs of this chapter.

Bouchard *et al* (1996) reviewed 15 studies of 'cognitive restructuring' in the treatment of schizophrenia, most of which were individual case studies or small case series using cognitive–behavioural approaches with medication-resistant delusions and/or hallucinations. They considered five of these studies to be methodologically rigorous and performed with people with schizophrenia, involving a total of 35 people, including a waiting list controlled trial with a sample of 20 conducted by our group (Garety *et al*, 1994). Bouchard *et al* (1996) focused on changes in positive symptoms as the main measure of outcome. They concluded that these studies suggest that cognitive approaches are effective to reduce or eliminate delusions and hallucinations in people with schizophrenia. In a detailed examination of the studies, however, they found that the effect may be greater on delusions than hallucinations, the former reliably showing substantial changes.

Randomised controlled trials, despite having limitations (such as problems of generalising from research to clinical settings), are more conclusive than case reports or case series as valid tests of the efficacy of various forms of psychological therapy (see Roth & Fonagy, 1996, for a full discussion). Two randomised controlled trials have recently been completed (Kuipers *et al*, 1997, 1998; Tarrier *et al*, 1998, 1999), while a third has just been published (Sensky *et al*, 2000).

Our London–East Anglia trial (Kuipers *et al*, 1997, 1998) compared CBT added to medication and case management with medication and case management alone (treatment as usual control). The trial participants were 60 people, randomly allocated to two groups: 28 in the therapy group, 32 in the control group. They had medication-resistant psychoses, predominantly a diagnosis of schizophrenia. In general, the participants were middle-aged, had a long history of illness (average about 13 years) with moderate levels of symptoms and had average IQ scores. There was a preponderance of men. The therapy was as described above and lasted for nine months. The therapists were all experienced clinical psychologists and engaged in supervision throughout the trial.

At the end of treatment only the CBT group improved significantly (Kuipers *et al*, 1997). The therapy group showed a 25% reduction in overall symptom scores as assessed by the Brief Psychiatric Rating Scale (BPRS; Overall & Gorham, 1962). Participants had a low drop-out rate from therapy (11%) and expressed high levels of satisfaction with treatment. They also expressed considerable hope that they would be able to make progress in the future. At this stage 50% of the treatment group showed a clinically significant improvement, compared with 31% in the control group. However, at follow-up, nine months later, the groups had diverged further. The CBT group showed a significant and continuing improvement in BPRS score reductions whereas the control group returned to baseline. Delusional distress and frequency of hallucinations were also significantly reduced in the treatment group. By this point, 65% of the treatment group showed a reliable clinical improvement on the BPRS measure, compared with only 17% of the control group. However, significant improvements were not shown in levels of depression on the Beck Depression Inventory, which had been achieved in our earlier study (Garety *et al*, 1994), or in general social functioning. There was no evidence that the improvements in the treatment group were attributable to medication; medication did not predict outcome, as both groups were reasonably well maintained on it (Garety *et al*, 1997). An economic evaluation provided an indication that the costs of delivering CBT (£123 per month at 1996 prices) were offset by reduced use of services, particularly in-patient days, in the treatment group over the follow-up phase (Kuipers *et al*, 1998). This is encouraging, although not definitive, evidence that CBT is a cost-effective intervention for this service user group. It also suggests that the changes in symptoms were relevant to relapse prevention. This implies that provision of psychological therapy can help to shift the delivery of services from reactive care to active inter-ventions, which serve as a form of secondary prevention.

We also conducted an analysis of factors that predicted good outcome in response to CBT (Garety *et al*, 1997). We found that key predictors before the start of treatment were a measure of cognitive flexibility concerning delusions and a greater number of recent admissions. The former variable, which represents a capacity, despite high delusional conviction, to contemplate that there may possibly be alternatives to one's beliefs, is consistent with other findings (Chadwick & Lowe, 1994) and suggests that the therapy outcome is in part due to specific effects on delusional thinking. Just as importantly, good outcome was not predicted by any demographic or clinical variables or by IQ. CBT is suitable for a wide range of patients, with differing levels of IQ and with varying symptoms and degrees of severity of problems.

A second randomised controlled trial, which took place in Manchester, has found similar effects, although it differs in a number of respects (Tarrier *et al*, 1998, 1999). In this study, CBT was somewhat narrower and consisted of three components: coping strategy enhancement, problem-solving training and relapse prevention work. It was carried out in 20 hourly sessions, twice each week, thus lasting only 10 weeks. The main aims were to reduce positive symptoms and to prevent relapse. In this study CBT was compared not only with a treatment as usual control, but also with a supportive counselling condition, which aimed to provide emotional support through the development of rapport and unconditional regard. Fidelity to these different interventions was independently assessed and strenuous efforts were made to ensure that the independent assessors of outcome were 'blind' to treatment condition. The participants (*n*=87), predominantly diagnosed as having schizophrenia, were demographically similar to those in our trial (Kuipers *et al*, 1997).

The results show that CBT was superior to routine care in reducing the number and severity of positive and negative symptoms, while the supportive counselling group showed intermediate levels of change (Tarrier *et al*, 1998). A criterion of 50% improvement on psychotic symptom scores was adopted to represent an important clinical improvement. At the end of the treatment phase, the groups differed significantly on this criterion: one-third of the CBT group, less than one-sixth of the supportive counselling group and one-ninth of the routine care made clinically significant improvements. Unlike the London–East Anglia study (Garety *et al*, 1997), in the Manchester study it was found that improvement was predicted by a shorter duration of illness and having less severe symptoms at entry to therapy. However, this latter analysis differed in identifying predictors of change in all three groups, rather than those specific to CBT. During the treatment phase, there were no relapses in the CBT and supportive counselling groups, while 14% of the treatment-as-usual group relapsed. This is not statistically significant, but suggests that both forms of psychological intervention may buffer against relapse during the period in which they are delivered. At follow-up, one year post-treatment, benefits of CBT were substantial compared with the treatment as usual control group. However, there were only a few advantages for CBT, compared with the supportive counselling group (Tarrier *et al*, 1999).

A third randomised controlled trial has recently been reported, the Wellcome study of CBT for neuroleptic-resistant schizophrenia in Newcastle and London (Sensky *et al*, 2000). They compared CBT delivered over nine months with a 'befriending' control condition. The results demonstrate that both groups improved significantly in terms of scores on a general symptom measure over the nine-month treatment period, with no differences between the groups. However, results at nine-month follow-up show that the improvements in the CBT group were maintained, while the befriending group scores reverted to baseline.

Both the Manchester and the Wellcome studies contrasted CBT with a psychosocial control condition, supportive counselling and befriending, respectively (Tarrier *et al*, 1998; Sensky *et al*, 2000). It is important to note that these alternative psychosocial approaches, designed to control for so-called 'non-specific' effects, showed therapeutic benefits, at least in the short term. This is interesting, since such interventions were not expected to exert powerful effects and many professionals would doubt that change could occur for people with psychosis as a result. It is intriguing to speculate which aspects of the interventions are helpful, bearing in mind that they were delivered by skilled therapists who set out to establish a therapeutic relationship, to use empathic counselling techniques and to talk reflectively about the lives and experiences of the service users. These are elements of all good psychological therapies and are not trivial. The quality of the therapeutic relationship is an important predictor of therapy success in general (Horvath & Symonds, 1991) and probably is particularly helpful for people with psychosis who often lack close supportive relationships. Part of the beneficial effect of more formal psychological therapies, such as CBT, will be attributable to such factors; in addition, it is becoming clear that CBT has specific effects of longer term change in symptoms.

Collectively, these three randomised controlled trials provide some support for the effectiveness of CBT for people with psychosis. The clearest effects have been in terms of reductions in symptoms, particularly the positive symptoms of delusions and hallucinations. The London–East Anglia trial found that distress associated with delusions reduced. We also found that the gains made in therapy were sustained or even increased nine months after the end of therapy, a finding that is echoed in the Wellcome study. This would suggest that this approach helps people to develop their own ways of dealing with difficulties, at least for nine months post-intervention, which is a strength of psychological as opposed to pharmacological interventions.

Work in the acute episode

A recent innovation has been the formal application of cognitive–behavioural approaches to acute episodes of psychosis (Drury *et al,* 1996). The aims of this are to hasten the resolution of positive symptoms and to promote full recovery, reducing the severity of residual symptoms. The approach as developed by Drury *et al* (1996) emphasises helping the patient to 'integrate' the psychotic breakdown, rather than 'seal over' the experience. 'Integration' refers to a set of attitudes about psychotic illness, in which it is perceived as a manageable, meaningful and containable experience (McGlashan & Levy, 1977). It is also hoped that by reducing the distress associated with the psychotic episode itself, subsequent traumatic responses and depression may be lessened.

Drury *et al* (1996) report a controlled trial of cognitive therapy with acute psychosis. Patients admitted to an acute psychiatric ward in Birmingham with an episode of functional psychosis (but not bipolar affective disorder or hypomania) were randomly allocated to cognitive therapy or an activity control condition, both in addition to standard care. In the cognitive therapy condition, the psychological intervention methods employed were not restricted to individual cognitive therapy, but included cognitive–behavioural group work, two family engagement sessions and regular structured activity. The total package therefore involved an intensive intervention programme averaging eight hours per week, with daily input over the admission. The individual cognitive therapy focused directly on the person's delusional beliefs, the distress caused and the evidence for the beliefs. The patient would then be invited to consider, in a collaborative manner, alternative constructions and meanings. Drury *et al* (1996) report that patients engaged very well with this approach and valued the fact that their beliefs were not dismissed or ignored. The activity control condition consisted of matched hours of flexible and low-key leisure and social activities away from the ward, together with informal supportive listening.

The results are impressive. The people in the cognitive therapy condition showed a significantly faster and more complete recovery from their psychotic episodes. The effect was most apparent for positive symptoms. At nine-month follow-up, the cognitive therapy group had significantly fewer positive symptoms than the activity control group: at this stage 95% of the cognitive therapy group and 44% of the activity group reported no or only minor hallucinations or delusions. The therapy group also had a significantly shorter stay in hospital.

This is an exciting study that indicates that cognitive–behavioural work with people during their acute episodes may be beneficial and cost-effective. A limitation of the study is the intensive input with multiple components, making inferences about the specific effect of cognitive therapy difficult. (It is noteworthy that a brief cognitive–behavioural intervention, with a specific focus on insight and treatment adherence ('Compliance therapy', see Chapter 3) has shown some benefits in terms of improved medication adherence, when offered during an acute admission (Kemp *et al*, 1996)). A number of other groups are following up Drury *et al*'s work, albeit focused on working with people with early episodes of psychosis, investigating the effects of less intensive programmes, with a more specific emphasis on CBT.

Work with people with early psychosis

A logical extension of Drury *et al*'s pioneering work is to work with people in the early stages of a psychotic illness; indeed one-third of their sample were in the first episode of psychosis. This development is particularly timely, since there is considerable international interest in providing more effective and more rapid interventions, whether pharmacological, social or psychological, to people in their first episode of psychosis (see McGorry, 1998). Combined interventions, incorporating optimal medication management, and psychosocial programmes with both individual and family intervention components have been advocated (Birchwood *et al*, 1998; Falloon *et al*, 1998) and shown to be beneficial (Linszen *et al*, 1996). However, there are no randomised controlled trials of CBT with early psychosis yet published. McGorry, Jackson, Edwards and colleagues in Melbourne, Australia have published a descriptive study of such work (Jackson *et al*, 1998), and a large multi-centre trial, Socrates, is under way in the UK, whose aims and methods are described by Haddock *et al* (1998).

Haddock *et al* (1998) describe their ongoing work with people with early (first or second episode) psychosis as broadly similar to the earlier work with people with medication-resistant psychosis (Tarrier *et al*, 1998). Therapy consists of four elements: assessment and engagement; formulation of key problems; interventions directed at positive and negative symptoms, depression and medication; and relapse prevention. The approach, as before, has a strong symptom focus: it is aimed at reducing symptoms and attempting to reduce symptom recurrence.

A rather different cognitively oriented psychotherapy for early psychosis (COPE) is described by Jackson *et al* (1998). COPE is aimed at assisting people to adjust in the wake of the first episode and focuses on issues of stigmatisation, views of the self and helping people to come to terms with understanding the illness and pursue life goals.

Cognitive and behavioural techniques are used to focus on depression and anxiety. Interestingly, Jackson *et al* (1998) note that COPE does not use the positive symptom-focused cognitive interventions developed in the UK, partly because COPE was developed before such approaches had become established, and partly because people with first episodes show a positive response to medication. COPE is generally offered on an out-patient basis, in 40-minute sessions, weekly or fortnightly.

Jackson *et al* (1998) report on an open trial of COPE, in which all the people who entered the early psychosis service in Melbourne, Australia (EPPIC), who met the criteria were offered COPE. Those who accepted were compared with a group who refused COPE. Both groups received the other services of EPPIC, which provides comprehensive and innovative biopsychosocial services. When first offered, it was intended that about 15 sessions of COPE should be a minimum; however, people chose to have widely varying numbers of sessions (from 2–40). A small control group mostly from outside the catchment area received only in-patient care. Clearly, the methodology of this study, in which there are clear biases in group selection and wide variability in the duration of treatment, means that the data can only be regarded as indicative. The results are mixed. There are indications that the COPE group improved significantly compared with the no treatment control group in terms of their attitudes to their illness and in negative symptoms, but did not show advantages compared with the refusal group. Indeed, this latter group was significantly less depressed at the end of treatment, but had also been less depressed than the COPE group at pre-treatment. Overall, the study suggests that COPE may improve understanding and insight, and aspects of functioning. A more rigorous study is needed, but it may also be that the addition of the more specific cognitive methods for positive symptoms would result in a more powerful and comprehensive treatment approach, which would then be similar to the individual component of Drury *et al*'s (1996) cognitive intervention.

Group CBT

Drury *et al* (1996) included a structured cognitive–behavioural group in their cognitive therapy programme for acute episodes, in addition to individual cognitive therapy. They considered that the group was an important component of treatment, enabling peer group relating and providing a setting of solidarity for bolstering self-regard through the challenging of negative social stereotypes (Birchwood *et al*, 1998). This is consistent with earlier research. Kanas (1986), in a review of group treatment with people with schizophrenia, found benefits with interaction-oriented group approaches, in contrast to insight-oriented approaches. Drury *et al*'s approach was a planned and systematic programme of eight sessions that addressed the following topics: introductory session; making sense of experience and symptoms; medication; stress management; early warning signs and relapse; coping with symptoms; and group cognitive therapy for delusions and hallucinations. As one element in an intensive treatment, the results of Drury *et al*'s (1996) study cannot confirm the specific benefits of the group approach. However, there is growing interest in applying cognitive–behavioural approaches in a group format, with people with both acute and medication-resistant psychoses (e.g. Gledhill *et al*, 1998). Controlled research of the effectiveness of such groups is needed.

Conclusions

Although the evaluation of CBT for psychosis is in its early stages, evidence is accumulating for its efficacy and cost-effectiveness. It is also developing rapidly, and becoming more person-centred rather than purely symptom-focused. We have found that the approach is highly acceptable to people, who often report that the detailed discussion of their beliefs and experiences, previously only treated as symptoms for a check-list, is immensely valued. For this reason, we have argued that the general approach can be adopted by mental health staff, in their interactions with service users, even without undertaking formal therapy (Fowler *et al*, 1998). However, the difficulty of engaging and working therapeutically with people with psychosis should not be underestimated. We have already highlighted the complexity and diversity of the problems of people with psychosis. A sound knowledge is required both of cognitive and other theories of psychosis and of cognitive therapy more generally, as well as good therapeutic skills. We recommend training and supervision as essential, both of which are currently in short supply. However, we cannot afford yet (if ever) to foreclose on precisely which approaches are most beneficial or for which people. In these exciting times for psychological approaches to psychosis, further research and development are needed to refine and clarify the details of CBT and to establish efficacy and effectiveness more firmly.

References

BECK, A. T. (1952) Successful out-patient psychotherapy of a chronic schizophrenic with a delusion based on borrowed guilt. *Psychiatry*, **15**, 305–312.

BENTALL, R. P. (1994) Cognitive biases and abnormal beliefs: towards a model of persecutory delusions. In *The Neuropsychology of Schizophrenia* (eds A. S. David & J. Cutting), pp. 337–360. London: Lawrence Erlbaum Associates.

BIRCHWOOD, M. (1996) Early interventions in psychotic relapse: cognitive approaches to detection and management. In *Cognitive–Behavioural Interventions with Psychotic Disorders* (eds G. Haddock & P. Slade). London: Routledge.

——, MASON, R., MACMILLAN, F., *ET AL* (1993) Depression, demoralisation and control over psychotic illness: a comparison of depressed and non-depressed patients with chronic psychosis. *Psychological Medicine*, **23**, 387–395.

——, TODD, P. & JACKSON, C. (1998) Early intervention in psychosis. *British Journal of Psychiatry*, **172** (suppl. 33), 53–59.

BOUCHARD, S., VALLIÈRES, A., ROY, M., *ET AL* (1996) Cognitive restructuring in the treatment of psychotic symptoms in schizophrenia: a critical analysis. *Behavior Therapy*, **27**, 257–277.

BUCHKREMER, G., KLINGBERG, S., HÖLLE, R. *ET AL* (1997) Psychoeducational psychotherapy for schizophrenic patients and their key relatives or care-givers: results of a 2-year follow-up. *Acta Psychiatrica Scandinavica*, **96**, 483–491.

CHADWICK, P. D. J. & BIRCHWOOD, M. (1994) The omnipotence of voices: a cognitive approach to hallucinations. *British Journal of Psychiatry*, **164**, 190–201.

——, —— & TROWER, P. (1996) *Cognitive Therapy for Delusions, Voices and Paranoia*. Chichester: Wiley.

—— & LOWE, C. F. (1990) Measurement and modification of delusional beliefs. *Journal of Consulting and Clinical Psychology*, **58**, 225–232.

—— & —— (1994) A cognitive approach to measuring and modifying delusions. *Behavioural Research and Therapy*, **32**, 355–367.

CLOSE, H. & GARETY, P. A. (1998) Cognitive assessment of voices: further developments in understanding the emotional impact of voices. *British Journal of Clinical Psychology*, **37**, 173–188.

DRURY, V., BIRCHWOOD, B., COCHRANE, R., *ET AL* (1996) Cognitive therapy and recovery from acute psychosis: a controlled trial. I. Impact on psychotic symptoms. *British Journal of Psychiatry*, **169**, 593–601.

FALLOON, I. R. H., COVERDALE, J. H., LAIDLAW, T. M., *ET AL* (1998) Early intervention for schizophrenic disorders. *British Journal of Psychiatry*, **172** (suppl. 33), 33–38.

FOWLER, D. & MORLEY, S. (1989) The cognitive-behavioural treatment of hallucinations and delusions: a preliminary study. *Behavioural Psychotherapy*, **17**, 267–282.

——, GARETY, P. A. & KUIPERS, E. (1995) *Cognitive Behaviour Therapy for Psychosis: Theory and Practice*. Chichester: Wiley.

——, —— & —— (1998) Cognitive therapy for psychosis: formulation, treatment, effects and service implications. *Journal of Mental Health*, **7**, 123–134.

FREEMAN, D. (1998) *Psychosis and Neurosis: Examining the Role of Anxiety in the Formation and Maintenance of Persecutory Delusions*. PhD thesis. London: University of London.

——, GARETY, P. A., FOWLER, D., *ET AL* (1998) The London–East Anglia randomised controlled trial of cognitive–behavioural therapy for psychosis. IV: Self-esteem and presercutory delusions. *British Journal of Clinical Psychology*, **38**, 113–154.

FRITH, C. D. (1992) *The Cognitive Neuropsychology of Schizophrenia*. Hove: Lawrence Erlbaum Associates.

GARETY, P. A. & HEMSLEY, D. R. (1994) *Delusions: Investigations into the Psychology of Delusional Reasoning*. Hove: Psychology Press.

——, KUIPERS, E., FOWLER, D. *ET AL* (1994) Cognitive behavioural therapy for drug-resistant psychosis. *British Journal of Medical Psychology*, **67**, 259–271.

——, FOWLER, D., KUIPERS, E., *ET AL* (1997) London–East Anglia randomised controlled trial of cognitive–behavioural therapy for psychosis. II: Predictors of outcome. *British Journal of Psychiatry*, **171**, 420–426.

GARETY, P. A. & FREEMAN, D. (1999) Cognitive approaches to delusions: a critical review of theories of evidence. *British Journal of Clinical Psychology*, **38**, 113–154.

GLEDHILL, A., LOBBAN, F. & SELLWOOD, W. (1998) Group CBT for people with schizophrenia: a preliminary evaluation. *Behavioural and Cognitive Psychotherapy*, **26**, 63–75.

HADDOCK, G. & SLADE, P. (1996) *Cognitive–Behavioural Interventions with Psychotic Disorders.* London: Routledge.

——, BENTALL, R. P. & SLADE, D. (1996) Psychological treatment of auditory hallucinations: focusing or distraction? In *Cognitive-Behavioural Interventions with Psychotic Disorders* (eds G. Haddock & P. Slade), pp. 45–70. London: Routledge.

——, MORRISON, A. P., HOPKINS, R. ET AL (1998) Individual cognitive–behavioural interventions in early psychosis. *British Journal of Psychiatry*, **172** (suppl. 33), 101–106.

HEMSLEY, D. (1994) Perceptual and cognitive abnormalities as the basis for schizophrenic symptoms. In *The Neuropsychology of Schizophrenia* (eds A. S. David & J. Cutting). Hove: Lawrence Erlbaum Associates.

HORVATH, A. O. & SYMONDS, B. D. (1991) Relationship between working alliance and outcome in psychotherapy: a meta-analysis. *Journal of Consulting and Clinical Psychology*, **38**, 139–149.

JACKSON, H., McGORRY, P., EDWARDS, J., ET AL (1998) Cognitively-orientated psychotherapy for early psychosis (COPE). *British Journal of Psychiatry*, **172** (suppl. 33), 93–100.

KANAS, N. (1986) Group therapy with schizophrenics: a review of controlled studies. *International Journal of Group Psychotherapy*, **36**, 339–351.

KEMP, R., HAYWARD, P., APPLEWHAITE, G., ET AL (1996) Compliance therapy in psychotic patients: randomised controlled trial. *British Medical Journal*, **312**, 345–349.

KINDERMAN, P. & BENTALL, R. P. (1997) Attribution therapy for paranoid delusions: a case study. *Behavioural and Cognitive Psychotherapy*, **25**, 269–280.

KINGDON, D. G. & TURKINGTON, D. (1994) *Cognitive Behaviour Therapy of Schizophrenia.* Hove: Lawrence Erlbaum.

KUIPERS, E., GARETY, P. A., FOWLER, D., ET AL (1997) The London–East Anglia trial of cognitive–behavioural therapy for psychosis. I: Effects of the treatment phase. *British Journal of Psychiatry*, **171**, 319–327.

——, FOWLER, D., GARETY, P. A., ET AL (1998) London-East Anglia randomised controlled trial of cognitive-behavioural therapy for psychosis. III: Follow-up and economic evaluation at 18 months. *British Journal of Psychiatry*, **173**, 61–68.

LINSZEN, D., DINGEMANS, P., VAN DER DOES, J. W., ET AL (1996) Treatment, expressed emotion and relapse in recent onset schizophrenic disorders. *Psychological Medicine*, **26**, 333–342.

McGLASHAN, T. & LEVY, S. (1977) Sealing over in a therapeutic community. *Psychiatry*, **40**, 55–65.

McGORRY, P. (ed.)(1998) Verging on reality. *British Journal of Psychiatry*, **172** (suppl. 33), 1–136.

——, CHANEN, A., McCARTHY, E. ET AL (1991) Post-traumatic stress disorder following recent onset psychosis. An unrecognised postpsychotic syndrome. *Journal of Nervous and Mental Disease*, **179**, 253-258.

MORRISON, A. P. (1994) Cognitive behaviour therapy for auditory hallucinations without concurrent medication: a single case. *Behavioural and Cognitive Psychotherapy*, **22**, 259–264.

OVERALL, J. E. & GORHAM, D. R. (1962) The brief psychiatric rating scale. *Psychological Reports*, **10**, 799–812.

PERRIS, C. (1989) *Cognitive Therapy for Patients with Schizophrenia.* New York: Cassel.

ROTH, A. & FONAGY, P. (1996) *What Works for Whom? A Critical Review of Psychotherapy Research.* New York: Guilford.

SHARP, H. M, FEAR, C. F., WILLIAMS, J. M. G., ET AL (1996) Delusional phenomenology – dimensions of change. *Behavioural Research and Therapy*, **34**, 123–142.

Sensky, T., Turkington, D., Kingdon, D., *et al* (2000) A randomised-controlled trial of cognitive–behavioural therapy for persistant symptoms in schizophrenia resistant to medication. *Archives of General Psychiatry*, **57**, 165–172.

Strauss, J. S. & Carpenter, W. T. (1981) *Schizophrenia*. New York: Plenum.

Tarrier, N. (1992) Management and modification of residual positive psychotic symptoms. In *Innovations in the Psychological Management of Schizophrenia* (eds M. Birchwood & N. Tarrier). Chichester: Wiley.

——, Beckett, R., Harwood, S., *et al* (1993) A trial of two cognitive–behavioural methods of treating drug resistant residual psychotic symptoms in schizophrenic patients: I. Outcome. *British Journal of Psychiatry*, **162**, 524–532.

——, Yusupoff, L., Kinney, C., *et al* (1997) The use of coping skills in the treatment of hallucinations and delusions in schizophrenia. In *Psychotherapy of Psychosis* (eds C. Mace & F. Margison), pp. 130–148. London: Gaskell.

——, , , *et al* (1998) Randomised controlled trial of intensive cognitive–behavioural therapy for patients with chronic schizophrenia. *British Medical Journal*, **317**, 303–307.

——, Withkowski, A., Kinney, C., *et al* (1999) Durability of the effects of cognitive–behavioural therapy in the treatmentof chronic schizophrenia. *British Journal of Psychiatry*, **174**, 500–504.

Zubin, J. & Spring, B. (1977) Vulnerability – a new view on schizophrenia. *Journal of Abnormal Psychology*, **86**, 103-126.

3 Compliance therapy: a collaborative approach to psychiatric medication

PETER HAYWARD, ROISIN KEMP and ANTHONY DAVID

In discussions of psychotherapeutic approaches to human difficulties and mental illness it is probably important to clarify and discuss the fundamental assumptions on which the various approaches are based. However, within a book considering various psychological approaches to serious mental illness, we can do this by pointing out how our approach resembles or differs from others.

Our own, admittedly imperfect understanding of psychodynamic approaches is that they seek to address the fundamental, often unconscious, deficits underlying psychiatric problems. For problems as drastic in their effects as those usually seen in the psychotic disorders, one might assume that the underlying problems are complex, and that addressing them would, therefore, be a difficult and time-consuming process. We might also presume that it would demand an extended period of cooperation from the patient and a considerable degree of skilled, individual attention on the part of the therapist.

The approach we describe here is very different in that it assumes that many, apparently fixed and on the surface, maladaptive positions are taken up for reasons that are accessible (i.e. within or close to conscious awareness) through discussion within a working therapeutic alliance. Furthermore, most actions follow directly from beliefs, which are likely to be biased but may be refined with simple explanation and experience. This assumption lies behind most cognitive–behavioural interventions. We are also mindful of the practicalities imposed by the setting in which we work. Hence, unlike some psychological interventions based on exploring supposedly unconscious motivation and seeking to effect fundamental change, our approaches have to be relatively easy to use and require both a much smaller commitment of resources from the UK NHS and much briefer commitment of time on the part of both patient and therapist. It was developed in the context of an acute admission ward serving a deprived area of inner city London, and was intended to work in conjunction with what might be called conventional medical treatment. We concentrated on medication, although this was not the sole focus of the intervention that we will describe and is clearly only one part, albeit an important one, of an effective therapeutic package.

It was also our intention that the skills involved could be taught to a variety of health professionals in a relatively limited period of time (although empirical evidence for this is only now being assembled). It is therefore based on four assumptions. While not arguing that these assumptions will be true of every patient with serious mental illness, we would suggest that they apply in a sizeable percentage of such cases, making this approach worth trying with almost all patients. These assumptions are:

(a) That treatment with neuroleptic medication will be, on balance, beneficial for most patients with psychosis. There may well be some patients for whom neuroleptics are not particularly effective or who suffer a prohibitively high level of side-effects. On the other hand, we are not aware of a credible alternative approach, and we believe that improving adherence with treatment and reducing conflict between the patient and health professionals will be, on balance, beneficial.

(b) Most patients, when on medication, will be capable of rational consideration of a variety of issues. Some patients may remain so paranoid or thought disordered, even on medication, that communication is significantly hampered, and with some there may be other barriers to communication, such as language problems or very low intelligence. But it is our experience that, with most patients, it is possible to enter into dialogue about their illness and its need for medication treatment, whatever their apparent level of 'insight' (McEvoy, 1998).

(c) Patients have a variety of beliefs, both positive and negative, regarding medication use. One can therefore think of these beliefs in terms of the Health Belief Model (Budd *et al*, 1996), which implies that the patterns of compliance and non-compliance can be explained in terms of the services user's beliefs about his or her 'illness'.

(d) Patients who do not comply with psychiatric medical treatment will, in some respects, resemble other patients who do not comply with optimal treatment for a variety of non-psychiatric illnesses, and may therefore be approached in similar ways. Certainly, the problem of non-compliance is not restricted to those with psychiatric disorders: it is seen across the spectrum of illness, and a variety of approaches have been suggested to reduce it (Sackett & Haynes, 1976; Becker & Rosenstock, 1984). It is our belief that, with appropriate modifications, a psychiatric patient who is non-adherent can be approached in a manner similar to any patient who does not choose to follow medical advice. As with any other patient, compliance can be increased by offering a regime that is, first of all, effective, and by minimising deterrent factors, whether they be side-effects, over-complex prescribing regimes, or difficulties in attending and receiving treatment (Cramer, 1995; Kemp & David, 1997). It can also be increased by ensuring a good relationship between patient and prescriber, one in which the patient feels respected and understood (Corrigan *et al*, 1990). With patients with serious mental illness, these factors may not be enough. We therefore developed a treatment protocol that we refer to as 'compliance therapy' (Kemp *et al*, 1996*a,b*, 1997, 1998), which was developed in the first instance using as a model 'motivational interviewing', a technique that has been developed to foster a variety of positive health behaviours (Rollnick *et al*, 1993). This chapter offers a brief description, with case examples, of this approach and highlights some of the specific barriers to acceptance of treatment with which our approach is intended to deal.

Barriers to compliance

Non-compliance with medical advice is not restricted to those with psychiatric illness. A simple vignette may illustrate this:

> Carl is a fit and healthy young medical student of 23. Since entering medical school he has been in the habit of drinking 2–3 pints of beer a day during the week, mostly in the evenings while studying. On the weekends he plays a great deal of sport and drinks fairly heavily with a group of friends, all of whom drink at least as much as he does. When receiving teaching on the effects of alcohol, he realises that he is drinking 35 to 40 units of alcohol per week, a level that, he is told, may cause long-term damage to his health. In spite of this, his drinking habits do not change.

The story of Carl is probably similar to many, or even most, ordinary people who commit a variety of health 'sins', either of commission (smoking, taking drugs) or omission (not exercising regularly, not flossing after every meal). One of the main reasons for Carl's continued drinking is that he probably does not experience what he perceives to be negative effects from his habit. Possible negative effects lie somewhere in the uncertain future, while the perceived positive effects of drinking are immediate. This effect can be seen in many psychiatric patients, especially, but not exclusively, in patients who lack 'insight'. Many patients with psychotic disorders may not perceive themselves as being ill: they may have delusional explanations for their periods of illness, or may attribute periods in hospital as due to outside forces. Similarly, some patients with grandiose delusions or manic mood state may view their so-called symptoms positively, and be reluctant to give them up (van Putten *et al*, 1976). Even for patients with insight, short-term relief from adverse side-effects may tempt them to under-dose themselves, while those who relapse while on medication may feel that continuing their treatment is futile.

The vignette hints at a second important cause of non-compliance: Carl may fear the attributions that his friends might make about him if he reduces his level of alcohol use. By the same token, acceptance of psychiatric medication can be seen as the acceptance of a psychiatric diagnosis. A review of the existing literature on stigma and mental illness supports the view that the lay public know relatively little about mental illness, and that they fear and distrust those who are mentally ill (see Rabkin, 1974; Hayward & Bright, 1997). This research also suggests that, in lay eyes, the main mark of psychiatric illness is that one is receiving psychiatric treatment: as Scambler (1984) says of another stigmatised condition, epilepsy, "In short, people saw *medical* diagnosis as certain to expose them to the harsh and injurious realities of *lay* ignorance, intolerance and prejudice". We feel that the existence of such stigmatising beliefs provides an important barrier to acceptance of medical treatment, and one that will often need to be addressed.

Two other factors are worth mentioning. Psychiatrists alone among medical professionals have the power to compel treatment. While no doubt necessary at times, this procedure may create resentment and the feeling of being demeaned; such negative feelings, if they exist, will certainly need to be addressed if one's goal is to create a more collaborative treatment relationship. Finally, some patients may well be so disorganised in their thoughts and actions that following a treatment regime is too difficult. Box 3.1 lists the main barriers to compliance.

Basic principles

The compliance therapy approach grew out of two strands of therapeutic work, the use of motivational interviewing in the substance

---

Box 3.1.
Barriers to compliance: a multi-dimensional scheme

The person
Culture, family, values and prejudices
Experiences and beliefs
Support network and milieu
Personality
Intelligence
Insight

The illness
Psychosis
Grandiosity
Depression
Cognitive impairment

The treatment
Doctor–patient relationship
Treatment setting
Effectiveness
Complexity
Side-effects
Stigma

---

misuse field (Rollnick *et al*, 1993) and recent development in cognitive–behavioural therapy (CBT) for psychosis (Garety *et al*, 1994; Kingdon *et al*, 1994; see also Chapter 2 of this book). These approaches all emphasise, in the first instance, a collaborative, non-judgmental approach. The service users's own model of the causes and effects of his or her difficulties is assessed in a non-confrontational way, and investigation of that model is used to find motives for the desired behavioural change. Compliance therapy, along with its two 'parents', emphasises the use of reflective listening, empathy and regular summarising of the service user's views to create rapport and build a therapeutic alliance. In motivational interviewing, the service user is encouraged to supply reasons for abstaining from drugs or alcohol: the pros and cons of abstinence are examined, and the goal is to help the service user see an abstinent lifestyle as the best way of attaining valued goals. By the same token, the goal of compliance therapy is to help the person with a long-term mental illness to see drug compliance as a useful tool for obtaining personally valued goals. Motivational interviewing shuns stigmatising labels: discussions about whether one really is 'an alcoholic' are avoided because they may lead to confrontation and interfere with the treatment alliance. By the same token, compliance therapy views acceptance of a diagnostic label like 'schizophrenia' as less important than promoting doctor–patient collaboration regarding medication regimes. From the foregoing introduction it should be clear that we do not use the term 'compliance' in an authoritarian fashion as has been assumed in some circles. Compliance with the medical treatment is the shared aim of patient and therapist (not unquestioning compliance with the doctor).

The trials of CBT for schizophrenia cited above emphasise a collaborative focus on target symptoms with the goal of relieving perceived distress. This principle is also a key aspect of compliance therapy: medication compliance is offered to the patient as a freely chosen strategy to deal with areas of perceived distress or difficulty. In addition, Kingdon & Turkington (1994) and Kingdon *et al* (1994) have developed the extremely useful strategy of employing what they term the "normalising rationale", whose purpose is to offer patients relatively non-threatening explanations for their symptoms. When using this technique, the therapist focuses on the continuities between psychotic symptoms and normal experience; as they say,

> '"… it can be suggested that evidence points to the conclusion that the symptoms the patient is experiencing are different in degree from, or are exaggerations of, normal responses to stress; they are not distinctively different in type." (Kingdon & Turkington, 1994)

The therapist can first suggest that in extreme situations, for example, those produced by prolonged sleeplessness, sensory deprivation or a high fever, most people will have abnormal experiences. If psychotic illness is viewed in terms of a diathesis–stress model, then the person can be described as someone with a somewhat lower threshold for such effects than other people and psychotic experiences, such as paranoid beliefs or auditory hallucinations, can be conceptualised as an exaggerated form of normal experience ('jumping to conclusions', 'being too self-conscious', or 'letting the imagination run away with itself'). Such an approach is designed to reduce the stigmatising effects of medication: rather than being 'drugs for crazy people', neuroleptics can be described as drugs to make the person more resilient or to relieve or reduce specific distressing experiences. Box 3.2 offers a summary of the basic general principles of the compliance therapy approach.

Three phases of compliance therapy

With these points in mind, we will give a brief outline of the compliance therapy approach. We describe the approach as involving three phases, but these are only intended as guidelines, indicating the tasks that

---

Box 3.2.
Basic principles of compliance therapy (adapted from Kemp et al, 1997)

Emphasis on personal choice and responsibility
Non-blaming atmosphere
Focus on eliciting patient's concerns
Express empathy
Support self-efficacy

Key techniques
Reflective listening
Regular summarising
Inductive questioning
Explore ambivalence: the good and bad things about treatment
Develop discrepancy between present behaviour and broader goals
Use normalising rationales

Avoid
Lecturing or preaching
Insisting on diagnostic labelling
Turning session into a debate
Asking a series of questions (instead use selective reflection)

---

the therapist will be trying to undertake. The overall style, throughout all three phases, is worth emphasising: it involves empathic, reflective listening, with frequent use of summaries of what the service user has said. Confrontational statements and giving direction are avoided, as are turning the therapy session into a series of questions. The main goal throughout is to understand the service user's perspective: if aspects of that perspective can be utilised to promote medication compliance, this is desirable, but any exercise that builds understanding and rapport is likely to be useful for long-term management.

Therapy is probably best begun when the patient is not acutely unwell, for example, when a hospitalised patient has begun to improve on medication. In the first phase of therapy, the goal is to establish the patient's stance towards medication. A key technique is the taking of an illness history. Due credence is given to any negative views that the patient may have about medication: these are not challenged at this point, but instead gentle enquiry is used to establish as many of the facts as possible of what happened. Certainly, a variety of unpleasant side-effects and adverse drug reactions seem to be inherent in most of the medications used in modern psychiatric practice; before being too quick to challenge a patient for 'not following doctor's orders', the therapist should consider how willing he or she would be to take a neuroleptic or mood stabiliser for an extended period of time.

In most cases, it is our experience that patient's discussing their illness history will seldom opt in the first instance for a medical explanation of their problems. They may focus on delusional explanations of their problems, or they may put the blame on others, perhaps using a paranoid style of explanation (e.g. 'the doctors are against me', or 'I'm the victim of black magic'). Paranoid ideas may serve a defensive function by bolstering low self-esteem in a competitive society (e.g. 'I have failed to gain status and wealth not due to lack of talent, but because my enemies have foiled me'). Stress, trauma and various external factors may also be blamed. If a link can be made between non-compliance and relapse, this should be gently pointed out to the patient, without emphasising it unduly at this point: it is probably better simply to comment on it, but noting it so that it can be referred to later in the therapy. The disadvantages of being unwell should be highlighted; this is worth mentioning because, as the patient improves, he or she may wish to forget or gloss over the more distressing aspects of acute illness. It may also be useful to highlight indirect benefits of staying well, such as better relationships with loved ones or being able to remain at work. Negative aspects of medication (e.g. dystonic reactions, weight gain, sexual problems, complicated regimens (see Box 3.1)) must be acknowledged although it is also important to bear in mind that these unfortunate factors may play into a person's already negative attitude and be given, by them, undue weight. If a patient chooses to focus on some adverse treatment experience (e.g. being forcibly medicated), this must also be acknowledged, but examples in which treatment has been useful can be pointed out. If the patient is resistant to any acknowledgement of the problem, gentle enquiry can be used to seek out areas of difficulty, such as relationships or accommodation, and it can be suggested that medication use might have some utility in those areas. If it proves impossible to convey that subjective benefits will accrue from taking medication and all else fails, it is worth raising the possibility that continued use of medication might help the patient to remain out of hospital, and that this possibility might deserve a trial.

In the second phase of the therapy, the key technique is to ask the patient to examine the pros and cons of medication use (see Box 3.2). This is the heart of the compliance therapy intervention, and is in keeping with the model of the patient as capable of rational choice. Patients may or may not behave in a rational manner, and, for legal purposes, they can be treated, for a set period of time, as lacking in the power of rational decision-making, in a similar way to being involuntarily medicated while detained on a section of the Mental Health Act. However, unlike some countries, in which the patient can be forced to accept medication over a prolonged period of time, patients in the UK cannot be forced to accept medication once their involuntary detention is finished except during a limited period of leave. Thus, we would argue, if patients cannot be given positive reasons for continuing their medication, they will discontinue it. Further, it is well worth making the effort to convince the patient that deciding to comply with prescribed medication is in no way an attempt to minimise a person's freedom and individuality. On the contrary, by taking medication, the person is more likely to retain his or her dignity and position as an individual in a free society and reduce the chances of being detained involuntarily.

That said, the therapist will often be greeted with a long list of 'cons'. These may include, in the first instance, the side-effects of psychiatric medication and the stigma of being someone who is being forced to take the medication. It may require more work to elicit the pros. Some of these may include a reduction in certain distressing experiences, improved sleep or better social or occupational functioning. Of course some patients may not connect these improvements with medication, and may have other explanations. Some of these explanations may be delusional (e.g. 'my voices have decided to leave me alone for a while'), while others may attribute this to external factors (e.g. 'hospitalisation has reduced my stress level'). In these cases, it is worth noting that the perceived benefits coincided with medication use, and that continuing medication might help to maintain them. The emphasis should fall on the benefits that may flow from continued compliance, especially in terms of the patient's own long-term goals. In general, positively reinforcing those attitudes that are congruent with therapeutic goals (or re-framing the patients' views in this way) is a valuable technique.

At the same time, the therapist may have to deal with those aspects of medication use that the patient perceives as negative. These must be acknowledged, and an honest effort made to understand the patient's views of these issues. One cannot promise that the patient will not experience side-effects or other unpleasant aspects of treatment, only that every effort will be made to minimise them. Misconceptions can be explored (e.g. 'I'm afraid of addiction'), and the issue of psychiatric stigma (e.g. what other people may attribute to a person 'on medication') may need to be addressed. The first may be allayed by accurate information or the analogy with maintenance therapy in other conditions such as diabetes, while concern about stigma must be acknowledged as being perfectly understandable, but the patient should be asked to consider whether or not the fears and prejudices of an uninformed public should prevent one from receiving a beneficial treatment. The normalising rationale, as explained above, may also be useful here. Finally, the patient must be asked to weigh up these pros and cons, and decide whether the possible drawbacks of compliance outweigh its benefits (see Box 2). The patient may conclude that the drawbacks are overwhelming, in which case his or her decision can, in most circumstances, be accepted along with 'an agreement to differ'. An excessively confrontational stance taken at this point runs the risk of alienating the patient and cutting off all lines of communication. In the event that the patient chooses not to comply, we would argue that those lines should be kept open for the future.

During the third phase of therapy, the benefits and drawbacks of continued, long-term compliance are discussed. This is only possible if the patient thinks that there may be some benefit in medication, following the exploration carried on in the second phase. The goal here is to offer arguments in favour of accepting, or, at the very least, trying out a long-term course of medication. A stress–vulnerability model is offered to the service user, with the goal of normalising long-term medication use, seeing it as analogous to the long-term treatment of chronic conditions like diabetes or asthma. The normalising rationale, as explained above, is very important here, and stigma may be an important issue, with the patient perhaps seeing the necessity of long-term medication as a diminishing of the sense of self. The existence of stigma cannot be denied, but it can be suggested that the patient should not give up something that might improve functioning and quality of life because of the prejudices of others (see Hayward & Bright, 1997); one can also point out that mental illness of various sorts affects more than 10% of the total population and that many gifted and creative individuals (e.g. Van Gogh, Spike Milligan or other cultural icons relevant to the patient) have suffered from it (see Jamison, 1993). Rather than seeing medication as something imposed from outside, the patient is encouraged to view it as a long-term strategy to improve personal functioning; bitterness about past involuntary treatment can be met with the suggestion that compliance is a way of receiving treatment on one's own terms and avoiding detention and forced medication in the future. The therapist can suggest relevant literature for the patient to read if appropriate but usually these concepts are simply discussed face-to-face. Other topics that may be useful include recognition of early signs of relapse and useful information on drug effects and side-effects. The use of maintenance medication is often described as a 'protective layer' or an 'insurance policy' that can be used to improve the chances that one stays well and out of hospital. Probably the most important point will be to make sure that the lines of communication remain open: should the patient stop complying and relapse, then this could be seen as a learning experience and a springboard for further compliance work. (For a fuller summary of the three phases, see Kemp *et al* 1996*a,b*; Kemp *et al* 1997.)

Case vignette

In order to illustrate these three phases of compliance therapy, we offer the following case vignette, a composite designed to illustrate the treatment in action:

> William is 26. He did well in secondary school and was enjoying studies in chemistry, which he wished to continue at university. However, after leaving school, he had his first breakdown and was forced to take the year off. During this episode he slept less and less and became agitated and unkempt. He believed that his family and members of his class were plotting to make him fail his exams, and he also heard denigrating, third person auditory hallucinations suggesting that he was incapable of work and a lazy and bad person. Following a year off, during which he received psychiatric treatment, he returned to college and had a second episode. During this episode he was detained in hospital and involuntarily medicated – he never resumed his studies. Instead, he worked at a number of casual jobs which he did not find satisfying. He also became interested in religion and philosophy and began reading various religious works on a rather non-selective basis.
>
> He is now in hospital following a third episode and a second involuntary admission. He had begun staying up late at night reading, sleeping less and less and isolating himself. He believed that his neighbours and workmates were plotting against him, and again began experiencing denigrating hallucinations. Once admitted he refused medication and had to be given an injection on two occasions.
>
> During the first phase of compliance therapy, William presented as very anti-medication and anti-psychiatry. He described the mental health establishment as "society's way of controlling geniuses" and viewed medication as a "chemical straight-jacket". He was particularly angry at the psychiatrist who treated him during his first episode, stating that "he and his drugs were worse than useless". Gentle probing revealed that he stopped his medication because of side-effects before his first hospitalisation. When asked about why he was in hospital, he described himself as "persecuted by mediocre people", and stated that nothing was wrong with him, although he then admitted that he had been hearing voices and not sleeping, and that these symptoms were now somewhat better. When asked why this was, his answers were evasive.
>
> During the second phase of therapy William was asked to think about the good and bad points of medication. At first he stated that he could think of no good points at all, but only bad ones. He described a number of very unpleasant side-effects, but it became clear that the most important negative effect from William's point of view was that medication took away his feeling of "creative inspiration". William dwelt at length on how wonderful this creative feeling was, but gentle inquiry revealed that it was not all positive: it also produced troubling insomnia and problems in his relationships with friends and family. When asked why he felt that friends and family had turned against him, he first suggested that they were involved in a conspiracy; however, when the

attitudes of other people were explored, William did admit that this seemed hard to believe. He also admitted that, since the medication had been started, he was sleeping much better and feeling less restless.

During the third phase of therapy, William continued to be of two minds about medication. At times, he was willing to admit that it might be responsible for his improved relationships with others. He also admitted that he was sleeping better, although he complained about being excessively tired. Stigma was an important issue for him at this point; he had invested a great deal in the belief that he had acquired some special knowledge and felt that to willingly take medication was to admit that he was "just another crazy person". The nature of mental illness was discussed, and it was pointed out that, whatever the cause of his experiences, they could still be seen as revelatory or mystical, even though they might also pose a serious threat to his health and well being. William felt well at the time of discharge, but it was suggested that further medication use could be seen as an 'insurance policy' to make sure that he stayed well. It was also suggested to him that by taking maintenance medication at a lower dose he could avoid the unpleasant experience of an involuntary admission involving high doses of involuntary medication. The fluctuating nature of William's insight made his prognosis a guarded one, but a good working relationship had been established, which hopefully could be used again in the event of relapse. It should be noted that while not all patients are as articulate and intelligent as William, lack of such attributes does not preclude a good response to compliance therapy (Kemp *et al*, 1996c).

Therapeutic strategies for improving compliance with medication

It would seem sensible to begin by informing patients about their prescribed treatment, including what it is and what it does, both positively and negatively. Many studies have shown that patients with schizophrenia have a poor knowledge of the drugs they take (Tempier, 1996). Regardless of this fact, Sackett & Haynes (1976) have cast doubt on whether, in fact, there is any relationship discernible from the general medical literature between patients' knowledge of disease or its treatment and compliance, and they concluded that patients' intelligence or educational achievement may also have little bearing on compliance. Factors that do emerge repeatedly are complexity of regimens, side-effects, health beliefs and 'discordance' between the doctor's and patient's therapeutic goals (Royal Pharmaceutical Society of Great Britain, 1997).

A number of trials have now been conducted, examining methods to improve compliance. These are summarised in Table 3.1. In general, it appears that psychoeducation on its own is not effective, or at least if

TABLE 3.1
A summary of intervention studies aimed at improving compliance in patients with psychosis

Authors	No. of subjects (including controls)	Follow-up	Comment
Seltzer *et al* (1980)	67 with mixed psychoses	5 months	Educational lectures in groups. Improved attitudes and objectively measured compliance. Non-randomised.
Boczkowski *et al* (1985)	36 out-patients	3 months	Behavioural training superior to psychoeducation. Very brief intervention.
Streicker *et al* (1986)	75 mostly recovered patients with schizophrenia	6 & 10 months	Education plus counselling. Increased knowledge but no sustained improvement in compliance.
Eckman *et al* (1992)	41 schizophrenia out-patients	1 year	Intensive multi-media small group sessions in medication self-management. Skills improved.
Lecompte & Pelc (1996)	64 DSM–III–R people with schizophrenia	1 year	Randomised trial of cognitive–behavioural programme. Length of subsequent hospitalisation in treatment group, 30 days *v.* 43 days in controls.
MacPherson *et al* (1996)	64 DSM–III–R people with schizophrenia	1 month	Psychoeducation; improved knowledge but not compliance.
Hornung *et al* (1998)	84 'regular attenders' *v.* 64 controls with DSM–III–R schizophrenia	1 year	Controlled prospective study of psychoeducation, medication training plus counselling and/or cognitive psychotherapy. Significantly improved attitudes to treatment but not compliance (already good).
Kemp *et al* (1998)	74 acute in-patients with psychosis	18 months	Randomised controlled trial of compliance therapy. Improved attitudes to medication, insight and compliance, and longer remission in treatment group.

DSM–III–R (American Psychiatric Association, 1987).

it is, the benefit is short lasting. More psychotherapeutic input of the following types needs to be given. Two studies (Lecompte & Pelc, 1996) plus our own (Kemp *et al*, 1996*a*; Kemp *et al*, 1998) have shown that hospitalisation and remission can both be changed for the better in tandem with compliance. The intervention in the former study was eclectic and included educational, cognitive and behavioural strategies as well as a focus on the therapeutic alliance. Subjects were selected on the basis of a good response to medication. As in Kemp *et al*'s study of compliance therapy, symptom scores were not noticeably better in the treatment group (as measured by the Brief Psychiatric Rating Scale; Lukoff *et al*, 1996) suggesting that benefits from improved compliance may go beyond the mere effects of medication and may in fact have more general positive effects.

Another factor to be considered is the intensity of the intervention. Boczkowski *et al* (1985) compared the effects of a behavioural-tailoring, which included practical guidelines such as stimulus cues to facilitate remembering and self-monitoring calendars. The individual sessions lasted only a maximum of 50 minutes in total. Seltzer *et al*'s (1980) intervention consisted of nine lectures given in small groups. However the intervention was not randomised, and the groups not well matched. Streicker *et al* (1986) studied the effects of six sessions of didactic education providing mainly medication information, and four of peer counselling, in enhancing compliance, spread over 10 weeks. Knowledge about medication was improved and retained at six-month follow-up. Attitudes to medication improved initially but reverted to baseline levels at follow-up. Actual compliance was not improved in the 10-month study period or beyond. Eckman *et al* (1990) investigated the potential of a behaviourally oriented programme in improving compliance and medication management skills in out-patients with schizophrenia. This was part of a comprehensive series of modules for training in social and independent living skills. In a multi-centre field trial, patients were administered a structured module by trained therapists, using behavioural techniques, in groups for about three hours a week over four months. The module used videotaped demonstrations, focused instruction, role plays, social and video feedback and practice in the 'real world'. The skill areas targeted included: benefits of antipsychotic medication; correct self-administration and evaluation of medication, including side-effects; and negotiating treatment with health care providers. The study showed that these skills could be learned and increasingly utilised over three-month follow-up. Compliance – taking the medication prescribed – as independently assessed, improved significantly from about 60% to 80%. Therefore, this was a group with relatively good baseline compliance. The module has also been investigated in a randomised controlled trial with a smaller group (*n*=41) (Eckman *et al*, 1992). A significantly greater improvement was seen in medication management knowledge and skills in subjects compared with controls, who received supportive group psychotherapy. The skills were retained over one year, although compliance data were not reported. Evidently this intervention is very promising but involves considerable input, which may not be easily adapted to the typical busy clinical setting in the UK.

The compliance therapy intervention used in Kemp *et al*'s (1996*b*, 1998) studies was deliberately kept simple and consisted of 4–6 sessions during hospital admission, each lasting less than one hour, with a view to it being taken up in non-research settings. The results of the study showed improvements (compared with a control group who had 'non-specific counselling' in addition, of course, to their routine clinical care) in attitudes to medication, insight (as measured by the Schedule for the Assessment of Insight (David, 1990; Kemp & David, 1997)) and the Global Assessment of Function (GAF; American Psychiatric Association, 1987). The last of these took longer to show an advantage in the intervention group. Compliance also improved; this was measured from ratings given by at least one keyworker per subject on the basis of their behaviour and attitudes over a period of weeks. A more quantitative assessment would have been valuable, but measurements of serum drug levels for example are rather invasive and may be misleading. The relevant clinical parameters – global rating of compliance, insight and overall functioning – improved by 15–20%. Survival curves showed a significant increase in the time before readmission, with the controls having approximately twice the risk of admission as those who received the intervention. The overall rates of readmission were high, the sample being a socially deprived inner city cohort, most of whom had experienced several previous relapses and remissions. At the end of the follow-up period about 50% in the compliance tharapy group had relapsed compared with about 70% of the controls.

Implications for the future

The research evidence presented above requires replication but its principal implication would seem to be that a counselling approach, based on treating the patient with psychotic illness as a rational decision maker, can significantly improve compliance with medication. The particular model that we have tested employs this therapy as an adjunct to routine patient care, but we believe that the same approach could be employed by the psychiatrists, nurses and keyworkers who deliver that care. So far this approach has not been tested, but we are hopeful that the methods of compliance therapy could improve drug compliance and patient quality of life when employed in this way. There are times, for example, in dealing with hostile or 'difficult' patients, when a third party, who is perceived by the patient as separate from the treating team, may be able to mediate between the patient and professionals, but we are inclined to believe that, most of the time, the type of approach that we are advocating, applied when the patient first encounters the mental health services, could result in better long-term relationships, leading to better compliance.

To take a broader, societal perspective, we believe that our research highlights a dilemma that will become increasingly salient in the future: the issue of individual liberty versus social protection. At least in the UK, successive governments have talked about protecting the public from the dangerous mentally ill, and have passed a number of laws designed to increase the ability of professionals to control those suffering from long-term mental illness (Holloway, 1996). However, they have so far not introduced the power to compel patients in the community to accept medication even though some authorities in the USA have argued that this would be beneficial to many of those patients (Torrey, 1997). Compliance therapy can be used in the context of involuntary care; as noted above, compliance with medication can be presented as a freely chosen strategy to avoid episodes of compulsion. In the study by Kemp *et al* (1998) about 50% of patients were detained under the Mental Health Act at inception. Although this was a rather poor prognostic indicator with respect to future compliance, it is evident from this and other studies that some patients, despite the (temporary) suspension of their rights to determine their treatment during a compulsory admission to hospital, may nevertheless respond well to treatment and, in retrospect, judge the coercion to have been in their best interests (Kane *et al*, 1983; Kjellin *et al*, 1997).

The compliance therapy model fits in very well with an alternative approach, one that emphasises the individual's right to control his or her own life and medical treatment. If our society does not choose to compel patients to accept treatment, then it must recognise that they are free to refuse treatment if they wish. In such a situation, an approach that recognises the patient's freedom and works with it would seem to be the one most likely to be successful and to foster the maximum of consensus between patients, carers and professionals.

References

AMERICAN PSYCHIATRIC ASSOCIATION (1987) *Diagnostic and Statistical Manual of Mental Disorders* (3rd edn, rev) (DSM–III–R). Washington, DC: American Psychiatric Association.

66   Hayward et al

BECKER, M. H. & ROSENSTOCK, I. M. (1984) Compliance with medical advice. In *Health Care and Human Behaviour* (eds A. Steptoe & A. Mathews), pp. 175–208. London: Academic Press.

BOCZKOWSKI, J. A., ZEICHNER, A. & DESANTO, N. (1985) Neuroleptic compliance among chronic schizophrenic outpatients: an intervention outcome report. *Journal of Consulting and Clinical Psychology.* **53**, 666–671.

BUDD, R. J., HUGHES, I. C. T. & SMITH, J. A. (1996) Health beliefs and compliance with antipsychotic medication. *British Journal of Clinical Psychology,* **35**, 393–397.

CORRIGAN, P. W., LIBERMAN, R. P. & ENGEL, J. D. (1990) From non-compliance to collaboration in the treatment of schizophrenia. *Hospital and Community Psychiatry,* **41,** 1203–1211.

CRAMER, J. A. (1995) Optimizing long-term patient compliance. *Neurology,* **45**, S25–S28.

DAVID, A. (1990) Insight and psychosis. *British Journal of Psychiatry,* **156**, 798–808.

ECKMAN, T. A., LIBERMAN, R. P., PHIPPS, C. C., ET AL (1990) Teaching medication management skills to schizophrenic patients. *Journal of Clinical Pharmacology,* **10**, 33–38.

——, WIRSHING, W. C., MARDER, S. R., ET AL (1992) Technique for training patients in illness self-management: a controlled trial. *American Journal of Psychiatry,* **149**, 1549–1555.

GARETY, P. A., KUIPERS, L., FOWLER, D., ET AL (1994) Cognitive behavioural therapy for drug-resistant psychosis. *British Journal of Medical Psychology,* **67**, 259–271.

HAYWARD, P. & BRIGHT, J. (1997) Stigma and mental illness: a review and critique. *Journal of Mental Health,* **6**, 345–354.

HOLLOWAY, F. (1996) Community psychiatric care: from libertarianism to coercion. Moral panic and mental health policy in Britain. *Health Care Analysis,* **4**, 234–244.

HORNUNG, W. P., KLINGBERG, S., FELDMANN, R., ET AL (1998) Collaboration with drug treatment by schizophrenic patients with and without psychoeducational training: results of a one-year follow-up. *Acta Psychiatrica Scandinavica,* **97**, 213–219.

JAMISON, K. R. (1993) *Touched with Fire: Manic–Depressive Illness and the Artistic Temperament.* New York: Free Press.

KANE, J. M., QUITKIN, F., RIFKIN, A., ET AL (1983) Attitudinal changes of involuntarily committed patients following treatment. *Archives of General Psychiatry,* 40, 374–377.

KEMP, R., DAVID, A. & HAYWARD, P. (1996*a*) Compliance therapy: an intervention targeting insight and treatment adherence in psychotic patients. *Behavioural and Cognitive Psychotherapy,* **24**, 331–350.

——, HAYWARD, P., APPLEWHAITE, G., ET AL (1996*b*) Compliance therapy in psychotic patients: randomised controlled trial. *British Medical Journal,* **312**, 345–349.

——, —— & DAVID, A. (1996*c*) Psychological predictors of insight and compliance in psychotic patients. *British Journal of Psychiatry,* **169**, 444–450.

—— & DAVID, A. (1997) Insight and compliance. In *Treatment Compliance and the Treatment Alliance in Serious Mental Illness* (ed B. Blackwell), pp. 61–84. The Netherlands: Harwood Academic Publishers.

——, HAYWARD, P. & DAVID, A. (1997) *Compliance Therapy Manual.* Macclesfield: Gardiner–Caldwell.

——, KIROV, G., EVERITT, B., ET AL (1998) Randomised controlled trial of compliance therapy: 18-month follow-up. *British Journal of Psychiatry,* **172**, 413–419.

KINGDON, D. G. & TURKINGTON, D. (1994) *Cognitive–Behavioural Therapy of Schizophrenia.* New York: Guilford Press.

——, —— & JOHN, C. (1994) Cognitive–behavioural therapy of schizophrenia. *British Journal of Psychiatry,* **164**, 581–587.

KJELLIN, L., ANDERSSON, K., CANDEFJORD, I. L., ET AL (1997) Ethical benefits and costs of coercion in short-term in-patient psychiatric care. *Psychiatric Services,* **48**, 1567–1570.

LECOMPTE, D. & PELC, I. (1996) A cognitive–behavioral program to improve compliance with medication in patients with schizophrenia. *International Journal of Mental Health,* **25,** 51–56.

LUKOFF, D., NUECHTERLEIN, K. H. & VENTURA, J. (1996) Manual for expanded BPRS. *Schizophrenia Bulletin*, **12**, 594–602.

MACPHERSON, R., JERROM, W. & HUGHES, A. (1996) A controlled study of education about drug treatment in schizophrenia. *British Journal of Psychiatry*, **168**, 709–717.

McEVOY, J. P. (1998) The relationship between insight in psychosis and compliance with medications. In *Insight and Psychosis* (eds X. F. Amador & A. S. David). New York: Oxford University Press.

RABKIN, J. (1974) Public attitudes towards mental illness: a review of the literature. *Schizophrenia Bulletin*, **10**, 9–33.

ROLLNICK, S., KINNERSLEY, P. & STOTT, N. (1993) Methods of helping patients with behaviour change. *British Medical Journal*, **307**, 188–190.

ROYAL PHARMACEUTICAL SOCIETY OF GREAT BRITAIN (1997) *From Compliance to Concordance*. London: Royal Pharmaceutical Society of Great Britain.

SACKETT, D. L. & HAYNES, R. B. (eds) (1976) *Compliance with Therapeutic Regimens*. Baltimore, MD: Johns Hopkins University Press.

SCAMBLER, G. (1984) Perceiving and coping with stigmatizing illness. In *The Experience of Illness* (eds R. Fitzpatrick *et al*), pp. 203–226. London: Tavistock.

SELTZER, A., RONCARI, I. & GARFINKEL, P. (1980) Effect of patient education on medication compliance. *American Journal of Psychiatry*, **25**, 638–645.

STREICKER, S. K., AMDUR, M. & DINCIN, J. (1986) Educating patients about psychiatric medication: failure to enhance compliance. *Psychosocial Rehabilitation Journal*, **4**, 15–28.

TEMPIER, R. (1996) Long-term psychiatric patients' knowledge about their medication. *Psychiatric Services*, **47**, 1385–1387.

TORREY, E. F. (1997) *Out of the Shadows: Confronting America's Mental Health Crisis*. New York: Wiley.

VAN PUTTEN, T., CRUMPTON, E. & YALE, C. (1976) Drug refusal in schizophrenia and the wish to be crazy. *Archives of General Psychiatry*, **33**, 1443–1446.

4 Psychoeducational multi-family groups: adaptations and outcomes

WILLIAM R. McFARLANE

Psychoeducation – basic concepts

The idea of working with the families of the severely mentally ill in order to affect the course of the illness goes back at least as far as the early 1950s when Bateson first formulated the notion of the 'double bind' and Jackson attempted to translate this theoretical construct into a treatment (Bateson *et al*, 1956). The family therapy that evolved from this source was unfortunately rooted in the notion that families had in some way caused the illness of their relative and that the illness itself was rather more a metaphor for trouble in the family than a biological reality. The treatment attempted to induce the family, through a variety of means, to change its behaviour towards the patient while simultaneously allowing the patient to get out of a dysfunctional role. These efforts were dismally unsuccessful. Families naturally resented the notion that they had caused the illness and patients were unable simply to shed their symptoms regardless of how clearly the supposed link between their illness and the family's dynamics was articulated. Predictably, family therapy as an organised body of theory and practice began to move away from the treatment of schizophrenia when success continued to elude it.

Yet living with an illness such as schizophrenia is difficult and confusing for patients and families alike. A well-functioning family under these circumstances has to possess the available knowledge about the illness itself and coping skills specific to the disorder, skills that are counter-intuitive and only nascent in most families. It is unrealistic to expect families to understand such a mystifying condition and to know what to do about it naturally. Given that perspective, the most adaptive family will be the one that has access to information, with the implication that the treatment system is a crucial source of that information. As to coping skills, many families have developed methods of dealing with positive and negative symptoms, functional disabilities and the desperation of their ill relatives through painful trial and error. These successes, however, are few and far between. So, a critical need is that families have access to each other to learn of other families' successes and failures and to establish a repertoire of coping strategies that are closely tailored to the disorder.

It took over 10 years for interest in involving families in the treatment of persons with severe mental illness to be revived, and then it emerged with an entirely different ideology. Investigators began to recognise the crucial role families played in outcome after a schizophrenic episode had occurred. They endeavoured to engage families collaboratively, sharing illness information and suggesting behaviours that promote recuperation as well as coping strategies to reduce their sense of burden (Goldstein *et al*, 1978; Anderson *et al*, 1980; Falloon & Liberman, 1983; Leff *et al*, 1983).

The group of interventions that emerged became known as 'family psychoeducation'. The approach recognises schizophrenia as a brain disorder that is only partially remediable by medication, and that families can have a significant effect on their relative's recovery. Thus, the psychoeducational approach shifted away from attempting to get families to change their 'disturbed' communication patterns towards educating and persuading families that how they behave toward the patient can facilitate or impede recovery. For example, a family might interfere with recuperation if in their natural enthusiasm to promote and support progress they create unreasonable demands and expectations.

Psychoeducation typically includes formal training sessions for a family or families, in an effort to teach as much as is currently known about the illness and to encourage their continued involvement with the treatment of their relative. For example, families are taught about negative symptoms of schizophrenia – that long periods of lethargy, anhedonia, passivity and social withdrawal typically follow an episode of more active, positive symptoms. With such knowledge families can better create a more low-key convalescent environment within which the patient can more naturally recuperate from a major psychotic episode. Clinicians work collaboratively with the family or families in resolving difficulties that are naturally generated by the illness. Research on the psychoeducational model, in particular the work of Anderson & Hogarty, Falloon, Leff & Goldstein, has led to a set of basic assumptions that underlie its application. These are outlined in Box 4.1.

The psychoeducational approaches have been remarkably effective in reducing rates of illness relapse when rigorously evaluated in

---

Box 4.1.

Psychoeducation – basic assumptions

(a)   Schizophrenia has a clear and demonstrable biological component. Numerous recent studies strongly support this perspective (Stevens, 1982; DeLisi *et al*, 1983; Weinberger *et al*, 1986).

(b)   Schizophrenia is a chronic illness characterised by episodes of up to two years in duration, during which either positive or negative symptoms of the illness, or both, may be in evidence, but these diminish slowly in the absence of stress (Hogarty & Ulrich, 1977).

(c)   The specific deficit in schizophrenia is one involving attention, arousal and under-functioning of the dorso-lateral frontal lobe, such that the patient's ability to gate stimuli adequately is impaired (Tecce & Cole, 1976).

(d)   Families can have an influence on this biological process such that they are either able to protect the patient from further relapses into illness or appear inadvertently to exacerbate them (Vaughn & Leff, 1976).

(e)   Familial behaviours can be most parsimoniously described as 'natural' responses to a difficult situation, and do not indicate anything about the level of functioning in the family (Leff &Vaughn, 1985).

(f)   Living with an ill relative has negative consequences for the family (Johnson, 1990).

(g)   The illness itself has a negative negative impact on the social support networks of both patient and family (Beels, 1981).

---

experimental outcome studies. The results of these studies are unusually consistent and point to a valid, reliable and quite robust main effect (Goldstein *et al*, 1978; Leff *et al*, 1982; Falloon *et al*, 1985; Leff & Vaughn, 1985; Hogarty *et al*, 1986; Tarrier *et al*, 1988; McFarlane, 1990).

Family psychoeducation – clinical methods

The basic psychoeducational model consists of four treatment stages that roughly correspond to the phases of an episode of schizophrenia, from the acute phase through the slow recuperative and rehabilitation phases (Anderson *et al*, 1986):

Joining

This stage refers to a way of working with a family or families that is characterised by collaboration in attempting to understand and relate to the family. The joining phase typically comprises 3–5 sessions in single- or multi-family format. The goals of this phase are: to establish a working alliance; to acquaint oneself with any family issues and problems that might contribute to stress either of the patient or the family; to learn of the family's strengths and resources in dealing with the illness; and to create a contract with mutual and attainable goals. Joining, in its most general sense, continues throughout the treatment, since it is always the responsibility of the clinician to remain an available resource for the family as well as their advocate in dealing with any other clinical or rehabilitation system necessitated by the illness of their relative. To foster this relationship, the clinician demonstrates genuine concern for the patient, acknowledges the family's loss and grants them sufficient time to mourn, is available to the family outside of the formal sessions, avoids treating the family as a patient or blaming them in any way, helps to focus on the present crisis and serves as a source of information about the illness.

Survival skills training/workshop

The family is invited to attend workshop sessions conducted in a formal, classroom-like atmosphere. Biological, psychological and social information about schizophrenia and its management is presented through a variety of formats, such as videotapes, slide presentations, lectures, discussion and question-and-answer periods. Information about the way in which the clinician and the family will continue to work together is also presented. Typically eight hours in length, several families attend the workshop at a time. The opportunity to interact with other families in similar situations greatly enhances the power of this portion of the intervention. The families are also introduced to the 'guidelines' for management of the illness. These consist of a set of behavioural instructions for family members, that integrates the biological, psychological and social aspects of the disorder with recommended responses: those that help to maintain a home environment that minimises relapse-inducing stress (see Box 4.2).

Re-entry

Regularly scheduled meetings twice-monthly focus on planning and implementing strategies to cope with the vicissitudes of a person recovering from an acute episode of schizophrenia. Major content areas include medication adherence, helping the patient avoid the use of street drugs and/or alcohol, the general lowering of expectations during the period of negative symptoms and an increase in tolerance for these symptoms. Two special techniques are introduced to participating members as supports to the efforts to follow family

---

Box 4.2.
Family guidelines for the management of schizophrenia

Things everyone can do to help make the process run more smoothly:

(a) **Go slow**. Recovery takes time. Rest is important. Things will get better in their own time.

(b) **Keep it cool**. Enthusiasm is normal. Tone it down. Disagreement is normal. Tone it down too.

(c) **Give each other space**. Time out is important for everyone. It's okay to reach out. It's okay to say 'no'.

(d) **Set limits**. Everyone needs to know what the rules are. A few good rules keep things clear.

(e) **Ignore what you can't change**. Let some things slide. Don't ignore violence.

(f) **Keep it simple**. Say what you have to say clearly, calmly and positively.

(g) **Follow the doctor's orders**. Take medications as they are prescribed. Take only medications that are prescribed.

(h) **Carry on business as usual**. Re-establish family routines as quickly as possible. Stay in touch with family and friends.

(i) **No street drugs or alcohol**. They make symptoms worse.

(j) **Pick up on early signs**. Note changes. Consult with your family clinician.

(k) **Solve problems step by step**. Make changes gradually. Work on one thing at a time.

(l) **Lower expectations, temporarily**. Use a personal yardstick. Compare this month to last month (Anderson *et al*, 1986).

---

guidelines (Falloon *et al*, 1985): (a) formal problem-solving; and (b) communications skills training. The application of either one of these techniques characterises each session. Further, each session follows a prescribed, task-oriented format or paradigm, designed to enhance family coping effectiveness and to strengthen the alliance between the family and the clinician.

Social/vocational rehabilitation

Approximately one year following an acute episode, most patients begin to show signs of a return to spontaneity and actively engage with those around them. This is usually the sign that the negative symptoms are lifting and that the patient can be challenged more intensively. The focus of this phase deals more specifically with the rehabilitative needs of the patient, addressing the two areas of functioning in which there are the most common deficits: social skills and their ability to gain and maintain employment. The sessions are used to role-play situations that are likely to cause stress for the patient if entered into unprepared. Family members are actively used to assist in various aspects of this training endeavour. Additionally, the family is assisted in rebuilding its own network of family and friends, which has usually been weakened as a consequence of the presence of schizophrenia in one of its members. Regular sessions are conducted on a once- or twice-monthly basis, although more contact may be necessary at particularly stressful times.

MFG psychoeducation

This section describes a treatment approach, the 'psychoeducational multiple family group' (McFarlane, 1990), which brings together aspects of family psychoeducation family and multi-family behavioural approaches. As such, it is a second-generation treatment model that incorporates the advantages of each of its sources, diminishes their negative features and leads to a number of synergistic effects that appear to enhance efficacy. Building on the psychoeducational family approach of Anderson *et al* (1986), the model has attempted to reflect contemporary understanding of schizophrenia from biological, psychological and social perspectives. It is built on the assumption that an effective treatment should address as many known aspects of the illness as possible, at all relevant system levels. Unlike the recent origins of psychoeducation, however, multiple family group work arose nearly three decades ago in attempts by Laqueur (1964, 1972) and Detre *et al* (1961) to develop psychosocial treatments for hospitalised patients with schizophrenia. Unlike family therapy during its early period, the emphasis was more pragmatic than theoretical. Indeed, the first reported successful experience with the modality emerged serendipitously from a need to solve ward management problems. In the process, Laqueur noted improved ward social functioning in patients who insisted on attending a group organised for visiting relatives. Detre *et al*(1961) started a multiple family group in order to encourage cooperation between resident psychiatrists and social workers on an acute in-patient service, but found a high level of interest in the group among patients and family members alike, as well as improvements in social functioning among patients and in family communication and morale. From these beginnings, the modality has grown steadily; most of the focus has continued to be the major psychiatric disorders (Strelnick, 1977; Benningfield, 1980; O'Shea, 1985).

Many clinicians have observed that specific characteristics of the multiple family group have remarkable effects on a number of social and clinical management problems commonly encountered in schizophrenia (Lansky *et al*, 1978; McFarlane, 1983). A critical goal of psychoeducation and family behavioural management is to reduce family expressed emotion and thereby to reduce the risk of psychotic relapse (Leff & Vaughn, 1985). The multiple family group (MFG) approach goes beyond the focus on expressed emotion, because families attempting to cope with schizophrenia inevitably experience a variety of stresses that secondarily put them at risk of manifesting exasperation and discouragement, as natural reactions (Johnson, 1990).

The common observation that many families with a member with schizophrenia seem more socially isolated has been partially confirmed by studies of social networks (Hammer, 1963; Brown *et al*, 1972; Tolsdorf, 1976; Garrison, 1978; Hammer *et al*, 1978; Pattison *et al*, 1979; Lipton *et al*, 1981; Potasznik & Nelson, 1984). Isolation of the family assumes significance when one considers the functions of a social network. Hammer (1981) has emphasised social and instrumental support, access to other people and resources, mediation of information, the placing of demands and the imposition of constraints, all of which are essential to developing skills for coping with a chronic mental disability. Lack of social support markedly increases vulnerability to ordinary stressors in both medical and psychiatric illness, while moderate network size and density interact to predict low relapse rates (Steinberg & Durell, 1968; Dean & Lin, 1977; Dozier *et al*, 1987). Although the lifetime risk of schizophrenia is about the same the world over, its course is more benign in developing non-industrialised cultures with a more permeable village social structure (World Health Organization, 1979). Thus, the social support available to the family may be one of the critical factors determining outcome; the lack of it appears to make everyone, especially the person with schizophrenia, more vulnerable to stress. Where social support is not available, the treatment context has to provide it.

With respect to the issue of stigma, while the available studies are in some conflict (Yarrow *et al*, 1955; Freeman & Simmons, 1961; Rabkin, 1974; Lamb & Oliphant, 1978), the conclusion can reasonably be drawn that a patient's family members do not automatically feel stigmatised, but often behave as if they do. Friends and relatives do tend to avoid them as if they are stigmatised. Thus, many families may be isolated and stigmatised, and may feel so as well, in combinations that may be complex and variable. These problems produce strains that are likely to lead to exasperation, a sense of abandonment and eventually demoralisation. These effects on the family are likely to interfere with their capacity to support the ill member and to assist in rehabilitation.

MFGs address these issues directly by increasing the size and complexity of the social network, exposing a given family to other families like themselves, providing a forum for mutual aid and providing an opportunity to hear the experiences of other adults who have had similar experiences and found workable solutions.

(a) In addition, psychoeducational MFGs reiterate and reinforce the information learned at coping skills workshops.
(b) Coupled with formal problem solving (Falloon *et al*, 1985), the group experience serves to enhance the family's available coping skills for the many problems encountered in the course of the patient's recovery and rehabilitation.

Multiple family psychoeducation – clinical methods

The psychoeducational MFG has been designed to counter family isolation and stigma, while incorporating the clinical methods that have been shown to alleviate expressed emotion and foster extended remission. The general character of the approach can be summarised as consisting of three components, roughly corresponding to the phases of the group.

In the first phase, the content of the model follows that of Anderson *et al* (1986), with its emphasis on joining in a collaborative alliance with family members, conducting an educational workshop and focusing on preventing relapse for a year or so after discharge from an acute hospitalisation.

Unlike the single-family psychoeducational approach, the format for treatment after the workshop is an MFG. The second phase involves moving beyond stability to gradual increases in patients' community functioning, a process that uses MFG-based problem-solving as the primary means for accomplishing social and vocational rehabilitation. This occurs roughly during the second year of the MFG. The third phase consists of deliberate efforts to mould the group into a social network that can persist for an extended period and satisfy family and patient needs for social contact, support and ongoing clinical monitoring. This format is also an efficient context in which to continue psychopharmacological treatment and routine case management.

Expansion of the families' social networks occurs through problem-solving, direct emotional support and out-of-group socialising, all involving members of different families in the group.

The multi-family group treatment approach is briefly described below and in detail in another volume (McFarlane, 2000).

Engagement and family education

The intervention begins with a minimum of three engagement sessions, in which the patient's primary clinician meets with the individual family unit, usually without the patient present. These are accompanied by separate meetings with the patient.

For both philosophical and practical reasons, we establish treatment plans based on the patient's and family's stated goals and desires. When 5–8 families have completed the engagement process, the clinicians, usually including the patients' psychiatrist, conduct an extensive educational workshop, again usually without patients. The biomedical aspects of schizophrenia are discussed, after which the clinicians present and discuss guidelines for the family management of both clinical and everyday problems in managing the illness in the family context.

The ongoing psychoeducational MFG

The first meeting of the ongoing psychoeducational MFG follows the workshop by one or two weeks; its format includes a fortnightly meeting schedule, a 1.5-hour session length, leadership by two clinicians and participation by 5–8 patients and their families. From this point forward, patients are strongly encouraged to attend and actively participate. The MFG's primary working method is to help each family and patient to apply the family guidelines to their specific problems and circumstances. This work proceeds in phases whose timing is linked to the clinical condition of the patients. The actual procedure uses an MFG-based problem-solving method adapted from a single-family version by Falloon & Liberman (1983). Families are taught to use this method in the MFG, as a group function. It is the core of the MFG approach, one that is acceptable to families, remarkably effective and nicely tuned to the low-intensity and deliberate style that is essential to working with the specific sensitivities of people with schizophrenia.

The first phase concentrates on problems being experienced by the patient as he or she begins to re-enter the world outside the protection of the hospital or clinic. A central goal during this phase is prevention of relapse, achieved primarily by limiting functional expectations and demands and artificially reducing the level of stimulation and stress in the social environment. That is, the family is recruited to institute a relatively simple, low-demand and low-intensity milieu at home, to the degree possible without totally disrupting family life. Beyond that general approach, the MFG maintains remission by systematically applying the group problem-solving method, case by case, to difficulties in implementing the family guidelines and fostering recovery.

The rehabilitation phase should be initiated only by patients who have achieved clinical stability by successfully completing this community re-entry phase. As stability increases, the MFG functions in a role unique among psychosocial rehabilitation models: it operates as an auxiliary to the *in vivo* social and vocational rehabilitation effort being conducted by the clinical team. The central emphasis during this phase is the involvement of both the family and the group in helping each patient to begin a gradual, step-by-step resumption of responsibility and socialising. The clinicians continue to use problem-solving and brain-storming in the MFG to identify and develop jobs and social contacts for the ill group members, to help individual patients obtain job placement and to find new ways to enrich their social lives.

In the current model for MFG sessions, a stable membership of 4–8 families meets with two clinicians on a fortnightly basis two years or more following the onset of an episode of schizophrenia. In most instances, the decision to have a given patient attend is based upon his or her mental status and susceptibility to the stimulation that such a group may engender.

The format of the sessions is closely controlled by the clinician, following a standard paradigm (see Box 4.3). This structure serves to reduce the likelihood that the sessions will turn into emotional 'pot-boilers' or non-productive gripe sessions that, given the nature of the illness, would not be rehabilitative for the patient or helpful to families. The task of the clinicians, particularly at the beginning, is to adopt a business-like tone and approach that promotes a calm

---

Box 4.3
Time structure of psychoeducational multi-family group sessions

Socialising with families and patients	15 minutes
A go-around, reviewing	20 minutes
(a) The week's events	
(b) Relevant bio-social information	
(c) Applicable guidelines	
Selection of a single problem	5 minutes
Formal problem-solving	45 minutes
(a) Problem definition	
(b) Generation of possible solutions	
(c) Weighing pros and cons of each	
(d) Selection of preferred solution	
(e) Delineation of tasks and implementation	
Socialising with families and patients	5 minutes
	Total: 90 minutes

group climate, oriented towards learning new coping skills and engendering hope.

Each session of the MFG begins and ends with a period of purely social chat, facilitated by the clinicians, the purpose of which is to give the patients and even some families the opportunity to re-capture and practice any social skills they may have lost due to their long isolation and exposure to high levels of stress. Following the socialising the clinicians specifically enquire as to the status of each family, offering advice based on the family guidelines or direct assistance, when it can be done readily. A single problem that has been identified by any one family is then selected and the group as a whole participates in problem-solving. This problem is the focus of an entire session, during which all members of the group contribute suggestions and ideas. The relative advantages and disadvantages are then reviewed by the affected family, with some input from other families and clinicians. Typically, the most attractive of the proposed solutions is reformulated as an appropriate task for trying at home and assigned to the family. This step is then followed by another final period of socialising.

Medication adherence often emerges as the problem. Some of the solutions that have been developed in MFGs have included the following:

(a) Reviewing the patient's immediate past history, drawing the contrast between life and function while on medication and while not on it. This intervention is most successfully aimed at patients who are considering cessation of medications primarily because they currently feel well. Here, the clinician's job has been to help the patient (and the family) come to the recognition of the need for maintenance doses of medication in order to avoid relapse and to allow the healing process to take place.

(b) Bolstering and supporting the families' beliefs that the medications are necessary. This would sometimes entail re-educating the family about medication and its effects on psychotic symptoms and differentiating the negative symptoms of the illness such as lethargy, inertia, withdrawal and anhedonia from true side-effects of the medications. This intervention is also most likely to succeed when the patient is still on medication but is considering cessation. However, it is a necessary first step to more direct interventions with the family if the patient does eventually become non-adherent with treatment.

(c) Careful enquiry as to why the patient wishes to stop medication and then an equally careful attempt to address the issues raised. These are usually unstated and sometimes not in the awareness of the affected person. The most common issues include stigmatisation of being mentally ill, undesirable side-effects, inconvenient times of administration and feelings of loss of personal control. These specific issues then become problems in themselves and are subjected to problem-solving techniques. It is absolutely necessary to respond to these issues as quickly as they are raised, rather than 'down-playing' the patient's complaints. Coupled with this approach is the importance of helping the patient to accept that they may be unavoidable, but are to be preferred to the return of symptoms and a relapse. It is often helpful to enter into a discussion of the various medications prescribed and a description of their specific side-effects and advantages as a means of de-mystifying them. Clinicians will need to be conversant with some of the advantages of newer atypical antipsychotic drugs as a possible solution to these kinds of complaints. The treating physician, if available, might be called into the session to do this as a means of reinforcing the message.

(d) Reviewing prodromal signs of relapse with both family and patient in order to heighten sensitivity to the issue. This intervention is most appropriately tried when the patient seems about to cease medication, despite the prior efforts of clinicians and family to convince him or her otherwise. It is essentially an 'upping of the ante' manoeuvre on the part of the clinician, preparing the family for what has not yet occurred, but nevertheless communicating the clinicians' beliefs that it will occur.

(e) Explaining how the patient's life will be more limited if prodromal or primary symptoms return. This should be done in enough detail to help the patient make a clear choice about stopping medication. It is helpful for the clinician to be well informed about the patient's past life, as well as hopes and aspirations. The thoroughness of the early joining process, especially regarding review of goals and the initial contracting, is crucial to making this intervention successful.

(f) Encouraging other patients to share their experiences about the dangers of stopping medication. This basically comes under the rubric of peer pressure, and it has been found to be very powerful if the patient connects with other patients in the group, and identifies with them.

(g) Encouraging the patient to make a connection between non-compliance and the return of prodromal or primary symptoms by the use of a diary kept daily by patient. This would most logically follow the patient's decision to stop medications or to cut them down below therapeutic levels. To be effective, this intervention must be combined with increased surveillance by the clinician and the family, with an increase in the contact between clinician, patient and family.

Research on MFG treatment

Early studies on MFG treatment were quasi-experimental or impressionistic (Berman, 1966; Lurie & Ron, 1972; Lansky *et al*, 1978; Falloon & Liberman, 1983). The positive effects reported in these uncontrolled studies are consistent with those measured in more recent experimental studies conducted by the author and described below.

The Bergen County (New Jersey) Study

Forty-one patients, with schizophrenia or schizoaffective disorder, were randomly assigned during an acute in-patient hospitalisation to one of three conditions:

(a) psychoeducational MFG;
(b) single-family psychoeducational treatment without inter-family contact;
(c) dynamically oriented multiple family therapy (McFarlane *et al*, 1995*a*).

Medication was used in all cases; dosage was determined by the staff psychiatrist for the patients and set at lowest effective dose levels. At four years after discharge, the psychoeducational MFG had a significantly longer time to first relapse than psychoeducational single-family treatment (Cox's coefficient=2.09; P=0.01). Final four-year relapse rates were 50% for psychoeducational MFG, 76.5% for psychoeducational single-family treatment and 57.1% for dynamically oriented multiple family therapy. What is suggested by the data is that there is a specific and independent MFG effect that appears to prevent or forestall relapse.

The New York State Study

This study utilised a two-cell design to compare psychoeducational multiple-family and psychoeducational single-family treatment, experimentally, over a two-year period (McFarlane *et al*, 1995*b*). The design included: random assignment; full specification of the test therapies; extensive training and ongoing supervision of experienced therapists by the project's supervisory staff; a standard-dose medication strategy and wide-ranging measurement of patient and family outcomes. The total sample consisted of 172 patients with DSM–III–R (American Psychiatric

Association, 1987) schizophrenic, schizoaffective or schizophreniform disorders, recruited and treated at six New York State public psychiatric facilities, encompassing a wide range of the public-service patient population in terms of chronicity, race, ethnicity, social class and geography. Four clinicians at each participating site assessed and treated nine patients. There were no significant differences at baseline between the treatment conditions on any of the measured variables.

One-year relapse outcome was determined using symptom criteria based on the Brief Psychiatric Rating Scale (BPRS; Overall & Gorham, 1962): 19.0% of multi-family group cases relapsed during the first year as compared with 28.6% of single-family treatment cases. The symptomatic relapse rates at two years were 28% and 42%, respectively; rates of clinically significant relapse (cases that met criteria for seven days) were 15.7% v. 26.8%, respectively. For cases completing the treatment protocol (80% of the sample) or when controlled for medication compliance, this was a statistically significant difference (*P*<0.05). The multiple-family result – an annual clinically-significant relapse rate of under 10% – compares quite favourably with expected relapse rates of about 40% using medication alone or with supportive individual therapy (Hogarty *et al*, 1979).

Among Caucasian families with patients who only partially remitted during the index admission, there was a marked difference in relapse, again favouring the MFG format: 17% v. 59%, at two years, using the more rigorous criteria. Interestingly, there was little difference in relapse rates between the modalities in minority (non-Caucasian) patients. For each one-point increase in the mean per-item score in BPRS, the risk of relapse increased by 39% in single-family treatment. In contrast, in the MFG cohort each one-point increase led to a reduction in risk of relapse by 42%. For those 96 cases discharged with essentially no positive symptoms (BPRS mean item score >2), there is no difference in relapse rate between treatment modalities (32.7% in MFGs v. 31.8% in single-family treatment). However, for those 76 cases who were symptomatic at discharge (BPRS>2), 19% of the MFG cases relapsed, while 51% of the cases assigned to single-family treatment relapsed. A Cox's analysis showed that, for patients discharged in a partially remitted state, being assigned to MFG treatment meant a risk of relapse only 28% of that of single-family treatment (2(2)=12.51, *P*< 0.01; (treatment)=–1.28, s.e.=0.46, *P*<0.01). This higher symptom subgroup accounts almost entirely for the difference in relapse outcomes between MFGs and single-family treatment. That is, in the highest risk sub-sample, the MFG relapse rates were actually lower than in more well-stabilised patients, while the opposite effect was observed in single-family treatment.

We compared the mean number of hospitalisations for the entire sample for two years prior to the study with hospitalisations during the study period. These rates dropped to about one-third of the sample's prior rate by the end of the two-year observation and treatment interval. The sample as a whole increased significantly in employment (full- or part-time competitive or sheltered job) from 17.3%, two months prior to the test treatments, to 29.3% during the 18–24 month period in treatment (χ^2=7.63, P=0.001). Although the MFG yielded a higher employment gain than single-family treatment (16% *v*. 8%), the difference was not statistically significant.

A final measure of effectiveness has to do with the relative expenditure of staff time in implementing a treatment. Because the MFG approach not only yields better outcome, but also requires exactly one-half the staff time expenditure of single-family treatment, the cost–benefit ratio (1:2.5) strongly favours the MFG format. The cost–benefit ratio between MFG and prior treatment, comparing hospitalisation costs before and during treatment, is 1:34. That is, for each dollar spent on family intervention in MFGs there is a $34 saving in hospitalisation costs during the second year of treatment. Furthermore, the psychosocial treatment appeared to affect pharmacological treatment. Medication compliance, as assessed by the treating psychiatrists, averaged close to 90% for the entire sample across the two years, increasing slightly over that period. The study was conducted in a large state hospital system, under less than ideal circumstances, yet the outcome was fairly dramatic, suggesting wide applicability to a variety of settings.

Merging multiple family psychoeducation and assertive community treatment

Assertive community treatment (ACT) is the most thoroughly studied, comprehensive, out-of-hospital service system for people with persistent psychotic disorders, with nine published controlled trials and several others under way (Olfson, 1990; Thompson *et al*, 1990; Stein & Santos, 1998). The original Madison-based Training in Community Living Programme was designed as an alternative to hospitalisation and showed dramatic results in its ability to maintain people with acute illnesses in the community (Stein & Test, 1980). Outreach, tightly organised teamwork and proactive, highly individualised treatment and rehabilitation planning were among the key elements of the model. Projects directly derived from the original Madison programme have established themselves as community-based intensive case management programmes, emphasising *in vivo* life-skills training, problem-solving, clinical management and advocacy for resources.

Shifting their focus to rehabilitation, many ACT programmes have helped patients learn vocational skills by using actual work placements in the community as the site for acquiring, relearning and practising them. On-the-job training, high counsellor contact and individualised placement planning, all key components of ACT rehabilitation, have been shown in uncontrolled studies to yield better placement ratios (Knoedler, 1979; Zadny & James, 1979; Worral & Vandergoot, 1982). Higher levels of vocational adjustment were achieved largely through direct advocacy and job coaching, bypassing conventional rehabilitation programmes. However, a comparison between ACT 'supported employment' and sheltered workshop placement did not yield significantly different competitive employment rates.

As a method that relies extensively on existing community resources and direct therapeutic support by a team of clinicians, ACT has shown a complicated relationship with the service user's family and to the concept of building supportive networks. Initially, ACT promoted 'constructive separation' of the patient from his or her family during crisis episodes. Further, patients were encouraged to live away from the family home and restrict their contact with family members, who usually were not included in the treatment effort. Conceptualisation which set the stage for the ACT approach made extensive reference to the family literature of the 1950s which emphasised pathogenic characteristics of the family bond in schizophrenia. More recently, ACT proponents have made more of an effort to include family members, but not systematically and not as an integral part of the patient's rehabilitation.

Family intervention approaches also have their limitations. When outcome is determined more by negative patient factors (e.g. chronic medication non-compliance, substance misuse, poor vocational achievement prior to onset of illness or severely debilitating negative symptoms), then family interaction and support, even if ideal, are less likely to positively affect course. Our studies have consistently shown that approximately 14% of the study patients suffered repeated relapses and re-hospitalisations: that is, without observable effects from family intervention. Also, because the family models conform to an out-patient therapy profile, they rely on conventional vocational rehabilitation services. If these are refused by the patient or are not available, rehabilitation is much less likely to occur. Some families, though involved and motivated, may simply be too burdened to devote the necessary energy to a lengthy treatment and rehabilitation effort.

Thus, from these considerations, we came to the conclusion that combining ACT with the psychoeducational MFG might lead to enhanced outcomes, compared to ACT or psychoeducation alone, because each compensates for what we see to be crucial deficiencies in the other model. Further, neither ACT nor single-family psychoeducation significantly expand the patient's or the family's social network, while an MFG, by definition, does exactly that, thereby potentially adding an additional increment of efficacy. We term the combined approach 'family-aided assertive community treatment' (FACT). This approach fosters maximum possible coordination between all the important people and social forces that influence a given patient. Although both of the source treatment models in FACT espouse and create continuity of care, each has been somewhat deficient in bringing all the components of the patient's treatment under one coordinated system.

FACT – clinical methods

The FACT approach involves a merging of interrelated elements of ACT with those of the psychoeducational MFG.

Integration of the patient's life into the community

As an alternative to hospitalisation, ACT provides the patient with a viable support system in the community. This calls for an assertive approach with considerable outreach and pro-active monitoring, in which ACT staff function as direct providers of individualised therapeutic and rehabilitation services, rather than as service brokers.

In vivo teaching of coping and problem-solving skills

To meet the demands of community life patients must not only have adequate access to all material resources, but must also learn how to use them effectively. In addition, problems of daily living and vocational adjustment arise frequently and require an array of problem-solving skills. As much as possible, teaching these skills takes place '*in vivo*': that is, directly in the natural settings of the patient.

Prevention of relapse and crisis intervention

Monitoring of social stressors, such as life events or transitions, and responding immediately and assertively to them are essential for the prevention of relapse. This requires an awareness of prodromal signs on the part of the treatment team. Medication management and monitoring is an integral feature of this approach and requires close collaboration with the prescribing psychiatrist, who is usually a member of the ACT team. The team is available on a 24-hour basis to respond to emergencies and is reachable by all concerned parties.

Graduated increase in patient responsibilities

The ACT approach maintains a continuous rehabilitative stance in looking for opportunities to help the patient move in the direction of his or her established goals and independence. An assertive, but graduated approach is maintained to support service users in their striving toward higher functional levels. However, we also recognise that precipitous and premature advances can contribute to the resurgence of prodromal symptoms and ultimately lead to a relapse. Therefore, an increase in support, careful preparation and symptom monitoring accompany any significant increase in functional demands.

Support and education of community members

Community members, especially the patient's family and employers, frequently react to patients' behaviour in ways not supportive of community tenure. The goal of the ACT team is to aid these key community members by providing them with ongoing support and guidance.

Team approach

ACT is provided by an interdisciplinary team whose members are known to all the team's service users and serve relatively interchangeable functions. It functions within a tightly organised and pragmatic structure, with an emphasis on goal-oriented treatment planning. Daily schedules and staff assignments are based on service user needs and staff availability.

Family engagement, goal-setting and education

The engagement and educational interventions begin with a minimum of three 'engagement' sessions, in which the patient's primary clinician meets with the individual family unit, usually without the patient present. These are accompanied by separate meetings with the patient. In carrying out rehabilitation, the essential starting point is goal-setting, with the patient as the central focus. For both philosophical and practical reasons, we emphasise the patient's perceived desires for their vocational and social lives as the nucleus of work by both the FACT team and the families in the MFG. Thus, the initial and crucial step is getting a sense of the patient's previous work history and his or her interests either in continuing a career already started or in changing directions. This occurs in the initial sessions held with the patient alone and in the joint patient–family sessions.

Next, the cohort of patients due to join the psychoeducational MFG meets together for nine goal-setting sessions beginning at about the same time as the engagement process with families, but separately from families. These meetings are class-like, in which the team teaches the patients how to set a goal, decide on the steps necessary for its achievement and how to deal with barriers that might impede success. When 5–8 families have completed the joining, the FACT team conducts the educational workshop, usually with patients present if they have been out of the hospital and stable for six months or so. In this presentation, we also closely follow Anderson's format (Anderson *et al*, 1986), except that we present the biomedical aspects of schizophrenia by showing a standardised videotape and have added new guidelines and other components specifically geared to the vocational rehabilitation phase.

Ongoing psychoeducational multi-family group

Following the workshop is the first meeting of the ongoing psycho-educational MFG; its format includes a fortnightly meeting schedule, with a 1.5-hour session length, leadership by two FACT clinicians and participation by 6–9 patients and their families. Patients are strongly encouraged to attend and actively participate.

The MFG is conducted in a manner similar to that described previously. The first phase concentrates on problems being experienced by the patient as he or she begins to re-enter the world outside the protection of the hospital or clinic. A central goal during this phase is prevention of relapse, achieved by limiting functional expectations and demands and reducing the level of stimulation and stress in the social environment. The rehabilitation phase in FACT should be initiated only by patients who have achieved clinical stability by successfully completing this community re-entry phase. As stability increases, the MFG functions in a role unique among psychosocial rehabilitation models: it operates as an auxiliary to the *in vivo* vocational rehabilitation effort being conducted by the clinical team. The central emphasis during this phase is the involvement of both the family and the group in helping each patient to begin a gradual, step-by-step resumption of responsibility and socialising. The clinicians continue to use group-based problem-solving and brain-storming to identify and develop jobs, to help individual patients obtain job placement or to enrich their social lives.

Family-based goal setting

Because this process inevitably involves some reduction or post-ponement of previously held vocational goals, and because those goals are often held as strongly by family members as patients themselves, the process and outcomes of the goal-setting classes are reported into the MFG as a regular part of each session. This allows each family to express doubts and reservations, opinions or possibly support, so that the final result of goal-setting is something that has been ratified by the patient's own family in the public arena of the MFG. Further, the other families in the group are aware of each patient's intentions, making the vocational progress of the group's patients the project of the entire group, which, in turn, helps to define a positive group identity. Reciprocally, the families' ideas, opinions and information can be taken back to the goal-setting class setting and incorporated into patients' rehabilitation aims.

Creating a compendium of potential jobs

After the group completes the goal-setting process, several group meetings are spent on developing a list of possible job opportunities among the members of the group's families and their extended kin. Potential jobs may be located in the homes or businesses of group members, in those of relatives and friends outside the group, in their work-places or in those of their kin. In this way, patients may work at jobs with members of other families in the group and/or their extended kin. Jobs may also be identified that are known to group members by simple informal connections, chance encounters (for instance, seeing 'help-wanted' signs) or through deliberate enquiry and community advocacy. Ultimately, families, in collaboration with the team and local family advocacy associations, may create jobs for the patients through community action. In general, such jobs are potentially less stressful, since they are embedded within the social network of the MFG and involve social connections that are inherently more familiar to the patients. To a large degree, we have modelled this approach after the usual methods – involving networks and personal connections – by which a mentally healthy individual obtains a job or job leads (Granovetter, 1974; Vandergoot, 1976; Roessler & Hiett, 1983). Family members may be asked to gather additional information on job possibilities between meetings, but actual job development is carried out by the team clinicians.

Individualised job-finding

After the completion of the job-opportunity compendium, the vocational or social rehabilitation process for each patient is broken down into steps that are attempted sequentially. The achievement of the next rehabilitative step, usually employment, is raised as a focus in the problem-solving portion of the MFG. The members of the group and their extended kin are polled for sources of jobs, job leads and even possibilities for job development, with specific reference to one particular patient in the group. In this brain-storming process, various ideas are generated from participants in the MFG. The patient and his or her family then review these suggestions and a final plan is developed. This usually involves job preparation, job development, coaching, planning and problem-solving, all carried out in the field by the FACT team. The results of these efforts are then reported back to the team during rounds, treatment planning and during the next MFG. If necessary, the process is repeated if initial results were disappointing.

Research on FACT

The FACT research project began in 1987, sponsored by the New York State Office of Mental Health and the New York State Alliance for the Mentally Ill (McFarlane *et al*, 1996). The FACT project used a two-cell experimental design: one combined the ACT treatment method with psychoeducational multi-family group (FACT), the other was ACT treatment with limited single-family crisis intervention. This design tested ongoing family participation in an MFG as a primary treatment factor.

The sample consisted of 72 patients at three community mental health centres in New York State. Patients were selected who met the following criteria: diagnosis (DSM–III–R schizophrenia, schizophreniform and schizoaffective disorders), associated complicating factors (homelessness, treatment non-compliance, substance abuse, criminal charges, suicidality), family availability and age (18–45 years). Analysis of baseline psychiatric and demographic data indicated that no differences existed between cohorts.

Hospitalisations declined from a pre-treatment mean of 1.85 hospitalisations per patient in the two years prior to treatment to a mean of 1.37 hospitalisations per patient during the two years of treatment ($t(52)=2.89$, $P < 0.01$), without significant differences between FACT and ACT. We found no difference in employment activity between the two cohorts at intake (11% of FACT patients were engaged in employment activity, versus 6% of ACT patients, $t(66)=0.62$, NS). Employment activity showed an increase in the first four months of treatment ($F(1, 52)=8.54$, $P< 0.01$) and patients were able to maintain this level for nearly the duration of the project. The maximum level of employment activity was 33%, achieved at the 20-month assessment point. After achieving this peak level, activity dropped off in the last four months of treatment, down to 17% ($F(1,52)=9.18$, $P<0.01$). We compared employment activity between FACT and ACT. At 12 months

FACT was superior to ACT: (a) in number of patients employed at any job, whether full-time, part-time, in a sheltered workshop, or as a volunteer – 37.0% *v.* 15.4%; and (b) in competitive employment – 16.0% *v.* 0%. Averaged over the full two years, there was a significant result in favour of FACT for sheltered work (18% of the FACT sample over two years *v.* 6% of the ACT sample; $t(51)=1.99$, $P=0.05$) and no difference for non-sheltered activity (patients showed an average of 10% non-sheltered work activity regardless of family involvement).

FACT as vocational rehabilitation

Because twice as many patients whose families were in psycho-educational multi-family groups were employed during the FACT study, the same approach to rehabilitation was used in this study. It was designed to provide focused support and training in work-related problem-solving skills, carried out in the context of an expanded and rehabilitation-oriented family and social support system. The goal of this combined treatment and rehabilitation approach was meaningful, competitive employment.

The study was designed to directly compare vocational and clinical outcomes in FACT with those in conventional vocational rehabilitation (CVR) and to assess clinical outcomes and their relationship to work outcomes. The principal differences between experimental conditions were that, in CVR: (a) there were no MFGs and no vocational specialists working closely with the clinicians; (b) all vocational rehabilitation was initiated by referral to the state-operated vocational rehabilitation agency; and (c) vocational rehabilitation staff, even if employed at site-affiliated rehabilitation services, worked on the basis of referral from the CVR clinicians and case managers.

The study was carried out in two typical community mental health centres that have close ties to excellent vocational rehabilitation services: one in an urbanised suburb of New York City and one in rural New York State. An individual was eligible for the study if he or she:

(a) was aged 18–55 years;
(b) had a diagnosis in either the schizophrenia spectrum (e.g. schizophrenic, schizoaffective, schizophreniform disorders) or the mood spectrum (e.g. major depressive, bipolar disorders);
(c) was not employed competitively for the past six months;
(d) had a family member available;
(e) stated explicitly that he or she wanted to work.

Once baseline data had been collected and the family engaged, subjects were randomly assigned to FACT or CVR, after which ACT and the MFGs commenced in the FACT-assigned cohort. ACT, an educational workshop, the ongoing MFG and team-integral vocational specialists were the experimental treatment variables.

Each FACT team in this study consisted of three primary staff (two social workers or psychiatric nurses with prior experience treating the study population and one vocational specialist), a senior clinician/ team leader and a psychiatrist. The staff to patient ratio was 1:8. The teams in this study were enhanced by the addition of vocational specialists who were trained in supported employment concepts and methods and co-led the MFGs.

The comparison rehabilitation model was implemented by clinicians (MSc-level) who worked in the same mental health centres as the FACT teams. The clinicians oversaw the CVR referral, followed-up when crises or drop-out interceded, arranged to place CVR drop-outs in other rehabilitation programmes and consulted on all decisions about rehabilitation programme changes and job placement. They carried out family crisis support, research assessment and tracking procedures. The CVR clinicians made referrals to the state-operated vocational rehabilitation service and assisted subjects to follow through on the assessment, training and placement phases.

Sixty-nine cases were admitted to the study. The sample was predominantly male, unemployed for over a year, with a schizophrenic disorder, a long and chronic course of illness, not living with family and lower levels of persistant psychotic symptoms and less severe substance abuse than in many samples in other clinical trials. To control for potential bias, prior employment was entered as a co-variable in all analyses of employment outcomes.

The FACT and CVR cohorts were similar in rates of sheltered and unpaid work, while there were dramatically fewer unemployed FACT subjects: 16.2% of the FACT cohort, *v*. 43.3% in CVR. More FACT subjects obtained competitive jobs. Averaged across all the three-month in-treatment assessment points, 28% of the FACT cohort held a competitive job, compared with 10% of those in CVR. Throughout the study, FACT subjects were significantly more likely to be employed than CVR subjects (ANCOVA, controlling for baseline employment and the site of treatment: $F(1,54)=7.72$, $P<0.01$). There was a slow and steady increase in competitive employment until it peaked at 12 months at 37%, compared with 8% in CVR ($F(1,56)=9.21$, $P<0.01$), after which there was a small decline, to 27% in FACT ($F(1,54)=5.11$, $P<0.05$). On the other hand, CVR competitive employment remained at essentially the same level throughout the study, ending at 8.0% below its baseline level. There were 26 jobs held by 17 FACT subjects, while six CVR subjects held eight jobs. The difference in amount of employment was not due to a 'revolving door' effect, in which subjects were continually fired and getting new jobs. Job duration for competitive jobs between FACT and CVR were similar: 6.9 months for FACT and 6.0 months for CVR. There was a trend towards FACT having greater total time employed in study: 10.4 months $v.$ 7.0 months ($P< 0.10$, $n=23$). For those with any competitive employment, FACT averaged \$1448 compared with \$320 for CVR (Mann–Whitney $z(22)=2.08$, $P=0.038$), and hourly wages were higher in FACT: \$6.34 versus \$3.64 (Mann–Whitney $z(22)=1.92$, $P=0.055$). At a mean of over \$6 per hour, these were not just minimum-wage positions. A major impediment to the employment effort was the recession of the early 1990s and the closing of the principal employer in one of the site counties mid-way through the study. Unemployment reached 11% by the end of the study. It became increasingly difficult to find competitive jobs for participants and for relatives in MFGs to identify potential jobs for participants, because several were themselves victims of the plant closing.

FACT and CVR were equally effective clinical treatments. For the subsample with schizophrenia, there were significant reductions in negative symptoms ($F(1,38)=6.03$, $P<0.05$) and general psychopathology ($F(1,38)=5.69$, $P<0.05$), indicating improvement or no change, respectively, for FACT and worsening for CVR. The total sample showed statistically significant improvements in positive symptoms ($F(1,14)= 5.94$, $P<0.05$), general psychopathology ($F(1,14)=5.40$, $P<0.05$) and affective symptoms ($F(1,13)=6.42$, $P<0.05$). As an increasing number of subjects became employed, the rate of hospitalisation did not rise.

Conclusion

The paradigm presented here for the treatment of schizophrenia is an educational and clinical management model that optimally aligns with, and supports, the family. Particularly in its multiple family format, psychoeducation is a powerful tool for the avoidance of future relapse and significant improvement in the quality of life for patients with severe mental illness and their families. The psychoeducational MFG approach represents the wedding of two powerful and well-established models of treatment, uniquely developed and suitable for alleviating the psychiatric and personal catastrophe that is schizophrenia. Because they promote repetition and structure at the expense of complexity, emotionality and diversity, they rarely make for great theatre, but they are quietly and gradually effective in promoting the restitution and the rehabilitation of the afflicted person, the relief of family burden and suffering and the re-balancing of family relationships.

In an effort to capitalise on the specific advantages and efficacies of ACT, MFGs and family psychoeducation, we have combined them in a more comprehensive treatment system, FACT. The unique component of the approach integrates the family in the ongoing treatment and rehabilitation work being conducted by the ACT clinicians. It is focused on patient vocational rehabilitation, step-wise functional progression, early crisis intervention and relapse prevention; it is as coordinated as possible with the team's work and plans.

For families, we encourage the expansion of their social networks by in-group cross-family problem-solving and social support and out-of-group socialising. Throughout, the aim is that the MFG becomes something of a task force, in which experts from various sectors of the patient's total network share experiences, information, planning and the creation of new ideas and options, especially in the difficult area of vocational rehabilitation. The professional team's job is then to take these possibilities and attempt to realise them. The assumptions are that all aspects of the patient's network should be brought to bear on the effort toward employment and that expanding that network through the natural connections in an MFG can gain each patient access to a greatly expanded pool of potential jobs and opportunities. This total process is a major contributor to the higher employment rates achieved to date in our experimental clinical trials of the FACT approach.

Training in family intervention varies between approaches, but for the psychoeducational, long-term clinical management approaches clinicians will require intensive workshop-style training and some supervision to realise fully the potential of the model. The psychoeducational MFG approach has been described in a treatment manual, that has been used to train a large cadre of practitioners in New York State, Illinois and Maine. They received intensive training in a two-day workshop, followed by at least one year of monthly group supervision. The focus in these training sessions has more recently been role-playing and planning of implementation, rather than conceptual presentation. The more practical and technical focus has proved to be more effective in helping clinicians, at least the more experienced individuals, to attain competence more systematically and rapidly than lecture/discussion formats. The supervision has focused on the engagement process and the execution of the problem-solving process in the MFG context. Recent trainees have universally been able to initiate successful MFGs if the administrative elements have supported their efforts.

The outcome data available and continuing to emerge suggests that these eminently teachable and practical approaches may be the most cost-effective psychosocial treatment yet developed for chronic and severe psychiatric disorders. These studies provide evidence that:

    (a) a multi-family group version of psychoeducation yields significantly fewer relapses than the single-family form and markedly fewer relapses in partially-remitted patients;

(b) there is a significant increase in employment in both forms of psychoeducational family treatment and a trend towards superiority for the MFG format;
(c) FACT yields better vocational outcome than ACT alone.

Ultimately, however, the most persuasive recommendation for this type of work is that it allows the family and patient to move this devastating illness off to a corner of their lives and proceed to live a bit more as their neighbours and friends do, something that until now has been all but impossible for most families.

References

AMERICAN PSYCHIATRIC ASSOCIATION (1987) *Diagnostic and Statistical Manual of Mental Disorders* (3rd edn, rev) (DSM–III–R). Washington, DC: APA.

ANDERSON, C. M., HOGARTY, G. E. & REISS, D. J. (1980) Family treatment of adult schizophrenic patients: a psychoeducational approach. *Schizophrenia Bulletin*, **6**, 490–505.

—, REISS, D. J. & HOGARTY, G. E. (1986) *Schizophrenia and the Family.* New York: Guilford.

BATESON, G., JACKSON, D. D., HALEY, J., ET AL (1956) Toward a theory of schizophrenia. *Behavioural Science*, **1**, 251–264.

BEELS, C. C. (1975) Family and social management of schizophrenia. *Schizophrenia Bulletin*, **13**, 97–118.

— (1981) Social support and schizophrenia. *Schizophrenia Bulletin*, **7**, 58–79.

BENNINGFIELD, A. B. (1980) Multiple family therapy systems. *Advances in Family Psychiatry*, **2**, 411–424.

BERMAN, K. K. (1966) Multiple family therapy: its possibilities in preventing readmission. *Mental Hygiene*, **50**, 367–370.

BROWN, G. W., BIRLEY, J. L. T. & WING J. K. (1972) Influence of family life on the course of schizophrenic disorders: a replication. *British Journal of Psychiatry*, **121**, 241–258.

DEAN, A. & LIN, N. (1977) The stress-buffering role of social support. *Journal of Nervous and Mental Disorders*, **165**, 403–416.

DeLISI, L. E., SCHWARTZ, C.C., TARGUM, S. D, ET AL (1983) Ventricular brain enlargement and outcome of acute schizophrenic disorder. *Journal of Psychiatric Research*, **9**, 169–171.

DETRE, T., SAYER, J., NORTON, A., ET AL (1961) An experimental approach to the treatment of the acutely ill psychiatric patient in the general hospital. *Connecticut Medicine*, **25**, 613–619.

DOZIER, M., HARRIS, M. & BERGMAN, H. (1987) Social network density and rehospitalization among young adult patients. *Hospital and Community Psychiatry*, **38**, 61–64.

FALLOON, I. R. H. & LIBERMAN, R. P. (1983) Behavioral family interventions in the management of chronic schizophrenia. In *Family Therapy in Schizophrenia* (ed W. R. McFarlane), pp. 141–172. New York, Guilford.

—, BOYD, J. L., McGILL, C. W, ET AL (1985) Family management in the prevention of morbidity of schizophrenia. *Archives of General Psychiatry*, **42**, 887-896.

FREEMAN, H. & SIMMONS, O. (1961) Feeling of stigma among relatives of former mental patients. *Social Problems*, **8**, 12.

GARRISON, V. (1978) Support systems of schizophrenic and non-schizophrenic Puerto Rican women in New York City. *Schizophrenia Bulletin*, **4**, 561–596.

GOLDSTEIN, M. J., RODNICK, E., EVANS, J., ET AL (1978) Drug and family therapy in the aftercare of acute schizophrenics. *Archives of General Psychiatry* **35**, 1169–1177.

94   *McFarlane*

GRANOVETTER, M. S. (1974) *Getting a Job: a Study of Contacts and Careers.* Cambridge, MA: Harvard University Press.

HAMMER, M. (1963) Influence of small social networks as factors on mental hospital admission. *Human Organization,* **22,** 243–251.

HOGARTY, G. E. (1981) Social supports, social networks, and schizophrenia. *Schizophrenia Bulletin,* **7,** 45–57.

—— & ULRICH, R. F. (1977) Temporal effects of drug and placebo in delaying relapse in schizophrenic outpatients. *Archives of General Psychiatry,* **34,** 297–301.

——, MAKIESKY-BARROW, S., & GUTWIRTH, L. (1978) Social networks and schizophrenia. *Schizophrenia Bulletin,* **4,** 522–545.

——, SCHOOLER, N. R. & ULRICH, R. F. (1979) Fluphenazine and social therapy in the aftercare of schizophrenic patients. *Archives of General Psychiatry,* **36,** 1283–1294.

——, ANDERSON, C. M., REISS, D. J., *ET AL* (1986) Family psychoeducation, social skills training and maintenance chemotherapy in the aftercare treatment of schizophrenia. *Archives of General Psychiatry,* **43,** 633–642.

JOHNSON, D. (1990) The family's experience of living with mental illness. In *Families as Allies in Treatment of the Mentally Ill* (eds H. P. Lefley & D. J. Johnson), pp. 31–64. Washington, DC: American Psychiatric Association Press.

KNOEDLER, W. H. (1979) How the Training in Community Living program helps patients work. *New Directions for Mental Health Services,* **2,** 57–66.

LAMB, H. R. & OLIPHANT, E. (1978) Schizophrenia through the eyes of families. *Hospital and Community Psychiatry,* **29,** 803–806.

LANSKY, M. R., BLEY, C. R., MCVEY, G. G., *ET AL* (1978) Multiple family groups as aftercare. *International Journal of Group Psychotherapy,* **29,** 211–224.

LAQUEUR, H. P. (1972) Mechanisms of change in multiple family therapy. In *Progress in Group and Family Therapy* (eds C. J. Sager & H. S. Kaplan). New York: Brunner/Mazel.

——, LABURT, H. A. & MORONG, E. (1964) Multiple family therapy, further developments. *International Journal of Social Psychiatry,* **10,** 69–80.

LEFF, J., KUIPERS, L., BERKOWITZ, R., *ET AL* (1982) A controlled trial of social intervention in the families of schizophrenic patients: two-year follow-up. *British Journal of Psychiatry,* **146,** 594–600.

——, ——, & —— (1983) Intervention in families of schizophrenics and its effect of relapse rate. In *Family Therapy in Schizophrenia* (ed W. R. McFarlane), pp. 173–187. New York: Guilford.

—— & VAUGHN, C. E. (1985) *Expressed Emotion in Families.* New York: Guilford Press.

LIPTON, F. R., COHEN, C. I., FISCHER, E., *ET AL* (1981) Schizophrenia: a network crisis. *Schizophrenia Bulletin,* **7,** 144–151.

LURIE, A. & RON, H. (1972) Socialization program as part of aftercare planning. *General Psychiatric Association Journal,* **17,** 157–16.

MCFARLANE, W. R. (1990) Multiple family groups in the treatment of schizophrenia. In *Handbook of Schizophrenia.* Vol. 4. (ed. H. A. Nasrallah), pp. 167–189. Amsterdam: Elsevier.

—— (1983) Multiple family therapy in schizophrenia. In *Family Therapy in Schizophrenia* (ed. W. R. McFarlane), pp. 141–172. New York: Guilford.

—— (2000) *The Multifamily Group.* New York: Oxford University Press (in press).

——, LINK, B., DUSHAY, R., *ET AL* (1995*a*) Psychoeducational multiple family groups: four-year relapse outcome in schizophrenia. *Family Process,* **34,** 127–144.

——, LUKENS, E., LINK, B., *ET AL* (1995*b*) Multiple-family groups and psychoeducation in the treatment of schizophrenia. *Archives of General Psychiatry,* **52,** 679–687.

——, DUSHAY, R. A., STASTNY, P., *ET AL* (1996). A comparison of two levels of family-aided Assertive Community Treatment. *Psychiatric Services,* **47,** 744–750.

OLFSON, M. (1990) Assertive community treatment: an evaluation of the experimental evidence. *Hospital and Community Psychiatry,* **41,** 634–641.

O'SHEA, M. D. (1985) Multiple family therapy: current status and critical appraisal. *Family Process,* **24,** 555–582.

OVERALL, J. E. & GORHAM, D. R. (1962) The brief psychiatric rating scale. *Psychological Reports*, **10**, 799–812.

PATTISON, E. M., LLAMA, R. & HURD, G. (1979) Social network mediation of anxiety. *Psychiatric Annals*, **9**, 56–67.

POTASZNIK, H. & NELSON, G. (1984) Stress and social support: the burden experienced by the family of a mentally ill person. *American Journal of Community Psychology*, **12**, 589.

RABKIN, J. (1974) Public attitudes toward mental illness: a review of the literature. *Schizophrenia Bulletin*, **10**, 9–33.

ROESSLER, R. T. & HIETT, A. (1983) Strategies for increasing employer response to job development surveys. *Rehabilitation Counselling Bulletin*, **26**, 368–370.

STEIN, L. I. & TEST, M. A. (1980) Alternative to mental hospital treatment I: Conceptual model, treatment program and clinical evaluation. *Archives of General Psychiatry*, **37**, 392–397.

—— & SANTOS, A. B. (1998) *Assertive Community Treatment of Persons with Severe Mental Illness.* New York: Norton.

STEINBERG, H. R. & DURELL, J. A. (1968) A stressful social situation as a precipitant of schizophrenia. *British Journal of Psychiatry*, **114**, 1097–1105.

STRELNICK, A. H. (1977) Multiple family group therapy: a review of the literature. *Family Process*, **16**, 307–325.

STEVENS, J. R. (1982) Neuropathology of schizophrenia. *Archives of General Psychiatry*, **39**, 1131–1139.

TARRIER, N., BARROWCLOUGH, C., VAUGHN, C., *ET AL* (1988) The community management of schizophrenia: a controlled trial of a behavioural intervention with families to reduce relapse. *British Journal of Psychiatry*, **153**, 532–542.

TECCE, J. J. & COLE, J. O. (1976) The distraction–arousal hypothesis, CNV and schizophrenia. In *Behavioural Control and Modification of Psychological Activity* (ed. D. I. Mostofsky). Englewood Cliffs, NJ: Prentice-Hall.

THOMPSON, K. S., Griffith, E. E. H., & Leaf, P. S. (1990) A historical review of the Madison model of community care. *Hospital and Community Psychiatry*, **41**, 625-634.

TOLSDORF, C. C. (1976). Social networks, support and coping: an exploratory study. *Family Process*, **15**, 407–417.

VANDERGOOT, D. (1976) A comparison of two mailing approaches attempting to generate the participation of businessmen in rehabilitation. *Rehabilitation Counselling Bulletin*, **20**, 73–75.

VAUGHN, C. E. & LEFF, J. P. (1976). The influence of family and social factors on the course of psychiatric illness: a comparison of schizophrenic and depressed neurotic patients. *British Journal of Psychiatry*, **129**, 125–137.

WEINBERGER, D. R., BERMAN, K. R. & ZEC, R. F. (1986) Physiologic dysfunction of dorsolateral pre-frontal cortex in schizophrenia. *Archives of General Psychiatry*, **43**, 114–135.

WORLD HEALTH ORGANIZATION (1979) *Schizophrenia: an International Follow-up Study.* Chichester: John Wiley & Sons.

WORRALL, J. D. & VANDERGOOT, D. (1982) Additional indicators of non-success: a follow-up report. *Rehabilitation Counselling Bulletin*, **26**, 88–93.

YARROW, M., SCHWARTZ, C., MURPHY, H., *ET AL* (1955) The psychological meaning of mental illness in the family. *Journal of Social Issues*, **11**, 12.

ZADNY, J. J. & JAMES, L. F. (1979) Job placement in state vocational rehabilitation agencies: A survey of technique. *Rehabilitation Counselling Bulletin*, **22**, 361–378.

5 Bringing into clinical practice skills shown to be effective in research settings: a follow-up of 'Thorn Training' in psychosocial family interventions for psychosis

IAN BAGULEY, ANTONY BUTTERWORTH,
KIERAN FAHY, GILLIAN HADDOCK, STUART
LANCASHIRE and NICK TARRIER

Background to the study

The incidence of serious mental illness such as schizophrenia has changed little over time and, despite the absence of rigorous diagnostic criteria, has remained at around one in 10 000 population each year. As a result of the chronicity of the illness, prevalence is greater than incidence, therefore the economic cost to health services is likely to be greater than a serious common physical illness such as coronary heart disease (Birchwood *et al*, 1988).

It has been estimated that the direct cost of schizophrenia to the UK mental health services in 1992/93 was about £1 billion, excluding the substantial indirect costs for residential care, income support and more general costs to families and society (Clinical Standards Advisory Group (CSAG), 1995).

This chapter refers to the situation in the UK where traditional treatments for patients suffering from schizophrenia have often consisted of regular attendance at an out-patient's clinic to see a psychiatrist and regular neuroleptic medication received from either a community psychiatric nurse (CPN) or from a specially run medication or 'depot' clinic. This treatment is usually supplemented with hospital admission at times of crisis (Woof *et al*, 1988; White, 1990).

The role of the CPN in the care of patients suffering from a serious mental illness has changed over the years (Woof *et al*, 1988; White, 1990). The first CPN service in the UK started in 1954 when two psychiatric nurses were seconded to posts to provide a 'follow-up' service for those patients discharged from long-term in-patient care (Moore, 1961). The 1970s saw the expansion of these CPN services and more than three-quarters of current services were established during that decade (Community Psychiatric Nurses Association, 1981). Although information about the development of CPN services is often unreliable and inaccurate, a pattern has emerged. While communtiy psychiatric nursing was intended initially to provide continuity of care to a wide range of patients (most notably those who were discharged from hospital), there has been a drift away from providing services to patients with a serious mental illness. This shift in role has been criticised, as has the tendency for CPNs to concentrate on the patient rather than including the family, who frequently bear the main burden of care (Brooker & Butterworth, 1991). The reasons for this change are complex; however, several recent health policy changes in the UK have had a major influence on the activities of CPNs. New policies allowed general practitioners (GPs) and health authorities to become commissioners of services while the provision of health care became the responsibility of self-governing NHS Trusts (Department of Health, 1989*a*). Related policy changes (Department of Health, 1989*b*) charged local authorities with:

(a) ensuring that the social needs of patients were assessed;
(b) that services based on the assessed needs were bought;
(c) that these services were managed and coordinated effectively.

These changes have had a major influence on the development of CPN services. Marum (1995) asserts that GP fund-holders had three main objectives:

(a) maintaining or increasing the amount of time that CPNs spent in the surgery;
(b) dismantling locality-based community mental health teams;
(c) increasing the availability of surgery-based counselling services.

Clearly, it would be difficult for any CPN team to focus effectively on patients with a serious mental illness, particularly if the interventions were to be long term, within an environment that appears to be changing in such a way to militate against research-based interventions.

Research suggests that if mental health professionals such as CPNs were able to use a more problem-centred approach with patients with a serious mental illness, then there would be significant benefits for patients, families and services (Brooker & Butterworth, 1993).

More recent changes in the provision of health care in the UK demand clinical practice that is based on sound research. 'Evidence-based practice' is rapidly becoming a purchasing catchphrase. However, if research- or evidence-based practice is going to be anything other than rhetoric, service managers at the highest level have a vital role to play (Woof, 1992). An important part of this role is to identify the training needs of those best in a position to deliver psychosocial approaches to patients and their families.

Research in the psychosocial treatment of psychosis in the late 1950s and early 1960s began to examine the factors that were thought to contribute to relapse, particularly in the context of post-hospital adjustment of patients discharged from a large psychiatric hospital in London (Brown *et al*, 1958). Brown (1959) studied a large subgroup of patients who had a diagnosis of schizophrenia and found that those patients who returned from hospital to live with a family or relative fared worse in terms of relapse than those patients who lived alone or in supported accommodation. Over the next 15 years, three broad themes began to emerge from the research:

(a) patients who returned to live with a family where relatives exhibited a high degree of expressed emotion, such as emotional over-involvement, hostility and criticism, were likely to relapse more quickly than those who returned to live with relatives who displayed a low level of expressed emotion, identified by the absence of hostility, critical comments or emotional over-involvement;

(b) contact time between the patient and relatives within high expressed emotion households;

(c) patients' adherence with medication were important predictive factors.

Those patients who spent less than 35 hours per week in face-to-face contact with a relative with a high level of expressed emotion and who complied with their medication relapsed less than those who had a high level of face-to-face contact and did not comply with their medication (Vaughn & Leff, 1976; Leff & Vaughn, 1980; Vaughn & Leff, 1981).

Over the last two decades a large number of prospective expressed emotion studies have been carried out in a number of countries and in different cultural settings confirming the robustness and predictive validity of the construct (e.g. India, China). Bebbington & Kuipers (1994) report an analysis of aggregated data from 25 expressed emotion studies that confirm the original findings of Brown *et al* (1962, 1972).

Family relationships clearly have an important role to play in the course of schizophrenia. The finding that a high level of expressed emotion is associated with significantly greater relapse rates has also been found to be robust by Butzlaff & Hooley (1998).

However, despite the research findings in expressed emotion, the exact nature of the relationship between relapse and ambient and acute stress is not well understood. It is also important to note that many families exhibit the characteristics of high expressed emotion at times of crisis and low expressed emotion at other times. Some studies suggest that around one-third of relatives, rated as showing high levels of expressed emotion during the acute phase of the illness while the patient was in hospital, were found to show low levels of expressed emotion following the patients' discharge when the acute symptoms had remitted (Brown *et al*, 1972; Dulz & Hand, 1986).

As a result of the expressed emotion research, problem-focused family interventions have developed and been shown consistently to decrease schizophrenic relapse in randomised controlled trials whereas non-problem-focused family interventions have not (Mari & Streiner, 1994).

While there is strong research evidence that family interventions are highly beneficial to patients and their carers, they are still not widely or routinely available in clinical practice. Recent changes in Government legislation demands that providers of mental health services supply a comprehensive service to patients with serious mental illness that takes into account the clinical and social needs of both the patients themselves and their families and carers. It is also expected that patients, families and carers should be included in the planning of care (Department of Health, 1989*a*, 1994). That this systematic, collaborative approach to the management of serious mental illness, does not routinely happen is demonstrated in the report of the CSAG into the standards of care for people with schizophrenia (CSAG, 1995).

The CSAG report found that training in interventions that were underpinned by sound research findings, more specifically, problem-centred psychosocial interventions, was given a low priority and that clinicians were often poorly trained and poorly managed within in-patient and community mental health teams. Few attempts were made to link training priorities to service priorities and little effort was made to discover the training needs of mental health professionals. The report states:

> "There was little systematic assessment of mental health nurses' training needs in psychological/family interventions, case man-agement approaches (including assertive outreach), and the assessment of the side-effects of medication." (CSAG,1995)

It seems clear so far that, while we have unequivocal research evidence of the benefits of problem-centred family interventions, services appear unable or unwilling to operationalise a policy based on such research. For services to reach the patient groups that most need them and to be clinically effective once reached, service managers have a significant contribution to make in terms of the clinical objectives and configuration of the service, so that it may more accurately reflect contemporary views on the management of serious mental illness.

Training in psychosocial interventions

Psychosocial interventions (PSI) describe the complex activities undertaken by clinicians and services that focus on improving the health and social situation of those service users who suffer from serious mental illness (Baguley & Baguley, 1999). Training programmes carried out throughout the north-west of England, particularly in Manchester, during the 1980s demonstrated that it was possible to train mental health professionals in the family intervention component of PSI and retain the efficacy that had been demonstrated within the research studies (Barrowclough & Fleming, 1986; Tarrier *et al.* 1988).

The model for these training programmes was described by Barrow-clough & Tarrier (1992) and mirrors the clinical model taught on the courses. Didactic teaching was followed up with practice in a role-play setting. Trainees were then required to carry out the interventions with a family. The results of these attempts to implement the skills were brought to clinical supervision the following week. Clinical supervision based on the experiences of the trainees was felt to be central to the acquisition of clinical skills.

A study funded by the Government, conducted at the University of Manchester during the 1980s and early 1990s, used this same model for training and supplemented it by asking trainees to submit audiotapes of their clinical sessions with service users. These audiotapes were used as a focus for the supervision sessions (Brooker & Butterworth, 1991; Brooker *et al*, 1994). Under this study two training programmes ran; the first trained nine CPNs and the second trained 10. Both courses were evaluated; the first study adopted a quasi-experimental design and the trainees were matched, on a number of demographic variables, with a CPN from their workplace. The matched CPN constituted the control group. Each CPN, in both the experimental and control groups, was asked to identify three patients with a diagnosis of schizophrenia who had a family.

All the CPNs in both groups were trained to reliably rate a symptom rating scale, the 'KGV' (Krawieka *et al*, 1977), and to use a measure of social functioning, the Social Functioning Scale (SFS; Birchwood *et al*, 1990). Data from these measures, along with a number of others, were collected pre-training (baseline), on completion of the training (post-training) and at one year follow-up. Although there were no significant differences between the patients in the experimental group compared to the control group at baseline, and both the experimental and control groups demonstrated improvements at post-training, only those service users in the experimental groups demonstrated significant improvements at follow-up.

The evaluation of the second course adopted a prospective, within-subject design. Each CPN acted as his or her own control and was required to work with six service users and their families, three in the experimental group and three in a control group. All of the families would be assessed and receive standard care for six months prior to the start of the training, and three would then go on to receive family interventions (Brooker *et al*, 1992).

The results of this study were very similar to the first study. Service users in the experimental group demonstrated significant improvements in both symptoms and social functioning that were not evident in the control group. There are clear methodological problems with this research. For example, there was no independent follow-up of the service users, and trainees were asked to work as normal with the service users in the control group as opposed to using the newly acquired family intervention skills. Despite these reservations the results are encouraging and suggest that clinical skills found to be effective within tightly controlled research studies can be taught to CPNs and retain their efficacy when used in a service setting.

However, despite the success of these training programmes, Brooker found that the trainees, once they returned to their area of work full-time, had difficulty integrating the skills into their everyday clinical work. It is difficult to draw clear conclusions from this study about the reasons that might underpin the difficulties around implementation. Former trainees themselves blamed service structure and the lack of support from managers and colleagues. An important point might be that the training focused only on family work and did not help trainees to address other problems that service users might have.

A similar study carried out in New South Wales, Australia, failed to engage trainees in the evaluation element of the programme. Only 44 out of 160 trainees agreed to take part in the treatment trial and of these, 28 saw only one family. Fifty-seven per cent of the families in the study were seen by six trainees (Kavanagh *et al*, 1993). There were some important differences between the Manchester and Australian studies: the Australian course lasted only 30–35 hours, less than half the time invested in the Manchester programme, and the Australian course did not appear to include supervision as an integral part of the course. A final important difference is that the Manchester teaching team made efforts to enlist the cooperation of the trainees' managers in the study, whereas the Australian study did not engage managers at all.

Barrowclough & Tarrier (1992) suggest that organisational change is of paramount importance if family interventions are to be implemented; they observe that organisations tend to have 'a homeostasis of inertia'. They further suggest that attention needs to be paid to the organisational culture in which the family intervention will be implemented and that organisational change is a slow process. An individual of senior status needs to be nominated as the agent of organisational change if such change is to be long lasting.

Georgiades & Phillimore (1975) suggest working with those who are supportive of change rather than those against change, and advocate the identification of teams of workers for the implementation of new approaches. This means working with that part of the system that has the ability and willingness to change. There are obvious advantages to working with individuals and groups who have the authority or independence to make their own decisions. It is also important that an appropriate level of commitment and involvement is obtained from those in top management positions to offer protection from burn-out and stress in team members.

Barrowclough & Tarrier (1992) also describe issues of service configuration and specifically the advantages of specialist teams over generic teams in terms of not diluting the intervention skill. As well as raising the profile of the work of the team such an approach would encourage staff to develop specialist skills and facilitate their career development.

The acquisition of clinical skills is a complex process, the success of which is underpinned by a number of important factors. These include practical training methods, which are more useful than traditional didactic teaching styles, clinical supervision that guides the practice of the trainee and understanding of, and support for, the work of former trainees by service managers and colleagues (Tarrier *et al*, 1998).

Mental health professionals should have access to skills-based training that has a positive impact on the symptoms and social functioning of patients. It is an approach that is welcomed by patients, families and carers, recognised as good practice by the Department of Health and encouraged by central government (Department of Health, 1994; Duggan, 1997).

Thorn Training

Outline

The Thorn Training Initiative was established in 1992 with funds from the Sir Jules Thorn Charitable Trust. Two centres (the University of Manchester and the Institute of Psychiatry, London) designed the Thorn Training to equip nurses with those psychosocial intervention skills (that had been validated as effective in sound research conditions) to improve the clinical symptoms and social functioning of people with a serious mental illness. After three years the training became multi-disciplinary. Research strongly suggests that multi-disciplinary teamwork is essential for effective clinical work (Muijen, 1992).

The course was taught in three modules:

(a) a problem-centred case management module;
(b) family work;
(c) psychological management of psychosis.

Case management module

The case management module, as well as giving trainees an opportunity to examine the literature that informs case management, was also a foundation module. Assessment is the cornerstone of intervention and a substantial amount of this first module was devoted to the training of students in the reliable use of a variety of structured assessments, for example, the KGV(M) modified psychiatric assessment scale (Krawieka *et al*, 1977) and the SFS (Birchwood *et al*, 1990). The KGV(M) is a semi-structured interview that comprises 14 items. Ratings for the first six are based on information gained through the questions asked at the time of the interview. These questions concern the patients' experiences over the previous four weeks. The questions in the interview are based on the psychosis section of the Present State Examination (PSE; Wing *et al*, 1974). Ratings for the remaining items are based on systematic observations during the interview itself. Its purpose is to provide a summary of the symptoms experienced by patients who have a serious mental illness. Ratings are made on a five-point Likert scale (zero means that the symptom was absent over the previous four weeks, four means the symptom has been present on the majority of days during the past four weeks). The scale covers positive and negative psychotic symptoms as well as affective symptoms. It is sensitive to small changes in symptom severity and trainees are asked to use this scale to monitor the progress of their patients. The SFS measures changes in the social functioning and competency skills likely to be affected following the onset of a serious mental illness.

Cognitive–behavioural family management module

This module gave trainees an opportunity to explore the literature that underpins this approach and offers training in family interventions. Although this module has a central theme of assessment, education strategies with families, stress management and problem-solving, trainees are encouraged to adopt a formulation-driven approach, that is, interventions driven by the assessed needs of the service users and families. Consequently, much of the training is directed by the clinical problems that trainees bring to the teaching and supervision sessions.

Psychological management module

This module introduces trainees to the growing literature that underpins those strategies that have proved effective in helping reduce the distress that patients experience as a result of psychotic phenomena. Included in this module are early warning signs, early interventions and focusing and distraction techniques.

In both the family management and psychological management modules, supervised clinical practice was a mandatory part of the course. The course was principally taught by a clinical psychologist and a psychiatric nurse, with additional teaching from people with expertise in particular areas such as medication, genetics, case management, suicide and dangerousness among others.

Evaluation of the training

The course was subjected to a rigorous evaluation process. The evaluation can best be described in three parts.

(a) An assessment of the trainee's knowledge via standard methods of academic progress, such as essays, case studies and multiple choice examinations.
(b) An assessment of the reliability of trainee's ratings for both the KGV and SFS. A researcher visited randomly selected patients to make an independent assessment of the latter's progress and around half of all patients were independently assessed. Assessment data were collected from the trainees at baseline and every three months following this. Independent data are collected at baseline and at one-year follow-up.
(c) A third component of the process involves an evaluation of the clinical skills of trainees. This involves the trainees making audiotapes of all their clinical sessions with patients and families and the recordings being analysed using a modified version of

the Cognitive Therapy Check-List (CTC; Young & Beck, 1980; Haddock & Kinderman, 1997). The aim of the study was to establish a substantial data set that can be used to evaluate the effectiveness of current training courses, in terms of impact on patients and improved knowledge and techniques of trainees, as well as to inform future training courses.

An evaluation of the Thorn Initiative has shown that Thorn trainees achieved statistically significant improvements in both knowledge and clinical skills (Devane *et al*, 1998). Patients treated by the Thorn trainees during the period of their training reported significant improvements in psychiatric symptoms and social functioning (see Table 5.1) (Lancashire *et al*, 1996, 1997).

The Schizophrenia Family Work Scale (SFWS) was used by Devane *et al* to rate the skills of the Thorn trainees carrying out family interventions. Alongside the SFWS, the Cognitive Therapy Scale (CTS; Young & Beck, 1980) was used to assess the skills the trainees used in their individual work. Tapes of clinical sessions submitted by the trainees were rated and compared with those tapes submitted by matched controls. This study found that there were no significant differences between the experimental group and the control group on the CTC. As a result of the low numbers of tapes of family intervention sessions submitted by the control group, it was impossible to make a comparison. However, it was clear that the trainees had good levels of general skills and adequate levels of more technical family work skill. A more detailed study showed that trainees demonstrated significant increases in clinical skills compared to controls who had received no training (Haddock *et al*, 2000).

TABLE 5.1

Scores on measures of psychiatric symptoms and social functioning of 27 patients with serious mental illness before and after 12 months of interventions provided by Thorn trained nurses

Measure and range of possible scores	Before		After		P*
	Median	Range	Median	Range	
KGV scale(0–32)	12	9–16	9	5–13	<0.01
Positive symptoms (0–12)	6	3–8	3	1.5–7.5	<0.01
Negative symptoms (0–12)	2	1–4	1	0–3	NS
Affective symptoms (0–8)	4	3–5	3	2–4	<0.01
Social Functioning Scale (0–268)	107	85–131	125	91–138	<0.01

* Wilcoxon matched-pairs signed-rank test.

Good quality training is necessary, but not sufficient, to enable former trainees to put what they have learned into routine practice. It was, therefore, regarded essential to follow up trainees after completion of their training to discover to what extent they had been able to continue using the knowledge and skills acquired in family work skills during the Thorn Training.

Evaluation of the use by trainees of family intervention skills on completion of training

The main aims of the study were to:

(a) discover the extent to which family interventions had been integrated into former trainees' day-to-day clinical work;
(b) examine the nature of the difficulties that former trainees experienced in applying the family interventions;
(c) determine if the study could predict which trainees would be more able to implement family intervention skills acquired during training.

Method

All former trainees (n=21) from the first two cohorts of the Manchester Thorn Initiative training programme were identified and professional and other background descriptive data were obtained from course documentation (see Table 5.2). All data from the course participants' case-loads were assessed using the main patient outcome measures pre- and post-intervention. These measures were verified by the course evaluator, who carried out the same measures with a randomly selected sample of approximately half of the patients independently.

A questionnaire identical to that used by the Australian study (Kavanagh *et al*, 1993) was administered to enable comparisons of the data between the two studies. The questionnaire included:

(a) 13 questions about the numbers of families that the former trainees had worked with for a minimum of three sessions since completing the course and the difficulties that the former trainees had experienced with this work;
(b) four questions specifically about supervision of family work;
(c) a problem matrix that asked respondents to rate 33 questions that describe the difficulties they had encountered when trying to implement family interventions in their place of work on a scale of zero (no difficulty) to four (extreme difficulty).

A total of 21 former trainees, 8 women and 13 men, were sent the questionnaire. The questionnaires were assertively followed up with

TABLE 5.2
*Professional and other background data on the trainees of Thorn trainees,
Cohorts 1 and 2 (n=21)*

	Range	Mean
Age (years)	28–44	35 (s.d.=4.9)
Mental health service experience (years)	3–20	9.4 (s.d.=5.3)
Gender		
Female	n=8, 38%	
Male	n=13, 62%	
Profession		
Nurse	100%	(100% RMN)
Current post		
Community based	n–16	76.2%
Ward based	n=2	9.5%
Manager	n=2	9.5%
Lecturer	n=1	4.8%
Qualifications		
Registered General Nurse	n=10	47.6%
Community psychiatric nursing certificate	n=6	28.6%
HV certificate	n=1	4.8%
Degree	n=4	19.0%
Nursing grade		
H	n=1	4.8%
G	n=10	47.6%
F	n=4	19.0%
E	n–2	9.5%
Lecturer	n–1	4.8%
Missing data	n=3	14.3%
Previous relevant training[1]		
Behaviour or cognitive–behavioural therapy (course ENB 650/655)	n=2	9.5%
Psychosocial Intervention Techniques	n=5	23.8%

1. Relevant training was defined as the course having had a cognitive or behavioural focus and included supervised clinical practice. RMN, Registered Mental Nurse.

telephone calls and reminder letters. All 21 questionnaires were returned, but one questionnaire was incomplete.

Results

Implementing family interventions

Trainees had completed the course between 6 and 18 months before completing the questionnaire (mean=11.14, s.d.=6.08). Table 5.3 shows that the mean number of families that each former trainee had worked with since completing the course was 2.5. Three trainees (15%) had worked with no families, and three with just one family. Five trainees

(25%) had worked with two families while the remaining nine trainees (45%) had worked with three or more families including three (15%) who had worked with more than five families.

Of the three people who had not used this approach with a family since completing the course, two nurses worked with teams dedicated to providing services for people with a serious mental illness. Both answered the question "What have been the main difficulties or challenges in using the approach?" by citing a lack of support, knowledge and understanding by managers regarding behavioural family work. Indeed, the majority (60%) of former trainees (see Table 5.5) specifically cited a lack of support by managers and/or colleagues as the main reason for difficulty.

Degree of difficulty in implementing family interventions

Former trainees were asked to rate the degree of difficulty that they had experienced in implementing family interventions on a five-point scale from zero (no difficulty) to five (impossible). The mean degree

TABLE 5.3
Number of families that trainees have worked with, using cognitive–behavioural techniques, since completing the course

Number of families worked with	% of trainees
0	15
1	15
2	25
3	30
5+	15
Group mean	2.5 families

No information was collected on the numbers of families or carers that trainees had worked with prior to coming onto the course.

TABLE 5.4
Degree of difficulty experienced by Thorn trainees on their return to service

Degree of difficulty	% of trainees
No difficulty	5
A little difficulty	15
Moderate difficulty	40
Very difficult	15
Extremely difficult	10
Impossible	15
Mean degree of difficulty	2.5

TABLE 5.5
Answers to the question asked of former trainees "What have been the main difficulties or challenges in using this approach?"

	%
Lack of support by managers and colleagues	60
Difficulty finding appropriate patients	20
Not having enough time	15
No difficulty	5

of difficulty was 2.5 (see Table 5.4). Eighty per cent experienced moderate and greater degrees of difficulty and only one person (5%) experienced no difficulty.

Tables 5.5 and 5.6 show additional difficulties encountered. Sufficient time for the interventions, time for appropriate supervision, the need for a co-worker and conflicting service demands were all cited as things that the mangers could influence in a way that would help the former trainees to carry out clinical work.

Problem matrix

The problem matrix asked people to rate 33 potential problem areas on a six-point scale reflecting the amount of difficulty experienced in

TABLE 5.6
Difficulties experienced in implementing cognitive–behavioural family work. Results expressed as: (a) the mean in a range of possible scores of 0–4; (b) rank order of difficulty; 1=greatest difficulty

	Manchester		Australia	
	Mean	(Rank)	Mean	(Rank)
Allowance of time from service to do the interventions	3.05	(1)	2.3	(2)
Integration with case-load or other responsibilities at work	2.95	(2)	2.4	(1)
Lack of support by managers	2.35	(3)	1.1	(19)
Availability of time in lieu or overtime for appointments	2.15	(4)	1.6	(7)
Access to supervision	2.11	(5)	1.4	(12)
Lack of knowledge/recognition by colleagues of the value of family work	1.75	(6)	1.0	(24)
Collaboration with co-therapist	1.63	(7)	0.9	(26)
Clashes of family sessions with crisis with other patients	1.63	(7)	1.4	(11)

that area. A score of zero indicated that there was no difficulty and a score of five indicated that the difficulty experienced was extreme.

Implementing cognitive–behavioural family interventions

On the problem matrix, the mean global score for implementing cognitive–behavioural family interventions in the former trainees work settings was 1.35 which is just above the 'little difficulty' level.

Dedicated time for implementation

Dedicated time, free from other service responsibilities, to carry out the interventions proved to be the most difficult area for the former trainees, with a mean score of 3.05, which indicates the 'very difficult' level.

Other areas of difficulty included integrating the approach with their existing case-load or other responsibilities at work, lack of support from managers, availability of time in lieu or overtime for appointments and access to supervision. All these items proved difficult for former trainees and were just above the 'moderately difficult' level on the matrix.

Summary of results

Our study shows that almost half of former trainees (45%) had used cognitive–behavioural family approaches with three or more families since completing the course (Table 5.3). Only three former trainees (15%) had not used the approach at all since finishing the course. It seems that the Thorn Training initiative has been comparatively successful in producing people to implement this approach. However, a look at the degree of difficulty experienced (Table 5.4) shows that 80% of trainees' scores indicated levels to be between 'moderately difficult' and 'impossible'. The former trainees were a very experienced group with a mean length of service of nearly 10 years. Most (just over three-quarters) were community nurses and just under half were senior clinician grade (Table 5.2).

Comparison with the Australian study

The main areas of difficulty reported by the students are represented in Table 5.6. The results are presented alongside the results of the similar Australian study. Integration with case-load and other responsibilities and time allowed to do the interventions were ranked as the most difficult area in both studies. This is in agreement with other work on barriers to effective implementation of behavioural approaches (Corrigan *et al*, 1992) where institutional constraints on trained resources are commonly reported.

Discussion

The aim of this study was to discover the extent to which psychiatric nurses trained in problem-centred family interventions were able to integrate these skills into their everyday clinical practice. Other follow-up studies of such psychosocial interventions courses (Kavanagh *et al*, 1993; Fadden, 1997) have shown a disappointing level of implementation.

Kavanagh *et al* (1993) suggest four main requirements if cognitive–behavioural interventions are to be integrated into standard clinical practice successfully:

(a) sufficient personnel and resources with the theoretical background and clinical skills to carry out the interventions;
(b) the service has an operational policy and philosophy consistent with the interventions;
(c) clinicians have access to good quality training;
(d) the service provides reinforcement for the continued use of interventions such as clinical supervision.

This last point is of particular interest as it has been recognised that positive reinforcement of behavioural change underpins many of the interventions offered to families (Falloon *et al*, 1984). It seems logical that a similar approach to trainees might improve implementation the of psychosocial interventions.

Another factor is that there may need to be a 'critical mass' of advanced level trainees, who get involved in local training and organisational change, before greater levels of clinical implementation occur.

Table 5.2 indicates that our study involved trainees who were predominantely CPNs, and only 9.5% of trainees were from in-patient wards. This reflects the poorer training opportunities offered to in-patient staff, who were also in the minority in other studies referred to in this paper. Not surprisingly, both Kavanagh *et al* (1993) and Fadden (1997) find that ward nurses are less likely to apply psychosocial approaches although they potentially have a vital role in identifying families at times of crisis when the chances of successful engagement are greater (Barrowclough & Tarrier, 1992).

Many of the trainees from this study went on to perform other roles within services and received promotion. Clarification is required whether, once in positions of seniority in management and training, their policies, service configurations and training priorities lead to the implementation of psychosocial interventions or not. Our data do not tell us if the small number of study participants who already had qualifications in cognitive–behavioural and/or psychosocial interventions before the course had greater success in implementing psychosocial interventions. Evidence from Kavanagh *et al* (1993) suggests that previous learning may be important when basic training differs between professions.

Fadden (1997) found that 40% of the families were seen by 8% of the trained therapists. This was similar to Kavanagh *et al* (1993) who found that 57% of families were seen by 6% of therapists. Fadden found that where therapists worked in communities rather than in-patient settings and the numbers of trained therapists in a service exceeded eight, then more families were seen by therapists.

Although in our study ex-trainees reported that services were unable to support psychosocial interventions, the reasons are likely to be more complex than those identified through the questionnaire used. There is no doubt that support from managers and access to appropriate clinical supervision is important. Similarly, the ability of the service to be flexible and accessible to patients is thought to be central to the provision of effective services for those suffering from serious mental illness (Onyett, 1992).

There is little recognition of the pressures that managers of mental health services are under from other areas such as primary health care and the reduction of in-patient beds. It is clear that if skills-based training courses are to be effective, managers, from line managers to those at board level, need to be actively involved in training and education along with clinicians.

If family interventions are going to be implemented, this may mean having specialist family intervention services, providing assertive community treatment programmes and having a service that is flexible and responsive to the needs of the patients and families. Service managers need to be mindful of the problems that may result as a consequence of providing a flexible service that will cross over professional boundaries (Barrowclough & Tarrier, 1992). Further studies are needed to clarify which aspects of the skills developed in training were utilised when the interventions were used.

In addition to the difficulties found in our study, Fadden (1997) found:

(a) an inability to find suitable families;
(b) the time-consuming nature of the interventions or requirement for out of hours working;

(c) difficulty in engaging families and poor motivation or unwillingness to cooperate on the part of family members.

Those unable to see families reported:

(a) difficulty in using the treatment manual;
(b) gaps in general clinical skill;
(c) lack of support for family interventions by colleagues.

Those working in in-patient settings had far more difficulty in implementing the approaches than did their community colleagues. CPNs had least difficulty engaging families, but felt that they had problems with their knowledge and skills in family interventions. Clinical psychologists had problems finding families, but had few problems with engagement.

The evidence from the Kavanagh and Fadden studies suggests that the training programmes evaluated may have been inadequate on a number of levels. First, the training was short and, although it may have introduced trainees to the background to family interventions, there might not have been enough time for trainees' to develop a more complete understanding of them. Second, although clinical supervision was available after the course had finished, few people took advantage of this. The courses were not linked to any academic programme. This makes it difficult to assess trainees understanding of the teaching materials. There is a mistaken assumption that because an intervention shows dramatic results within a controlled research study it can be transferred to a standard service setting and retain its potency.

The Thorn Training programme differed in a number of ways. The training was carried out over a period of one academic year and on completion the trainees were awarded a Diploma in Nursing Studies. This had a number of benefits: the trainees attended the teaching centre one day per week for training, and clinical supervision and the requirement to submit essays and complete examinations meant that the course teaching team were able to monitor the students' understanding of the teaching materials. Transferring these clinical skills into their place of work was facilitated through the clinical supervision. An important part of the research strategy for this programme was to examine whether the interventions could be used in standard practice and still retain the potency demonstrated in the controlled studies.

The trainees' academic performance was good on both training programmes and was consistent with undergraduate diploma-level work carried out in other academic institutions. The course had an external examiner from another university and the course teaching team comprised, as part of its academic contracts, external examiners for academic courses in other universities.

Trainees were required to audiotape all of their clinical work and submit the tapes to the course teaching team. The tapes involving family work were used as a focus for the clinical supervision sessions on family interventions. Separate supervision sessions were held for other skills taught on the course. In addition to providing material for clinical supervision, these tapes enabled the course teaching team to map the clinical progress of each trainee towards the acquisition of a satisfactory level of competency.

However, it is important to note that although we did receive letters of support from the trainees' managers, there was no other contact with them. Nor was there any provision for ongoing supervision once the trainees had completed the course. We did offer to provide facilities for a peer support group and this was taken up by the trainees: ex-trainees continue to meet up some five years later around four times a year. That the ex-trainees themselves manage this peer support group gives us reason to think that this approach is one that they believe has much to offer the patients with whom they work.

Many of the discussions within this peer group focus on service delivery and change management strategies. This supports the view of Milne (1984) that, despite training in interventions and highly motivated staff, the approaches cannot be implemented when the system in which they work remains unchanged. Brooker *et al* (1996) suggest that effective psychosocial interventions in a research setting are not implemented in routine practice because of the competing needs of service users who are at risk. The latter are more likely to be offered interventions than those with less acute needs but for whom planned interventions would be helpful.

Though there is overwhelming research evidence that these therapies are effective in reducing the problems identified, the studies referred to in this chapter indicate the very variable extent to which they are actually utilised in ordinary clinical settings following training of clinical staff. The Thorn Training programme and other training experiences indicate that teaching must be continually reinforced after training through clinical case supervision over a sustained time period. Clarification is also needed on what organisational changes need to be made when a model effective in a research project is to be transferred into a standard clinical setting.

It has been proposed that there are benefits to 'giving psychology away' to other professional groups. Milne (1984) provides evidence that providing psychological skills training for nurses results in effective workers. The development of the behavioural nurse therapist in the 1970s is an earlier example and was based on a premise that psychiatric nurses were ideally placed to deliver specialised interventions (Marks, 1973; Marks *et al,* 1977; Brooker & Brown, 1986). Follow-up studies demonstrated that the majority of trainees, following training, were involved in direct clinical work and were central to the implementation of the approaches. A lack of clinical career structure however prevents them from continuing clinical work above a certain nursing grade as a CPN.

Other factors affecting training outcome

Course design and content

In Australia, Kavanagh *et al* (1993) found that in training their multi-disciplinary group there was considerable variance in the retention of the theory underpinning the practice. This was particularly true of cognitive–behavioural approaches: 70% could not recall enough of this material to allow them to use it competently. This figure does not include non-responders to the follow-up and the total could be higher. Psychologists reported a lower overall difficulty in retaining under-standing of the intervention than nurses. They suggest that this may be because the psychologist undergoing this additional training has previous knowledge and training in cognitive–behavioural approaches that fit conceptually with the type of family interventions taught, but it cannot be assumed that this is always the case.

Expectations of former trainees

Patience with the approach is clearly important in the complex relationships that family interventions demand. The approaches are seductive, in the sense that they are based on research evidence, offer real hope for patients and their families and provide workers with a structure and purpose. However, results are not instant and considerable patience and commitment are required to see a family intervention through (Anderson *et al*, 1986). Lack of progress is a real issue identified by all the surveys discussed here, but realistic time scales for behavioural change are more often measured in months and years than weeks (Anderson *et al*, 1986; Barrowclough & Tarrier, 1992). It appears that this lack of progress may be based on the unrealistic expectations of some of the former trainees and this is to some extent supported by the follow-up studies when former trainees have pointed to poor motivation on the part of the families.

Conclusion

The Thorn Training programme described in this chapter was an attempt to build upon previous work in the area of psychosocial interventions. There is evidence that family interventions particularly have much to offer both patients and families in terms of reduced symptoms and increased social functioning for patients allied to reductions in perceived burden for carers. It is also evident from the research that it is possible to teach family interventions to CPNs and retain the efficacy that was evident in the randomised controlled trials. Whilst there is evidence that the Thorn Training programme did train psychiatric nurses to use family interventions to an adequate level, that is, a level that has demonstrable benefits to patients, it is also clear that post-training ex-trainees have few opportunities to use the skills.

Although the reasons for this are complex, the research seems to suggest that a number of areas need to be addressed. First, it appears as if the providers of education need to work much more closely with services to which trainees will return in order to help identify and reduce potential barriers to later implementation in those services. Conversely, service providers could work closely with education providers to identify barriers to implementation that could be reduced if addressed through education programmes.

A new training programme run at the University of Manchester, the Collaboration On Psychosocial Education (COPE), represents a collaborative relationship between a number of education and service providers who, along with education purchasing consortia and the regional health authority, are responsible for targeting psychosocial intervention training throughout the north-west of England. These training programmes aim to provide accessible skills-based training at both undergraduate and postgraduate level for all those disciplines who work in mental health.

To supplement the training, services are offered the use of a management consultancy service as part of the contract with the university. In addition, the university is also training clinical supervisors from across the region in order to provide this service within the trainees' place of work.

With an increased focus on good quality skills training it is important that education providers and service providers work together to ensure that the mental health workforce has access to high quality skills-based training that is both relevant and locally supported in its implementation.

References

ANDERSON, C. M., REISS, D. J. & HOGARTY, G. E. (1986) *Schizophrenia and the Family*. New York: Guilford Press.

BAGULEY, I. & BAGULEY, C. (1999) Psychosocial interventions with people and psychosis. *Mental Health Care*, **2**, 314–317.

BARROWCLOUGH, C. & FLEMING, I. (1986) Training direct care staff in goal planning with elderly people. *Behavioural Psychotherapy*, **14**, 192–209.

—— & TARRIER, N. (1992) *Families of Schizophrenic Patients. Cognitive Behavioral Intervention.* London: Chapman & Hall.

BEBBINGTON, P. E. & KUIPERS, L. (1994) The predictive utility of expressed emotion in schizophrenia: an aggregate analysis. *Psychological Medicine*, **24**, 707–718.

BETZLAFF, R. L. & HOOLEY, J. M. (1998) Expressed emotion and pyschiatric relapse: a meta-analysis. *Archives of General Psychiatry*, **55**, 547–552.

BIRCHWOOD, M., HALLETT, S. & PRESTON, M. (1988) *Schizophrenia: An Integrated Approach to Research and Treatment.* London: Longman.

——, SMITH, J., COCHRANE, R., *ET AL* (1990) The social functioning scale: the development and validation of a scale of social adjustment for use in family intervention programmes with schizophrenic patients. *British Journal of Psychiatry*, **157**, 853–859.

BROOKER, C. & BROWN, M. (1986) A national follow-up survey of practicing nurse therapists. In *Psychiatric Nursing Research* (ed. J. Brooking), pp. 177–193. Chichester: Wiley.

—— & BUTTERWORTH, T. (1991) Working with families caring for a relative with schizophrenia: the evolving role of the community psychiatric nurse. *International Journal of Nursing Studies*, **28**, 189–200.

——, TARRIER, N., BARROWCLOUGH, C., *ET AL* (1992) Training community psychiatric nurses for psychosocial intervention: report of a pilot study. *British Journal of Psychiatry*, **160**, 836–844.

—— & BUTTERWORTH, T. (1993) Training in psychosocial intervention: the impact on the role of community psychiatric nurses. *Journal of Advanced Nursing*, **18**, 583–590.

——, FALLOON, I., BUTTERWORTH, A., *ET AL* (1994) The outcome of training community psychiatric nurses to deliver psychosocial intervention. *British Journal of Psychiatry*, **165**, 222–230.

——, REPPER, J & BOOTH, A. (1996) The effectiveness of community mental health nursing: a review. *Journal of Clinical Effectiveness*, **1**, 44–49.

BROWN, G. W. (1959) Experiences of discharged chronic mental hospital patients in various types of living group. *Millbank Memorial Fund Quarterly*, **37**, 105–131.

——, CARSTAIRS, G. M. & TOPPING, G. (1958) Post-hospital adjustment of chronic mental patents. *Lancet*, **ii**, 685–689.

——, MONCK, E. M., CARSTAIRS, G. M., *ET AL* (1962) Influence of family life on the course of schizophrenic illness. *British Journal of Preventive and Social Medicine*, **16**, 55–68.

——, BIRLEY, J. L. T. & WING, J. K. (1972) Influence of family life on the course of schizophrenic disorders: a replication. *British Journal of Psychiatry*, **121**, 241–258.

BUTZLAFF, R. L. & HOOLEY, J. M. (1998) Expressed emotion and psychiatric relapse: a meta-analysis. *Archives of General Psychiatry*, **55**, 547–552.

CLINICAL STANDARDS ADVISORY GROUP (1995) *Schizophrenia 1.* London: HMSO.

COMMUNITY PSYCHIATRIC NURSES ASSOCIATION (1981) *Community Psychiatric Nursing Services Survey.* Bristol: Community Psychiatric Nurses Association.

CORRIGAN, P. W., KWARTMAN, W. Y. & PRAMANA, W. (1992) Staff perception of barriers to behaviour therapy at a psychiatric hospital. *Behaviour Modification*, **64**, 132–144.

DEPARTMENT OF HEALTH (1989a) *Working for Patients.* London: HMSO.

—— (1989b) *Caring for People.* London: HMSO.

—— (1994) *Working in Partnership: a Collaborative Approach to Care.* London: HMSO.

DEVANE, S. M., HADDOCK, G., LANCASHIRE, S., *ET AL* (1998) The clinical skills of community psychiatric nurses working with people who have severe and enduring mental health problems: an empirical analysis. *Journal of Advanced Nursing*, **27**, 253–260.

DUGGAN, M. (1997) *Pulling Together.* London: Sainsbury Centre for Mental Health.

DULZ, B. & HAND, I. (1986) Short-term relapse in young schizophrenics: Can it be predicted and affected by the family (CFI), patient and treatment variables? An experimental study. In *Treatment of schizophrenia: Family assessment and Intervention* (eds M. J. Goldstein, I. Hand & K. Hahlweg), pp. 46–54. Berlin: Springer-Verlag.

FADDEN, G. (1997) Implementation of family interventions in routine clinical practice following staff training programme: a major course for concern. *Journal of Mental Health*, **6**, 599–612.

118 Baguley et al

FALLOON, I., BOYD, J. & McGILL, C. (1984) *Family Care of Schizophrenia.* London: Guildford.

GEORGIADES, N. J. & PHILLIMORE, L. (1975) The myth of the hero-innovator and alternative strategies for organizational change. In *Behaviour Modification with the Severely Retarded* (eds C. C. Kiernan & F. P. Woodford), pp.124–139. Amsterdam: Associated Scientific.

HADDOCK, G. & KINDERMAN, P. (1997) *The Modified Cognititve Therapy Checklist: The Socrates Scale.* Manchester: University of Manchester.

——, DEVANE, S., BRADSHAW, T., ET AL (2000) The aquisition of cognitive–behavioural therapy skills by mental health professionals working with severe mental health problems. *Behavioural and Cognitive Psychotherapy,* in press.

KAVANAGH, D. J., CLARK, D., PIATKOWSKA, O., ET AL (1993) Application of congnitive-behavioural family interventions in multi-disciplinary terms: What can the Matter be? *Australian Psychologist,* **28**, 1–8.

KRAWIEKA, M., GOLDBERG, D. & VAUGHAN, M. (1977) A standardised psychiatric assessment scale for chronic psychotic patients. *Acta Psychiatrica Scandinavica,* **55**, 299–308.

LANCASHIRE, S., HADDOCK, G., BUTTERWORTH, T., ET AL (1996) Training mental health professionals to use psychosocial interventions with people who have severe mental health problems. *Clinician,* **14**, 32–40.

——, HADDOCK, G., TARRIER, N., ET AL (1997) Effects of training in psychosocial interventions for community psychiatric nurses in england. *Psychiatric Services,* **48**, 39–41.

LEFF, J. P. & VAUGHN, C. (1980) The interation of life events and relatives expressed emotion in schizoprenia and depressive neurosis. *British Journal of Psychiatry,* **136**, 146–153.

MARI, JAIR DE JESUS & STREINER, D. L. (1994) An overview of family interventions and relapse on schizophrenia: meta-analysis of reseach findings. *Psychological Medicine,* **24**, 565–578.

MARKS, I. M. (1973) Psychiatric nurses as therapists: developments and problems. *Nursing Times,* **69**, 137–138.

——, HALLAM, R. S., CONNELY, J., ET AL (1977) *Nursing in Behavioural Psychotherapy.* London: Royal College of Nursing.

MARUM, M. (1995) The NAFP straw poll. *Fundholding Summary,* February, 2–4.

MILNE, D. (1984) *Training Behaviour Therapists: Methods, Evaluations and Implementation with Parents, Nurses and Teachers.* London: Croom Helm.

MOORE, S. (1961) A psychiatric outpatient nursing service. *Mental Health Bulletin,* **20**, 51–54.

MUIJEN, M. (1992) The balance of care. In *Innovations in the Psychological Management of Schizophrenia: Assessment, Treatment and Services* (eds M. Birchwood & N. Tarrier), pp. 253–275. Chichester: John Wiley & Sons.

ONYETT, S. (1992) *Case Management in Mental Health.* London: Chapman & Hall.

TARRIER, N., BARROWCLOUGH, C., & D'AMBROSIO, P. (1988) A training programme in psychosocial interventions with families with a schizophrenic member. *Behavioural Psychotherapist,* **27**, 2–4.

——, HADDOCK, G., & BARROWCLOUGH, C. (1998) Training and dissemination: in research to practice in innovative psychosocial treatments for schizophrenia. In *Outcome and Innovation in Psychological Treatment of Schizophrenia* (eds T. Wykes & N. Tarrier) Chichester: John Wiley and Sons.

VAUGHN, C. E. & LEFF, J. P. (1976) The influence of family and social factors on the course of psychiatric illness: a comparision of schizophrenic and depressed neurotic patients. *British Journal of Psychiatry,* **129**, 125–137.

—— & LEFF, J. P. (1981) Patterns of emotional response in relatives of schizophrenic patients. *Schizophrenia Bulletin,* **7**, 43–44.

WHITE, E. (1990) *The Third National Quinquennial Survey of Community Psychiatric Nursing Services.* Leeds: CPNA Publications.

WING, J. K., COOPER, J. E., & SARTORIUS, N. (1974) *The Measurement and Classification of Pschiatric Symptoms: an Instruction Manual for the Present State of Examination and CATEGO Programme.* London: Cambridge University Press.

WOOF, K. (1992) Service Organisation and Planning. In *Innovations in the Psychological Management of Schizophrenia: assessment, Treatment and Services* (eds M. Birchwood & N. Tarrier), pp. 277–304. Chichester: John Wiley & Sons.

——, GOLDBERG, D. P., & FRYERS, T. (1988) The practice of community psychiatric nursing and mental health social work in Salford: some implications for community care. *British Journal of Psychiatry*, **152**, 783–792.

YOUNG, J. & BECK, A. T. (1980) *Cognitive Therapy Scale: Rating Manual.* Philadelphia, PA: Centre for Cognitive Therapy.

6 Group therapy and schizophrenia: an integrative model

NICK KANAS

Group therapy is an especially valuable treatment modality, since its interpersonal nature allows patients to improve their ability to relate to other people, to share ways of coping with their symptoms, and to gain support and test reality during the sessions.

Clinical issues

Traditional models of treatment

There have been three traditional group therapeutic approaches for patients with schizophrenia: the educative, the psychodynamic and the interpersonal. The educative approach emphasises the biological aspects of this disorder. Therapy groups using this model try to help the members learn to cope with the symptoms of the illness and to deal with the real problems that these symptoms produce. Typical techniques include lectures, question and answer periods, problem-solving, advice-giving, role-playing and homework assignments between the sessions.

The psychodynamic approach emphasises the psychological aspects of schizophrenia. These groups try to help the members understand how long-term, intra-psychic problems and maladaptive behaviours interfere with their lives, with the hope of lessening the impact of these difficulties and improving ego functions. Techniques include the encouragement of open discussions initiated by the patients, uncovering of important unconscious issues and interpretations of transference.

The interpersonal approach places great importance on the relationship aspects of schizophrenia and attempts to help the group members become less socially isolated and improve their ability to interact with other people. Techniques include: facilitating discussions of interpersonal problems; encouraging patients to relate to each other during the sessions using structured exercises and other interaction-oriented techniques; and interpreting maladaptive interactions that are observed in the group.

Integrative model

As a result of a series of clinical research projects that took place over two decades, my colleagues and I have developed a biopsycho-social treatment model for people with schizophrenia known as the 'integrative approach'. Like the educative model described above, it helps patients learn ways of coping with psychotic symptoms in a safe, supportive environment. As with the psychodynamic approach, the integrative groups use open discussions where the members generate the topics. The effects of long-term problems on current functioning may be examined, and ego functions such as reality sense and reality testing may be strengthened. Like the interpersonal approach, a major goal of the integrative model is to help the members become less isolative and improve their relationships through the discussions as well as through the experiences the patients have in interacting with each other during the sessions.

Treatment goals

There are two major goals in the integrative group approach. The first goal is to help the members learn ways to cope with their psychotic symptoms, such as hallucinations and delusions. The second goal is to help the patients learn ways to improve their interpersonal relationships.

In open groups on shorter term acute-care in-patient units, the main focus is to help the members deal with the symptoms of their disease, and interpersonal problems usually are considered in reference to the psychotic state. In out-patient groups that are newly formed or are short term, discussions focus on both symptoms and interpersonal issues. After a closed group has met for some time, issues concerning relationships tend to dominate, although long-standing problems and maladaptive behaviours may be discussed as well.

Structural issues

The overwhelming majority of patients in the integrative groups have a diagnosis of schizophrenia, although a few suffer from related conditions: schizophreniform, schizoaffective and delusional disorders. High functioning patients may find discussions related to psychotic symptoms irrelevant to their needs and they are best referred for a different therapy. Patients with memory deficits gain little from these groups, and acutely manic or antisocial individuals may disrupt the process. Patients with concurrent substance misuse may be treated in our groups, so long as they are abstinent and are being followed up elsewhere for their problems with alcohol or other drugs.

In-patient integrative groups are open to frequent new referrals and usually meet for 45 minutes, three times a week. Sessions are not held with fewer than three patients, and more than eight make the group hard to manage. In the out-patient setting, the groups are closed or 'slow' open and meet for 60 minutes once a week. To compensate for drop-outs, the groups usually start with 8–10 patients, hoping to retain an average of 6–8 as the sessions progress.

Most of the patients take antipsychotic medications. Patients are discouraged from using group time to discuss medication dosage and side-effects, although feelings about having to take such drugs often are shared by the members. Patients who have technical questions or concerns about their prescriptions are referred back to their physicians.

A co-therapy approach is useful in integrative groups, since sessions can be chaotic at times, and it is easier for two therapists rather than one to maintain control and deal with unsafe situations. Two leaders also can model non-psychotic interactions and provide feedback in reality-testing situations. Finally, when a therapist is on vacation or is ill, the group still can be held. The gender, age and professional background of the therapists are not important, so long as both are well trained to do the group and are seen as being equally involved by the patients.

The therapists should be active and directive in keeping the members focused on the topic. Interventions need to be clear, consistent and concrete. Comments should be made supportively and diplomatically, and the therapists should be open and willing to give their opinions about important matters. Discussions that focus on the here-and-now are more productive than those that focus on the there-and-then.

Discussion topics

Useful discussion topics in integrative groups should focus on the specific needs of people with schizophrenia. Examples of helpful topics with acutely ill patients or early in the life of the group include: hallucinations and delusions, disorganised thinking, relations with others and emotional themes that typically are well tolerated by the group members, such as loneliness, depression and despair. Any topic that produces anxiety can cause regression and an intensification of symptoms in patients with schizophrenia, so caution needs to be exercised around issues related to anger, aggression and sexual orientation or identity. Issues that reveal unconscious conflicts and flood the members with painful insights also should be avoided.

In groups with stable patients or later in the life of the group, the above topics still may be discussed. In addition, long-standing maladaptive patterns of behaviour and interactions with others can be discussed. These patients are better able to tolerate sensitive, emotional topics than their more acute counterparts, although therapists still need to be careful about issues that produce anxiety.

Topics may be developed by discussing them in general terms first and then applying them to the group members, or by asking all of the patients to comment on an issue through a 'go-around'. A typical session proceeds by identifying an appropriate topic for discussion, then generalising it to all the members, and finally asking them to share coping strategies. These strategies often centre around decreasing the amount of stress in the patients' lives or providing more stimulation when their environment is impoverished.

When the members are interacting productively around topics that are related to their needs, then the therapists should remain quiet. However, when the group members cannot stay on a topic, are quiet or persist in discussing irrelevant issues, then the therapists should intervene to provide structure or to help the patients focus on an issue. When the environment is tense or unsafe, the therapists should change the subject or comment on the potential for danger and suggest a break in the discussion.

Cost-effectiveness issues

Integrative schizophrenia groups have been used in a variety of in-patient and out-patient settings in the USA and elsewhere (e.g. UK, Russia), and they have been found to be useful and cost-effective. Patients receive help for their psychotic symptoms and for their interpersonal problems. Typically, there is a high rate of attendance in these groups. In-patients often follow up with similar groups as out-patients, which improves their clinical course. In co-therapy groups, the staff-to-patient ratio is still a respectable 1:3 or 1:4, which is more cost-effective than individual 1:1 therapy. For many patients, participation in the groups obviates the need for individual therapy, since group therapy for people with schizophrenia has been found to be as or more effective than individual therapy in controlled studies. Short-term, time-limited integrative groups lasting for 12 weekly sessions have been found to be safe and beneficial, as will be described in detail below (Kanas *et al,* 1988; 1989*a*). In the out-patient setting, these represent a less expensive alternative to long-term group therapy, which has frequently been used with patients with schizophrenia (Kanas, 1986), since nearly half of the patients believe that one 12-week course is beneficial, and they elect to be discharged from the group.

Research issues

Effectiveness of traditional approaches

I have conducted a literature review of controlled studies that involved therapy groups with patients with schizophrenia that dated back to the time when antipsychotic medications began to be used in the clinical setting. The review spanned over 40 years from 1950 to 1991. Studies were obtained through a detailed examination of *Index Medicus* and subsequent study references, and were all in the English language. To be included in the review, all studies had to compare: at least one group therapy condition with a no-group-therapy control condition; had to include at least 50% of subjects with schizophrenia or statistically describe the effects of the groups on those with schizophrenia; had to evaluate outcome using at least one major outcome measure; and had to indicate the duration of treatment. Forty-six studies were found that met these criteria. Meta-analytical techniques could not be used due to the great variability across studies, the subjectivity inherent in selecting the most representative measure from a given study and the difficulty in calculating an effect size from those studies that adequately presented the statistical metrics. Consequently the studies were rated in terms of whether they concluded that group therapy was significantly more effective, no different than, or less effective than the control condition. In addition, the 57 groups involved in these studies were classified as being insight-oriented, interaction-oriented or other/unspecified in order to evaluate if any one of these clinical approaches was more beneficial than the others.

The results of the review (Kanas, 1986, 1996) found that group therapy was effective for patients with schizophrenia in both in-patient and out-patient settings. Overall, 70% of the studies found that it was significantly better than the no-group-therapy control condition. There was a trend for long-term in-patient groups lasting longer than 36 sessions to be more effective than shorter term groups. Insight-oriented approaches that emphasised uncovering issues and psychodynamic issues were less effective than interaction-oriented approaches that emphasised interpersonal problems and relationship issues in the here-and-now. Overall, 33% of the insight groups versus 78% of the interaction groups were significantly better than their corresponding no-group-therapy controls, and this difference itself was significant using Fisher's exact test.

Effectiveness of the integrative model

The integrative approach has developed from and been modified by a series of empirical studies conducted by my colleagues and myself since 1975. These studies have examined both outcome and group process and have been performed in both the in-patient and out-patient setting at a variety of hospitals and clinics.

In-patient studies

The first study took place on a 25-bed psychiatric clinical research unit located in a large military teaching hospital (Kanas *et al*, 1978, 1980). Subjects included active duty personnel, their dependents and military retirees who were randomly assigned to one of three experimental conditions: insight-oriented group therapy, activities-oriented task group or no group control condition. Both psychotic and non-psychotic subjects participated in each condition for one hour three times per week (controls were given free time on the ward during this time). They were evaluated shortly after admission and after eight experimental days (which averaged 20 days post-admission for all three conditions) by nurses blind to condition on a number of standard measures of symptomatology and a behavioural measure that quantified a patient's ward privileges using a 1–9 scale. Medication usage and individual therapy time also were recorded for all subjects.

Eighty-six in-patients completed this study, 44% of whom had a psychotic disorder (nearly all schizophrenia). Most subjects improved over the 20 days, and there were no significant differences in improvement rates, in medication usage or in individual therapy across the three conditions (Kanas *et al*, 1980). However, significantly more patients with psychosis assigned to group therapy got worse than those patients with psychosis assigned to the other two conditions. For example, on an overall severity of illness scale, 38% of patients with psychosis in group therapy were worse after 20 days, compared with 17% in the activities group and none in the control condition. Similarly, 56% of patients in group therapy dropped in ward privilege status, compared with 17% of the activities patients and 20% of the controls. There were no significant differences in decrement rate across conditions for non-psychotic patients. Thus, it appeared that insight-oriented group therapy may have been harmful for in-patients with acute psychosis during the first three weeks of hospitalisation as compared with tha activities group and the control condition.

As a result of these findings, I began developing a supportive group therapy treatment model for patients with schizophrenia that did not utilise insight-oriented, uncovering techniques but focused on ways that the patients could cope with psychotic symptoms and improve their interpersonal relationships. This format gradually evolved into the integrative approach, discussed in detail above.

The initial investigation used an exploratory method of investigation with an open design and only post-treatment measures of patient satisfaction and helpfulness. The study was carried out at a Department of Veterans' Affairs hospital (Kanas & Barr, 1982). A discharge questionnaire was given to 22 male in-patients with schizophrenia who had participated in the group for an average of nine sessions. On the questionnaire, 95% rated the group as having been 'very helpful' or 'somewhat helpful'. Significantly more patients below the median age of 29.5 years found the group 'very helpful' than patients above the median age, and significantly more people with non-paranoid schizophrenia found the group 'very helpful' than those with paranoid schizophrenia. In rating 13 statements that described possible therapeutic factors, the patients valued the group more as a place to express emotions, to learn ways of relating better with others and to cope with psychotic experiences than as a place to gain insight into the causes of their problems or to receive practical advice on their illness, medications or economic situation.

In the second Veterans' Affairs in-patient study, the characteristics of the group were evaluated using the Hill Interaction Matrix (HIM; Hill, 1961, 1965), a well-known process measure that categorises therapy groups in terms of what is being discussed (content style) and the manner in which the groups help the members learn about themselves (work style). The four content style categories (topic, group, personal and relationship) and the four active work style categories (conventional, assertive, speculative and confrontive) interact to form a matrix of 16 cells. The category and matrix scores for a group being studied can then be compared with similar scores from a normative sample of 50 therapy group sessions. We used a form of the Hill Interaction Matrix called the HIM–G, which is composed of 72 items rated by a group observer that describe qualities of the group member interactions that are characteristic of the session being evaluated.

In this study (Kanas *et al*, 1985), a trained evaluator observed seven consecutive tri-weekly sessions of the schizophrenia group through a one-way mirror, during which time 11 different male patients participated. By category, the schizophrenia group fell into the typical ranges of the normative sample except for the confrontive category, which was at the 97th percentile. Group resistance was scored as occurring less than 1% of the time and never involved more than one group member per session. Participation was spread out among the members, who were seen as being open and assertive in stating their positions. Overall, the therapists were scored as participating 10–20% of the time.

To test the robustness of this treatment approach, this HIM–G study was replicated five years later on the same unit, using a different rater, different patients and different therapists (Kanas & Smith, 1990). Twelve consecutive tri-weekly sessions were evaluated, which consisted of 11 different male patients, and the confrontive work style category again defined the uniqueness of the group, this time at the 98th percentile. The rank order of the 16 matrix cells from this study was compared with the rank order from the original study using the Spearman rank-order correlation the two rankings correlated significantly. Once again, group resistance was low (scoring at 1–5% of overall group activity) and the therapists were moderately active (26% of the time). Thus, the environment of the group looked very much like that of the earlier group, supporting the robustness and replicability of the treatment model.

In another in-patient study, the group process was assessed using the short form of the Group Climate Questionnaire (GCQ S; MacKenzie, 1983), which consists of 12 descriptive statements that are rated on seven-point Likert scales after each session by either the patients or the therapists. Eleven of the scales are used to construct scores on three group climate dimensions: engaged (indicating group cohesion), avoiding (indicating reluctance to face problems) and conflict (indicating interpersonal friction). The 12th scale is a measure of general anxiety.

In this study (Kanas & Barr, 1986), 34 consecutive sessions of our tri-weekly in-patient schizophrenia group were evaluated at a Veterans' Affairs hospital by the group leaders. In addition, important topics that were discussed during the sessions were recorded and later the contents were analysed. During the three-month study period, 22 male patients participated in the group. There was no difference between the schizophrenia group and MacKenzie's normative sample of 12 out-patient groups composed of patients with neurotic and characterological disorders in the avoiding dimension, but our group scored significantly lower in the engaged and conflict dimensions. These findings may have reflected the negative effect of rapid patient turnover on group cohesion in the in-patient setting as well as the fact that the group format encouraged safety and minimised the expression of interpersonal anger. MacKenzie does not report normative anxiety scale values, but our mean score of 2.58 would fall between the verbal descriptions of 'somewhat' and 'moderately' on the GCQ–S. Topics related to encouraging contact with others were discussed most frequently during the sessions, followed by issues related to the expression of emotions, reality-testing and giving advice on medications or discharge planning.

I conducted another process study in an open in-patient schizophrenia group at a general hospital in a large city in England (Kanas, 1996). The patients were from two unlocked units, each with 20 beds. The group met twice weekly for 45-minute sessions, and the first 10 sessions of the group's existence were evaluated using the GCQ–S. Twelve male and eight female patients participated during this time, with each session averaging six patients and two therapists. After each session, the group leaders agreed upon a consensus rating for the 12 GCQ–S statements and upon the major topics that were discussed. This group scored significantly higher than the above American Veterans' Affairs in-patient group in the engaged dimension and significantly lower in the avoiding dimension. Although the conflict score also was lower, this was not significant. The mean anxiety scale score of 1.30 also was significantly lower than the corresponding score for the Veterans' Affairs group.

Thus, the British group seemed to be more cohesive and less avoidant and tense than the American group, possibly reflecting the presence of females in the former. Generally, it is believed that women are more supportive and emotionally expressive than men in therapy groups (Lazerson & Zilbach, 1993), and there is some evidence that personal growth groups with women are more cohesive than all-male groups (Taylor & Strassberg, 1986). Perhaps women played a similar role in our schizophrenia groups. It is also possible that non-specific cultural factors accounted for the observed differences of these two groups.

The topics that were discussed in the British group were similar to those that were brought up in the Veterans' Affairs group. Of the 26 topics that were recorded, 11 dealt with ways to cope with hallucinations and delusions, and nine dealt with improving interpersonal relationships. Thus, the patients with schizophrenia in both settings seemed to discuss issues that were congruent with their needs and with the group goals.

Out-patient studies

Encouraged by the above in-patient experiences, the integrative treatment model was applied to the outpatient setting. Using the GCQ–S and a content analysis of discussion topics, a schizophrenia group was studied during the first six months of its existence at a university psychiatric out-patient clinic. The six-member group met weekly for one hour, and 26 sessions were evaluated on the GCQ–S by the two group leaders (Kanas *et al*, 1984). The attendance rate was 88%. The overall mean GCQ–S dimension scores did not differ significantly from the means in MacKenzie's out-patient normative sample. As in the in-patient group (Kanas & Barr, 1986), the anxiety score of 2.63 was between the verbal descriptions of 'somewhat' and 'moderately' on this scale. There was a tendency for the engaged scores to increase and the conflict scores to decrease over time. Topics related to the encouragement of contact with others were discussed most frequently, followed by issues pertaining to reality testing, to the expression of emotions and to advice-giving, in that order.

Since the early 1980s, there has been much interest in short-term, time-limited therapy groups for non-psychotic out-patients. These typically meet for 8–16 sessions and are characterised by careful patient selection, realistic goals and directive therapists (Klein, 1985). The integrative group approach was adapted to treat people with schizophrenia in out-patient groups that met for 12 weekly one-hour sessions. The goals were tightly focused on helping the patients improve their relationships and learning ways of coping with their symptoms.

The first study of this format was conducted at a university out-patient clinic (Kanas *et al*, 1988). Seven patients began, and five (three men, two women) completed the 12-week course. The attendance rate was 80%. The patients filled out several outcome measures before and after participating in the group, and at termination they completed the discharge questionnaire that was used in an earlier study (Kanas & Barr, 1982). A nurse-observer recorded the discussion topics. Four months after the group ended, the patients were contacted by phone and interviewed about their ability to relate with others, their ability to cope with psychotic experiences and their treatment progress. Although there were no significant pre-/post-group differences in symptoms, there was a significant improvement in the predicted direction on the Social Avoidance and Distress Scale (SAD; Watson & Friend, 1969). On the discharge questionnaire, the members all rated the group as being 'very helpful' or 'somewhat helpful'. The rank order of therapeutic factors correlated significantly with the rank order from our earlier in-patient study (Kanas & Barr, 1982) using the Spearman rank-order correlation. The members valued the group more for helping them relate better with others, test reality and cope with psychotic experiences than as a place to gain insight or to receive advice about their illness, medications or economic situations. This paralleled the content analysis of discussion topics, which showed that relationship and reality-testing issues were discussed more often than issues related to advice-giving, the group itself or the expression of emotions. During the structured telephone interviews four months after the group ended, four of the five patients reported gains in their ability to interact with other people, and two of them believed that they were coping better with psychotic experiences. None of the patients had been hospitalised. Two felt that their group experience was too short, and three said that it had been just right in length.

A follow-up controlled study of this short-term, time-limited format was conducted at a Veterans' Affairs out-patient clinic (Kanas *et al*, 1989*a*). Fourteen patients began the study in one of two groups, and 12 (eleven men, one woman) finished. The patient attendance rate for the two groups was 89%. Nine additional patients were assigned to a waiting list control condition, and they did not differ demographically from their counterparts in the groups. Both group and control patients were given the 90-item Symptom Check-List (SCL–90; Derogatis *et al*, 1973) and the SAD initially and after completing their respective experimental condition (about four months for each), and group discussion topics were recorded. All patients were contacted four months later and asked a series of questions similar to those in the previous study.

On the SCL–90, the group patient scores dropped in all nine symptom dimensions, and two of these decreases (anxiety and somatisation) were significant when compared to the waiting list patients using an analysis of variance. There was a non-significant decrease in group patient SAD scores. Topics dealing with relationships and coping with psychotic experiences were most frequently discussed, followed by topics pertaining to the therapy group, the expression of emotions and advice-giving. In the four-month follow-up interview, all of the group patients found their experience to be very helpful or somewhat helpful. Three said it was too short, and nine thought it was about the right duration. Four months after the group ended, 88% of the patients acknowledged that they were relating better with other people, and 63% said they were coping better with their psychotic symptoms. The comparative numbers for the waiting list control patients were 11% and 0%, respectively. These group–control differences were significant using the Fisher exact test. There were no significant interval differences between the two conditions in terms of general psychological problems, antipsychotic medication dose, hospitalisation status, out-patient therapy, living arrangements, job or disability status, legal status or physical condition. It is noteworthy that the two significant differences were in the two areas most congruent with the group goals and with the types of topics most often discussed in the sessions. This suggests that a short-term time-limited therapy group for people with schizophrenia can have an impact for up to four months after the group ends in specific areas that are the focus of the discussions.

The university and the two Veterans' Affairs groups described above all were evaluated by the co-therapists using the GCQ–S (Kanas *et al*, 1989*b*). The three groups did not generally differ from each other on any of the dimension scores, although one of the Veterans' Affairs groups scored significantly higher than the other two on the engaged subscale, it experienced no drop-outs and had a much higher attendance rate (99%). The composite mean dimension scores for the three groups did not differ from MacKenzie's out-patient normative sample in the engaged dimension, but they scored significantly lower in avoiding and conflict dimensions. The dimension scores varied high and low about the mean from session to session, and there was no evidence of sequential developmental stages (MacKenzie, 1983; MacKenzie & Livesley, 1983). Like the long-term group described earlier (Kanas *et al*, 1984), there was a tendency for the engaged scores to increase and the avoiding and conflict scores to decrease as time went on. The overall attendance rate was 86%, and the drop-out rate was 19%.

Twelve Veterans' Affairs patients who finished one of the earlier groups within the past two years were contacted, and seven (58%) agreed to participate in a second 'repeater' group. One of these dropped out after the third session, leaving six (five men, one woman) to complete the sequence. Like its predecessors, the group consisted of 12 one-hour weekly sessions, and the goals and topic areas were similar to the first group's. The repeater patients seemed to deal with relationship and symptomatic issues more efficiently than before and to discuss more sophisticated topics that included a recognition of long-standing maladaptive patterns of behaviour. The patient attendance rate was 89%. At the end of the group, five members rated it as very helpful and one said it was somewhat helpful. A trained rater evaluated sessions on the HIM–G (Kanas & Smith, 1990). The confrontive work style category again defined the uniqueness of the group at the 98th percentile. Using the Spearman rank-order correlation, a ranking of the 16 matrix cells describing this group correlated significantly with each of the two in-patient groups already described, suggesting that a similar process was operating in these groups. Also similar to the findings from the two previous in-patient groups, the total group resistance was low (1–5% of overall group activity), and the therapists were moderately active overall (26% of the time). Thus, in terms of the content and work constructs of the HIM–G, the environments of our short-term out-patient and in-patient groups are quite similar.

Conclusions

Although my review of the literature indicates a lack of high quality randomised studies, these findings offer tentative support for the view that the integrative group therapy treatment approach is effective and safe and can reliably be taught to new therapists. It appears to be acceptable to patients with schizophrenia and to complement the benefits from antipsychotic medication. It is effective and may be used with other psychosocial treatment approaches that are being given concurrently. It also has been used successfully in a variety of in-patient and out-patient treatment settings in the USA, UK, Russia and elsewhere.

Future research directions include examining the outcome and process of the integrative group model in large controlled studies using follow-ups of a year or more. In addition, it would be useful to study which patients benefit most from variations in the treatment approach, such as long- versus short-term groups. Finally, the influence of various cultural and gender patient ratios on the integrative group process would further delineate important treatment characteristics and encourage the use of this method in multi-cultural and international settings. These activities would supplement the empirical work that has been done to date and hopefully would further support the value of this treatment method for patients with schizophrenia.

References

DEROGATIS, L. R., LIPMAN, R. S. & COVI, L. (1973) SCL-90: an out-patient psychiatric rating scale – preliminary report. *Psychopharmacology Bulletin*, **9**, 13–28.
HILL, W. F. (1961) *Hill Interaction Matrix (HIM) Scoring Manual.* Los Angeles: Youth Studies Center, University of Southern California.
—— (1965) *Hill Interaction Matrix (HIM) Monograph.* Los Angeles: Youth Studies Center, University of Southern California.
KANAS, N. (1986) Group therapy with schizophrenics: a review of controlled studies. *International Journal of Group Psychotherapy*, **36**, 339–351.
—— (1996) *Group Therapy for Schizophrenic Patients.* Washington, DC: American Psychiatric Press.
——, ROGERS, M., KRETH, E., *ET AL* (1978) Psychiatric research in a military setting: evolution of a study on inpatient group psychotherapy. *Military Medicine*, **143**, 552–555.
——, ——, ——, *ET AL* (1980) The effectiveness of group psychotherapy during the first three weeks of hospitalization: a controlled study. *Journal of Nervous and Mental Disease*, **168**, 487–492.
—— & BARR, M. A. (1982) Short-term homogeneous group therapy for schizophrenic in-patients: a questionnaire evaluation. *Group*, **6**, 32–38.
——, DILELLA, V. J. & JONES, J. (1984) Process and content in an out-patient schizophrenic group. *Group*, **8**, 13–20.

——, BARR, M. A. & DOSSICK, S. (1985) The homogeneous schizophrenic in-patient group: an evaluation using the Hill Interaction Matrix. *Small Group Behavior,* **16,** 397–409.

—— & —— (1986) Process and content in a short-term inpatient schizophrenic group. *Small Group Behavior,* **17,** 355–363.

——, STEWART, P. & HANEY, K. (1988) Content and outcome in a short-term therapy group for schizophrenic outpatients. *Hospital & Community Psychiatry,* **39,** 437–439.

———, DERI, J., KETTER, T., *ET AL* (1989*a*) Short-term outpatient therapy groups for schizophrenics. *International Journal of Group Psychotherapy,* **39,** 517–522.

——, STEWART, P., DERI, J., *ET AL* (1989*b*) Group process in short-term out-patient therapy groups for schizophrenics. *Group,* **13,** 67–73.

—— & Smith, A. J. (1990) Schizophrenic group process: a comparison and replication using the HIM–G. *Group,* **14,** 246–252.

KLEIN, R. H. (1985) Some principles of short-term group therapy. *International Journal of Group Psychotherapy,* **35,** 309–330.

LAZERSON, J. S. & ZILBACH, J. J. (1993) Gender issues in group psychotherapy. In *Comprehensive Group Psychotherapy* (3rd edn) (eds H. I. Kaplan & B. J. Sadock), pp. 682–693. Baltimore, MD: Williams & Wilkins.

MACKENZIE, K. R. (1983) The clinical application of a group climate measure. In *Advances in Group Psychotherapy: Integrating Research and Practice* (eds R. R. Dies & K. R. MacKenzie), pp. 159–170. New York: International Universities Press.

—— & LIVESLEY, W. J. (1983) A developmental model for brief group therapy. In *Advances in Group Psychotherapy: Integrating Research and Practice* (eds R. R. Dies & K. R. MacKenzie), pp. 101–116. New York: International Universities Press.

TAYLOR, J. R. & STRASSBERG, D. S. (1986) The effects of sex composition on cohesiveness and interpersonal learning in short-term personal growth groups. *Psychotherapy,* **23,** 267–273.

WATSON, D. & FRIEND, R. (1969) Measurement of social-evaluative anxiety. *Journal of Consulting and Clinical Psychology,* **33,** 448–457.

7 Preventing relapse and readmission in psychosis: using patients' subjective experience in designing clinical interventions

LARRY DAVIDSON, DAVID A. STAYNER,
MATTHEW J. CHINMAN, STACEY LAMBERT
and WILLIAM H. SLEDGE

"In order to arrive at what you do not know
You must go by a way which is the way of ignorance."
(T. S. Eliot, *Four Quartets*, 1971, p. 127)

The downsizing of large, public mental hospitals and continuing decreases in length of acute in-patient stays have led to the creation of a new kind of 'chronicity' in some individuals with serious mental illness. Rather than languishing on the abandoned back wards of state hospitals, these individuals experience a repetitive, cyclic pattern of brief in-patient stays and a lonely, isolated and invisible life on the streets and in the prisons of our towns and cities. Unable to establish and maintain a life outside of institutions, such individuals have become disaffiliated both from their natural communities and from the mental health system. The resulting phenomenon of the 'revolving door' patient has become of increasing concern to a number of constituency groups, including consumer advocates, family members, mental health providers, clinical administrators and public policy-makers (Cotterill & Thomas, 1993; Pfeiffer *et al*, 1996). In addition to a negative clinical impact on the course and outcome of their psychiatric conditions, the recurrent hospitalisation of these patients creates a significant burden on the mental health system. It utilises costly police, accident and emergency and in-patient services; and thereby accounts for a disproportionate share of the limited resources allocated for mental health treatment (Dietzen & Bond, 1993; Wasylenki, 1994).

A number of approaches have been developed to address the problems of relapse and readmission in individuals with serious mental illness. To date, these approaches have included patient and family psychoeducation, intensive case management, assertive community treatment and intramuscular medication administration (Anderson *et al*, 1980; Leff & Vaughn, 1981; Falloon, 1985; Hogarty *et al*, 1991; Gaebel *et al*, 1993; Goldstein, 1994; Soni *et al*, 1994; Scott & Dixon, 1995). The most promising recent advance in this area has been a further development in the psychoeducational approach to working with patients and families that has come to be called 'prodromal recognition and early intervention'. Based primarily on the work of Falloon (1992) and Birchwood (1995), this approach involves identifying the unique early warning signs and prodromal symptoms that typically precede a relapse for an individual, educating the patient and his or her family about these signs and symptoms, and instituting a system for the monitoring and identification of these signs and symptoms as they emerge in order to allow for early intervention to prevent a full-blown episode of disorder. Although this approach has been shown to be effective in preventing relapses and readmissions for some patients (Birchwood *et al*, 1989; Hertz & Lamberti, 1995), there are several reasons to think that it will be limited in its application to the 'revolving door' patients described above.

A core assumption of the prodromal recognition and early intervention approach is that readmissions are caused primarily by relapses or exacerbation of the patient's disorder. In this way, this approach to relapse prevention is based on a medical model of serious mental illness as a prolonged disorder that involves an underlying vulnerability and the possibility for repeated recurrences of active episodes of disorder. In this model, hospitalisation is viewed as bringing about a remission in symptoms, with patients being discharged in a stable enough condition to resume their care on a conventional out-patient basis with the addition of a strategy for the close monitoring of early warning signs of impending relapses. Given the realities and parameters of current clinical practice, there are several limitations to such a model of relapse and readmission, particularly when applied to patients with histories of multiple hospitalisations.

First, significant decreases both in hospital beds and in length of stay have raised the threshold for hospitalisation considerably. Patients are no longer hospitalised for relapses or exacerbation in symptomatology alone, but only for when these symptoms or deterioration in functioning lead them to be at risk of hurting themselves or others, or to be unable to care for themselves. Lengths of stay averaging at this time between 5 and 10 days mean that patients also are no longer being discharged in remission or in stable condition, but simply as soon as their most troubling, active and visible symptoms abate. Second, these patients face a number of social and environmental stressors in the community: the lack of a supportive environment and poverty, that both further complicate their recovery upon discharge and also may lead them to view the hospital as a positive alternative to life on the streets (Appleby *et al*, 1996; Drake & Wallach, 1988, 1992; Green, 1988; Kent *et al*, 1995; Kent & Yellowlees, 1995; Klinkenberg & Calsyn, 1996). Finally, these patients often choose not to follow through with out-patient treatments and medication following discharge, thereby rendering early intervention strategies ineffective.

In this chapter, we describe our own failures in attempting to apply the approach of prodromal recognition and early intervention to preventing relapse and readmission in patients with serious mental illness who have histories of multiple hospitalisations. We then describe how, in recognising the limitations of this approach, we were able to benefit from the lessons patients had to teach us about the reasons for their readmissions and the factors that potentially would contribute to increasing their community tenure. Going 'the way of ignorance' and following our patients' lead required shifting from an objective and external perspective that emphasised the visible signs and symptoms of the disorder and their treatment to a subjective and internal perspective that emphasised the patients' experiences of their disorders and their day-to-day attempts to cope with these less visible experiences in an often unfriendly and stark environment.

Included in these less visible experiences were social and cognitive deficits that have recently come to be conceptualised as negative and cognitive symptoms of psychosis (Davidson & McGlashan, 1997), as well as the impact of these deficits on the patients' capacities for problem-solving, establishing and maintaining social relationships, self-esteem and sense of identity. Grounding our approach to preventing readmission in a broader understanding of these subjective experiences then led us to design a novel clinical intervention that focuses on the fostering of mutual support and remoralisation in the context of a community milieu that provides an alternative both to life on the streets and to life in the hospital. We describe the development of this integrated, community-based clinical and peer support programme, and then provide outcome data suggesting its effectiveness in preventing readmission for patients with multiple hospitalisations. We then close with a brief discussion of the implications of this shift in perspective and resulting outcomes for future programme development and evaluation efforts.

Failure of the objective paradigm

The original impetus for our attempts to address the problems of relapse and readmission in patients with psychosis was derived from some unexpected findings of an earlier study that involved a controlled clinical and cost-effectiveness trial of a crisis respite alternative to acute in-patient care. In this study (Sledge *et al*, 1996*a,b*), we examined direct mental health service utilisation and costs for acutely ill patients treated in a day hospital/crisis respite programme as compared with those in an in-patient programme. A total of 197 patients were randomly assigned to either of the conditions and followed up for up to 10 months post-discharge. Overall, the day hospital/crisis respite programme was significantly less costly than the in-patient programme, yet it produced comparable clinical outcomes through the 10-month follow-up period. On average, day hospital/crisis respite costs were 80% of the in-patient condition costs, with these cost differences almost entirely attributable to reduced costs at the index admission.

The present study was stimulated by the unexpected findings of this earlier study related to re-hospitalisation and its costs among study patients. Specifically, we found that 39% of the patients admitted to in-patient care and 37% of those admitted to the respite programme experienced at least one readmission within the 10 months following their index hospitalisation, for an average of 46 (in-patient) and 45 (respite) bed-days, respectively. Most striking was the fact that readmissions accounted for approximately 28% (US\$9638) and 36% (US\$9667) of the total direct costs of treatment for patients in the in-patient (US\$33 917) and respite (US\$26 820) conditions respectively during their 10 months of participation in the study. The difference is accounted for by the higher index admission costs for in-patient care. Since the conclusion of this study, we have monitored readmission rates for patients in our own out-patient clinic, and over two years (July 1994–July 1996) we consistently have found 30% of those patients admitted to our own in-patient units to be readmitted there during the year following discharge. Seventy per cent of those readmitted annually were readmitted within the first three months post-discharge from the index hospitalisation.

This high rate and cost of re-hospitalisation, which we found reflected in the broader literature (Kissling, 1994; Wasylenki, 1994; Weiden & Olfson, 1995; Klinkenberg *et al*, 1996), then became the target of our efforts. Following the work of Birchwood and Falloon already described, our initial approach to this problem was grounded in the objective and external perspective of conventional clinical programmes, emphasising the disease and its vicissitudes. Symptoms, disability, early recognition of prodromal signs and symptoms and adherence with medication were the phenomena that we addressed in our initial clinical intervention and research strategy. We focused on patients with a history of two or more hospitalisations within the previous year. During their in-patient stay, we educated these patients about their disorders, assisted them in identifying their unique 'relapse signature' (or pattern of prodromal symptoms and other early warning signs of relapse) and attempted to involve them with their out-patient clinician in developing an 'action plan' that stipulated what they should do in the case of the appearance of their relapse signature in order to avert a full-blown episode of disorder and consequent readmission to the hospital.

Some of this work was carried out individually between the patient and his or her clinician, but most was carried out in a twice-weekly in-patient relapse prevention group. We also instituted twice-weekly relapse prevention groups in the out-patient clinic in order to provide for close monitoring of symptoms following discharge. Our intent was to engage patients in these groups while still in the hospital, in the hope that they then would continue to attend after discharge. One clinician co-led all four groups, providing for some continuity through discharge.

For the first three months of this initiative, patients completed the relapse signature check-lists and participated in both in-patient and out-patient groups while in the hospital. Following discharge, however, not a single patient (out of the 36 who were eligible) returned to the out-patient relapse prevention groups . These patients continued to be readmitted to the hospital with the same presenting issues at about the same rate as before implementation of the programme. Although we continued at first to focus on the need to increase these patients' compliance with out-patient care, we soon realised that our efforts were failing to persuade them of the benefits we expected them to gain from these services. Following discharge, these patients continued to be as unstable and as unmotivated for treatment as they had been before admission, with their risk for readmission obviously remaining high as well. With this robust and consistent finding of the ineffectiveness of this programme staring us in the face, we began to recognise the limitations of this approach and decided to reconsider our initial conceptualisation of this problem.

Using a subjective paradigm in designing a new approach

We needed to develop a new approach that built on the awareness of the limitations of our initial approach. We acheived this by turning to the patients themselves to see what they could teach us about the problem and its possible solutions. Such a turn involved a shift in perspective from the objective and external, disorder-based perspective of conventional clinical programmes (in which the professionals have the answers) to the subjective and internal, individual-based perspective of first-person experience (about which only the patients themselves can inform us) (Davidson & Cosgrove, 1991; Davidson *et al*, 1995; Davidson, 1997). Such a shift allowed us to broaden our initial clinical frame to include a better understanding of the additional needs and issues challenging these patients that also contributed to their repeated admissions, as well as the community context and social – environmental precipitants for their readmissions. Finally, this broader understanding of the processes of relapse and readmission suggested several new directions for programme development and intervention.

To gain access to the subjective perspective, we used phenomeno-logical and participatory methods of data collection and analysis (Giorgi, 1970; Wertz, 1983; Whyte, 1989, 1991; Rogers & Palmer-Erbs, 1994; Davidson, 1994). As we have described elsewhere (e.g. Davidson, 1997; Davidson *et al*, 1997, 1998), these methods build upon the early work of the German philosopher Edmund Husserl. Husserl's (1983, 1989, 1970) use of the term 'phenomenology' refers to a subjective, reflective method for the rigorous and systematic study of experience that has come to be adopted within the human and social sciences for the purpose of delineating the salient features and structures of human existence. First applied in psychiatry by Jaspers, different variants of this method have been used both in Europe and in North America to explore within an empathic attitude the inner lives of people with a variety of psychiatric disorders, including schizophrenia, mania, depression, obsessions, phobias and anxiety (for a review of pheno-menological studies of psychosis, see Davidson, 1994). We have argued (Davidson, 1997) that the use of a phenomenological method with individuals with schizophrenia necessarily requires a participatory model of enquiry as well, involving these individuals in the overall research enterprise as collaborators and consultants as well as participants.

The combination of phenomenological and participatory methods involved several steps. First, we conducted open-ended interviews following discharge with 12 patients who had had two or more hospitalisations within the last year. The interviews were relatively unstructured to allow the patients to describe their experiences leading up to, during and following their most recent hospitalisation, rather than to have them address specific issues that we assumed to be relevant (e.g. relapse). Patients also were asked to focus on their experiences of the new relapse prevention interventions in which they participated

during their hospitalisation, the factors that led to their not participating following discharge and anything they would find useful in
preventing future admissions.

Second, all interviews were transcribed verbatim and analysed
according to the following established qualitative procedures. Each
interview was reviewed independently by each of three investigators.
Each investigator reviewed each transcript to identify and code
the interview data for recurrent themes that characterised each
participant's experience, before bringing the themes together through
a 'cut and paste' method into a narrative summary for that participant.
The narrative summary served to retell the participant's story in a
thematic way, placing the recurrent and salient themes identified in
the interview in the temporal context of the participant's on-going
life. Following the completion of 12 narrative summaries by each
investigator, all three investigators then met to review each of their
summaries for each participant, comparing and contrasting the themes
they had each identified and coming to a general agreement on the
operative and important themes in each story.

Once a consensus had been reached on a narrative summary for
each of the interview transcripts, the investigators then reviewed the
12 summaries as a whole, initially in an independent fashion and then
again coming together as a group. This review entailed identifying themes
that were common across the participants, as well as areas in which the
participants might have differed. Each investigator composed a general
summary of these themes, which once again retained the narrative structure
of the initial summaries. The investigators then compared and
contrasted these general summaries to produce a general structural
summary of the findings common to all investigators (Giorgi, 1970;
Davidson, 1994; Davidson *et al*, 1995).

As a third step, once we had reached an initial draft of the major
themes that we had identified and their interrelationships in the form
of a general structural summary, we reconvened a group of the original
participants and asked for their appraisal of our tentative understanding of their responses. We asked them to identify issues or
experiences that we had missed, and to comment on whether or not
we had captured their concerns in the way we had framed the themes
that we had identified.

Utilising these methods, we discovered three major themes dominating the interviews with these patients (Davidson *et al*, 1997). Our
understanding of their experiences led us to hypothesise that these
three themes of social isolation, demoralisation and disconnection
from out-patient mental health and substance misuse services and
community supports acted to mediate the deteriorations in clinical
and functional status that precipitated their readmissions. Following

a brief description of each theme and its role in rehospitalisation, we will describe the intervention that we designed based on this understanding and in further collaboration with the patients themselves (for more detail on the collaborative process, see Davidson *et al*, 1997).

Social isolation

The most striking feature of these interviews was the fact that our agenda of preventing readmission was not shared by the patients themselves. Rather than describing hospitalisation as something to be avoided, patients described several attractions to the hospital that made it a place that they appreciated being able to return to when needed. These attractions included safety, respite, food and privacy. Most important to participants, however, was the care and concern they experienced in the hospital. One patient, for example, described how he had come to appreciate the hospital more each time he had been admitted, because the staff knew him better and his sense of being cared about had grown during each hospitalisation.

The importance of such experiences of being cared about was emphasised repeatedly by participants in describing their most recent hospitalisation. For instance, one patient described the most important benefit of hospitalisation as "just the support I got while I was there". Even the strictures and loss of freedom several participants identified as major drawbacks of being hospitalised were overshadowed by the caring nature of the milieu in which they occurred. After bemoaning rules about cigarette smoking, for example, one patient described how staff members "watch you". When the interviewer queried him on this response, he explained, "It's alright, I don't mind. They take care of me while I'm here, you know, they watch me, give me my medications, take care of me".

This appeal of the hospital becomes understandable when juxtaposed to descriptions of what patients' lives were like outside of the hospital. Several patients described hospitalisation as a vacation, as it provided respite from their lives in the community; characterised by one patient as: "homeless, broke, unemployed. The same harsh feeling everyday". The starkest contrast drawn between life in the hospital and life in the community was again in the area of caring and concern. Patients' descriptions of life in the community were striking in their absence of any mention of supportive friends or family. One patient spoke directly of his lack of social support in the community in contrast to the hospital when he said, "At home you don't have to listen to nobody but yourself. When you come into a hospital it's different. You're around a whole bunch of people that care about you". Others described needing 'somebody to talk to', a need unmet in the community that led patients to appreciate having a doctor appear at their bedroom door each morning in the hospital to ask how they had slept the night before. This sense of being cared about and listened to in the hospital provided a welcome relief from patients' feelings of being alone and abandoned on the outside, where there may have been no one who even knew or cared that they existed, much less how they had slept the night before.

Demoralisation

In addition to being lonely, all of the patients interviewed expressed a profound sense of demoralisation that involved feelings of power-lessness, fatalism and apathy in the face of their symptoms and other problems in living. For instance, asked if there was anything that she could do to cope with her illness or make things better, one patient could only state, "just take my medicine and pray". Far from feeling that they could intervene early to prevent relapse, patients drew a blank when asked what they could do to prevent future readmissions. Said another: "I can't answer that one. Nobody knows the future. I could be talking to you today and end up back in the hospital tomorrow". A few patients spoke of trying to ward off the effects of their symptoms through vague attempts to 'keep stress free', to rest or 'go slow', or to keep their minds 'occupied'. Their overall sense, however, was one of having little or no control over their illness, as described by one participant who said that all that he could do was to stay quiet and "do what the doctor says". This lack of control extended beyond their symptoms to their lives in general, as captured by one patient whose mental illness was simply the last item in a long list of things in his life that he could not change. For many participants, this sense of hopelessness and helplessness was derived from repetitive experiences of dysfunction and failed attempts at relating and coping with their condition, which by this point in their course of illness was fading into an increasing sense of apathy. A patient described: "The symptoms are still there, I'm still suffering, (but) my reaction to my suffering is less, less fierce now. I'm becoming cold about it ... I don't mean I don't care no more, but, you know, I'm living in the situation for a long time and my reaction to it is, like, numbed".

Disconnection from out-patient services and community supports

The last major theme was that the patients saw treatment and other supports as being of little use to them in dealing with the situations described above. While most spoke of taking their medications as perhaps the only thing they could do, few expressed even a rudimentary understanding of their illness or how treatment might be helpful. For example, one patient could think of only one thing that she could do when she felt that she was getting worse: "I just know when I get too sick ... it's time to come (in to the hospital)". As described above, however, coming in to the hospital was not primarily understood in terms of the treatment that would be received there as much as the respite and care it provided. What is conventionally conceptualised as treatment appeared to be experienced by these patients more like classroom exercises for which they would be graded, having no more relevance to, or impact on, their symptoms and lives than a history lesson. As one patient described: "It was like going to school (and) I passed ... I passed with flying colours. Everybody loved me after I left that place".

Compliance of this kind in the hospital did not translate into meaningful connections for patients between out-patient treatment and their risk for rehospitalisation. Out-patient treaters were uniformly described as unhelpful and relatively peripheral to the process of readmission, except in cases in which they had had to commit someone involuntarily. In one such case, the participant had seen his out-patient treater's role as solely one of social control, responding to the question of how his out-patient clinician could be more helpful to him by saying that he could "stay away from me". In general, patients reported being uninterested in any group activities such as the initial relapse prevention groups, as they did not see any benefit in sitting around with other people and focusing only on their problems. In addition to being uninterested, patients identified lack of transportation as a barrier to keeping out-patient appointments or attending the relapse prevention or other groups. Given the limited relevance of treatment to their lives, they did not see it worth the effort and inconvenience required to obtain transportation to the mental health centre to make it to these activities.

From preventing re-hospitalisation to promoting community integration

We took these data to hold several important implications for our efforts to prevent re-hospitalisation. It was evident first that preventing readmissions would remain our agenda only until the time that patients were able to find the appealing features of the hospital – such as respite, privacy, safety and above all care – in the community. In addition, our efforts to educate patients about their disorders and involve them collaboratively in the process of identifying early warning signs were undermined by their feelings of hopelessness about their possibilities for improvement and helplessness to do anything on their own behalf. Finally, these efforts were further undermined by the patients' disconnection from treatment and their believing there was no benefit from remaining in treatment once discharged.

On the other hand, these data also suggested a possible direction for the design of a new intervention that was more consistent with these patients' needs and experiences. This direction involved moving beyond an exclusive focus on the management of the more visible signs and symptoms of the disorder to providing a supportive and therapeutic milieu in the community that could serve several functions. These functions included:

(a) offering patients a social support network and sense of belonging outside of the hospital that could rival the sense of camaraderie they experienced in the hospital;

(b) enhancing patients' sense of hopefulness, efficacy and mastery over the various aspects of their disability, including the less visible social and cognitive deficits that impacted on their ability to negotiate community living and their self-esteem;

(c) engaging patients in the out-patient services and community supports that could be useful to them in maintaining community tenure. We now turn to describing the programme we developed to achieve these aims.

Components of the 'Engage Programme'

To achieve these aims, we re-conceptualised the out-patient component of the original relapse prevention initiative to be an intensive, assertive outreach intervention, named the 'Engage Programme', that augmented standard out-patient care. This programme's primary focus was to engage patients in social connections with each other and in out-patient services and community supports during the three-month period following discharge in which they were most vulnerable to readmission. Its primary vehicle for accomplishing these aims was the creation of a therapeutic milieu in the community in which the patients could participate together in mutual support, collaborative decision-making and problem-solving, and pro-social community activities.

In order to establish and maintain this milieu, the Engage Programme employed three major structures: (a) consumer-run outreach and peer support; (b) twice-weekly community-based group treatment; and (c) clinical coordination and consultation. These three structures were interrelated in the following way: during and following hospitalisation for up to three months post-discharge, patients received visits from outreach staff who offered them assistance in meeting their basic needs and provided them with transportation to social and recreational outings in the community, abstinence-based and other mutual support groups, and the twice-weekly groups. These groups met in the community and were co-led by a clinical psychologist, rehabilitation therapist and an outreach worker. Encouraging patients' participation in mutual support and collaborative decision-making and problem-solving, these groups provided the core of the therapeutic milieu. In addition to organising and providing transportation to the groups and outings, these staff focused on engaging patients in a working alliance with their out-patient clinicians. This involved bringing patients to their appointments and consulting out-patient clinicians on patients' immediate goals and needs and ways to involve them more collaboratively in their care. At the end of the three-month intervention, patients who had not been readmitted 'graduated' to a less intensive mutual support group and were expected to continue to work with their out-patient clinician and to participate in abstinence-based and other mutual support groups and social activities in the community. The interventions to be offered in each of these three components, and the ways in which they target the three primary issues of social isolation, demoralisation and disconnection from services and supports are described in detail in Boxes 7.1a–7.1c. A brief description of each of these components follows.

Consumer-run outreach and mutual support

As soon as a patient was admitted to the hospital who had had at least one prior hospitalisation within the previous year, Engage consumer outreach staff visited the person in the hospital and invited him or her to join the Engage Programme. As soon as the patient was able to leave the unit, these staff offered to provide transportation to and from the twice-weekly groups that met in the community. Following discharge, patients were visited in their homes by the outreach staff, who brought them a 'welcome basket' of food, toiletries and other useful items, and who offered to provide transportation for them to the twice-weekly groups, weekly social and recreational outings, on-going abstinence-based and mutual support groups and out-patient treatment appointments. In addition, the outreach staff conducted an interest survey and assessed the patient's needs and goals, and offered to work with the patient on a time-limited basis to address any of these issues. These case management functions were conducted in collaboration with the patient's out-patient clinician. Consumer staff also organised and hosted weekly, low-cost social and recreational outings in the community which had as their only function allowing

Box 7.1a
Engage Programme interventions by domain – social isolation

Assist group members to engage in and maintain social connections with other group members.
(a)   Encourage members to share their experiences of social disconnection and isolation.
(b)   Assertive community outreach:
(i)   provide transportation to groups for 3 months, then as indicated;
(ii)   maintain twice-weekly telephone or personal contact with members for three months, then as indicated;
(iii) assist members to get half-price bus passes;
(iv)   encourage members to accompany each other to assist in learning bus routes.

Facilitate and encourage specific acts of mutual support and reciprocity among members.
(a)   Recognise and encourage expressions of caring, camaraderie, and friendship among group members.
(b)   Assist members to recognise and respect social cues and personal boundaries in their interactions.
(c)   Three home visits are made to new members by peer support staff to provide home supplies and lists of local community resources, and to help members fill out personal interest inventories.

Facilitate local community outings and activities with group members.
(a)   Provide planning, financial support and transportation for once-weekly, local community outings led by peer support staff.
(b)   Enhance members' independence and familiarity and connections with affordable, local community activities and resources.

Create and maintain group rituals and celebrations.
(a)   Assist members to remember and celebrate milestones in recovery and avoiding rehospitalisation.
(b)   Enhance members' connections with seasonal rhythms and with local events and celebrations.

Facilitate participative group planning to increase members' personal investment in upcoming meetings, activities and events.

patients to experience the positive features of community living, to have fun and to become friends. Low-cost activities were encouraged, as these would be activities that patients would be more likely to continue on their own once they graduated from the programme. To date, outings have included such events as minor league baseball games, picnics and hikes in a state park and apple- and pumpkin-picking.

Box 7.1b
Engage Programme interventions by domain – demoralisation

Assist group members to recognise and share problems and limitations they face and changes that occur.

(a)   Encourage members' self-disclosure and expressions of hope in the possibility of change and recovery.

(b)   Encourage members to recognise and share constructive downward and upward social comparisons.

(c)   Encourage members to face and share their struggles with constricted resources in treatment and social benefits, and help them apply for needed assistance.

Facilitate participatory decision-making and planning among group members.

(a)   Help members to recognise how their decisions and actions have an impact on the group and other members.

(b)   Help members make specific, constructive plans for unstructured time, such as weekends.

(c)   Recognise and strengthen experiences of mutual accountability and responsibility among members.

Provide individually tailored, flexible support to group members experiencing crises.

(a)   Increase engagement and contact intensity (including daily telephone contact if indicated).

(b)   Provide transportation to extra out-patient department appointments and intermediate care facilities if indicated.

(c)   Provide out-patient department clinicians with assessments of functional deterioration and crisis intensification.

(d)   Advocate for inter-treater meetings to plan special support and outreach efforts.

Facilitate the emergence and recognition of group members' natural interests.

(a)   Encourage members to state preferences and interests in participatory planning for meals, community outings and in group celebrations.

(b)   Encourage members to initiate activities with others who share their interests.

(c)   Recognise members' particular strengths, skills and natural leadership roles in outings and activities.

(d)   Recognise and encourage members to share ways that their interests motivate initiative and enhance engagement in local community activities.

Twice-weekly community-based group treatment

Twice-weekly Engage group meetings were held outside the mental health centre at a community location, with the focus of the groups on

---

Box 7.1c

Engage Programme interventions by domain – disconnection from out-patient mental health and substance misuse services and community supports

Help group members to recognise and face symptoms and destructive patterns of relating as these become evident in the lived interactions of the group milieu.

Help group members recognise and remember changes and improvements in their symptoms and problems.

Connect group members with abstinence-based mutual support groups for substance misuse.

(a)   Support members' engagement in these groups by rewarding it with positive group recognition.

(b)   Encourage members to connect with sponsors.

(c)   Assist members with transportation if indicated.

(d)   Facilitate group celebrations of turning points and milestones in recovery, e.g. one year of 'clean time'.

Assist group members to recognise and experience themselves as collaborative partners in their ongoing treatment.

(a)   Help members to recognise their fears of medication side-effects and stigma.

(b)   Assist members to honestly face struggles between acquiescence, resistance and adherence to their treatment – and increase their cooperation.

Assist group members to connect experienced stress with symptom exacerbation.

(a)   Facilitate problem-solving and planning strategies to help members reduce the impact of some stressors.

(b)   Assist members to find activities and other strategies for reducing experienced stress.

Advocate for flexible, collaborative treatment planning with out-patient treaters and other service agencies.

(a)   Initiate inter-treater contact and meetings and provide transportation to out-patient meetings as indicated.

Provide out-patient clinicians with information about members' daily lives and environment, and assessments of functional disabilities, capacities, interests and strengths as these emerge in group interactions and activities.

Consult out-patient clinicians and other service providers regarding frustration and demoralisation around group members' continuing problems.

---

promoting mutual support among patients, instilling hope for recovery, involving patients in collaborative decision-making and modelling appropriate self-care (including the use of medications and abstaining from alcohol and other drugs). The cornerstone of this approach was an emphasis on cultivating group norms that involved patients caring for each other and working on the shared task of staying in the community together. The group leaders facilitated the development of a sense of belonging and cohesiveness both within the group and outside of the group, by encouraging patients to spend time with each other doing things together in the community.

In addition to fostering social support, a number of strategies were included in the groups and community outings to instill hope and provide patients with concrete evidence of their own efficacy and of the possibility of their achieving some level of mastery over their condition. The role of the consumer outreach staff within the groups included instilling hope and providing role models for patients through disclosure of their own histories of disability and their strategies for effective coping, enhancing group members' own coping and problem-solving skills. Lunch was provided once a week during one of the groups, and planning for what to have for lunch and where to go on the weekly outings was left up to the patients themselves, providing them with tangible evidence of their own agency and decision-making abilities. Group rituals and celebrations, similar to those in abstinence-based '12-step' groups, were established based on patient input, such as a 'graduation ceremony' in which a certificate of achievement was presented to patients who successfully completed the three-month period post-discharge without being rehospitalised. As patients neared graduation, they were invited to start making the transition to a graduation group that met once per week at the local service user-oriented social club. They were expected to arrange their own transportation to this group and to provide their own lunch, and were able to participate in this group in addition to their out-patient care for up to one year post-discharge, with periodic reunions with the members of the Engage groups.

Clinical coordination and consultation

The clinician and rehabilitation therapist who co-led the twice-weekly Engage groups maintained close communication with patients' out-patient clinicians, arranged for patients to be dropped off at their clinicians' offices after groups or other outings, and consulted the patients' clinicians about ways to engage and maintain the patients in treatment. This consultation's primary focus was to demonstrate to patients that treatment could be of direct benefit to them; highlighting for clinicians ways to enable their patients to make use of treatment in an active, collaborative and constructive way that promoted their recovery and enabled them to reclaim their lives in the community.

The consultation had three phases:

(a) helping clinicians to get past their own frustration in relation to patients who historically have not shown up for appointments or used treatment only sporadically;

(b) providing information to clinicians about members' daily lives, living environments, functional disabilities, strengths and goals in order to facilitate a working alliance;

(c) helping clinicians to reframe symptoms and substance misuse as barriers to a patient's achieving a fulfilling life in the community, and to reframe treatments, including medication and participation in abstinence-based mutual support groups, as useful tools for patients' recovery.

Results

The design of our initial evaluation of the effectiveness of this programme entailed a pre- and post-intervention comparison of the group that received the intervention and a non-random comparison of the intervention group and a similar group that did not receive the intervention. The outcome measures were utilisation of in-patient services, including the number of admissions and number of hospital days. Data have been collected on the first 46 patients to be eligible for the Engage Programme since these programme revisions were implemented. All patients who had had two admissions (including the index admission) within the last 365 days were eligible if they also lived in the greater New Haven area (and were eligible to receive out-patient services at our community mental health centre), except those who were patients in an assertive community treatment programme or in supportive housing. We reasoned that exclusion of these patients was warranted, since patients in these programmes already were receiving intensive, scarce and costly services, and that this intervention, the Engage Programme, would duplicate many of those services. Furthermore, we intended the intervention to be reserved for patients who did not yet qualify for this level of service intensity, but who were, nonetheless, at risk for readmission.

All patients were recruited for this pilot study while in-patients at the community mental health centre (during their index hospitalisation). Of the 46 patients who initially were eligible to be referred to the Engage Programme, 19 were referred and 27 were not. The reasons for non-referral included four categories: (a) patients who were discharged or who eloped from the in-patient unit before they could be referred (n=9); (b) patients who were discharged with an alternative disposition that precluded their participation, such as to a partial hospital programme (n=9); (c) patients who were referred but declined to participate in the intervention (*n*=6); and (d) patients who were transferred to another catchment area and thereby were no longer eligible (*n*=3). Of the 19 patients who were referred to the programme, four moved soon after discharge out of the catchment area and thereby also became ineligible. Data are presented for the 15 patients who participated in the programme and the 24 patients who did not participate in the programme but who remained within the catchment area, thereby allowing us to track their service utilisation post-discharge.

All 39 patients participated in the original relapse prevention module while on the in-patient unit, consisting of twice-weekly groups focused on educating them about their early warning signs and encouraging them to develop an action plan with their out-patient clinician to monitor their symptoms and intervene early following discharge to prevent a relapse. Upon discharge, the 24 comparison group patients who were not in the Engage programme received standard out-patient care, while patients in the Engage Programme in addition to standard out-patient care also received outreach services from the consumer staff and participated in the twice-weekly Engage groups and weekly social and recreational outings, as described above.

Table 7.1 presents demographic and diagnostic characteristics for the patients in each condition. The patients were roughly comparable

TABLE 7.1
Demographic and diagnostic characteristics for patients by condition

Demographic/ diagnostic category	Demographic/ diagnostic subtype	Engage programme + standard care (n=15)	Standard care only (n=24)
Gender	Male	60.0%	58.3%
	Female	40.0%	41.7%
Age	Range	21-60	19-63
	Mean	37.8	33.8
Race/ ethnicity	Caucasian	53.3%	50.0%
	African American	40.0%	29.2%
	Hispanic origin	6.7%	20.8%
	Other	6.7%	20.8%
Diagnosis	Schizophrenia/ schizoaffective	40.0%	41.7%
	Major affective disorder	46.7%	58.3%
	Personality disorder only	13.3%	0.0%
Co-occurring disorders	Co-occurring personality disorder	20.0%	54.2
	Co-occurring substance misuse disorder	46.7%	45.8%

TABLE 7.2
Service utilisation for one year prior to index admission

Variables	Engage Programme + standard care (n=15)	Standard care only (n=24)
Readmissions	24	45
Mean admissions per patient (s.d.)[1]	1.60 (1.18)	1.88 (1.90)
In-patient days	462	842
Mean in-patient days per patient (s.d.)[2]	30.08 (35.45)	35.08 (32.32)

1. Difference not statistically significant, $t(37)=-0.50$, $P=0.620$.
2. Difference not statistically significant, $t(37)=-0.39$, $P=0.700$.

across conditions, with the following exceptions: there were more patients with personality disorders only in the Engage Programme and more patients with co-occurring personality disorders in the standard care only condition; there were more African American patients in the Engage Programme; and there were more patients of other races and of Hispanic origin in the standard care only condition. Consistent with the literature on patients with multiple hospitalisations (Green, 1988; Cotterill *et al*, 1993; Gaebel *et al*, 1993; Soni *et al*, 1994; Weiden *et al*, 1995; Kent *et al*, 1995; Kent & Yellowlees, 1995; Appleby *et al*, 1996; Klinkenberg *et al*, 1996; Pfeiffer *et al*, 1996), overall these patients were likely to be male, in their 30s and with co-occurring substance misuse disorders.

Independent sample *t*-tests were used to assess the differences between the Engage and standard care only groups during the year

TABLE 7.3
Service utilisation for 90 days post-discharge

Variables	Engage Programme + standard care (n=15)	Standard care only (n=24)
Readmissions	2	10
Mean admissions per patient (s.d.)[1]	0.13 (0.35)	0.42 (0.72)
In-patient days	7	122
Mean in-patient days per patient (s.d.)[2]	0.42 (0.72)	5.08 (10.38)

1. Difference not statistically significant, $t(35.48)=-1.64$, $P=0.110$.
2. Difference statistically significant, $t(30.80)=-2.09$, $P=0.045$.

prior to, and 90 days post-discharge from, the index admission on readmission rates and in-patient days. During the year prior to their index admission, the admission rates and average number of in-patient days per patient were similar across the Engage and standard care only groups (see Table 7.2). As could be expected due to the shorter time period, both the Engage Programme participants and the patients in the standard care only group had less admissions and in-patient days at the end of 90 days post-discharge than at one year prior to the index admission (see Table 7.3). The readmission rate for Engage participants was about one-third less compared to the standard care only group, however, perhaps because of the small sample size, this difference was not statistically different. The average number of in-patient days per patient for the Engage participants was 92% less than the standard care group, and this difference was significant (see Table 7.3).

Discussion

The data presented in Tables 7.2 and 7.3 are certainly suggestive of the potential effectiveness of this new intervention in preventing readmissions among individuals with serious mental illnesses, particularly among those with psychosis. The power of this programme appears to lie in its ability to engage patients both in therapeutic and in social and recreational activities in the community, and in its offering patients a supportive community as an alternative to returning to the hospital. There are a number of limitations to the present study, however, which we are currently addressing in a prospective, randomised controlled design. These include: difficulties in determining the equivalency of the comparison groups due to lack of randomisation; lack of information related to changes in symptoms, social functioning and quality of life; lack of information related to costs of services and potential cost savings generated by the intervention; and lack of information related to the enduring nature of the gains that appear to have been brought about by the intervention during the first three months post-discharge.

While we must await the results of the clinical trial currently under way to draw stronger conclusions about the effectiveness of this novel intervention in preventing readmissions and promoting community tenure among individuals with psychosis, we already have learned an instructive lesson from this exercise that has implications for future programme development and evaluation. This implication is the value of including the subjective frame of reference of the patients themselves in our understanding of, and approach to, their difficulties. Broadening our initial conceptualisation of the problem of recidivism

154   *Davidson et al*

to include patients' experiences allowed us to discover and appreciate the importance of the less visible – but equally distressing – elements of their day-to-day struggles in the community. These elements had more to do with cognitive and negative symptom deficits associated with their disorders and with the social–environmental contexts of their lives than with the more prominent and visible signs and symptoms of psychosis that had been the focus of conventional relapse prevention efforts.

The social isolation and demoralisation that had resulted from repeated failures at attempts to establish social relationships and negotiate community living appeared to be potent factors in precipitating readmissions for these patients. It was only through an understanding of the role of these issues in the patients' experiences that we then were able to develop a psychosocial intervention to address these concerns, which offered the patients a more attractive alternative both to life on the streets and to life in the hospital. Future efforts to design psychological and social interventions would benefit from a similar path, starting from 'the way of ignorance' to explore first what concerns, needs and challenges patients experience. Securing a subjective perspective as the ground for our approach will prevent us from simply rehashing our own preconceived, largely medical, notions of disorder, and will assure the relevance of our interventions to our patients' day-to-day lives, thereby increasing the likelihood of their using these strategies in their recovery.

References

ANDERSON, C. M., HOGARTY, G. & REISS, D. J. (1980) Family treatment of adult schizophrenic patients: a psychoeducational approach. *Schizophrenia Bulletin*, 6, 490–505.
APPLEBY, L., LUCHINS, D. J., DESAI, P. N., *ET AL* (1996) Length of inpatient stay and recidivism among patients with schizophrenia. *Psychiatric Services*, 47, 985–990.
BIRCHWOOD, M. (1995) Early intervention in psychotic relapse: cognitive approaches to detection and management. *Behavior Change*, 12, 2–19.
——, SMITH, J., MACMILLAN, F., *ET AL* (1989) Predicting relapse in schizophrenia: the development and implementation of an early signs monitoring system using patients and families as observers, a preliminary investigation. *Psychological Medicine*, 19, 649–656.
COTTERILL, L. & THOMAS, R. (1993) A typology of care episodes experienced by people with schizophrenia in an English town. *Social Science and Medicine*, 36, 1587–1595.
DAVIDSON, L. (1994) Phenomenological research in schizophrenia: from philosophical anthropology to empirical science. *Journal of Phenomenological Psychology*, 25, 104–130.
—— (1997) Vulnérabilité et destin dans la schizophrénie: prêter l'oreille á la voix de la personne. (Vulnerability and destiny in schizophrenia: hearkening to the voice of the person.) *L'Evolution Psychiatrique*, 62, 263–284.
—— & COSGROVE, L. (1991) Psychologism and phenomenological psychology revisited, Part I: The liberation from naturalism. *Journal of Phenomenological Psychology*, 22, 87–108.

——, Hoge, M. A., Merrill, M. E., *et al* (1995) The experiences of long-stay inpatients returning to the community. *Psychiatry*, **58**, 122–132.

—— & McGlashan, T. H. (1997) The varied outcomes of schizophrenia. *Canadian Journal of Psychiatry*, **42**, 34–43.

——, Stayner, D. A., Lambert, S., *et al* (1997) Phenomenological and participatory research on schizophrenia: Recovering the person in theory and practice. *Journal of Social Issues*, **53**, 767–784.

——, —— & Haglund, K. E. (1998) Phenomenological perspectives on the social functioning of people with schizophrenia. In *Handbook of Social Functioning in Schizophrenia* (eds K. T. Mueser & N. Tarrier), pp. 97–120. Needham Heights, MA: Allyn & Bacon.

Dietzen, L. L. & Bond, G. R. (1993) Relationship between case manager contact and outcome for frequently hospitalized psychiatric clients. *Hospital and Community Psychiatry*, **44**, 839–843.

Drake, R. E. & Wallach, M. A. (1988) Mental patients' attitudes toward hospitalisation: a neglected aspect of hospital tenure. *American Journal of Psychiatry*, **145**, 29–34.

—— & —— (1992) Mental patients' attraction to the hospital: correlates of living preference. *Community Mental Health Journal*, **28**, 5–12.

Eliot, T. S. (1971) *The Complete Poems and Plays, 1909–1950*. New York: Harcourt, Brace & World.

Falloon, I. R. H. (1985) *Family Management of Schizophrenia*. Baltimore, MD: Johns Hopkins.

—— (1992) Early intervention for first episodes of schizophrenia: A preliminary exploration. *Psychiatry*, **55**, 4–15.

Gaebel, W., Frick, U., Kopcke, W., *et al* (1993) Early neuroleptic intervention in schizophrenia: are prodromal symptoms valid predictors of relapse? *British Journal of Psychiatry*, **163**, 8–12.

Giorgi, A. (1970) *Psychology as a Human Science: a Phenomenologically Based Approach*. New York: Harper & Row.

Goldstein, M. J. (1994) Psychoeducational and family therapy in relapse prevention. *Acta Psychiatrica Scandinavica*, **89** (suppl. 382), 54–57.

Green, J. (1988) Frequent rehospitalisation and noncompliance with treatment. *Hospital and Community Psychiatry*, **39**, 963–966.

Herz, M. I. & Lamberti, J. S. (1995) Prodromal symptoms and relapse prevention. *Schizophrenia Bulletin*, **21**, 541–550.

Hogarty, G. E., Anderson, C. M. & Reiss, D. J. (1991) Family psychoeducation, social skills training and maintenance chemotherapy in the aftercare treatment of schizophrenia: II. Two-year effects of a controlled study on relapse and adjustment. *Archives of General Psychiatry*, **48**, 340–347.

Husserl, E. (1970) *The Crisis of European Sciences and Transcendental Phenomenology* (trans by D. Carr). Evanston, IL: Northwestern University Press.

—— (1983) *Ideas Pertaining to a Pure Phenomenology and to a Phenomenological Philosophy. First Book: General Introduction to a Pure Phenomenology* (trans F. Kersten). The Hague: Nijhoff.

—— (1989) *Ideas Pertaining to a Pure Phenomenology and to a Phenomenological Philosophy. Second book: Studies in the Phenomenology of Constitution* (trans R. Rojcewicz & A. Schuwer). Boston: Kluwer Academic Publishers. (Originally published in 1952)

Kent, S., Fogarty, M. & Yellowlees, P. (1995) A review of studies of heavy users of psychiatric services. *Psychiatric Services*, **46**, 1247–1253.

—— & Yellowlees, P. (1995) The relationship between social factors and frequent use of psychiatric services. *Australian and New Zealand Journal of Psychiatry*, **29**, 403–408.

Kissling, W. (1994) Compliance, quality assurance and standards for relapse prevention in schizophrenia. *Acta Psychiatrica Scandinavica*, **89** (suppl. 382), 16–24.

KLINKENBERG, W. D. & CALSYN, R. J. (1996) Predictors of receipt of aftercare and recidivism among persons with severe mental illness: a review. *Psychiatric Services*, **47**, 487–496.

LEFF, J. A. & VAUGHN, C. (1981) The role of maintenance therapy and expressed emotion in relapse of schizophrenia: a two-year follow-up. *British Journal of Psychiatry*, **139**, 102–104.

PFEIFFER, S. I., O'MALLEY, D. S. & SHOTT, S. (1996) Factors associated with the outcome of adults treated in psychiatric hospitals: a synthesis of findings. *Psychiatric Services*, **47**, 263–269.

ROGERS, E. S. & PALMER-ERBS, V. (1994) Participatory action research: implications for research and evaluation in psychiatric rehabilitation. *Psychosocial Rehabilitation Journal*, **18**, 3–12.

SCOTT, J. E. & DIXON, L. B. (1995) Assertive community treatment and case management for schizophrenia. *Schizophrenia Bulletin*, **21**, 657–668.

SLEDGE, W. H., TEBES, J. K., RAKFELDT, J., *ET AL* (1996a) Day hospital/crisis respite care v. inpatient care. Part I: Clinical outcomes. *American Journal of Psychiatry*, **153**, 1065–1073.

——, TEBES, J. K., WOLFF, N., *ET AL* (1996b) Day hospital/crisis respite care vs. inpatient care. Part II: Service utilization and costs. *American Journal of Psychiatry*, **153**, 1074–1083.

SONI, S. D., GASKELL, K. & REED, P. (1994) Factors affecting rehospitalisation rates of chronic schizophrenic patients living in the community. *Schizophrenia Research*, **12**, 169–177.

WASYLENKI, D. A. (1994) The cost of schizophrenia. *Canadian Journal of Psychiatry*, **39** (suppl. 2), S65–S69.

WEIDEN, P. J., & OLFSON, M. (1995) Cost of relapse in schizophrenia. *Schizophrenia Bulletin*, **21**, 419–429.

WERTZ, F. J. (1983) From everyday to psychological description: analyzing the moments of a qualitative data analysis. *Journal of Phenomenological Psychology*, **14**, 197–241.

WHYTE, W. F. (1989) Advancing scientific knowledge through participatory action research. *Sociological Forum*, **4**, 367–385.

—— (1991) *Participatory Action Research*. Newbury Park, CA: Sage Publications.

8 Crisis residential care for patients with serious mental illness

WAYNE S. FENTON and LOREN R. MOSHER

In recent years, the efficacy of treatments prescribed for patients with schizophrenia has increasingly been put to the test in rigorously designed randomised clinical trials. As reflected in a comprehensive review of the empirical basis for the treatment of schizophrenia commissioned by the US Agency for Health Care Policy and Research, substantial data derived from randomised clinical trials support the efficacy of a range of psychosocial and pharmacological interventions in schizophrenia (Lehman *et al*, 1995, 1998*a*). Among psychosocial treatments, family interventions (Dixon & Lehman, 1995), case management and assertive community treatment (Scott & Dixon, 1995*a*) and social skills training (Scott & Dixon, 1995*b*) have demonstrated efficacy in reducing relapse and/or improving functional outcome for patients with schizophrenia. In addition, a more recently completed randomised clinical trial demonstrates that a disorder-specific individual psychotherapy can yield progressive advances in social and vocational functioning not otherwise possible (Hogarty *et al*, 1997*a,b*). This empirical research forms the scientific basis of modern treatment planning, and suggests that a model that integrates biological and psychosocial treatment modalities will result in better and more individualised patient care (Fenton & McGlashan, 1997).

How well are scientific advances in treatment transforming care delivered to patients in existing service systems? A recent study from the USA suggests that treatment as actually delivered more often than not falls short of what would be recommended based on the best evidence of efficacy (Lehman *et al*, 1998*b*). In a survey of 719 patients with schizophrenia receiving care in two states, for most empirically derived treatment recommendations less than half of patients were receiving treatment that met recommendation criteria. Overall, rates of conformance were lower for psychosocial than for pharmacological treatment recommendations. Although the authors could not determine whether this relative lack of access to psychosocial treatment was due to absence of availability or inadequate use of existing services, in many areas fiscal constraints limit the widespread implementation of treatments of demonstrated efficacy (Mosher, 1983).

In many parts of the world, including the USA, a public mandate to provide care to an expanding population within a fixed budget limits the dissemination of research advances into service delivery systems. Consequently, relatively few patients have access to the best scientifically informed treatment. Across many countries and jurisdictions, the largest portion of direct health care costs expended in caring for patients with schizophrenia and other serious mental illnesses continues to be allocated to hospital-based in-patient care (Evers & Ament, 1995; Thompson *et al*, 1995; Knapp, 1997). Given fixed or contracting budgets, developing cost-effective alternatives to hospital care is required to allow the funding of new and effective psychosocial and pharmacological treatments (Stoline & Sharfstein, 1996).

Based on these considerations, we undertook an effort to evaluate the clinical effectiveness and cost of a non-hospital-based treatment alternative for voluntary patients with severe mental illness who would normally require hospital care for an exacerbation of illness. Clinical and economic outcome assessment suggests that, for many patients, acute care provided in a specialised treatment home can deliver outcomes comparable to hospital care with the potential for significant savings. Within an organised health service with a fixed budget, we suggest that savings might be invested in making optimum community-based supportive and preventative care more widely available.

Crisis residential treatment model

Crisis residential alternatives are homes in neighbourhoods that are staffed and organised to accept and treat acutely decompensated patients in lieu of voluntary admission to a psychiatric ward of a general hospital or state psychiatric facility. Originating in a climate of anti-medical ideology in the 1960s, the first-generation crisis residential concept began with experimental efforts to treat psychosis in a normalising and non-stigmatising (i.e. non-medical) setting with no neuroleptic medication. In a randomised study narrowly focused on young adults newly diagnosed with schizophrenia and treated with no or minimal antipsychotic medications, Mosher and colleagues demonstrated that care in a home-like acute residential facility (Soteria) generated patient outcomes comparable or superior to treatment in the in-patient unit of a mental health centre (Mosher *et al*, 1995; Mosher & Menn, 1978; Matthews *et al*, 1979).

In subsequent decades, modifications and adaptations of the Soteria model were developed to meet the needs of more typical patients with long-standing and recurrent mental illness who, while living in the community, are intermittently in need of acute care. Second-generation crisis residential services provide both pharmacological and psycho-social care and have five major characteristics:

(a) they provide housing during a crisis;
(b) their services are short term;
(c) they provide acute treatment and support services;
(d) they serve small groups (6–8 service users);
(e) they are used to avoid hospitalisation.

These programmes typically operate as one component of integrated out-patient community support and crisis response systems. While many clinical and anecdotal reports describe the operation and utility of these programmes (Matthews *et al*, 1979; Kresky-Wolff *et al*, 1984; Weisman, 1985; Rappaport *et al*, 1987; Stroul, 1987, 1988; Bond *et al*, 1989; Budson, 1994; Bourgeois, 1995), rigorous data supporting their efficacy has been lacking.

Concerns about missed medical diagnoses and professional liability accruing from the failure to hospitalise patients who are psychotic and/or suicidal has generated resistance to widespread replication of pilot or demonstration programmes (Stroul, 1988). In addition, partly because of a lack of efficacy data, funding for crisis residential services has not been integrated into nationally mandated benefit programmes. As a result, these services are still rare in the USA and elsewhere. Our study of crisis residential care was designed to rigorously assess the efficacy of this service in the hopes of generating data to guide funding decisions.

Treatment settings

Crisis residential service

McAuliffe House is an eight-bed crisis alternative located in a ranch-style house in a residential neighbourhood in Rockville, Maryland. The programme is staffed by two graduate counsellors 24 hours a day under the direction of an clinical social worker level programme director. During the residential treatment episode, medical responsibility for each patient's care is maintained by the patient's out-patient psychiatrist who prescribes or changes psychotropic medications, and orders out-patient laboratory assessments and other medical evaluations as indicated. In this way, the patient's general medical status is evaluated by the physician who has been providing ongoing out-patient care. Each newly admitted patient is also evaluated by a consulting psychiatrist who, in addition to providing a written second opinion, meets with programme staff each week to assist in treatment planning, monitor progress and provide staff supervision. Among other purposes, the second opinion provides documentation that an independent physician has examined the patient and determined treatment in the non-hospital alternative to be medically appropriate. This limits the professional liability concerns of the referring and treating clinician.

The McAuliffe programme model was based on Soteria and Crossing Place, and has been described in detail elsewhere (Mosher & Menn, 1978; Matthews *et al*, 1979; Kresky-Wolff *et al*, 1984; Weisman, 1985; Rappaport *et al*, 1987; Stroul, 1987, 1988; Bond *et al*, 1989; Budson, 1994; Mosher *et al*, 1995). Beyond a supportive environment, supervised medication self-administration and the availability of one to one staff monitoring, formal treatment is not provided in the alternative. Rather, continued participation in ongoing community-based treatment, rehabilitation, school, work or other activities is supported to an extent allowed by patients' symptoms. If needed, programme staff provide transportation to these appointments or activities. Emergency back-up for the residential alternative is provided by a mobile treatment team if evaluation for involuntary hospitalisation becomes necessary. The efficacy of the model is thought to derive from a normalising home-like environment that minimises stigma, loss of esteem and assumption of the sick role while allowing patients to maintain continuity with out-patient treatment providers and community supports (Mosher *et al*, 1986; Mosher & Burti, 1994; Bourgeois, 1995; Herrell *et al*, 1996). From the time of admission, if able, patients may visit family or friends, have visitors and attend work or other scheduled community activities. The house culture promotes responsible conduct from patients as members of a temporary family who share the tasks of shopping, cooking and keeping the house tidy.

General hospital service

The bulk of short-term acute care in the catchment area is provided on the psychiatric unit of general medical hospitals. These units typically treat voluntary patients with public funding admitted through the emergency department. If these patients cannot be stabilised within several weeks, transfer to a centralised state hospital for longer term care is employed. For this study, the control treatment site was

Montgomery General Hospital, Olney, Maryland, a 229-bed Joint Commission Accreditation of Health Care Organizations-accredited general hospital that since 1971 has operated a 31-bed in-patient psychiatric treatment unit supported by a day hospital and out-patient clinic. Hospital care includes medical assessment, individual psychotherapy, group therapy and pharmacological management generally provided by hospital-based specialists.

Study methods

Setting and subjects

Located just outside Washington, DC, Montgomery County, Maryland has a population of approximately 800 000 residents. The home of the National Institute of Mental Health, and the Food and Drug Administration, the county is among the most educated and affluent in the USA. Nonetheless, 10% of county residents live below the federal poverty line, and homelessness, particularly among the seriously mentally ill, is a significant problem. The waiting list for public housing exceeds seven years. Adult patients under the care of the Montgomery County, Maryland Department of Health and Human Services (DHHS) were eligible for participation in this study. As the sole local public mental health authority, the DHHS manages a comprehensive network of services that supports approximately 1600 adults with serious and persistent mental disorders at any given time. Annually, about 12% of these patients experience an illness exacerbation requiring one or more hospitalisations.

Patients who met the following criteria were referred for randomisation:
  (a) were judged by their treating clinician to be in need of hospital level care;
  (b) were judged not to require acute general medical care or detoxification;
  (c) had Medicaid or Medicare (government subsidised) funding;
  (d) were willing to accept voluntary placement.

Voluntary patients experiencing acute psychosis, depression, suicidality, homicidality or concomitant substance misuse were not excluded from randomisation.

Assignment procedures

The International Research Review Board (IRB) admission procedures were as follows. First, at the time of crisis assessment, a DHHS clinician and the patient agreed on the need for in-patient treatment. Second, after determining that the patient met eligibility criteria, the clinician contacted the department's 24-hour crisis centre, which randomly assigned the patient to one or other treatment condition according to a computer-generated pattern to which referring clinicians were blind. Third, following admission, the patient was approached to provide written informed consent to participate in subsequent study procedures and assessments.

Because all admissions were voluntary, both referring clinicians and randomised patients were free to decline admission after learning the assignment. Overall, 27 of 185 randomised subjects (14%) declined admission after receiving assignment. While these patients were not allowed admission to the treatment option to which they were not assigned, they were free, with their clinicians' assistance, to seek admission to one of the other in-patient programmes in the area. An additional 11 patients withdrew consent for assessment interviews, and 11 either did not arrive at their assigned placement or left within 24 hours. Unsuccessful entry was more common among those assigned to the hospital ($n=42$) than those assigned to the alternative ($n=24$). As this trend was noted early in the study, the ratio of random assignments was set at 10:7 to favour hospital placement. Nonetheless, the final sample included 69 alternative and 50 hospital participants.

Background demographic, diagnostic and case mix data were collected on all randomised patients to allow a comparison of patients treated in each setting and evaluate potential biases introduced by the necessity of obtaining patient and clinician consent following randomisation.

Outcome assessment

Process measures

Since maintenance of continuity with community support is considered a key feature of treatment in the alternative, the percentage of patients who saw their out-patient clinician, visited their residence and had a trial at their day activity during the treatment episode was assessed in each setting. Since closer management of psychotropic medications is a significant potential advantage of the hospital, the proportion of patients who had a medication change during the treatment episode was coded.

Discharge quality

Discharge quality was assessed at the time of discharge interview by rating patients' knowledge of prescribed medications, date and time of aftercare appointment, plans for transportation to aftercare appointment and familiarity with aftercare clinicians, and by rating anticipated aftercare housing and community support activities.

Clinical effectiveness

Clinical programme effectiveness was assessed by evaluating changes in patient symptom severity, patient satisfaction with treatment episode and percentage of patients successfully discharged to the community. Psychosocial functioning, service utilisation and life satisfaction in the six months before and after the treatment episode were evaluated as secondary measures of clinical effectiveness. Randomised patients were assessed by a member of the research team at three time points: (a) within 48 hours of admission (mean=28, s.d.=13); (b) within 48 hours of discharge (mean=20, s.d.=26); and (c) six months following admission (mean=7.6, s.d.=3.5).

Symptom severity was rated at each time point using the Positive and Negative Syndrome Scale (PANSS; Kay *et al*, 1992). Patient satisfaction with episode treatment was measured at discharge using a 10-item satisfaction survey based in part on the Quality of Life Scale (Lehman, 1988). Discharge was considered successful if the patient was returned to the community and unsuccessful if the treatment episode ended in transfer to another in-patient facility.

At admission, data concerning premorbid functioning, illness onset, severity and history as well as psychosocial functioning and service utilisation over the prior six months were collected using an interview schedule based on our earlier work on the prediction of outcome in serious mental illness (Fenton & McGlashan, 1986, 1991). Psychosocial functioning and six-month service utilisation were again assessed at six-month follow-up. Psychosocial functioning during each six-month period was assessed in the domains of family, social and romantic relationships, work performance, living situation and service utilisation. Patient satisfaction ratings in each of these areas were obtained on a scale from one (extremely dissatisfied) to seven (extremely satisfied). Data concerning episodes of homelessness and arrests were collected via patient interview for each six-month period. Axis I, Axis II and substance misuse diagnoses were established through administration of the Structured Clinical Interview for DSM–III–R (SCID and SCID–II; Spitzer *et al*, 1990) during the treatment episode. Assessment and statistical procedures have been described in detail previously (Fenton *et al*, 1998).

Results

Study population

Between July 1992 and December 1994 a total of 185 individuals who met entry criteria were randomised and 119 (64%) successfully entered the study. To determine whether the 66 unsuccessful admissions differed from the 119 successful admissions, the sub-samples were compared across seven demographic, six treatment history, three diagnostic, four personal history and seven prognostic/illness severity variables based on information coded from their out-patient charts. The subsamples did not differ significantly on any of these 27 variables, suggesting that the study sample adequately represented the total sample of patients referred for in-patient treatment.

The average age of the final treated sample was 37 years (s.d.=10); 62/119 (52%) were male and 38/119 (32%) were non-Caucasian. Most patients were never married (81/119; 68%) and 21/119 (18%) were divorced. The diagnostic distribution of the sample by DSM–III–R criteria was schizophrenia (33/119; 28%), schizoaffective disorder (31/119; 26%), bipolar disorder (25/119; 21%), major affective disorder (25/119; 21%) and other (5/119; 4%). The mean age of illness onset for patients was 16 years (s.d.=9) and mean age at first hospitalisation was 23 years (s.d.=9). Study patients had an average of 13 (s.d.=14) lifetime hospitalisations and a cumulative lifetime average of 43 months (s.d.=70) of prior psychiatric hospitalisation. The large standard deviation of duration of prior hospitalisation reflects the sample inclusion of both younger seriously ill individuals as well as patients who had been institutionalised for a long time, discharged from state hospitals and residing in the community. Core case mix variables rated at admission for the hospital and alternative study patients are shown in Table 8.1. Patient groups randomised to the two treatment settings did not differ at the $P < 0.05$ level on any variables studied.

Clinical process

Clinical process measures obtained in the crisis residential and hospital setting are summarised in Table 8.2. Compared with hospitalised patients, patients in the alternative treatment group were significantly more likely to have seen their out-patient clinician during the treatment episode, were more likely to have visited their residence during the treatment episode and were more likely to have had a trial of their day activity during the treatment episode. On the contrary, hospitalised patients were more likely than alternative patients to have had a medication change during the treatment episode. Thus, in relation to the major hypothesised advantage of each setting (maintenance of continuity with community supports for the alternative; closer medication management for the hospital), clinical process measures in the treatment sites emerged as predicted.

TABLE 8.1
Demographic, diagnostic and treatment history characteristics of hospital (n=50) and alternative (n=69) treated patients at admission

Demographic/prognostic	Hospital		Alternative	
Age, years (s.d.)	37	(10)	38	(11)
Gender (female: *n* (%))	25	(50)	32	(46)
Marital status (married: *n* (%))	5	(10)	1	(1)
Ethnicity				
Caucasian, *n* (%)	37	(74)	44	(64)
Black, *n* (%)	7	(14)	19	(28)
Other, *n* (%)	6	(12)	6	(9)
Parent SES (s.d.)	2.6 (1.5)	*n*=46	2.8 (1.4)	*n*=60
Lifetime aquisition of skills/interests (0, none; 4, significant skills)	2.1	(1.0)	2.0	(1.0)
Diagnostic				
Axis I (*n*, %)				
Schizophrenia/schizoaffective/ other psychoses	30	(60)	36	(52)
Bipolar	9	(18)	16	(23)
Other major affective disorder	9	(18)	15	(22)
Other DSM–III–R	2	(4)	2	(3)
Comorbid drug or alcohol dependence	14	(28)	17	(25)
Comorbid Axis II (among those non-schizophrenia, schizoaffective, bipolar)	9/11	(82)	13/18	(72)
Treatment history				
Age (years) at illness onset (s.d.)	16 (8)	*n*=47	16 (9)	*n*=61
Age (years) at 1st out-patient contact	20 (10)	*n*=47	20 (9)	*n*=63
Age (years) at 1st hospitalisation	23 (9)	*n*=47	23 (9)	*n*=63
Number of prior hospitalisations	12 (12)	*n*=46	14 (16)	*n*=61
Months in lifetime in prior hospitalisations	42 (77)	*n*=48	43 (65)	*n*=69
Ever arrested (*n*, % yes)	20/46	(43)	24/60	(40)

No significant difference (*P*<0.05) between hospital and alternative on any variable

Discharge quality

Measured indices of discharge quality included the patient's discharge destination (residence *v.* shelter or homeless) and planned or actual participation in aftercare activities. As indicated in Table 8.3, discharge quality was roughly comparable for the two treatment settings. Patients treated in the non-hospital alternative were somewhat more likely to have actually begun an aftercare activity during the treatment episode; slightly fewer hospital-treated patients had no planned aftercare activity. Patient's ability at discharge to fully or partially state key elements of their aftercare plan is shown in Table 8.4. Most patients in

166   *Fenton & Mosher*

Table 8.2
Crisis residential and hospital care

	Crisis residential	Hospital	χ^2	P
Saw out-patient clinician	53/58 (92%)	16/47 (34%)	38.1	0.0001
Visited residence	46/58 (79%)	15/47 (25%)	22.0	0.0001
Trial at day activity	23/33 (70%)	8/32 (25%)	11.3	0.0008
Medication change	29/60 (48%)	36/47 (77%)	7.7	0.006

Table 8.3
Dicharge quality: Crisis residential and hospital care

	Crisis residential	Hospital	χ^2	P
Discharge destination				
Residence	51/59 (86%)	40/47 (85%)		
Shelter	5/59 (9%)	4/47 (10%)		
Street	3/59 (5%)	3/47 (6%)	0.08	0.96
Discharge activity				
None	25/59 (49%)	18/47 (38%)		
Planned	5/59 (14%)	16/37 (34%)		
Begun	22/59 (37%)	13/37 (27%)	6.27	0.05

both settings were aware of the time of their aftercare appointment, had met their aftercare physician and had planned transportation. No significant differences across sites emerged.

Clinical effectiveness

Length of stay for the patients treated alternatively (18.7 days, s.d.=13.8) was significantly longer than that for patients who were treated in hospital (11.7 days, s.d.=8.2; t=3.19, d.f.=117, $P<0.002$). Symptom severity at admission and discharge for patients treated in each setting are shown in Table 8.5. Repeated measures analysis of variance using total PANSS score as the dependent variable indicated a statistically significant time effect (F=52.94, d.f.=2/220, $P<0.0001$) but no significant treatment site (F=0.23, d.f.=1/110, P=0.64) or treatment site by time interaction (F=1.18, d.f.=2/220, P=0.31). *Post hoc* t-tests showed that psychopathology for both hospitalised patients and patients treated using the residential alternative decreased significantly from admission to discharge and the decrease in both settings was maintained at six-month follow-up. No hospital–alternative differences were significant at $P<0.05$.

TABLE 8.4
Patient knowledge of aftercare: Crisis residential and hospital care

	Crisis residential			Hospital			χ^2	P
	No	*Partial*	*Yes*	*No*	*Partial*	*Yes*		
Patient knows date/time aftercare	6 (10%)	14 (24%)	38 (66%)	11 (23%)	9 (19%)	27 (57%)	3.30	0.19
Patient knows current medications	2 (3%)	10 (27%)	41 (68%)	6 (13%)	12 (26%)	29 (62%)	3.65	0.16
Patient knows aftercare transportation	5 (9%)	–	53 (91%)	2 (4%)	–	45 (96%)	0.25	0.62
Patient has met aftercare physician	3 (5%)	–	55 (95%)	6 (13%)	–	41 (87%)	1.10	0.30

TABLE 8.5
Admission and discharge psychopathology[1]: crisis residential and hospital care

	Crisis residential		Hospital	
Admission	87	(s.d.=24)	89	(s.d.=25)
Discharge	72	(s.d.=27)	69	(s.d.=16)
Six-month follow-up	73	(s.d.=22)	69	(s.d.=18)

1. Positive and Negative Symptom Scale (see text for ANOVA).

PANSS levels

At admission, psychopathology scores for both patient groups were in the range reported for acutely decompensated in-patients entering pharmacological protocols, and patients in both patient groups showed significant improvement over the course of the treatment episode.

Mean total patient satisfaction with acute episode care did not differ between settings, (hospital:5.1, s.d.=0.93; alternative:5.1, s.d.=0.84; P=0.84). Of 10 areas rated, patient satisfaction differed significantly between settings on only one: patients receiving the alternative treatment were significantly more satisfied with facility-provided food (hospital:4.7, s.d.=1.2; alternative:5.2, s.d.=1.4; P=0.023). Effect sizes for the differences between groups on the other nine rated areas varied from 0.01 to 0.31.

Overall, 108/119 (91%) of patients were stabilised during the treatment episode and returned to the community. Treatment failure rate (transfer to another in-patient facility) was 9/69 (13%) in the alternative and 2/50 (4%) in the hospital (χ^2=1.85, d.f.=1, P=0.17). One-third (3/9) of alternative treatment patients requiring transfer accepted voluntary hospitalisation; the remainder required involuntary commitment. Beyond the police intervention needed for commitment, no serious adverse events occurred among patients receiving alternative treatment requiring transfer to an in-patient unit.

Ninety-five per cent (113/119) of patients were located for follow-up interview. One patient (alternative treatment group) died from suicide between discharge and follow-up. Table 8.6 shows acute care use, psychosocial functioning and patient satisfaction over the six months prior to and following index admission. No main effects or interaction between time of assessment and treatment site were significant at Bonferroni-corrected α levels. Acute care use, psychosocial functioning and satisfaction with one's life and physical health services over the six months following admission, therefore, were comparable for patients treated in the hospital and the alternative.

Preliminary cost estimates

Cost estimates for health services vary depending upon from whose perspective they are viewed. From the perspective of state or national health services, for example, costs may be reduced by limiting services. These same service reductions, however, may increase costs from the perspective of family members who must take time from work to care for ill relatives. Since our study was designed to inform state mental health funding policy, treatment episode costs are analysed from the perspective of state and local government who pay for care rendered to disabled individuals with serious mental illness.

TABLE 8.6

Acute, psychosocial functioning and satisfaction with health services among hospital and alternative treated patients during six months prior to and after treatment episode

	Hospital		Alternative	
	Prior to	Following	Prior to	Following
Utilisation of acute care				
Percentage with non-index acute admissions	46.0% (23/50)	62.5% (30/48)	55.1% (38/69)	58.7% (37/63)
Non-index acute admissions (*n*)	-.22 (50) (s.d.=2.05)	1.77 (48) (s.d.=3.32)	1.19 (69) (s.d.=1.62)	1.30 (63) (s.d.=1.88)
Non-index days in acute care	21.40 (50) (s.d.=38.98)	28.13 (47) (s.d.=45.47)	18.96 (67) (s.d.=31.97)	27.39 (61) (s.d.=46.13)
Psychosocial functioning				
Percentage with any paid work	28.0% (14/50)	16.7% (8/48)	29.0% (20/69)	23.4% (15/64)
Social contacts (0, no meetings with friends; 5, more than 2 meetings with friends per week)	2.89 (45)	2.09 (47)	2.57 (63)	2.52 (60)
Percentage homeless in six months	20.0% (10/50)	18.8% (9/48)	21.7% (15/69)	23.1% (15/65)
Percentage arrested in six months	0/40	0/48	5.8% (3/51)	4.8% (3/63)
Patient satisfaction				
Life satisfaction	4.01 (48)	4.24 (48)	3.94 (63)	4.01 (48)
Satisfaction with mental health services	4.57 (46)	5.13 (48)	5.07 (59)	4.57 (46)
Satisfaction with physical health services	4.97 (35)	5.27 (30)	4.98 (42)	4.90 (40)

Costs reported here are adjusted to reflect dollars in the fiscal year 1993. Hospital bed rates are set using a methodology imposed by the State of Maryland Hospital Cost Review Commission. These rates reflect what the state actually pays for a day of in-patient care. Hospital physician services, medications, laboratory services and ancillary charges are valued based on the state payment schedule to treatment facilities, pharmacies and laboratories.

Bed cost in the crisis residential alternative is based on county contracted *per diem* rate. Since patients treated in the alternative continue to rely on their community providers for care, these costs must also be accounted for. The volume of additional treatment services (physician, case manager, residential counsellor visits; substance misuse treatment, psychiatric rehabilitation programme days; general medical and laboratory assessments; emergency services; and police intervention) used by patients during their treatment episode in the alternative was estimated based on a detailed review of source documents for 14 patients receiving alternative treatment. An average cost per day for these additional county-provided services was estimated based on provider salary, health department budget and service volume data. Medication costs for patients in both settings are based on state reimbursement rates adjusted to 1993 dollars.

Cost estimates

A full cost-effectiveness analysis of the two service models described here is currently being conducted, so only basic cost parameters are reported here. Average hospital *per diem* bed cost in 1993 was US$384.00. Ancillary services including clinical services, pharmacy, laboratory and radiology for a sample of 10 hospitalised patients averaged an additional US$114.78 per day for a total average hospital cost estimate of US$498.78 per day. The crisis residential *per diem* rate was US$123.29. The cost of community services used by a sample of alternative patients during the treatment episode averaged an additional US$38.66 per day for a total cost of US$161.95 per day. A rough estimate of mean treatment episode cost (cost per day×length of stay) was US$5935.48 for hospital-treated patients and US$3044.66 for patients receiving alternative treatment.

Costs were adjusted to reflect the differential treatment failure rate in the two settings based on the assumption that patients failing treatment in the alternative were transferred (3/9) or committed (6/9) to a general hospital and were treated over the average length of stay required for patients treated in a general hospital. Hospital treatment failure cost was estimated based on the assumption that these patients experienced a second course of general hospital treatment. Based on these assumptions, adjusted treatment episode cost was US$6172.90 for hospital and US$3890.37 for alternative treatment patients. Because these estimates are sensitive to the assumptions upon which they are based, however, they must be considered preliminary.

Discussion

Mental illnesses such as schizophrenia, schizoaffective disorder and bipolar disorder are often recurrent, with exacerbations and remissions superimposed on varying degrees of prolonged disability. Care for patients with these severe disorders accounts for the use of nearly half (43%) of mental health resources, with the largest proportion of expenditure allocated to hospital in-patient care (Thompson *et al*, 1995). It is widely recognised that providing needed services to this population within budgetary constraints requires the management of costly in-patient utilisation (Sharfstein *et al*, 1993; Frank *et al*, 1994).

In this study voluntary adult patients with severe and persistent mental illness and a history of multiple prior in-patient care episodes were prospectively assigned at the time of illness exacerbation to an acute psychiatric ward of a general hospital or an acute residential alternative programme. Overall, 87% of patients receiving care in the alternative were successfully treated and returned to the community. This relatively low failure rate is consistent with those reported in other studies of alternatives to psychiatric hospitalisation (Brook *et al*, 1976; Kresky-Wolff *et al*, 1984; Weisman, 1985; Walsh, 1986; Bond *et al*, 1989). Patient acceptance of the alternative acute care setting is reflected in satisfaction ratings and a higher percentage of successful placements in the intention to treat sample. Both episode and six-month clinical outcome measured in the domains of symptom improvement, psychosocial functioning, acute care service utilisation and patient satisfaction were comparable for the hospital and alternative treatment cohorts.

Our preliminary cost estimates suggest that, despite a significantly longer length of stay, treatment episode cost in the alternative averaged US$2890.82, that is, 49% less than the hospital treatment cost. The data indicate that, for most patients studied, the residential alternative model delivered outcomes comparable to hospital care at a substantially reduced cost per treatment episode. When the additional costs incurred by patients who could not be managed and required transfer to a hospital were estimated, the alternative's cost advantage narrowed to $2282.53, representing a 37% saving over hospital costs. Because these estimates are based on charges, however, they must be interpreted with caution (Evers *et al*, 1997; Wolff *et al*, 1997). A detailed analysis of the six-month cost of care for patients treated in the two acute care models studied here is under way. Nonetheless, it is both intuitively obvious and clear from the data that the major determinant of the cost difference between the two models of care is the lower hotel (room and board) cost associated with care in a community home compared with a hospital.

Using comprehensive cost estimation, Sledge *et al* (1996*a,b*) recently described a model of acute care that combined day hospital and residential respite care for voluntary patients that generated outcomes comparable to hospital care at a significantly reduced operating cost. The crisis care model described here differs from that described by Sledge *et al* in our use of an eight-bed rather than a four-bed facility, the use of non-medically trained crisis staff and our reliance on ongoing community treatment resources rather than a day hospital to provide medical care and structure during the crisis episode. For these reasons, we suspect the total programme cost of the McAuliffe crisis residential model to be less than that of the day hospital/respite care model studied by Sledge and colleagues.

Our results must be considered in light of this study's strengths and limitations. This investigation took place in a functioning mental health system where both acute hospital and alternative services were in place prior to the study. The patient sample was restricted to public beneficiaries disabled by clearly documented severe and persistent mental illness characterised by repeated in-patient hospitalisations. For these reasons, findings should be broadly applicable to patient populations in public mental health systems in other jurisdictions.

While the naturalistic setting of this study provides a favourable environment to test the programme model's effectiveness, it also results in limitations. The necessity of obtaining patient consent may introduce a selection bias that cannot be measured and many patients developed a preference for the non-hospital treatment setting. Any biases due to self-selection, however, did not result in significant differences between successfully and unsuccessfully admitted patients on any of 27 demographic and clinical characteristics, and the randomisation procedure produced comparable subject groups for the two treatment sites.

The results reported here are clearly restricted to voluntary psychiatric admissions not requiring detoxification or acute general medical intervention. In the fiscal year 1993, 52/509 (10%) of admissions among DHHS-enrolled patients were involuntary. In addition to involuntary patients and those requiring general medical evaluation and management, a clinical review of crisis residential treatment failures suggests that acutely manic and agitated patients who have not slept in one or more days might best be managed in the hospital setting where aggressive pharmacological intervention can interrupt a cycle of deteriorating agitation, insomnia and disorganisation.

Our findings suggest that crisis residential care can be added to the list of community-based interventions with demonstrated effectiveness (Polak & Kirby, 1976; Fenton *et al*, 1979; Stein & Test, 1980; Kiesler, 1982; Burns & Santos, 1995). In systems where acute in-patient care accounts for a significant proportion of mental health expenditure for patients with serious mental illness, substituting crisis residential care for hospital care for voluntary patients may be among the few remaining methods of generating funds required to increase the availability of new pharmacological and psychosocial treatments. When more readily accessible, these treatment should improve patients' functional outcomes and reduce the need for future acute care.

A fully integrated mental health system requires an optimal balance of acute care, extended care and hospital and community-based treatment services (Rothbard *et al*, 1998). Clearly residential alternatives cannot replace all hospital care (Gudeman & Shore, 1984). In an era characterised by fixed or shrinking resources, however, a re-examination of this balance and the adoption of technologies that can provide comparable outcomes at a lower cost should be a priority (Detsky & Naglie, 1990; Laupacis *et al*, 1992).

Data from this study were successfully used by local health planners and legislators to justify developing a permanent funding stream for crisis residential care as part of the State of Maryland's health care reform initiatives.

Acknowledgements

We thank St Luke's House, Inc. (McAuliffe House), Montgomery General Hospital and the Montgomery County, Maryland Department of Health and Human Services for their assistance.

This study was supported by grant no. SM49102 from the Community Support Program, Center for Mental Health Services, Substance Abuse and Mental Health Services Administration.

References

BOND, G. R., WITHERRIDGE, T. F., WASMER, D., ET AL (1989) A comparison of two crisis housing alternatives to psychiatric hospitalization. *Hospital and Community Psychiatry*, **40**, 177–183.

BOURGEOIS, P. (1995) Crossing Place: a community based model for acute care. In *Alternatives to Hospitalization for Acute Care* (ed. R. Warner), pp. 61–69. Washington, DC: American Psychiatric Association Press.

BROOK, B. D., CORTES, M., MARCH, R., ET AL (1976) Community families: an alternative to psychiatric hospital intensive care. *Hospital and Community Psychiatry*, **27**, 195–197.

BUDSON, R. D. (1994) Community residential and partial hospital care: low-cost alternative systems in the spectrum of care. *Psychiatric Quarterly*, **65**, 209–220

BURNS, B. J. & SANTOS, A. B. (1995) Assertive community treatment: an update of randomized trials. *Psychiatric Services*, **46**, 669–675.

DETSKY, A. S. & NAGLIE, G. (1990) A clinician's guide to cost-effectiveness analysis. *Annals of Internal Medicine*, **113**, 147–154.

DIXON, L. B. & LEHMAN, L. B. (1995) Family interventions for schizophrenia. *Schizophrenia Bulletin*, **21**, 631–644.

EVERS, S. M. A. A. & AMENT, A. J. H. A. (1995) Costs of schizophrenia in The Netherlands. *Schizophrenia Bulletin*, **23**, 141–154.

——, WIJK, A. S. V. & AMENT, A. J. H. A. (1997) Economic evaluation of mental health interventions. A review. *Health Economics*, **6**, 161–177.

FENTON, F. R., TESSIER, L. & STRUENING, E. L. (1979) A comparative trial of home and hospital psychiatric care. One year follow-up. *Archives of General Psychiatry*, **36**, 1073–1079.

FENTON, W. S. & MCGLASHAN, T. H. (1986) Prognostic scale for chronic schizophrenia. *Schizophrenia Bulletin*, **13**, 277–286.

—— & —— (1991) Natural history of schizophrenia subtypes. II: Positive and negative symptoms: long-term course. *Archives of General Psychiatry*, **48**, 978–986.

—— & —— (1997) We can talk: individual psychotherapy for schizophrenia. *American Journal of Psychiatry*, **154**, 1493–1495.

——, MOSHER, L. R., HERRELL, J. M., ET AL (1998) Randomized trial of general hospital and residential alternative care for patients with severe and persistent mental illness. *American Journal of Psychiatry*, **155**, 516–522.

FRANK, R. G., MCGUIRE, T. G., REGIER, D. A., ET AL (1994) Paying for mental health and substance abuse care. *Health Affairs*, **1**, 337–342.

GUDEMAN, J. E. & SHORE, M. F. (1984) Beyond deinstitutionalization: a new class of facilities for the mentally ill. *New England Journal of Medicine*, **311**, 832–836.

HERRELL, J. M., FENTON, W. S., MOSHER, L. R., ET AL (1996) Residential alternatives to hospitalization for patients with severe and persistent mental illness: should patients with comorbid substance abuse be excluded? *Journal of Mental Health Administration*, **23**, 348–355.

HOGARTY, G. E., KORNBLITH, S. J., GREENWALD, D., ET AL (1997a) Three year trials of personal therapy among schizophrenic patients living with or independent of family. I: Description of study and effects on relapse. *American Journal of Psychiatry*, **154**, 1504–1513.

———, GREENWALD, D., ULRICH, R. F., ET AL (1997b) Three year trials of personal therapy among schizophrenic patients living with or independent of family. II: Effects on adjustment of patients. *American Journal of Psychiatry*, **154**, 1514–1524.

KAY, S. R., OPLER, L. A. & FISHBEIN, A. (1992) *Positive and Negative Syndrome Scale (PANSS) Rating Manual*. Toronto: Multihealth Systems Inc.

KIESLER, C. A. (1982) Mental hospitals and alternative care: non-institutionalization as potential public policy for mental patients. *American Psychologist*, **37**, 349–360.

KNAPP, M. (1997) Costs of schizophrenia. *British Journal of Psychiatry*, **171**, 509–518.

KRESKY-WOLFF, M., MATTHEWS, S., KALIBAT, F., ET AL (1984) Crossing Place: a residential model for crisis intervention. *Hospital and Community Psychiatry*, **35**, 72–74.

LAUPACIS, A., FEENY, D., DETSKY, A. S., ET AL (1992) How attractive does a new technology have to be to warrant adoption and utilization? Tentative guidelines for using clinical and economic evaluations. *Canadian Medical Association Journal*, **146**, 473–481.

LEHMAN, A. F. (1988) A quality of life interview for the chronically mentally ill. *Evaluation and Program Planning*, 11, 51–62.

—, THOMPSON, J. W., DIXON, L. B., ET AL (1995) Schizophrenia: treatment outcomes research (Editors' introduction). *Schizophrenia Bulletin*, 21, 561–566.

—, STEINWACHS, D. M., & THE CO-INVESTIGATORS OF THE PORT PROJECT (1998a) At issue: translating research into practice: the schizophrenia patient outcomes research team (PORT) treatment recommendations. *Schizophrenia Bulletin*, 24, 1–10.

—, — & — (1998b) At issue: translating research into practice: patterns of usual care for schizophrenia: initial results from the schizophrenia patient outcomes research team (PORT) client survey. *Schizophrenia Bulletin*, 24, 11–20.

MATTHEWS, S. M., ROPER, M. T., MOSHER, L. R., ET AL (1979) A non-neuroleptic treatment for schizophrenia: analysis of the two-year post-discharge risk of relapse. *Schizophrenia Bulletin*, 5, 322–333.

MOSHER, L. R. (1983) Alternatives to psychiatric hospitalization: why has research failed to be translated into practice? *New England Journal of Medicine*, 309, 1579–1580.

— & MENN, A. Z. (1978) Community residential treatment for schizophrenia: two year follow-up. *Hospital and Community Psychiatry*, 39, 715–723.

—, KRESKY-WOLFF, M., MATTHEWS, S., ET AL (1986) Milieu therapy in the 1980s. A comparison of two residential alternatives to hospitalization. *Bulletin of the Menninger Clinic*, 50, 257–268.

— & BURTI, L. (1994) *Community Mental Health: a Practical Guide*. Washington, DC: Norton.

—, VALLONE, R., & MENN, A. (1995) The treatment of acute psychosis without neuroleptics: six-week psychopathology outcome data from the Soteria project. *International Journal of Social Psychiatry*, 41, 157–173.

POLAK, P. R. & KIRBY, M. W. (1976) A model to replace psychiatric hospitals. *Journal of Nervous and Mental Disease*, 162, 13–22.

RAPPAPORT, M., GOLDMAN, H., THORNTON, P., ET AL (1987) A method for comparing two systems of acute 24-hour psychiatric care. *Hospital and Community Psychiatry*, 38, 1091–1095.

ROTHBARD, A. B., SCHINNAR, A. P., HADLEY, T. P., ET AL (1998) Comparison of state hospital and community-based care for seriously mentally ill adults. *American Journal of Psychiatry*, 155, 523–529.

SCOTT, J. E. & DIXON, L. B. (1995a) Psychological interventions for schizophrenia. *Schizophrenia Bulletin*, 21, 621–630.

— & — (1995b) Assertive community treatment and case management for schizophrenia. *Schizophrenia Bulletin*, 21, 657–668.

SHARFSTEIN, S. S., STOLINE, A. M. & GOLDMAN, H. H. (1993) Psychiatric care and health insurance reform. *American Journal of Psychiatry*, 150, 7–18.

SLEDGE, W. H., TEBES, J., RAKFELDT, J., ET AL (1996a) Day hospital/crisis respite care versus inpatient care, part 1: clinical outcomes. *American Journal of Psychiatry*, 153, 1065–1073.

—, —, Wolff, N., et al (1996b) Day hospital/crisis respite care versus inpatient care, part II: service utilization and costs. *American Journal of Psychiatry*, 153, 1074–1083.

SPITZER, R. L., WILLIAMS, J. B. W., GIBBON, M., ET AL (1990) *Structured Clinical Interview for DSM–III–R (SCID)*. Washington, DC: American Psychiatric Press.

STEIN, L. I. & TEST, M. A. (1980) Alternative to mental hospital treatment. I: Conceptual model, treatment program and clinical evaluation. *Archives of General Psychiatry*, 37, 392–397.

STOLINE, A. M. & SHARFSTEIN, S. S. (1996) Funding the continuum of care: a rational social policy for the care and support of persons with schizophrenia. In *Handbook of Mental Health Economics and Health Policy I, Schizophrenia* (eds M. Moscarelli, A. Rupp, & N. Sartorius), pp. 475–493. New York: John Wiley & Sons.

STROUL, B. A. (1987) *Crisis Residential Services in a Community Support System*. Rockville, MD: National Institute of Mental Health, CSP.

Fenton & Mosher

—— (1988) Residential crisis services: a review. *Hospital and Community Psychiatry*, **39**, 1095–1099.

THOMPSON, J. W., BELCHER, J. R., DEFORGE, B. R., *ET AL* (1995) Trends in the inpatient care of persons with schizophrenia. *Schizophrenia Bulletin*, **21**, 75–85.

WALSH, S. F. (1986) Characteristics of failures in an emergency residential alternative to psychiatric hospitalization. *Social Work and Health Care*, **11**, 53–63.

WEISMAN, G. K. (1985) Crisis-oriented residential treatment as an alternative to hospitalization. *Hospital and Community Psychiatry*, **36**, 1302–1305.

WOLFF, N., HELMINIAK, T. W. & TEBES, J. K. (1997) Getting the cost right in cost-effectiveness analyses. *American Journal of Psychiatry*, **154**, 736–743.

9 Patients with psychosis, psychotherapy and reorganisation of 'the self'. One model of individual therapy: description and pilot study

ROBERTA SIANI and ORAZIO SICILIANI

Three years ago the Psychotherapy Service of Verona University started a two-year outcome study to evaluate the results of psychodynamic psycho-therapy combined with medication in the treatment of schizophrenia. The approach chosen was derived from Kohut's self psychology (Kohut, 1977, 1978, 1984, 1987, 1990, 1991, 1996) with some technical adaptations for the treatment of patients with schizophrenia (Siani, 1992a,b) (the Verona University Research in Self Psychology Psychotherapy). An experimental design was set up with control group patients treated with psychotropic drugs alone (Siani & Siciliani, 1995).

An application of Kohut's psychotherapy centred on the self was chosen as the treatment method both for daily practice in our psychotherapy service and for our controlled outcome study for the following reasons.

(a) Kohut's approach was originally elaborated to treat more difficult cases, for example, patients suffering from severe 'narcissistic disorders' and those who drop out from traditional psycho-analytical approaches (Kohut, 1977, 1996).

(b) Self psychology considers and treats the patient as a subject who models him- or herself on the therapeutic relationship. The approach encourages flexibility and modification of technique in order to turn the patient's resistances into 'driving forces' for the therapeutic processes and goals (Kohut, 1979, 1991). This considerably reduces the risk of drop-out.

(c) In this way, psychotherapy 'centred on the self' can be carried out with patients with psychosis (Siani, 1992*a*; Shapiro, 1995; Lichtenberg *et al*, 1996). Moreover, it is suggested that schizophrenic disorders can be treated by means of a particular form of 'corrective emotional experience' centred on the self (Tolpin, 1983; Kohut, 1984; Siani *et al*, 1996).

Methodological advances in therapeutic technique and outcome evaluation

Narcissistic needs

Early psychoanalytical views considered internal 'drives' as the primary motivational needs of all individuals. External events were seen as triggers, releasing inherent patterns requiring satisfaction. The emphasis was on the internal world. This view has changed and greater emphasis nowadays is placed on the interaction between internal and external events. Kohut's self psychology considers relationships as primary needs of everyone and motivation coming from a search for 'cohesion of the self' through relationships with others. While Kernberg (1974) sometimes seems to consider narcissism as usually pathological, Kohut suggests that it is normal to satisfy some narcissistic needs of the self in a relationship. Significant people act as 'self-objects', that is, narcissistic objects of the self.

> "There is no mature love in which the love-object is not also a self-object ... there is no love relationship without mutual (self-esteem enhancing) mirroring and idealisation." (Kohut, 1977)

A self/self-object relationship is also present in a psychotherapeutic relationship that mobilises some of the patient's early dynamics towards the parental self-object. The way in which the therapist may act as a self-object may take different forms. These have been termed 'mirroring', 'idealising' and 'twinship' self-objects.

Mirroring transferences reflect the grandiose exhibitionistic elements of the self – just as a mother picks out her child from all other children as special, eliciting a 'gleam in the mother's eye', so the patient hopes the therapist will see him or her as special. Failure of mirroring in childhood leads to lack of cohesion in the self.

In idealising transferences the individual experiences the other as perfect, thereby vicariously strengthening his or her defective self-esteem.

In the twinship self-object transferences the individual feels unsure of his or her talents and abilities, and turns to a phantasied alter-ego whose qualities are more grounded and who provides an externalised self-object to whom he or she can resort at times of loneliness and desolation.

Whether the therapist acts as a self-object or a drive-object largely depends on the way the therapist works. He or she will be a self-object when 'accompanying' the patient in an empathic way in the evolution of his or her transference dynamics (Mitchell, 1988). He or she will be a drive-object for the patient when 'interpreting' destructive or other impulses or when defending him- or herself from them by giving interpretations on the defences of the patient (Kohut, 1971, 1990). White & Weiner (1986) give a good example of the different consequences of a therapeutic response that bears in mind the narcissistic needs of the patient, compared with a response that tries to support the patient's ego resources:

Patient: Well, the holiday season is approaching, and I suppose you are going to attend that conference in New York and leave me to my own devices for a week.

Therapist: Yes, I had planned to mention it in today's session, as a matter of fact. But you know, you have been able to weather these separations for a couple of years now, so perhaps it won't be as difficult as you expect this year.

Patient: Oh, sure! Well, my parents always took off for ... right after Christmas leaving me with ... I used to dream that they would ... let me come along or that they would go in the summer with me, instead of shipping me and my brother off to camp. So, when they finally got around to inviting me, it was too late. I had my own friends and commitments by then, and I didn't care any more about being with my own parents.

Therapist (still focusing on the reality of the patient's improved ability to bear what the therapist regarded as separation anxiety): But wasn't it good that you could develop your own friends and interests and not feel left out by your parents anymore?

Patient: And I guess you're saying I should do the same thing now – develop my own support system and not care when you go on vacations. I have to warn you, though, that when that happens, I stop caring about you or needing what you have to give me, and I'm likely to stop coming, whether you think I'm ready to leave or not.

Therapist (sensing that his intervention did not have the soothing effect that he had hoped and wondering if an idealisation issue was involved): I guess you would like me to arrange for you to go with me on this holiday trip, just as you would have liked your parents to have arranged it.

Patient: Well, sure, I think my father could have afforded it at least once. He was a college professor, and it would have been great to go with him and my mother to ... I felt sad that he never thought of what fun it would be for both of us – and my brother too.

Therapist (realising that his empathic approach had brought up a disappointed idealisation issue with important self-feelings attached, but also anxious that he might be stirring up an expectation that he could not fulfill): Well, for us to have experiences like that ... But we can imagine here what it would be like to go to London together.

Patient: Oh! I know it wouldn't be possible. I think I would even feel too self-conscious being with you in a non-therapeutic setting. But I imagine you would be stimulating to walk through London with. I bet you know a lot about English literature.

Therapist (smiling): Well, thank you, that's a nice idea. (Here the therapist lets himself be idealised a bit, undoubtedly some relief that the patient's grasp of reality is enough to keep him from starting to demand in actuality what the therapist suggested having a fantasy about.)

The important outcome of this therapeutic exchange is the emergence of the patient's repeated experiences of being disillusioned about his father's insensitivity to his needs: for example, the de-idealisation of a parent imago and the patient's expectation that the therapist, in leaving him at a holiday time, has the same insensitivity. When the patient experienced the therapist's empathy about his sense of being ignored, it became possible to partly satisfy his need for idealising the therapist as a parent imago through fantasy.

The wise therapist neither gives a single interpretation nor does he or she consider any non-acceptance of his or her interpretation as resistance. He or she is led by the patient, accepting the object functions that the patient gives him at that moment. By working in this way, the patient comes to a self-object relationship. By accepting the functions that the therapist is allocated, the patient's self-esteem is restored and once the latter is more solid then the affects connected with separation may be more tolerable without damaging self-esteem. In psychotic states we consider it necessary to restore the patient's self-esteem, which has been fragmented by the psychotic process.

Pre-eminence of the relationship

We use Kohut's self psychology in the treatment of psychotic disorders because the model of the self is interpersonal. It gives effective guidelines on how to establish a therapeutic relationship with such patients positing a central role for empathy as a therapeutic factor (Ornstein, 1979, 1990;

Kohut, 1982, 1987, 1991). Particular importance is paid to the role of aggression, which is not assumed to be primary, as it might be in more classical theory, that is, an inherent drive. In the Kohutian relational model, a patient's aggressive attack is seen differently and is reacted to differently. For example, when a patient shows aggression in the course of a psychotherapy session, with no external events to the setting that could have frustrated him, the relational model does not make reference to the patient's basic drives. However, it makes the therapist think about what he or she might have said or done to have frustrated the patient's narcissistic needs, provoking reactive rage ('narcissistic rage'). When the patient brings rage to a session caused by external frustration, it is necessary to understand what happened earlier outside the setting that could have hurt the patient and his or her fragile self-esteem. For example, critical or ironic behaviour by the family or similar behaviour within the health service or psychiatric staff may all cause frustration. Therapy relates these external events to what happens in the therapeutic setting to ensure a close 'fit' between the patient's experience and the therapist's understanding. However, even if the rage seems reactive to an external event and the patient extends it to the figure of the therapist, it is necessary to try to understand why he or she is doing so. It is possible to surmise whether the patient considers the therapist an 'accomplice' of people outside the therapeutic situation, or if the external frustration has activated the recollection of previous occasions in which the therapist was a frustrating factor or not very empathic. These examples indicate that it is important first to deal with countertransference and that, before understanding what goes on in the patient's mind, it is important to pay attention to and then try to clarify and understand what is going through the therapist's mind. This takes us to the second main focus in the techniques based on self psychology – empathy.

Therapeutic factor of 'empathy'

Empathy is 'putting oneself in the patient's shoes' or "the ability to experience what another person experiences, though usually, and appropriately, to an attenuated degree" (Kohut, 1984). It is a central therapeutic factor in self-psychological approaches to psychosis and it brings a broad range of consequences.

First of all, empathy enables patients to feel understood when they have difficulty in verbalising their own feelings and emotions or veil their own discomforts with elusive reasoning (as in people with psychosis). Empathy is also "vicarious introspection" (Kohut, 1971). This is a hypothetical way of seeing the patient's inner world that the therapist keeps to him- or herself until confirmation or denial is found in the words or in the evolution of the patient's transference.

Second, empathy helps to understand the 'self-object function' that the patient ascribes to the therapist. Often with people with psychosis this is an idealised 'archaic omnipotent self-object' function, a direct or unrealistic extension of a fragmented 'grandiose self' (Siani, 1992*a,b*).

Third, empathy is the starting point of the next phase of the therapeutic process and of the corrective emotional experience. The therapist, after accepting the function of self-object, which the patient gives him from time to time, can cautiously change these functions by introducing two other important therapeutic factors.

Optimal frustrations

These are bearable when they are non-traumatic, because they are accompanied by the empathy of an authentic acceptance that the patient is doing his or her best.

Reality confrontations

These are confrontations that the patient him- or herself can, when ready, install between his or her usual way of seeing him- or herself and the way in which others see him or her from time to time. Here the role of the 'empathic mirror' of the therapist becomes fundamental. The way the therapist shows acceptance of the patient's transferences and the way in which he or she shows his negative reactions are pivotal. For example, if the therapist is annoyed or irritated by a request, attitude or an accusation by the patient, in some way the therapist might reveal his or her state of mind at certain points. Adequate empathic behaviour is not equivalent to a stereotypical acceptance or to a benevolent indifference, but rather to a live and 'decipherable' behaviour that allows the patient to become aware of the effects that he or she unconsciously produces in others.

Finally, in particular cases, the 'empathic understanding' technique enables the therapist to deal individually with the patient with psychosis and even with one of the parents (Siani, 1996). The therapist's immersion in countertransference towards a patient's mother appeared more reliable in the work with the daughter than anything else. It gives the therapist empathic understanding, through 'vicarious introspection', of the patient's experience towards the maternal figure that the patient had difficulty in expressing.

From 'explanation' to 'use' of the self-object functions

The issue is still debated as to whether Kohut felt that an interpretation phase was necessary after the work of the empathic understanding phase (Goldberg, 1978, 1983, 1988, 1992; Mitchell, 1988; Lichtenberg, 1989; Ornstein, 1990, 1995; Shane & Shane, 1996; Stolorow & Atwood, 1996). This is because change in the self psychology model is not necessarily tied to the verbalisation of insight but more to the consolidation of a corrective emotional experience.

The use of interpretation must be considered in the different therapeutic circumstances between narcissistic personality disorders, borderline disorders and psychotic and schizophrenic disorders (Siani *et al*, 1996).

Narcissistic defences

In all these disorders the transference dynamics and narcissistic resistances are not interpreted initially as 'defences', but first supported (during the empathic understanding phase) and only later interpreted in relation to the dynamics of the transference and countertransference: for example, the fear of becoming too dependent on a therapist who still does not appear trustworthy enough, metaphorically as in:

"the fear of finding oneself abandoned by the therapist in the middle of the stream" (Kohut, 1977).

This approach is similar to many psychoanalytical approaches, particularly those that place an emphasis on developing a therapeutic alliance with the patient throughout treatment (Sandler & Freud, 1985; Lachmann & Bebee, 1992).

Reconstruction

Contemporary anxieties may be interpreted in the classical analytical technique in terms of the patient's real or fantasied earlier relationships. In self psychology with narcissistic and borderline personalities there is some prompting of meaningful 'memories' of childhood experiences with parental figures that allow the patient to see some connection with present transference dynamics (Kohut, 1984).

However, with patients with psychosis this two- or three-dimensional view is often not possible to achieve for a long time by the very nature of the disorders of thinking and reflecting. The therapist's activity is focused on the empathic understanding of the self-object functioning required of him or her and the need of the patient to 'borrow' the therapist's personality in the course of corrective emotional experiences (Pao, 1983; Siani, 1992*a*).

Functional rehabilitation of the self and the corrective emotional experience

It is important to remember the distinction between 'defences' and 'compensations' presented in Kohut's (1977) self psychology. Defences such as delusions in psychotic states are considered as operations used by the patient to hide or to cover both a 'defect in the cohesion of the self' and a tendency to split and to disintegrate in the face of unbearable anxiety. Compensations, for example, the 'ambitendency' between searching for help and avoiding relationships (Pao, 1979; Feinsilver, 1986), are considered as operations that, as well as reflecting the split-self, allow adaptation by using tolerable existential states of mind even if this severely limits interpersonal relationships (Siani, 1992*b*).

Psychotherapeutic work is used to induce a passage from delusional projection to a cautious awareness of interpersonal and social relations. Defences are challenged within the safety of the self-object relationship and compensations carefully defined and worked on. This is an example of 'functional rehabilitation for the self', which may be complemented by psychosocial rehabilitation. However, the latter could also induce a crisis if compensations have not been fully worked through because the patient can suddenly retreat into regression and feel invaded by others (Siani, 1996).

Psychoanalysts have been discussing for a long time whether the 'true' therapeutic factor with people with psychosis is through the therapist's 'understanding' or through the patient's 'attachment' to the therapist (Gitelson, 1962; Winnicott, 1971; Rosenfeld, 1987). According to Kohut it can be said that both comprehension and attachment are needed since both are required for the development of mental 'structures'. In the end in many cases, the patient is able to recover some independence through identification with the therapeutic functions of the therapist and then, through internalisations, by absorbing it after having modified it according to his or her emotional needs (see Siani *et al*, 1996). This has been named the 'transmuting internalisation of the self-object' (Kohut & Wolf, 1978; Kohut, 1990, 1991).

This corrective emotional experience is possible with patients with psychosis (Tolpin, 1983) as long as the therapist uses his or her 'self-object' functions in a certain way, and is able to count on the help of staff who can take charge of the problems that a person with psychosis continues to pose outside the individual therapy setting. Such an integrated strategic approach enables therapy to procede safely (Siani *et al*, 1990).

Guidelines to the Verona technique 'centred on the self'

Guidelines to our approach to psychotic patients are summarised below (Siani, 1992*b*). According to Kohut (1984), three major constituents of the self have serious defects in psychotic disorders (i.e. the pole of ideals, the pole of ambitions and the intermediate area of skills). This psychopathology can be illustrated by a diagram that points out the double vertical split between the 'reality ego' sector (A), psychotic 'defensive structures' (C) and 'compensatory structures' of the self (D). Referring to our diagram (Fig. 9.1), the therapeutic process works in different ways at different times on the various sectors of the self.

A working alliance is established at the 'reality ego' sector level (Sector 1a) through a simple form of empathy developed through adequate understanding and acceptance of the patient's defensive inhibitions.

The therapist abstains from all interpretation of repressed aspects of early self-object relationships (Sector 1b) that cannot be revived in the psychotic transference. It is our practice to replace the traditional interpretation phase by empathic responses, appropriately differentiated and then deepened.

The therapist puts him- or herself in resonance[1] with the symptomatic defences of the patient with psychosis (in the second sector). Through this, he or she understands the defensive significance of the patient's delusional world and accepts the delusions, using the assigned functions of mirroring or twinship archaic self-object. This enables the therapist to turn the defences of the patient to his or her best advantage.

Finally, the therapist tries to strengthen and expand the patient's compensatory structures; to this purpose he or she can accept some transference merging using a 'higher form of empathy' (Kohut, 1982) in order to respond to the patient's narcissistic needs, which are archaic but not pathological *per se* (in the third sector).

---

1. To put oneself in resonance with a delusion is not the same as saying that the therapist shares the patient's ideas, but that he or she shares the basic anxieties that are standing below the delusion. Kohut (1978) stated that it makes little difference what the analyst does so long as he or she understands what is going on in the patient. At times it is possible to help the patient find a connection between present and past experiences, but more often one has simply to make the patient experience that "the sustaining echo of empathic resonance is indeed available in this world" (Kohut, 1984).

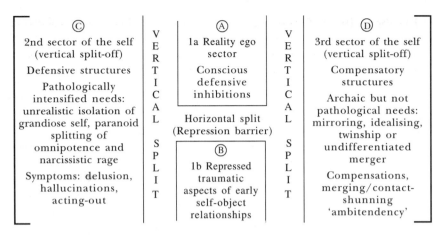

Fig. 9.1 Diagram of schizophrenic psychopathology informed by
self psychology (adapted from Siani, 1992a,b).

Methodology of evaluation: *the Karolinska Psychodynamic Profile*

The most difficult methodological problem was the choice of psycho-metric instrument for the assessments. The rating scales and structured interviews of clinical status that are used in controlled studies on symptomatic and clinical effectiveness, such as those of the National Institute of Mental Health study of brief psychotherapy for depression (Elkin *et al*, 1989), are not suitable for dealing with medium- to long-term analytical psychotherapy. Kernberg & Clarkin (1992) wrote,

> "for years the evaluation of a presumed structural and character change in psychodynamic psychotherapies has been obstructed by a lack of instruments to assess these changes."

In psychoanalysis, outcome studies have changed since 1980 to include those examining the therapeutic 'process'. Luborsky's studies on the 'core conflictual relationship theme' (CCRT) have given interesting results (Luborsky *et al*, 1988, 1990). But 'process research' does not easily permit studies with control cases.

A new psychometric instrument, the Karolinska Psychodynamic Profile (KAPP) (Weinryb & Rössel, 1991), validated by Weinryb *et al* (1991a,b, 1992) enables intermittent longitudinal evaluation to assess possible changes over time of the psychodynamic organisation of the personality, using Kernberg's structured interview procedure,

(Kernberg, 1984). This procedure can also be applied to control group subjects who are not in psychotherapy. The KAPP, therefore, enables long-term and controlled outcome studies on the psychostructural effects of the psychodynamic psychotherapies.

The validity of the Italian version of the KAPP (Weinryb & Rössel, 1993) was assessed in two of our studies (Siani & Siciliani, 1995; Turrina *et al*, 1996). This version has shown very good values for both inter-rater and test–re-test reliability (the mean agreement coefficient, ρ, ranged from 0.75 to 0.96). It can also discriminate between three main profiles of personality organisation (see Fig. 9.2) – neurotic, borderline and psychotic – in agreement with the psychostructural dimensions of Kernberg & Clarkin (1992) (see also Weinryb *et al*, 1997).

Patients with both anxiety disorders and dysthymic or mild to moderate depressive disorders share the neurotic profile. Patients with schizophrenia or with bipolar and major depressive disorders share the psychotic profile. The borderline profile is shared by patients with specific personality disorders (ICD–10; World Health Organization, 1992) and, in particular, those that DSM–IV (American Psychiatric Association, 1994) coded as borderline and narcissistic personality disorders. The borderline profile is intermediate between psychotic and neurotic profiles, but it is even more severe than psychosis in the subscale of 'body self'.

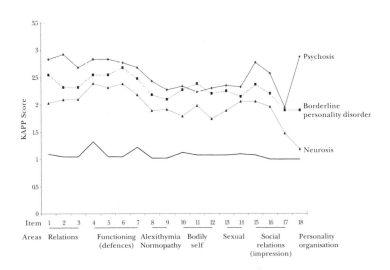

Fig. 9.2 The main KAPP psychostructural profiles: for psychotic, borderline and neurotic personality organisations (adapted from Siani & Siciliani, 1995).

Case–control experimental design

The experimental design involved 50 out-patients consecutively taken into treatment in 1994 at the Community Psychiatric Service of Verona University. Every third case was enrolled into the control group. This control group resulted in 16 patients being treated with psychotropic drugs alone while the other 34 were enrolled into the psychotherapy intervention group.

All the patients in the psychotherapy group were treated by means of individual psychotherapy centred on the self. It was carried out by one therapist (R.S.), with a median frequency of 118 sessions per patient over two years. Psychotherapy ended around then in one-third of the cases because the improvement was sufficient to satisfy both patient and therapist, but continued in the other two-thirds. In the psychotropic drug control group the median was of 10 consultations per patient in two years. The randomised assignment to the treatment

TABLE 9.1
Psychotherapy group and control group: socio-demographic characteristics and diagnostic composition

	Psychotherapy group[1]	Control group[2]
Age, years (s.d.)	32 (11)	34 (12)
Gender	Female (65%)	Female (62%)
Sociocultural status	Middle class	Middle class
Diagnostic composition (psychostructural and ICD–10)		
ICD–10 codes		
Schizophrenic disorders	n=8	n=3
Schizoaffective disorder	n=1	n=1
Major depressive disorders	n=1	n=1
Structural		
Psychosis	n=10 (29.5%)	n=5 (31.0%)
ICD–10 codes		
Borderline personality disorder	n=6	n=3
Narcissistic personality disorder	n=4	n=2
Structural		
Borderline	n=10 (29.5%)	n=5 (31.0%)
ICD–10		
Anxiety disorders	n=8	n=3
Dysthymic disorder	n=3	n=1
Mild/moderate depressive disorder	n=3	n=2
Structural		
Neuroses	n=14 (41%)	n=6 (38%)

1. Psychotherapy alone or plus medication.
2. Psychotropic drugs alone.

groups resulted in two groups similar in gender (2/3 women), average age (32–34 years), sociocultural level (middle class) and distribution of diagnostic groups, according to the ICD–10 (see Table 9.1).

At the psychotherapy unit in our service patients were admitted in the post-acute phase, so for 18 cases it was possible to avoid using psychotropic drugs (psychotherapy alone subgroup). For the other 16, psychotherapy was combined with the use of psychotropic drugs, which were prescribed for clinical reasons to 90% of patients with psychosis and to 30% of both patients with neurotic and borderline disorders (psychotherapy plus drugs subgroup). Of the 34 cases in psychotherapy, 10 had a psychotic disorder, 10 a borderline disorder and 14 a neurotic disorder.

All 50 patients were assessed three times by means of the KAPP: at the beginning ('baseline score'), after two months and after two years of treatment (single-blind assessment by two different raters).

Results

The analysis of variance for repeated measures (see Table 9.2) was carried out on the total KAPP score, as a global index of personality organisation. This showed highly significant differences ($P<0.0001$) both over time and in the interaction between treatments and times. There was minimum improvement at two months, while after two years the patients in psychotherapy showed an improvement of 30% (compared with baseline KAPP score). The improvement among the control patients treated with psychotropic drugs alone was only 2%, even if they responded well both symptomatologically and clinically (two-year relapse rate: 6% for both treatments).

The Sheffé test analysis of variance did not reveal any significant difference in terms of KAPP total score improvement between the two subgroups in psychotherapeutic treatment, that is, psychotherapy alone and psychotherapy plus drugs. The improvement has been calculated as percentage ratio between final reduction in score and starting score ([baseline score minus two-year score/baseline score]×100).

As regards diagnostic categories (see Table 9.3), the analysis of variance showed significant differences between times but not in the interaction between times and diagnostic subgroups. After two years patients with psychosis receiving psychotherapy showed an improvement of 26% (compared with baseline KAPP total score); patients with personality disorders and patients with neurotic disorders showed improvements of 31% and 32.6%, respectively: the difference between those with psychosis and those without psychosis was non-significant ($F=2.43$, $P=0.10$).

TABLE 9.2
Results in the treatment groups over time: Kapp total score at baseline, two months and two years

Groups of treatment	KAPP total score			Improvement (A−C/A)×100	
	A Baseline Mean (s.d.)	*B 2 months Mean (s.d.)*	*C 2 years Mean (s.d.)*	*Mean (s.d.)*	*F* / *P*
Psychotherapy alone (*n*=18)	37.1 (5.2)	36.5 (4.9)	25.4 (3.7)	30.85 (8.4)[1]	Time F=91.51 P<0.0001
Psychotherapy plus psychotropic medication (*n*=16)	44.7 (5.4)	44.1 (5.9)	31.6 (5.3)	29.45 (7.3)[1]	F=332.8 P<0.0001
Psychotropic medication alone (*n*=16)	39.6 (5.2)	38.8 (6.4)	38.8 (5.8)	2.09 (3.7)[1]	Treatment xtime
Analysis of variance for repeated measures					F=74.21 P<0.0001
Total (*n*=50)	40.3 (6.1)	39.7 (6.5)	31.7 (7.4)	21.21 (14.9)	

1. Sheffé test (into analysis of variance): NS, psychotherapy alone *v.* psychotherapy plus psychotropic medication; $P<0.05$, psychotherapy alone *v.* psychotropic medication alone; $P<0.05$, psychotherapy plus psychotropic medication *v.* psychotropic medication alone.

TABLE 9.3

Psychotherapy group results for diagnostic subgroups over time. KAPP total score at baseline, two months and two years

Diagnostic subgroups	KAPP total score					Improvement $(A-C/A)\times 100$	
	A Baseline Mean (s.d.)	B 2 months Mean (s.d.)	C 2 years Mean (s.d.)	F P		F P	Mean (s.d.)
Psychotic disorders (*n*=10)	45.9 (5.7)	45.4 (6.8)	34.0 (4.2)	Time		25.95 (4.9)[1]	F=2.43
Personality disorders (*n*=10)	42.3 (5.4)	41.7 (4.3)	29.0 (3.3)	F=365.0 P<0.0001		31.12 (5.2)[1]	P<0.1
Neurotic disorders (*n*=14)	35.7 (3.7)	35.0 (3.6)	23.8 (2.9)	Diagnosis ×time		32.61 (9.9)[1]	
Analysis of variance for repeated measures				F=0.52 NS			
Total (*n*=34)	40.6 (6.5)	40.1 (6.6)	28.3 (5.4)			30.20 (7.8)	

1. Sheffé test (into analysis of variance): NS, in each comparison between the diagnostic subgroups.

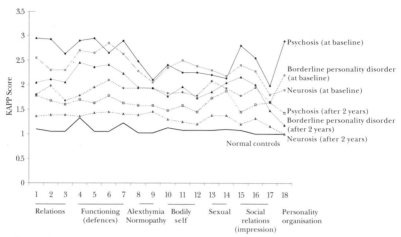

Fig. 9.3 Outcome in the psychotherapy group showing change from KAPP baseline profiles to those of two years later. Median test compares the KAPP median scores of borderline v. the medians of psychotic and neurotic profiles, before and after psychotherapy

Nevertheless, a non-parametric analysis performed on the single KAPP items and subscales (KAPP 'areas') showed that psychotherapy affects different areas of personality organisation, depending on the diagnostic categories. Figure 9.3 shows the 18-item profile of the KAPP of the 34 patients in psychotherapy, in baseline and final profiles for each of the three psychostructural diagnostic subgroups: psychosis ($n=10$), borderline personality disorder ($n=10$) and neurotic disorder ($n=14$ cases). After two years of treatment, in all three diagnostic subgroups the KAPP final profiles are lower (therefore less pathological) than the initial ones, but with different area profiles and with median values that differ significantly ($P<0.001$, median test). Of course, the final profile reached by patients with neurotic disorders is the closest to the normal subject profile (see Siani & Siciliani, 1995). However, by analysing the scores item by item, the patients with borderline personality disorders attain a significant decrease in the greatest number of items (14/18), followed by patients with neurotic disorders (11/18) and patients with psychosis (8/18) (Wilcoxon test for paired differences).

The patients with psychosis (see Fig. 9.4) show a significant improvement in the following items of the KAPP:

(1) intimacy and reciprocity in relationships;
(2) dependency;
(3) controlling traits in the area of object-relations;
(4) frustration tolerance and coping;

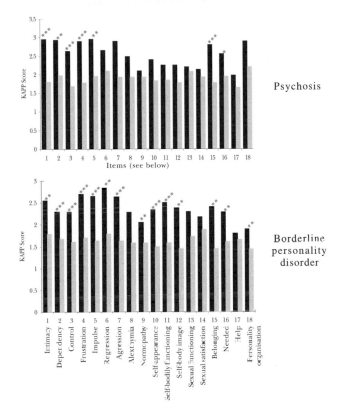

Fig. 9.4 Changes in each KAPP item after two years of psychotherapy in the subgroups of psychosis and borderline personality disorders (below). Wilcoxon test for paired differences compares baseline with two-year item scores: *P<0.05, **P<0.02, ***P<0.01, Wilcoxon test for paired differences (two-tailed); ■, baseline score; ▨, psychotherapy.

(5) impulse control;
(7) coping with aggressiveness (in the area of defences);
(15) sense of belonging;
(16) feeling of being needed (by someone) (in the area of social relations).

Items 6 and 11 also improved in the neurosis group: that is, regression in the service of the ego, and bodily functioning linked to self-esteem. Patients with borderline personality disorder improved even in the comprehensive personality organisation (Item 18) and in all three items of the bodily self and self-esteem, namely: Item 10, bodily appearance; Item 11, bodily functioning; Item 12, current body image (see Table 9.4).

TABLE 9.4

Psychotherapy group two-year outcome among diagnostic subgroups: median values of improvement[1] in each of the KAPP

Diagnostic subgroups	Area 1 Relationships	Area 2 Functioning (defences)	Area 3 Alexthymia Normopathy	Area 4 Bodily self	Area 5 Sexuality	Area 6 Social relationships (perception)
Psychosis (*n*=10)	**35.5**	32.3	13.4	20.0	7.4	27.2
Narcissistic/borderline personality disorders (*n*=10)	27.0	38.0	**29.3**	**36.8**	16.3	24.0
Neuroses (*n*=14)	33.3	**40.2**	19.9	30.0	**23.7**	31.2
Personality disorder *v.* psychosis	P<0.05	P<0.05	NS	P<0.05	P<0.05	NS
Personality disorder *v.* neuroses	NS	NS	NS	NS	NS	NS

1. Area improvement=(area baseline score−final area score/area baseline score)×100. The greatest area improvement value is emphasised in bold. Median test compares personality disorder with psychosis and neurosis subgroups.

To sum up, Table 9.4 compares the median values of improvement for pathologies regarding the six area-subscales of the KAPP.

Among the patients with psychosis there is a greater improvement of 35.5% in Area 1 – interpersonal relationships ($P<0.05$, median test). The best result with respect to defences and coping (improvement of 40% in Area 2) is in the group with neurotic disorders (which improved significantly also in Area 5 – sexuality). Body self linked to self-esteem improved most in the patients with borderline personality disorders (an improvement of 37% in Area 4).

Discussion

These results must be interpreted with maximum caution, for at least three sets of reasons:

(a) the limited number of 'cases' and therefore of diagnostic subgroups for comparison;

(b) the experimental design introduced a selective bias in that it only enrolled out-patients of the community psychiatric service and not the more severe or acute in-patients admitted to the psychiatric ward. It also ruled out more severe psychopatho-logical conditions associated with alcohol or drug addiction and organic-psychogeriatric pathology (which are dealt with by other public health services);

(c) the methodological innovations, such as psychotherapy 'centred on the self' and the KAPP (Wilczek *et al*, 1998; Svanborg *et al*, 1999) do not allow direct comparison with the results of studies carried out with more traditional methods.

With these limitations, we can discuss the more obvious points of the results. First of all, the study, not surprisingly, supports the expectation that psychotropic drugs alone would not modify the stable traits of personality evaluated by KAPP. On the other hand, the use of these drugs has made it possible to carry out psychotherapy especially with the more clinically disturbed cases. Second, the different responsiveness to psychotherapy of patients with borderline and psychotic disorders, in favour of those with borderline disorders, is in agreement with current literature (Kernberg *et al*, 1972, 1989; Waldinger & Gunderson, 1987).

The most meaningful result is the lack of significant differences in the comparison between patients with borderline and neurotic disorders in each of the KAPP 'areas' and in the total score. Patients with borderline disorders, compared with patients with neurotic disorders, obtained improvement in a larger number of 'single variables' of personality; in particular in the items of body self-image in relation to self-esteem and comprehensive personality organisation.

This finding suggests that borderline patients, even if the starting level of the KAPP profile is more severe than neurotics, after two years of psychotherapy 'centred on the self', reach improvements that do not differ significantly from those of patients with neurotic disorders (with peak results in the area of the self and self-esteem), according to the theory, technique, and clinical observations of self psychology (Goldberg, 1978; 1983; 1988; 1992; White & Weiner, 1986; Wolf, 1988; Monsen *et al*,1995).

The great improvement of patients with psychosis in this study in the area of interpersonal relationships seems to be unusual compared with other literature (see Gunderson *et al*, 1984; Weber *et al*, 1985; McGlashan & Keats, 1989). We should take into account that the marked improvement of patients with psychosis that we observed in the area of interpersonal relationships should emphasise especially the severity of the starting point (archaic and fragmented object-relations), rather than the quality of the level achieved which has not gone beyond that of narcissistic self-object relationships.

This fact (together with the significant results obtained with patients with psychosis in defensive coping and in subjective perception of social relations and the poor results on alexithymic traits and on regression in the service of the ego) seems congruent with the technical specificity of psychotherapy 'centred on the self'. As we have underlined in the methodology, this approach prioritises therapeutic work on object-relations and the development of compensatory defences and self esteem in social relations, rather than promoting a verbalisation of insight.

The results obtained by patients with psychosis seem to support our choice in adapting self psychology technique to treat these patients, where psychotherapy 'centred on the self' seems a valid alternative to the 'expressive–supportive' approach, bearing in mind the results obtained by Gunderson *et al* (1984). However, it is not possible to compare the outcome of the two approaches due to the methodology of the two evaluations. This was rather brief in Gunderson's study, although detailed with regard to 'process' rather than 'outcome' as in Luborsky & Crits-Christoph (1990).

In conclusion, our data underline two fundamental guidelines of self psychology: (a) to strengthen the 'working alliance' through empathic understanding; and (b) to avoid all 'narcissistic injury' to the patient through management of the countertransference and allowing a major function of the therapist to be an empathic mirror.

Acknowledgements

We wish to thank Cesare Turrina of the University of Brescia and Sabrina Fossella of the University of Verona for their contribution in the outcome assessment as the external blind raters of the KAPP administration. The Verona University Research on Self Psychology Psychotherapy study was financed by the Ministero dell'Università e della Ricerca Scientifica e Tecnologica (funds 60%, MURST, 1996–1997).

References

AMERICAN PSYCHIATRIC ASSOCIATION (1994) *Diagnostic and Statistical Manual of Mental Disorders* (4th edn)(DSM–IV). Washington, DC: APA.

ELKIN, I., PARLOFF, M. B. & HADLEY, S. W. (1989) NIMH treatment of depression collaborative research program: general effectiveness of treatment. *Archives of General Psychiatry*, **46**, 971–982.

FEINSILVER, D. B (1986) *Towards a Comprehensive Model For Schizophrenic Disorders.* Hillsdale, NJ: Analytic Press.

GITELSON, M. (1962) The curative factors in psychoanalysis: the first phase of psychoanalysis. *International Journal of Psychoanalysis*, **43**, 194–205.

GOLDBERG, A. (1978) *The Psychology of the Self: a Case Book.* New York: International University Press.

—— (1983) *The Future of Psychoanalysis.* New York: International University Press.

—— (1988) *Progress in Self Psychology*, Vol.4. Hillsdale,NJ: Analytic Press.

—— (1992) *Progress in Self Psychology*, Vol.8. Hillsdale, NJ: Analytic Press.

GUNDERSON, J. G., FRANK, A. F., KATZ, H. M., ET AL (1984) Effects of psychotherapy in schizophrenia. II. comparative outcome of two forms of treatment. *Schizophrenia Bulletin*, **10**, 564–598.

KERNBERG, O. F. (1974) Contrasting viewpoints regarding the nature and psychoanalytic treatment of narcissistic personalities. *Journal of the American Psychoanalytical Association*, **22**, 215–240.

—— (1984) *Severe Personality Disorders.* New Haven, CT: Yale University Press.

——, BURNSTEIN, E., COYNE, L., ET AL (1972) Psychotherapy and psychoanalysis: final report of the Menninger Foundation's Psychotherapy Research Project. *Bulletin of the Menninger Clinic*, **36**, 1–275.

——, SELZER, M., KOENIGSBERG, H., ET AL (1989) *Psychodynamic Psychotherapy of Borderline Patients.* New York: Basic Books.

—— & CLARKIN, J. F. (1992) Treatment of personality disorders. *International Journal of Mental Health*, **21**, 53–76.

KOHUT, H. (1971) *The Analysis of the Self.* London: Hogarth.

—— (1977) *The Restoration of the Self.* New York: International University Press.

—— (1978) *The Search for the Self – Vols. 1 & 2* (ed. P. Ornstein). New York: International University Press.

—— (1979) The two analyses of Mr. Z. *International Journal of Psychoanalysis*, **60**, 3–27.

—— (1982) Introspection, empathy and the semicircle of mental health. *International Journal of Psychoanalysis*, **63**, 395–414.

—— (1984) *How Does Analysis Cure?* Chicago: University of Chicago Press.

—— (1987) *Seminars* (ed. M. Elson). New York: Norton.

—— (1990) *The Search for the Self – Vol. 3* (ed. P. H. Ornstein). New York: International University Press.

—— (1991) *The Search for the Self – Vol. 4* (ed P. H. Ornstein). New York: International University Press.

—— (1996) *The Chicago Institute Lectures* (eds P. & M. Tolpin). Hillsdale, NJ: Analytic Press.

—— & WOLF, E. S. (1978) The disorders of the self and their treatment: an outline. *International Journal of Psychoanalysis*, **59**, 413–425.

LACHMANN, F. & BEBEE, B. (1992) Representational and self-object transferences: a developmental perspective. In *Progress in Self Psychology, Vol.8* (ed A. Goldberg), pp. 3–15. Hillsdale, NJ: Analytic Press.

LICHTENBERG, J. D. (1989) *Psychoanalysis and Motivation*. Hillsdale, NJ: Analytic Press.

——, LACHMANN, F. & FOSSHAGE, J. L. (1996) *The Clinical Exchange: Techniques Derived from Self and Motivational Systems*. Hillsdale, NJ: Analytic Press.

LUBORSKY, L., CRITS-CHRISTOPH, P. & MINTZ, J., ET AL (1988) *Who Will Benefit from Psychotherapy? Predicting Therapeutic Outcomes*. New York: Basic Books.

—— & —— (1990) *Understanding Transference: the CCRT Method*. New York: Basic Books.

MCGLASHAN, T. H. & KEATS, C. J. (1989) *Schizophrenia: Treatment Process and Outcome*. New York: International University Press.

MITCHELL, S. A. (1988) *Relational Concepts in Psychoanalysis: an Integration*. Cambridge, MA: Harvard University Press.

MONSEN, J., ODLAND, T., FAUGLI, A., ET AL (1995) Personality disorders and psychosocial changes after intensive psychotherapy: a prospective follow-up study of an outpatient psychotherapy project, 5 years after and of treatment. *Scandinavian Journal of Psychology*, **36**, 256–268.

ORNSTEIN, P. H. (1979) Remarks on the central position of empathy in psychoanalysis. *Bulletin of the Association of Psychoanalytical Medicine*, **18**, 95–108.

—— (1990) Introduction: the unfolding and completion of Heinz Kohut's paradigm of psychoanalysis. In *H.Kohut. The Search for the Self – Vol. 3* (ed P. H. Ornstein), pp. 1–82. New York: International University Press.

—— (1995) Critical reflections on a comparative analysis of 'Self Psychology and intersubjectivity theory'. In *Progress in Self Psychology, Vol. 11* (ed A. Goldberg), pp. 11–58. Hillsdale, NJ: Analytic Press.

PAO, P. N. (1979) *Schizophrenic Disorders: Theory and Treatment from a Psychodynamic Point of View*. New York: International University Press.

—— (1983) Therapeutic empathy and the treatment of schizophrenia. *Psychoanalytical Inquiry*, **3**, 145–167.

ROSENFELD, H. (1987) *Impasse and Interpretation*. London: Tavistock.

SANDLER, J. & FREUD, A. (1985) *The Analysis of Defense*. New York: International University Press.

SHANE, M. & SHANE, E. (1996) Self psychology in search of optimal. In *Progress in Self Psychology, Vol. 12* (ed A. Goldberg), pp. 37–54. Hillsdale, NJ: Analytic Press.

SHAPIRO, S. (1995) *Talking with Patients: A Self Psychological View of Creative Intuition and Analytic Discipline*. Northvale, NJ: Aronson.

SIANI, R. (1992*a*) Facilitating and therapeutic functions of the empathic understanding. In *USA–Europe Conference on Facilitating Climate for the Therapeutic Relation in Mental Health Services* (eds P. Borri, R. Quartesan & P. Moretti), pp. 67–79. Perugia: ARP.

—— (1992*b*) *Psicologia del Sé: da Kohut alle Nuove Applicazioni Cliniche*. Turin: Boringhieri.

—— (1996) Organisation of care and prevention of drop-out and burnout in a psychiatric team. *International Journal of Mental Health*, **25**, 50–57.

——, SICILIANI, O. & BURTI, L. (1990) Psychotherapy for psychotics in the mental health service. In *USA–Europe Joint Meeting on Therapies and Psychotherapy of Schizophrenia* (eds P. Borri & R. Quarteson), pp. 125–137. Perugia: ARP.

——— & SICILIANI, O. (1995) Valutazione della psicoterapia mediante il Karolinska Psychodynamic Profile (KAPP): Verona University Research on Self Psychology Psychotherapy. *Quaderni Italiani di Psichiatria*, 14, 293–374.

———, FOSSELLA, S. & SICILIANI, O. (1996) An application of Kohut's Self Psychology to psychotherapy of borderline and psychotic patients. In *Borderline and Psychotic Disorders: Therapeutic Strategies* (eds P. Borri, P. Quartesan, P. Moretti, *et al*), pp. 63–77. Perugia: ARP.

STOLOROW, R. D. & ATWOOD, G. E. (1996) The intersubjective perspective. *Psychoanalytical Review*, 83, 181–194.

SVANBORG, P., GUSTAVSSON, J. P. & WEINRYB, R. M. (1999) What patient characteristics make therapists recommend psychodynamic psychotherapy or other treatment forms? *Acta Psychiatrica Scandinavica*, 99, 87–94.

TOLPIN, P. (1983) Corrective emotional experience: a self psychological re-evaluation. In *The Future of Psychoanalysis* (ed. A. Goldberg), pp.121–130. New York: International University Press.

TURRINA, C., SIANI, R., REGINI, C., *ET AL* (1996) Inter-observer and test–retest reliability of the Italian version of the Karolinska Psychodynamic Profile in two groups of psychiatric patients. *Acta Psychiatrica Scandinavica*, 93, 282–287.

WALDINGER, R. & GUNDERSON, J. (1987) *Effective Psychotherapy with Borderline Patients*. Washington, DC: American Psychiatric Press.

WEBER, J. J., BACHRACH, H. M. & SOLOMON, M. (1985) Factors associated with the outcome of psychoanalysis: report of the Columbia Psychoanalytic Center Research Project (Parts I and II). *International Review of Psychoanalysis*, 12, 127–262.

WEINRYB, R. M. & RÖSSEL, R. J. (1991) Karolinska Psychodynamic Profile (KAPP): Manual. *Acta Psychiatrica Scandinavica*, 83 (suppl. 363), 1–23.

———, ——— & Åsberg, M. (1991a) The Karolinska Psychodynamic Profile. I. Validity and dimensionality. *Acta Psychiatrica Scandinavica*, 83, 64–72.

, ——— & ——— (1991b) The Karolinska Psychodynamic Profile.II. Interdisciplinary and cross-cultural reliability. *Acta Psychiatrica Scandinavica*, 83, 73–76.

———, GUSTAVSSON, J. P., ÅSBERG, M., *ET AL* (1992) Stability over time of character assessment using a psychodynamic instrument and personality inventories. *Acta Psychiatrica Scandinavica*, 86, 179–184.

——— & RÖSSEL, R. J. (1993) Karolinska Psychodynamic Profile (Italian version). *Psichiatria e Psicoterapia Analitica*, 12, 85–114.

———, ———, GUSTAVSSON, J. P., *ET AL* (1997) The Karolinska Psychodynamic Profile (KAPP): studies of character and well-being. *Psychoanalytic Psychology*, 14, 495–515.

WHITE, M. T. & WEINER, M. B. (1986) *The Theory and Practice of Self Psychology*. New York: Brunner-Mazel.

WILCZEK, A., WEINRYB, R. M., GUSTAVSSON, J. P., *ET AL* (1998) Symptoms and character traits in patients selected for long-term psychodynamic psychotherapy. *Journal of Psychotherapy and Practice and Research*, 7, 23–34.

WINNICOTT, D. W. (1971) *Playing and Reality*. London: Tavistock.

WOLF, E. S. (1988) *Treating the Self*. New York: Guilford.

WORLD HEALTH ORGANIZATION (1992) *The ICD–10 Classification of Mental and Behavioural Disorders: Clinical Descriptions and Diagnostic Guidelines*. Geneva: WHO.

10 Integrating intensive psychosocial and low-dose neuroleptic treatment: a three-year follow-up

JOHAN CULLBERG, GRETA THORÉN,
SONJA ÅBB, AGNES MESTERTON
and BODIL SVEDBERG

This is a pilot study lying behind the Parachute Project, a Swedish multi-centre study, which will extend the study in terms of numbers of patients treated and seek further clarification of the effective outcome issues and develop the research methodology.

Alanen *et al* (1991), Ciompi *et al* (1993), Mosher *et al* (1995), McGorry *et al* (1996) and others have opened up new and constructive ways of treating patients with first-episode psychosis. The common trait is a high emphasis on psychosocial and psychotherapeutic aspects of care combined with using neuroleptic medication in minimal dosage and only when needed. Immediate results seem to be superior to those of control groups or in naturalistic studies. However, long-term follow-up results often show less clear conclusions. One reason for this may be that the clinical follow-up periods were brief and, later on, when in need for further clinical help, the patients were obliged to turn to ordinary psychiatric services, which seemed to extinguish the results obtained.

In a review article about research on neuroleptic use and psychodynamic treatment (Cullberg, 2000) it was summarised that in many cases intensive psychosocial support can considerably reduce or make neuroleptic medication unnecessary with no increased risk of adversive effects. If, however, neuroleptic treatment is completely removed from schizophrenia treatment, the results are worse.

This chapter investigates the effects of a clearly defined psycho-socially based 'need-adapted care' compared with the effects of 'care as usual' for an analogous patient cohort treated four years earlier (Alanen *et al*, 1994).

Six principles of need-adapted care

We formulated these principles on the basis of a summary of the relevant literature and our own earlier experience.

Early intervention

This intervention had a particular emphasis on being in the patient's home. The aim was that a special psychosis team should take full responsibility for every patient with first-episode psychosis as soon as the patient asked for psychiatric care. Because of a lack of emergency resources this often means cooperation with standard psychiatric facilities during the first day or night.

Crisis and psychotherapeutic approach

The psychotherapy is mainly of a crisis intervention type during the acute stage, trying to understand the nature of the stress and conflict situation, to lessen the dramatic aspects of the psychosis and to give realistic hope. A supportive individual crisis intervention is followed – after one or several months or even years – by a more systematic therapy of a psychodynamic or cognitive approach according to needs and resources. By that time the patient usually is no longer psychotic or is less psychotic and the patient's wish and need to understand more deeply the dynamic background for his or her problems may be evident. Alternatively, the patient may wish for a cognitive approach to deal with depressive or remaining psychotic manifestations. This means meetings 1–2 times a week over several months for up to a year or more, sometimes including family members.

Family orientation

The patient's family (if existent) is regularly invited, preferably starting immediately but mostly within one week, for repeated family meetings. Often a 'family map' is constructed during the first meetings, which are continued with a supportive, problem-solving and pedagogical content. Some families need extended contact of a supportive or systemic kind.

Continuity and easy accessibility

Continuity and easy accessibility to the team through one or two personal contacts was offered over five years, the prerequisites being laid through the early contact with the patient and his or her family. (After five years most long-term psychoses seem to adjust and the risk of relapse is reduced (Bleuler, 1974).)

The optimal and lowest possible dose of neuroleptic medication

Anxiety and insomnia are primarily relieved with benzodiazepines when psychological support is not enough. In case of a fresh psychotic episode, neuroleptic medication is usually abstained from during the first 1–2 weeks in order to observe the patient's needs and to see if the psychosis disappears without medication. When psychotic symptoms are prevailing or disturbing, neuroleptic treatment is given. The dose is mostly very low at the start (about 50 mg chlorpromazine equivalents) and slowly increased. In cases of difficulties with the patient in remembering his or her oral medication, depot medication in low doses may be preferable. Thus, it is only rare that medication for side-effects is necessary. Lithium and antidepressants are used when needed.

Need-adapted overnight care

All patients are supported in continuing to live at home. When needed, crisis beds are offered in a relaxed and personal small-scale surrounding where occasionally relatives can also stay. In cases of danger, standard in-patient facilities are used.

Setting

A special mobile team was initially formed with a few members of staff. When complete, the team was staffed with five people where both medical expertise as well as dynamic and cognitive psychotherapeutic competence was represented. In the fifth year of the project 14 staff members, including the overnight crisis bed service, were engaged in the full-time project. Presently, around 70 patients continue to be followed up in different stages of acute psychosis, recovery and rehabilitation. For administrative reasons, however, the project was terminated in 1997 for any new patients and their care was integrated into ordinary psychiatric services.

After one year of the project the out-patient unit was complemented with a small apartment with three crisis beds. One person staffed this unit during the night and two during the daytime. It was open 24 hours a day throughout the year. Every patient accepted by the project could use the crisis beds at any time when considered to be in need of it. Since it was run as an out-patient facility this could be done without many formalities. The centre was situated in an active living area of the city with a personal and relaxed interior. The patients paid a small amount for overnight stay and meals. Later on, three more beds were made available in an adjacent apartment for more long-stay needs. In cases of very disturbing psychotic symptoms or high suicidal risk, the ordinary hospital in-patient resources could still be used.

Material and methods

Project group

Every patient with first-episode psychosis who came to public psychiatric care in an inner city catchment area of 95 000 inhabitants was included in the study between September 1993 and September 1995. (Private psychosis care is practically non-existent.) Patients with predominating organic or drug-related psychosis were not included. The diagnoses (DSM–IV; American Psychiatric Association, 1994) were re-evaluated (J.C., S.Å.) several times to ensure a proper evaluation of the 'real' diagnosis behind the first-episode psychosis that led to care. The patients have also been subjected to a number of psychological and medical assessments and investigations (not presented in this paper). The Global Assessment of Functioning (GAF; American Psychiatric Association, 1994) is an assessment of global mental functioning (<60 means to be in need of psychiatric help; >40 overtly psychotic). The Brief Psychiatric Rating Scale (BPRS; Ventura *et al*, 1993), a symptom scale, was expressed in terms of the mean value for positive symptom items: suspiciousness, hallucinations and unusual thought content. Negative symptom items were: self-neglect, blunted affect and emotional withdrawal. A score of one indicates no symptoms; two, a very mild degree of symptoms; three a mild degree; etc.

Retrospective comparison group

Every patient with first-episode psychosis from the same area and two other inner city areas have been identified according to the same criteria from the years 1991 and 1992. At that time no special facilities were available for this patient group, which may be looked upon as having been 'treated as usual'. This means that the patients were treated *ad hoc* and no special effort was made to secure continuity of care or follow-up. The standard treatment was neuroleptic medication on presentation with supportive psychotherapy and in-patient treatment. Psychotherapy in a more specialised sense was practically non-existent, as was family directed crisis intervention in the acute phase. In aftercare a few patients received in-patient treatment in small treatment units.

Originally, a personal follow-up of this comparison group was intended, but only 50% of the patients accepted to see the investigator. Therefore, follow-up was performed by means of records and other statistics. Extensive staff questioning, manual and also database case finding searches were undertaken to collect these cases at the different psychiatric clinics. Missing cases are difficult to estimate, but are probably minimal. The diagnoses (DSM–IV) were assessed by two specialised psychiatrists (A.M. and J.C.).

In the comparison group, prescription of neuroleptics and other medication has been assessed according to psychiatric records at different periods in the patient's care. Also different aspects of care consumption have been recorded. Ordinary in-patient (hospital) treatment has been separated from low-staffed non-hospital overnight treatment.

Results

At this point a three-year follow-up is available for only 22 subjects from the project group. The other 10 cases have been followed up for between 2.5 and 3 years. These are, however, counted here as having been followed up for three years. The project group is similar to the comparison group regarding age, gender (see Table 10.1) and diagnostic distribution (see Table 10.2). Because of a mistake, affective psychoses were not included in the comparison group.

Neuroleptic consumption

Neuroleptic consumption (see Table 10.3) is significantly lower in the project group, both regarding the number of patients using neuroleptic medication at the different intervals and regarding the

TABLE 10.1
Social data at entrance

	Project group	Comparison group
n	32	72
Age	29	30
Male gender (%)	51	51

TABLE 10.2
Diagnostic distribution (DSM–IV)

	Schizo-phrenia syndromes	Delusional syndrome	Brief psychosis	Psychosis unspecified	Affective psychosis
Project group, n=32 (%)	56	9	16	13	6
Comparison group, n=72 (%)	61	17	13	10	†

† not completed due to error.

TABLE 10.3
Neuroleptic medication

	First week	At 12 months	At 30–36 months
Neuroleptic medication (%)			
Project group (n=32)	62	25	45
Comparison group (n=71)	62	63	71
Mean dosage, mg cpz equiv/day for patients on medication			
Project group	140	84	62
Comparison group	204	198	192

cpz, chlorpromazine equivalents.

actual prescribed dosage. (Five or six cases have been unmedicated most of the time because of the patients' refusal – efforts have been made repeatedly to negotiate about medication. Their status was not grave enough to permit compulsory medication for a prolonged time.) Almost every patient among those with diagnoses of schizophrenia received medication eventually. Because of the generally low doses (rarely more than 1–2 mg/day of flupenthixol or risperidone) and slow increase of doses, practically no patient needed anticholinergic medication. One or two cases received lithium, and antidepressants have been used when needed. Benzodiazepines were generally used initially for anxiety relief and sleeping difficulties.

In-patient care consumption

In-patient care consumption in the project group is significantly lower for the project group (see Table 10.4). (The mean number of in-patient days of the project group at Year 3 is calculated on the 22 patients who

TABLE 10.4
In-patient days per patient (total groups)[1]

	Year 1	Years 2+3
Project group (*n*=32)		
Psychiatric clinic	20	8
Crisis unit	8	35
Total	28	43
Comparison group (*n*=71)		
Psychiatric clinic	42	37
'Treatment unit'	2	32
Total	44	69
P	<0.02	<0.002

1. Ten out of 32 patients in the project group have only been observed for 2.5–2.9 years.

have reached that time period.) Interestingly, the large part of the day and night care could be provided by the crisis unit that was made available during the last part of the first project year. At that time the need for in-patient care became drastically lowered.

Cost saving

The cost saving regarding diminished overnight care for each patient during the first year was calculated at £4220 and for each of the two subsequent years was calculated at £6111. In reality, the saving is lower because of the larger out-patient staff resources of the project organisation.

GAF and BPRS scores

These figures (see Table 10.5) have only been obtained for the project group. The GAF and BPRS were not measured at the entrance of the study. According to the BPRS, 39% of the schizophrenia group was symptom-free at three-year follow-up and so was 79% of the non-schizophrenia psychosis group. Those with residual symptoms generally exhibit them to a moderate degree only. The GAF values at the follow-up show a mean value of 55 for the schizophrenia group and 75 for the non-schizophrenia group.

Project group

Sixteen per cent of the project group were on a pension due to ill health, compared with 39% in the comparison group (see Table 10.6). The total amount of sick pension and sick leave (longer than six months) is about the same in the groups. A sick pension implies

TABLE 10.5
Follow-up of patients with first-episode psychosis after 2–3 years

	Schizophrenia syndromes	Other psychoses	Total
n	18	14	32
No symptoms (%)	39	79	56
Positive psychotic symptoms (%)	61	21	44
Mean BPRS value positive symptoms	3.2	1.8	2.9
Negative symptoms (%)	50	0	28
Mean BPRS value negative symptoms	2.3		1.6
GAF	55	75	64
	(35–85)	(40–85)	(35–85)

acceptance of permanent disability, while sick leave implies the continuing possibility of temporary disability.

Discussion

The main results of this study lie in the feasibility of caring for all cases in a psychosis population with fewer in-patient days and considerably lower doses of neuroleptic medication than is usually recommended. The outcome regarding symptom load and functional state is good. The difference from other first-episode projects is difficult to estimate. The reason for this is that outcome must be regarded from several aspects: symptom load, working abilities, life quality, etc. In the project group fewer patients were on sick pensions than in the comparison group.

The very low dose of neuroleptic medication is in accordance with research on the D_2 dopamine receptor binding capacity, which shows a satisfactory saturation at much smaller doses (2–4 mg haloperidol) than was previously believed (Nyberg *et al*, 1995). That such a low dose strategy is eminently feasible is in accordance with McEvoy *et al* (1991).

TABLE 10.6
Sick leave >6 months and sick pension

	Intake	1 year	3 years
Project group (%)	*n*=32		
Sick leave	3	41	38
Pension	–	6	16
Comparison group (%)	*n*=71	*n*=70	*n*=69
Sick leave	10	37	14
Pension	4	11	39

This low dose regimen also makes 'negative symptoms' less of a problem – they are often caused by elevated neuroleptic levels. It has been the philosophy of the project to encourage the patient to take neuroleptic medication in cases where such medication was regarded as useful, that is, sooner or later in most of the schizophrenia cases. However, we tried to listen to and, as much as possible, respect the patient's arguments in situations when the patient was not destructive. In five cases, patients with schizophrenia have not been willing to continue medication in spite of its good effects during brief compulsory hospitalisation.

The need for compulsory care or more secure environments has demanded an average of less than one psychiatric in-patient bed at any one time for the total group nowadays of 70 patients. The number of beds in the crisis centre also seems to be sufficient. In spite of the service users often being acutely psychotic and the openness of the unit, no serious incident has happened in this cohort.

The comparison with the treatment as usual group is less reliable because of the lack of a prospective control group. Generally, psychiatric beds have been somewhat reduced in these last years. This reduction is, however, much less than the difference in this study. If the results in this and similar studies are possible to replicate, it will be an argument for a significant change of the organisation for the care of the group of patients with first-time psychosis and possibly also for other psychiatric patients.

The high number of sick pensions and amounts of sick leave are a reflection of the unemployment problems for this group of young people. Many of the patients in the project group are subjects of rehabilitation measures and in the meantime have sick leave.

This has been a pilot study to help with the design of a new multi-centre project for patients with first-episode psychosis in 19 psychiatric clinics (Parachute Project) throughout Sweden where the outcome will be compared with a prospective control group.

Acknowledgement

This project has been realised thanks to the generous funding of the Stockholm County Council.

References

ALANEN, Y. O., LEHTINEN, K., RÄKKÖLÄINEN, V., *ET AL* (1991) Need-adapted treatment of new schizophrenic patients: experiences and results of the Turku Project. *Acta Psychiatrica Scandinavica*, **83**, 363–372.

——, UGELSTAD, E., ARMELIUS, B.-Å., *ET AL* (1994) *Early Treatment for Schizophrenic Patients. Scandinavian Psychotherapeutic Approaches.* Oslo: Scandinavian University Press.

AMERICAN PSYCHIATRIC ASSOCIATION (1994) *Diagnostic and Statistical Manual of Mental Disorders* (4th edn)(DSM–IV) Washington, DC: American Psychiatric Association.

BLEULER, M. (1974) The long-term care of the schizophrenic psychoses. *Psychological Medicine,* **4**, 244–254.

CIOMPI, L., ZUPPER, Z., AEBI E., *ET AL* (1993) Das Pilotprojekt? Soteria Bern? Zur Behandlung akut Schizophrener. II. Ergelbnisse einer vergleichenden prospektiven Verlaufstudie über 2 Jahre. *Nervenarzt,* **64**, 440–450.

CULLBERG, J. (2000) Neuroleptic treatment and psychodynamic treatment in psychosis. In SBU (Swedish Council on Technology Assessment in Health Care) report on treatment with neuroleptics. *Acta Psychiatrica Scandinavica,* in press.

McEVOY, J. P., HOGARTY, G. E. & STEINGARD, S. (1991) Optimal use of neuroleptics in acute schizophrenia: a controlled study of neuroleptic threshold and higher haloperidol dose. *Archives of General Psychiatry,* **48**, 739–745.

McGORRY, P. D., EDWARDS, J., MIHALOPOULOS, C., *ET AL* (1996) EPPIC: an evolving system of early detection and optimal management. *Schizophrenia Bulletin,* **22**, 305–326.

MOSHER, L. R., VALLONE, R. & MENN, A. (1995) The treatment of acute psychosis without neuroleptics: 6-week psychopathology outcome data from the Soteria project. *International Journal of Social Psychiatry,* **41**, 157–173.

NYBERG, S., FARDE, L., HALLDIN, C., *ET AL* (1995) D_2 Dopamine receptor occupancy during low-dose treatment with haloperidol decanoate. *American Journal of Psychiatry,* **152**, 173–178.

VENTURA, J., GREEN, M. F. SHAUER, A., *ET AL* (1993) Training and quality assurance with the Brief Psychiatric Rating Scale. *International Journal of Methods in Psychiatric Research,* **3**, 221–244.

11 Early intervention in psychosis: the TIPS project, a multi-centre study in Scandinavia

JAN O. JOHANNESSEN, TOR K. LARSEN, THOMAS McGLASHAN and PER VAGLUM

The suffering connected with schizophrenia spectrum disorders for the patients, their families and society is very great. In many cases treatment efforts have had only limited, if any, impact on the course of the disorder. On the other hand, in some cases it seems possible to reverse a psychotic process and to help the patient recover. What are the factors determining this difference in outcome? There is now tentative evidence supporting the hypothesis that the timing of the treatment may actually influence prognosis. Intervention at the earliest stages of the illness's development may reduce the extent, and the morbidity, of psychotic disorders (Wyatt, 1995; McGlashan, 1998).

The costs of schizophrenia are high (Davies *et al*, 1994). In Norway 60% of the psychiatric health care budget is used for the treatment and care of patients with schizophrenia (Rund, 1994). In all NATO countries combined, the costs connected with this disorder are estimated at over 1% of the gross national budget (Mednick & McGlashan, 1996). While the worldwide rate of new cases (incidence) is low (1 in 10 000 per year) (Johannessen, 1985), the lifetime prevalence of the disorder is high (1% of the population) and the disorder often results in chronic deficits in mental functioning. Ten per cent of all citizens with disabilities in Norway suffer from schizophrenia. There is no single disorder whether in somatic medicine or in psychiatry with comparable costs (Andreassen, 1991; Fog, 1996). Despite the development of structured individual and family therapy, modern neuroleptics and psychosocial rehabilitation programmes, too many patients do poorly or commit suicide (McGlashan & Johannessen, 1996).

210

In this chapter we will present arguments for early detection and intervention in psychosis, and describe an ongoing multi-centre project in Scandinavia with the specific aim of reducing duration of untreated psychosis (DUP). It is called the TIPS study (early treatment and identification of psychosis). This chapter will focus on strategies for educating the public, health professionals and schools about the early signs of psychosis, discuss our preliminary experiences and present some early results from this project.

Prevention in psychosis

In a way, we can say that the concept of early intervention now appearing in modern psychiatry is a way of rediscovering the past. Sullivan wrote in 1927: "the psychiatrist sees too many end states and deals professionally with too few of the prepsychotic", and "the great number of our patients have shown for years before the break, clear signs of coming trouble" (see Sullivan, 1994). The implication is that functional psychoses (i.e. schizophrenia) can be looked upon as a dynamic process with stages of development. This framework holds the possibility of modifying, delaying and perhaps even preventing deterioration in the course of the disease. While the evidence to date does not prove that early intervention with known treatments can change the natural history of schizophrenia, it is promising enough (for both biological and psychosocial treatments) to support further investigation (McGlashan & Johannessen, 1996).

The idea of prevention in psychosis has been in focus for the last decade (Birchwood, 1992; McGlashan, 1996; McGorry *et al*, 1996). Can the positive results in somatic medicine with early diagnosis of disorders such as cancer or heart diseases be translated to the field of psychiatry (Larsen & Opjordsmoen, 1996)? Three levels of prevention have been defined: primary, secondary and tertiary (McGlashan, 1996). Primary prevention is equivalent to reducing the incidence of a disorder; secondary prevention means reducing the prevalence of the disorder; and tertiary prevention means decreasing the morbidity of the disorder, that is, to bettering the long-term prognosis. Schizophrenia can be seen as a disorder that develops through different phases or stages: the premorbid, prodromal and psychotic phases end up in a more or less deficit phase depending on the duration of illness, number of relapses, etc. The relationship between the different types of prevention and the stages of illness in schizophrenia is outlined in Fig. 11.1.

Tertiary prevention in schizophrenia has been studied most. Wyatt (1991) reviewed studies suggesting that the long-term outcome of schizophrenia is better for patients treated earlier with neuroleptics.

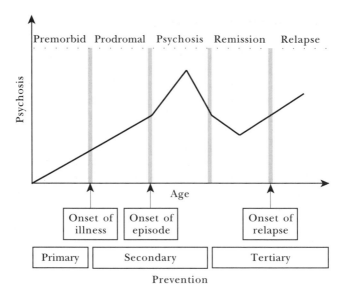

Fig. 11.1 *Stages of schizophrenia and prevention types*

Hogarty *et al* (1986) and Heinrichs *et al* (1995) have shown that structured long-term treatment with psychosocial intervention such as family treatment, supportive psychotherapy and the monitoring of early symptoms of relapse can improve the long-term outcome. Loebel *et al* (1992) and others found that longer duration of illness before treatment was correlated with poor outcome. Lieberman *et al* (1996) hypothesised a morbid process of active neuronal loss during periods of acute symptoms that, if not counteracted, produced lasting impairments. Wyatt & Green (1995) indicate that early treatment not only decreases the morbidity associated with schizophrenia, but also prevents detrimental changes related to untreated psychosis.

Regarding secondary prevention, in principle there may be little difference between relapse prevention and the prevention of first outbreak of psychosis. Relapse rates can be significantly reduced through a systematised mapping of early warning signs. Birchwood (1992) has introduced a practical clinical model for the identification of the prodromal symptoms of relapse in schizophrenia – the 'relapse signature'. Family studies involving psychoeducation have shown that family therapy can reduce the relapse rates to 20% in a two-year follow-up period (Leff, 1994). The combination of low expressed emotion, family therapy and medication can reduce relapse even more. McFarlane *et al* (1995) asserts that relapse rates involving the multi-family group approach can reduce relapse to 6–7% on an annual basis. The necessary conditions for developing psychosis are environmental stress and a vulnerability to psychosis (McGlashan, 1996). High expressed emotion can be looked upon as an expression of a high basic stress level in the milieu of the patient. In psychosis the capacity to handle additional stress will be reduced. Stress reduction thus reduces relapse rates significantly. Together with easy access to the health services, this may be the most important feature of family intervention programmes. Such programmes also educate parents and patients about preventive intervention upon early warning signs of relapse. As described above, Leff's research shows reduced relapse rates by reducing expressed emotion in high expressed emotion families (Leff, 1994). The principles of this approach could be adopted with people who have not yet suffered a break but are at risk and living in high expressed emotion families.

DUP

The DUP is defined as the time between the onset of first psychotic symptoms and first adequate treatment. The operationalised definitions are given later in this chapter. Many studies of first-episode psychosis, both those carried out retrospectively and prospectively, show that DUP is very long: on average between one and two years. Johnstone *et al* (1986) found a variation from less than two months (32%) to longer than one year (30%), despite the presence of overt and often severe symptomatic behaviours in many cases. Loebel *et al* (1992) found a mean DUP of 52 weeks, and a mean duration of untreated illness (DUI) of 151 weeks. Haas & Sweeney (1992) found mean DUP symptoms before hospitalisation of three years. Beiser *et al* (1993) found that patients with schizophrenia had a mean DUP of 56 weeks (median 8.2) and in addition a mean duration of prodromal symptoms of 112.8 weeks (median 52.7). From Germany, Haefner *et al* (1993) reported a mean DUP of 2.1 years and a mean duration of 4.6 years from the earliest sign of mental disorder until first admission for schizophrenia (Johannessen *et al*, 1999).

This means that people can live for long periods of time within society suffering severe symptoms of mental illness such as delusions, hallucinations or severe thought disorder, without getting proper treatment. It also means that they may be more likely to develop a longer, more chronic disturbance as a result of not getting earlier treatment.

In summary, the investigations reported above offer two compelling observations:

(a) the relationship between DUP and treatment response appears robust and less confounded by inter-correlation with other prognostic determinants;
(b) there is a consistency in the findings of the length of DUP in contemporary clinical samples (Larsen *et al*, 1996).

Early detection and intervention programmes

Intervention at the prodromal level

The prodromal phase refers to non-specific symptoms such as anxiety and depression that precede the onset of psychosis. Falloon (1992) conducted a pioneering project on early detection in the prodromal phase of psychosis in Buckinghamshire, England between 1984 and 1988. Early detection of potential psychosis (i.e. within the prodromal period before onset) was based on educating family practitioners to recognise prodromal symptoms and to refer such cases to the mental health team for assessment, early detection and treatment, if appropriate. The mental health services worked in close cooperation with the primary health services. During this four-year period, 16 patients with prodromal symptoms were detected, one of whom developed schizophrenia. Compared with earlier epidemiological studies within the same area, 10 new cases of schizophrenia were expected during this time period. The reduction in annual incidence was impressive: 0.75 per 100 000 compared to the expected 7.4 per 100 000. This study highlights the potential gains of early detection and intervention by focusing on the prodromal phase of psychosis. It also suggests that the deterioration underlying psychosis may be less irreversible and resistant to intervention than has been assumed for almost a century.

The study has some limitations: the number of patients is low, and the variation compared with the historical control could be coincidental. The strategy of prevention at the prodromal level is also problematic, due to the non-specific nature of the symptoms (Larsen *et al*, 1996), and the danger of falsely labelling people who would never actually have developed psychosis as 'pre-psychotic' or 'prodromal' to the disorder. The concept of 'prodromal symptoms' is also poorly defined, and might be of questionable predictive value (McGorry *et al*, 1995).

At the Early Psychosis Prevention and Intervention Centre (EPPIC) in Melbourne, Australia, the psychiatric health service programmes are designed towards offering early detection and the development of specialised treatment for early psychosis. They have demonstrated a significant improvement in symptomatic and functional outcome, but have not been able to establish a correlation between improved outcome and lower DUP. They evaluated the effect of EPPIC (1993, *n*=51) compared to pre-EPPIC populations (1989–92, *n*=51) and concluded that there was no statistical significant difference in DUP, the mean DUP being reduced from 237 days (pre-EPPIC) to 191 days (EPPIC) (McGorry *et al*, 1996). They conclude that the improved short-term outcomes that they demonstrated are derived from more phase-specific and intensive treatment than from earlier provision of treatment.

Development of early detection strategies in Rogaland County, Norway

Background

Due to reorganisation of the psychiatric health services in Rogaland in the early 1980s with a gradual closing down of the state hospital, there was an increasing interest in structuring the treatment of schizophrenia. The basic organising principle was continuity of care, as reflected on two levels, between different levels of health services, and in the relationship between the patient and therapist. The latter principle meant that the same therapist would follow the patient during the whole treatment process, from the first out-patient admission to the stay on the in-patient ward and through aftercare and rehabilitation. Thus, the clinicians have to follow the patient from the start of the disorder until recovery or chronicity. Based upon clinical impressions and follow-up studies (Johannessen, 1996), we developed an interest in establishing more systematic treatments for early schizophrenia. We developed a 10-point treatment programme for first-episode schizophrenia, based upon a comprehensive treatment approach (see Box 11.1). We decided to give priority to first-episode psychosis, and to concentrate treatment efforts towards this group, regarding chronicity as a possible result of a failure to implement adequate treatment during this time. Therefore, it became clear to us in the late 1980s that a very worthwhile goal would be to get people with psychotic conditions into treatment at an earlier stage of the illness in the hope that this would lead to a more successful intervention and outcome.

Schizophrenia Days

Schizophrenia Days, established in 1989, was the natural result of this development. It is a week-long conference about psychoses for

---

Box 11.1.
Treatment programme for first-episode schizophrenia

(a) Early diagnosis;
(b) Comprehensive treatment;
(c) Continuity.

Ideally we try to get into a position where we can treat in the prodromal phase. The basic principles of the treatment are:

(a) A thorough diagnostic evaluation and mapping of problems, tentatively within the first week of his or her involvement with the psychiatric service.
(b) Minimum one-year stay in the ward if necessary, at first admission (i.e. a guarantee of the necessary time as an in-patient).
(c) Two hours of adapted individual psychotherapy weekly with an experienced psychotherapist or a resident undergoing psychotherapeutic training.
(d) Stable, interested primary nurse, under instruction, i.e. the patient shall not be followed up by nurse/student who intends quitting the service within one year.
(e) Adapted housing-facility outside the family (e.g own apartment, collective, halfway house, etc.).
(f) Financial independence through health insurance or the equivalent.
(g) Employment/occupational training in cooperation with social security authorities.
(h) Contact with the family of a minimum of once a month during the first half-year; later regular contact is offered according to particular needs.
(i) The necessary medical/psychopharmacological treatment.
(j) Out-patient treatment after discharge, if necessary compulsory

These conditions can be adjusted depending on particular judgements, and should be motivated by the individual situation and explicitly in relation to the need of the patient and the treatment plan.

---

professionals and the public, held each year in the middle of the town centre (in the town's Culture House). It aims to enhance knowledge about schizophrenia and severe functional psychiatric disorders among those working in the mental health field as well as among lay people. It includes arts such as theatre, cinema and picture exhibitions, public lectures, political conferences, etc. The information provided for the public has been especially directed towards young people. Television stations as well as local newspapers give a broad coverage of these events. Schizophrenia Days are now visited by approximately 1000 professional people and 2000–4000 lay people each year. In this way, the whole population of the county (370 000) has been receiving information on schizophrenia on a yearly basis. Through Schizophrenia Days we have succeeded in involving a diverse group of people. In the organising committee, we have gathered the town mayor, the theatre and cinema directors, librarians, schoolteachers, representatives for national and local health authorities, clinicians, patients and relatives. School classes have been invited to attend special lectures and to develop projects around psychiatric and psychological themes.

Our aims relating to lay persons have been:

(a) to acquaint people with the term schizophrenia in the same way they are acquainted with other medical terms such as cancer or heart disease;
(b) to reduce the fear and stigma connected with severe mental disorder;
(c) to decrease the fear and stigma associated with the psychiatric health services, that is, help people understand that psychiatry is out to help, not to harm.

Parallel to this we have developed an institution called the Psychiatric Information Foundation, which develops and distributes material with information on psychiatric disorders and mental health service questions. This non-profit organisation, originating from within Rogaland Psychiatric Hospital, publishes information about psychiatric disorders for patients, relatives, health workers, social workers, schools and the public.

Pilot study

During the years 1993–94, we carried out a follow-up study of first-episode schizophrenia in order to find out if secondary prevention could be carried out in Rogaland. The inclusion criteria were a first episode of non-affective psychosis, in people of 15–55 years residing in the county. We also did a review of conceptual and ethical problems related to the idea of early intervention in psychosis.

Onset measures and DUP – definitions

We found that the definitions of DUP and onset of psychosis, etc. were quite vague and unspecific in earlier studies (Larsen *et al*, 1996). We defined onset of psychosis operationally using the Positive and Negative Syndrome Scale (PANSS):

> "A score of four or higher on PANSS (positive subscale), and manifestation of psychotic symptoms such as delusions, hallucinations, thought disorder or inappropriate/bizarre behaviour in which the symptoms are not apparently due to organic causes. These symptoms must have lasted throughout the day for several

days or several times a week, not being limited to a few brief moments." (Kay *et al*, 1987)

DUP was defined as the time interval between onset of psychotic symptoms and hospitalisation for psychosis or initiation of adequate treatment. Adequate biological treatment was defined as the prescription of antipsychotic medication given in sufficient time and amount that would lead to clinical response in the average non-chronic patient with schizophrenia (e.g. haloperidol 5 mg a day for three weeks). If patients had already received treatment according to this definition, they were excluded from the study.

Results

We found that the DUP was also very long in our county; the mean DUP was 114 weeks, s.d.=173.6 and the median was 26 weeks. We found that longer DUP was associated with poorer work performance, decreased social and global functioning in the year prior to admission and a more insidious onset of psychosis with more negative symptoms at hospitalisation. Longer DUP was not associated with age at onset of psychosis. Males had a significant longer DUP than females (154 weeks *v.* 39 weeks). We also found other strong gender differences: male patients were more often single; had a lower educational status; a higher rate of unemployment; were younger at onset; and had lower Global Assessment of Functioning (GAF; American Psychiatric Association, 1987) during the last year before hospitalisation. We found that males scored poorer at the level of premorbid functioning and deteriorated faster than females, especially closer to onset (Larsen *et al*, 1996).

When we studied the pathways to care of the subsample with schizophrenia (*n*=34), we found that the major obstacles against receiving treatment were passive and active withdrawal and a poor social network (Larsen *et al*, 1998). We also found that a majority of long DUP (DUP>54 weeks) cases had bizarre symptoms at hospitalisation, but not at the earlier phases of psychotic development. At present we are completing the five-year follow-up of the sample, the data are not yet available. At one-year follow-up we found that 56% were in remission, 18% had suffered multiple relapses and 26% had been continuously psychotic. Both poor premorbid functioning and long DUP were significantly correlated with more negative symptoms and poorer global functioning at one-year follow-up. Long DUP was also significantly correlated with more positive symptoms. Even when we controlled for other factors, including premorbid functioning and gender, DUP was a strong predictor of outcome. To a limited degree premorbid functioning and DUP interact, but DUP seems to have an independent influence on outcome.

Overall, there was a delay in detection and DUP was correlated with poor outcome. These findings strengthened our resolve to establish health service programmes for early detection and treatment of first-onset psychosis.

TIPS (early treatment and identification of psychosis)

The TIPS project is a multi-centre study involving three geographical areas, comparable in both demographic features and in the mixture of urban and rural features. The areas are Rogaland County and Oslo County, both in Norway, and Roskilde County in Denmark.

The project has the following goals:

(a) To explore whether it is possible to reduce the DUP within a geographical area (Rogaland County). The programme for the reduction of DUP includes:
   (i) informing the public;
   (ii) educating professional health care workers, school teachers, etc.;
   (iii) establishing a highly responsive early detection team.
(b) To investigate the resistances to reducing DUP, and, as part of this, to study whether public knowledge about psychosis and early signs of psychosis can be changed via educational campaigns.
(c) To describe the clinical problems of patients referred to the early detection team.
(d) If DUP can be reduced in Rogaland, to see whether the reduction improves prognosis for patients with a first-episode non-affective functional psychosis.
(e) To explore the short- and long-term outcome (five years) when such patients are offered an optimal treatment programme of two years' duration, including psychotherapy, medication and a psychoeducational family programme.
(f) To explore what problems the psychiatric health services will meet on trying to establish an optimal treatment programme for patients with first-episode psychosis, and what modifications (if any) are necessary when this presumptive optimal treatment is offered to patients with very short DUP.

Design

The project is a prospective, longitudinal multi-centre study of patients with first-episode psychosis from three counties (Rogaland and Ullevål in Norway and Roskilde in Denmark). Patients in all three counties are similarly assessed at the start of treatment, at one, two and five years. The study compares patients in Rogaland whose illnesses were detected early (experimental county) with the patients detected 'as usual' in the other counties (comparison sites). Patients will be included over a four-year period (1997–2001). Inclusion criteria are listed in Box 11.2.

The ideal design for testing the causal relationship between DUP and prognosis would be to randomise consecutive cases of first-episode psychosis to active treatment versus a long no-treatment waiting list control. The ethical side of this is at best questionable, given that active psychosis, especially first-episode, is a treatable, medical emergency. The project's design is, therefore, a 'quasi'-experimental design because randomisation cannot be used.

A standard treatment protocol is used in all three study populations to minimise the effect of treatment on the dependant variables (outcome) and to maximise the effect of differences in the independent variable (DUP) (McGlashan, 1996). We also compared the Rogaland early detection sample with the 1993–1994 Rogaland first-episode sample described earlier. This historical control design has the advantage that the demographic variances between samples are likely to be small. The disadvantage of historical control designs is non-measurable sources of variance, known as cohort effects. In order to minimise measurement variance in the historical control comparison we therefore use the same assessment methods in our new sample.

BOX 11.2.
TIPS inclusion and exclusion criteria

Living: within the catchment area
Age: between 18 (15 in Rogaland) and 65 years
Fulfil the criteria of DSM–IV: schizophrenia, schizotypal disorder, schizoaffective disorder, delusional disorder, brief psychotic episode, affective psychosis with mood incongruent delusions, psychotic disorder
Active psychosis: with symptoms that cannot be explained by organic disorders. On PANSS, the patient must acheive a score of 4 on one or more of the positive Items 1,3,5,6 or 9
Actual episode: is the first psychotic episode not already adequately treated according to a definition
No contraindication: to use of medication
No neurological or endocrine disorders: related to the psychosis
IQ: above 70
Able and willing to give informed consent

Assessment

When a patient with a possible first episode of psychosis is identified, the detection team carries out a PANSS interview describing actual symptoms and makes a GAF assessment. All detection team members are trained raters in these manuals. If this preliminary assessment by the detection team concludes that a first episode of psychosis is probably present, the assessment team carries out the rest of the assessment interviews. The assessment team consists of research scientists trained to reliability in diagnosis, etc. Patients who meet the inclusion criteria enter the study and receive the standard treatment protocol, after giving informed consent. Patients who refuse to participate will be offered the same treatment programme. Weekly case conferences with all TIPS clinicians and researchers are organised to discuss difficult cases. The different interviews are listed in Fig. 11.2.

A Structured Clinical Interview for DSM–IV Axis 1 disorders (SCID–P; Spitzer *et al*, 1990) is carried out as soon as possible. In addition, assessment of premorbid functioning (Premorbid Adjustment Scale, PAS; Canon-Spoor, *et al*, 1982), social functioning (Strauss & Carpenter,

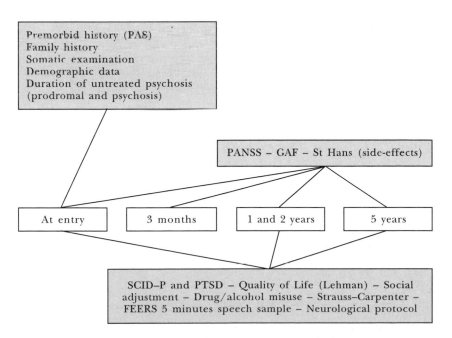

Fig. 11.2 Assessment for included patients

1974), quality of life, deficit symptoms, drug/alcohol misuse, life events, expressed emotions, duration of untreated psychosis and duration of prodromal symptoms is conducted by the assessment team.

Standard treatment

Background

In order to study whether a reduction in DUP will lead to a better outcome, we must control for other factors that are known to influence outcome. Therefore, a standard treatment protocol has been developed. The following treatment package is therefore provided in all three counties participating in the TIPS study. It consists of three elements based upon a review of studies on optimal treatment of psychosis (PORT) (Lehman & Steinwachs, 1998). These elements are:
  (a) active outreach supportive therapy;
  (b) medication;
  (c) psycho-educative family work (multi-family groups).

The basic treatment requisite is continuity of care. The treatment period is at least two years for all elements. In addition to these three core elements, we offer a need-specific treatment according to the individual patient's needs. The treatment protocol includes guidelines for supportive psychotherapy and medication, and for the family work. Psychosocial (re)habilitation is an important component of the treatment efforts aimed at patients with first-episode psychosis. The patients' needs in these areas show considerable variations, and the local rehabilitation resources could also vary. These elements are an integrated part of the individual treatment provided.

Organisation of the treatment programme

Treatment team

Continuity of treatment is secured by teams who work with the patient for at least two years. This team consists of the patient's individual psychotherapist and primary nurse. In some of the cases the main focus will be individual psychotherapy, but this will not be the most relevant in all cases. In our model the psychotherapist has the main responsibility for all aspects of the treatment.

Active outreach supportive psychotherapy

The supportive, active outreach psychotherapy guarantees a minimum of one psychotherapeutic contact per week with an experienced psychotherapist, either a psychiatrist or psychologist. The main focus of the therapy is supportive, psychodynamically based, with the therapist as an active coordinator of the different therapy elements. The psychosocial needs of the individual patient beyond the standardised treatment elements are tailored according to his or her specific needs. The treatment has a minimum guaranteed duration of two years. The emphasis on continuity of care is based upon the psychological needs of patients experiencing a psychological disintegration. We believe that the disintegration of the psychological structures pathognomonic for psychosis can probably be reduced by stable external structures, and the inherent anxiety and suffering requires time, stability and a stable relationship between patient and therapist to re-establish a psychic structure where structure has been dissolved. What the patient with psychosis needs least are new, quickly broken relationships. The therapy aims at being phase-specific and need-oriented. Patients' needs vary, as will the frequency of meetings between therapist and patient and the length of each session. The supportive elements will always be an important part of psychodynamically- oriented psychotherapy for this group of patients. In some cases the therapist will, for long periods, work primarily at establishing contact and/or getting the patients to come to sessions. Other patients can be strongly motivated for psychological treatments and an insight-oriented process. The therapist has to be flexible and also willing to give practical help. A main focus will be helping the patient to develop internal coping strategies and to enhance consciousness of personal vulnerability, and thereby enhance the understanding for and the acceptance of illness-related experiences and the need for treatment. There will also be a focus on accepting loss in a way that avoids demoralisation, preserves hope and encourages reintegration into society. Active outreach approaches are also an explicit responsibility for the psychotherapist, and will, for example, include calling the patient if he or she does not show up for an appointment and being willing to go to the patient's home on some occasions. The duration of the sessions should be at least 30 minutes a week.

Medication

The medication is based on treatment with olanzapine as first choice, risperidone as second choice and perphenazine as third choice. Maximum dosage of olanzapine is 20 mg per day, with recommended dosage 10 mg. For risperidone the recommended dosage is 1–4 mg per day, with a maximum dosage of 6 mg.

Family work

The model of the family work is based on extensive studies of the international research done on what is considered to be the best help for the families. Few studies on family intervention have been carried out on first-episode samples. Most studies have been in relation to patients with a more chronic course of illness. McFarlane *et al* (1995), in their work with multi-family groups, documented that this approach has a good effect on first-episode psychosis and their families. In first-episode samples, the patients will be very different, and the prognosis will also vary. Hence the content of the education given is broader spectrum, open-minded about outcome and crisis-oriented.

The family work consists of the following three elements:

(a) single family meetings;
(b) multi-family groups;
(c) a workshop for the families.

In the single-family meetings, the family meets with the individual therapist at least three times during the first weeks after the patient has been admitted to the TIPS project. The meetings can be with or without the patient, depending on the patient's condition.

A multi-family group consists of 5–6 families and has two group leaders. The sessions last for at least 90 minutes, and have a supportive non-threatening atmosphere. They meet every second week, and focus on problem-solving, crisis management, communication training and education about psychiatric disorders.

A one-day educational workshop is conducted for new participants. Participants can be siblings, close friends, teachers and other people the patient wants to include. The content of this workshop is as follows:

(a) information on psychiatric health services;
(b) information on psychosis;
(c) possible outcome/prognosis;
(d) stress vulnerability model;
(e) experiences of being a relative;
(f) what relatives can do to help;
(g) treatment and coping.

Early detection of psychosis programme in Rogaland

The main goal for the project in Rogaland County is to explore whether it is possible, through a massive information and education system, to reduce DUP. This programme was started on 1 January 1997, and will last for four years. The early detection programme in Rogaland has two elements: (a) the TIPS education programme; and (b) detection teams.

The main focus is on easy access to the treatment systems. The information campaigns try to enhance the public's knowledge of psychiatric disorders in general and on early signs of serious psychiatric disorders in particular, that is, to change the help-seeking behaviour of the population. We try to achieve this by reducing stigma, and providing information about severe mental disorders as well as about help that is available. The educational programme is based on the general information work carried out during the last 10 years, as outlined earlier in the chapter. The core elements are:

(a) information for the public;
(b) information for health professionals;
(c) information for schools (teachers and pupils).

General population

In January 1997 all households in the county (180 000) received a 12-page brochure with information about the project. The main statement in the brochure was:

"Psychiatric disorders have at least one thing in common with other disorders, the chance of getting well is better when treatment is started as soon as possible."

The brochure contained a section with general information about the early symptoms of psychosis and a symptom check-list describing different grades of severity. The psychosis detection team was introduced and emphasis put on how to get in touch with them. The main elements in the information campaign towards the public are:

General information available through mass media

(a) Free advertisements:
    (i)   local radio;
    (ii) local television;
    (iii) local newspapers.
(b) Paid advertisements:
    (i)   local radio;
    (ii)   local television;
    (iii) local newspapers;
    (iv)   local cinema;
    (v)   household brochure;
    (vi)   postcards;
    (vii) flyers;
    (viii) car stickers;

(ix) t-shirts;
(x) other brochures.

Lectures for the public

(a) Public meetings, etc.

General information material given

(a) What is psychosis?
(b) An outline of psychosis.
(c) What is schizophrenia?
(d) An outline of schizophrenia?

We have whole page advertisements in the newspapers on a regular basis. The first series was based on the theme 'myths and reality', where each advertisement carried a scene from the movie *One Flew Over the Cuckoo's Nest* (myth) opposed to a picture of people working in the detection team (reality). These newspaper advertisements were coordinated with advertisement campaigns in the commercial radios and local television stations.

Professional health workers

We developed:

(a) Educational programmes for general practitioners (GPs), psychiatric nurses and other people working within the general health service system and the psychiatric health service systems.
(b) A check-list and a rating manual based on the DSM–III–R (American Psychiatric Association, 1987) prodromal symptoms, and the PANSS. This was introduced to all the GPs in the region.
(c) A video with a 'patient' experiencing vague psychotic symptoms for a seminar lasting for 3–4 hours and consisting of:
    (i) two lectures describing the TIPS project and presenting the detection teams;
    (ii) the TIPS video;
    (iii) ratings of the TIPS video using the TIPS manual;
    (iv) clinical discussion of cases.

We have similar seminars for psychiatric nurses and other mental health professionals. The GPs also receive a letter twice a year with an update on the forthcoming results of the study, and with an appeal to refer patients as soon as possible when they suspect a possible serious psychiatric disorder in young people.

Schools

The main elements of the school information campaigns are:

(a) obligatory courses for all teachers, counsellors and school psychologists;
(b) educational programmes for the teachers to use in their teaching on psychological subjects;
(c) a video illustrating prodromal and early signs of psychosis;
(d) information brochures;
(e) posters;
(f) flyers;
(g) specifically designed newspaper advertisments;
(h) special education programmes for pupils.
(i) special education programmes for teachers consisting of a video, a lecture and a rating on prodromal signs;
(j) separate programme for school psychologists.

We enjoy close cooperation between the county's offices for health services and school authorities. This has made it possible to establish a constructive dialogue with the high schools and the teachers. As Olin & Mednick (1996) have shown, teachers in the high schools are often able to recognise early signs of serious psychiatric disorders among young people. The video *Something is Wrong With Monica* was made in cooperation with the school authorities and shows a 16-year-old girl gradually drifting into psychosis. This video has been used in the education of both teachers and pupils. All pupils at high school level have also received an information brochure on early signs of serious psychiatric disorders, and general information on how to seek help. This will be repeated on an annual basis.

Early detection team

A major prerequisite for doing early intervention work is to establish a system with easy access. Based on the experiences of Falloon (1992) and McGorry *et al* (1996), we established two detection teams, one in each of the sectors of the county (see Assessment section). The detection teams consist of psychiatrists, psychologists, psychiatric nurses and social workers. The teams are on call for referrals from 8 am to 3.30 pm, Monday to Friday. There is an answering machine outside these hours. In addition, the doctor on call at the psychiatric hospital will take over the detection functioning in weekends, but only assess emergency cases. The detection teams work together with the county out-patient units, and are considered a part of the regular psychiatric health services in the county. The pathways from the first contact with the detection team to final inclusion in the study are described in Fig. 11.3.

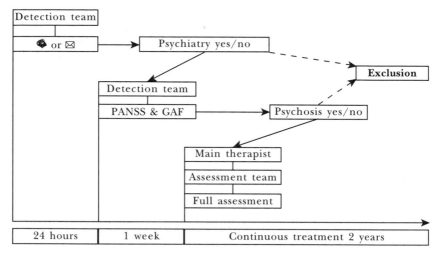

Fig. 11.3 Detection team flow-chart

The detection teams will make an initial assessment over the telephone, and the first decision is whether there is a psychiatric problem or not. If it is a possible psychiatric case, the detection teams will meet the patient or the referring persons wherever is convenient: at home, at school, in a GP's office or at the detection team office. The teams are very mobile, and work with an active outreach attitude. We give a 24-hour guarantee of assessment, which means that the patient will be met by the detection team within 24 hours after contact is established. In most cases the assessment will be concluded within only a few hours. The detection team carries out a preliminary PANSS and a GAF rating.

When the detection team has established that a psychiatric disorder is probable, the patient will be referred to a more extensive, scientifically based evaluation by the assessment team. They will decide whether or not the patient is suffering from a first episode of psychosis. Patients meeting the inclusion criteria will enter the study and receive the standard treatment protocol, after giving informed consent.

Patients who are not included in the project will receive information on how and where to secure help. Patients with non-psychotic disorders will be referred to the ordinary out-patient units. Those with a tentative diagnosis of 'at risk for developing psychosis' (possible prodromal cases) are referred to a special prodromal clinic. For patients who are at risk, but refuse treatment, the detection team will make an

TABLE 11.3
Patients referred to the detection team during 1997

	All patients n=306	Patients with psychiatric problems n=161	Patients with first episode psychosis n=31
Gender (% male)	61	70	81
Mean age (s.d.)	25.3 (10.3)	23.3 (6.8)	23.7 (5.9)
Prodromal symptoms, mean (s.d.)	7.4 (3.5)	8.2 (3.2)	9.8 (3.5)
Referred by (%):			
Patient	17	5	3
Mother	15	13	10
Father	5	6	7
Other family	13	9	7
School	10	12	13
Friends	3	1	0
Social office	3	4	3
Others	17	24	18
General practitioner	11	17	23

appointment to telephone or see the patient within days, weeks or months in order to remain in contact.

Preliminary results

Early detection work

During the first year of TIPS, the early detection teams received a total of 299 referrals. In Table 11.1 we have divided the referred patients into three categories: (a) all patients; (b) patients with psychiatric problems; and (c) patients with first-episode psychosis.

In all three groups there was a predominance of male patients. Fifty per cent of the cases had possible psychiatric problems and were assessed with PANSS and GAF rating scales. Twenty-eight cases had a first-episode psychosis. It seems that the specificity of our detection system is quite high. Almost 10% of all referrals had a first-episode psychosis and more than 50% of those that were screened as having a possible psychosis were actually experiencing a first episode of psychosis. One of the important findings from these early experiences with our system is that both the family and schools (teachers, school-nurses, etc.) use the detection teams actively. Thirty-four per cent of the cases with psychiatric problems and 29% of the first-episode cases were referred from the family (most often from mother). The GPs however, also refer approximately 25% of the cases in the group with psychiatric problems and psychosis. These findings indicate that family and the schools are able to identify patients with emerging psychosis or actual psychosis.

There is always a built in fear in our psychiatric health service systems that 'opening up' and lowering the treatment inclusion threshold will result in an overwhelming number of new cases. Our experience is that this fear is unfounded. In fact it is the opposite; we must actively encourage people in trouble to contact help delivery systems.

Reduction of DUP

The preliminary results for the historical comparison between the pilot study sample (1993–94) and the patients detected in the TIPS experimental county during 1997 are presented in Table 11.2.

The findings indicate that that education and early detection can be successful in reducing DUP. The pilot-study DUP was 2.1 years (mean; 26 weeks median). In the first year of the TIPS, the DUP fell to 17 weeks (mean; 12 weeks median). In both samples, 65% of the cases were males. The TIPS early detection sample is younger both at onset of psychosis and at hospitalisation, but the differences do not reach statistical significance. These findings look very promising, but more patients need to be included in the early detection group in order to see whether or not this trend is lasting and of clinical significance.

TABLE 11.2
Duration of untreated psychosis changes. Historical control study v. TIPS early detection sample; preliminary results (modified from Larsen et al, 1998)

	Pilot study 1993–94 n=43	TIPS early detection 1997 n=32	P values[1]
Gender (% male)	65.1	65.6	NS
Age at onset of psychosis, mean (s.d.)	26.3 (8.4)	24.1 (8.7)	NS
Age at hospitalisation, mean (s.d.)	28.4 (8.3)	25.1 (7.9)	NS
DUP in weeks, mean (median)	114.2 (26.0)	17.2 (12.0)	0.001

1. Mann–Whitney *U*-test.

General knowledge of psychiatric disorders

Is it possible to enhance the public knowledge of serious psychiatric disorders? In cooperation with an opinion poll company we collected data about knowledge of and attitude towards psychiatric disorders in the total population in the county prior to and one year after the information campaign had started. The results are shown in Figs 11.4a and 11.4b.

The results show that general knowledge about psychosis among our population was significantly better after one year of the public information campaigns. The main source of peoples' knowledge was the newspapers. These results are only preliminary and will be followed up on an annual basis.

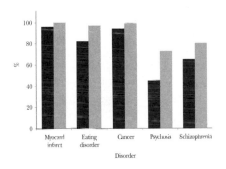

Fig. 11.4a Psychiatric disorders: general knowledge and attitude. Do patients know a lot about the disorder? ■, *1996;* ■, *1998.*

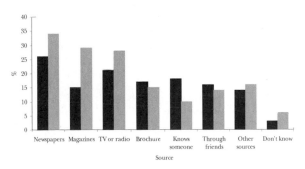

Fig. 11.4b Psychiatric disorders: How did you get your knowledge regarding schizophrenia? ■, *1996;* ■, *1998.*

Conclusions

Our preliminary results regarding the possibility of reducing the DUP through extensive information campaigns directed towards the public and special target groups are promising. The fear of mental health workers being overwhelmed by referrals if the threshold for referral is lowered seems unwarranted. Groups that do not normally refer patients to the psychiatric health services, such as family, teachers, social workers, etc. do so when they are invited, and the referrals seem appropriate. It seems that the groups at which the information campaigns have been aimed have responded and helped us detect patients earlier. The preliminary results are very positive, and we have so far achieved a major reduction in the DUP. The information campaigns seem well worth the money spent. The costs for the information campaigns were approximately one million Norwegian Krona per year (£80 000). This equals approximately half of the expenses that an average local supermarket store uses for advertisements on a yearly basis. It is also the equivalent to the one-year costs of treating a patient with chronic schizophrenia. However, the impact that such a reduction of DUP may have on clinical outcome has not yet been established, although the preliminary results so far are promising. The final comparison between the DUPs in the historical control and the present study, and the comparison with the Oslo and Roskilde samples are still awaiting analysis.

References

AMERICAN PSYCHIATRIC ASSOCIATION (1987) *Diagnostic and Satistical Manual of Mental Disorders* (3rd, edn)(DSM–III–R). Washington,DC: APA.

ANDREASSEN, N. C. (1991) Assessment issues and the cost of schizophrenia. *Schizophrenia Bulletin*, **17**, 475–481.

BEISER, M., ERICKSON, D., FLEMING, A. E. J., ET AL (1993) Establishing the onset of psychotic illness. *American Journal of Psychiatry*, **150**, 1349–1354.

BIRCHWOOD, M. (1992) Early intervention in schizophrenia: theoretical background and clinical strategies. *British Journal of Psychiatry*, **31**, 257–258.

CANON-SPOOR, H. E., POTKIN, S. G. & WYATT, R. J. (1982) Measurement of premorbid adjustment in chronic schizophrenia. *Schizophrenia Bulletin*, **8**, 470–484.

DAVIES, L. M. & DRUMMOND, M. F. (1994) Economics and schizophrenia: the real cost. *British Journal of Psychiatry*, **165** (suppl. 25), 18–21.

FALLOON, I. R. H. (1992) Early intervention for first-episode of schizophrenia: a preliminary exploration. *Psychiatry*, **55**, 4–15.

FOG, R. (1996) Schizophrenia research. *Journal of the Danish Medical Association*, **150**, 42–69.

HAAS, G. L. & SWEENEY, J. A. (1992) Premorbid and onset features of first-episode schizophrenia. *Schizophrenia Bulletin*, **18**, 373–386.

HAEFNER, H., MAURER, K., LOEFFLER, W., ET AL (1993) The influence of age and sex on the onset of the early course of schizophrenia. *British Journal of Psychiatry*, **162**, 80–86.

HEINRICHS, D. W., HANLON, T. E. & CARPENTER JR, W. T. (1995) The Quality of Life Scale: an instrument for rating the schizophrenia deficit syndrome. *Schizophrenia Bulletin*, 10, 388–398.

HOGARTY, G. E., ANDERSON, C. M. & REISS, D. J. (1986) Family education, social skills, training and maintenance chemotherapy in the aftercare of schizophrenia. *Archives of General Psychiatry*, 43, 633–642.

JOHANNESSEN, J. O. (1985) The epidemiology of schizophrenia in a Norwegian county. *Nordic Journal of Psychiatry*, 39, 217–223.

—— (1996) The outcome of first-time diagnosed schizophrenia in Rogaland, Norway. *Dialog*, 2, 19–22.

——, LARSEN, T. K. & McGLASHAN, T. H. (1999) Duration of untreated psychosis: an important target for intervention in schizophrenia. *Nordic Journal of Psychiatry*, 53, 275–283.

JOHNSTONE, E. C., CROW, T. J., JOHNSON, A. L., ET AL (1986) The Northwick Park study of first episode schizophrenia: I. Presentation of the illness and problems relating to admission. *British Journal of Psychiatry*, 148, 115–120.

KAY, S. R., FISZBEIN, A. & OPLER, L. A. (1987) The Positive and Negative Syndrome Scale (PANSS) for schizophrenia. *Schizophrenia Bulletin*, 13, 261–276.

LARSEN, T. K. & OPJORDSMOEN, S. (1996) Early identification and treatment of schizophrenia: conceptual and ethical considerations. *Psychiatry*, 59, 371–380.

——, McGLASHAN, T. H. & MOE, L. C. (1996) First-episode schizophrenia: 1 early course parameters. *Schizophrenia Bulletin*, 22, 241–256.

——, JOHANNESSEN, J. O. & OPJORDSMOEN, S. (1998) First-episode schizophrenia with long duration of untreated psychosis. *British Journal of Psychiatry*, 172 (suppl. 33), 45–52.

LEFF, J. P. (1994) Stress reduction in the social environment of schizophrenic patients. *Acta Psychiatrica Scandinavica*, 89 (suppl. 384), 133–139.

LEHMAN, A. F. & STEINWACHS, D. M. (1998) At issue. translating research into practice: the schizophrenia patient outcome research team (PORT) treatment recommendations. *Schizophrenia Bulletin*, 24, 1–10.

LIEBERMAN, J., KOREEN A. R., GEISLER, S. H., ET AL (1996) The psychobiology of first-episode psychosis. In *First International Conference on Strategies for Prevention in Early Psychosis*, pp. 15.

LOEBEL, A. D., LIEBERMAN, J. A., ALVIR, J. M. J, ET AL (1992) Duration of psychosis and outcome in first-episode schizophrenia. *American Journal of Psychiatry*, 50, 369–376.

McFARLANE, W. R., LINK, B., DUSKAY, R., ET AL (1995) Psychoeducational multi family groups: four-year relapse outcome in schizophrenia. *Family Process*, 34, 127–144.

McGLASHAN, T. H. (1996) Early detection and intervention in schizophrenia: research. *Schizophrenia Bulletin*, 22, 327–345.

—— (1998) Early detection and interaction of schizophrenia: rationale and research. *British Journal of Psychiatry*, 172 (suppl. 33), 3–6.

—— & JOHANNESSEN, J. O. (1996) Early detection and intervention with schizophrenia: rationale. *Schizophrenia Bulletin*, 22, 201–222.

McGORRY, P. D., McFARLANE, W. & PATTON, G. C. (1995) The prevalence of prodromal features of schizophrenia in adolescence: a preliminary survey. *Acta Psychiatrica Scandinavica*, 92, 241–249.

——, EDWARDS, J., MIHALOPOULOS, C., ET AL (1996) An evolving system of early detection and optimal management. *Schizophrenia Bulletin*, 22, 305–326.

MEDNICK, S. & McGLASHAN, T. (1996) *Early Detection and Intervention with Psychosis: Opportunities for Preventing Chronicity*, pp. 1–10. Dochecht: Kluwer for NATO International Scientific Exchange Programmes, Advanced Study Institute.

OLIN, S. S. & MEDNICK, S. A. (1996) Risk factors of psychosis: identifying vulnerable populations premorbidly. *Schizophrenia Bulletin*, 22, 223–240.

RUND, B. R. (1994) Schizophrenia, how much do we use on treatment and research? *Journal for the Norwegian Medical Association*, 21, 2682–2683.

SPITZER, R. L., WILLIAMS, J. B. W., GIBBON, M., *ET AL* (1990) *Structured Clinical Interview for DSM–III–R – Patient Edition (SCID–P)*. Washington, DC: American Psychiatric Press.

STRAUSS, J. S. & CARPENTER, JR, W. T. (1974) The prediction of outcome in schizophrenia: II. Relationships between predictor and outcome variables. *Archives of General Psychiatry*, **31**, 37–42.

SULLIVAN, H. S. (1994) The onset of schizophrenia. Classic articles 1927. *American Journal of Psychiatry*, **151** (suppl. 6), 135–139.

WYATT, R. J. (1991) Neuroleptics and the natural course of schizophrenia. *Schizophrenia Bulletin*, **17**, 325–351.

—— (1995) *The Cost of Schizophrenia*. American Psychiatric Association, Symposium no. 18. Washington, DC: American Psychiatric Press.

—— & GREEN, M. F. (1995) *Early Treatment Improves the Outcome of Schizophrenia*. American Psychiatric Association, Symposium No. 98D. Washington, DC: American Psychiatric Press.

12 The Finnish integrated model for early treatment of schizophrenia and related psychoses

YRJÖ O. ALANEN, VILLE LEHTINEN,
KLAUS LEHTINEN, JUKKA AALTONEN
and VILJO RÄKKÖLÄINEN

The overall goal of the Finnish integrated model has been to develop a treatment for new patients with schizophrenia that is: (a) predominantly psychotherapeutic; (b) comprehensive within psychodynamic and systemic basic orientations; and (c) widely applicable to public psychiatric health care.

One of our central premises was the fact, known already to Bleuler (1911), that schizophrenic disorders form a very heterogeneous group with regard to their clinical symptoms, prognosis and the patients' psychological and social condition. This also leads to a diversity of therapeutic challenges. People suffering from schizophrenia should, therefore, be met flexibly and individually in each case, on the basis of both an individual and interactional interpretation of the situation and it is from these that the therapeutic needs should be defined. This is why the Finnish model was named 'need-adapted treatment of schizophrenia-group psychoses' (Alanen et al, 1991; Alanen, 1997a).

The heterogeneity of psychoses within the schizophrenia group is also perceptible with regard to their aetiology. It is most probable that the aetiological factors are multifactorial, both multi-faceted and multi-layered, and differently weighted in different cases (Alanen, 1997a, b). We recognise the role of biological and genetic vulnerability factors but also the connections with disorders of human personality development and the prevalence of psychosocial precipitating factors at the onset of the psychosis (Räkköläinen, 1977).

Because of the dominating reductionistic views of the nature of schizophrenia, a model like ours, integrated and based on a comprehensive psychotherapeutic orientation, is apt to arouse resistance. This may be especially true of many biologically oriented researchers, encouraged to study brain functions as biochemical or by means of the new imaging methods, or trying to identify chromosomal regions likely to contain 'schizophrenia-susceptibility' genes applying methods of new molecular genetics. It may then be too easily forgotten that interactional relationships with other people are an integral part of human biology, necessary for our growth into adult individuals and crucial to include in our therapeutic endeavours. Fleck (1995) recently described in a critical survey the dehumanising developments in contemporary American psychiatry, leading to a view of patients as containers of neurochemical aberrations, in place of the emphasis placed earlier on interviewing skills and understanding patients in terms of their personal development. Management programmes have displaced psychotherapeutic treatment and psychiatrists have been reduced to the role of diagnostician and writers of drug prescriptions.

The mode of treatment adopted in our work as researchers, clinicians or psychotherapists may come to be regarded as the only correct approach. Our view becomes blinkered, effectively shielding the clinician from seeing the usefulness of any other approach. An integrated model of treatment may stimulate resistance by implying that one's own way of thought and action is not necessarily the only one and this may be experienced as a narcissistic blow.

We would like to challenge the belief that a psychotherapeutic approach to psychoses is not possible in public health care because of the extensive staff resources required. From our experiences with the need-adapted model, this is not true. Not all people with schizophrenia need long-term individual psychotherapy in order to be treated adequately.

Core model

Development

Our approach was developed over three decades in connection with the Turku Schizophrenia Project (Alanen, 1997*a*; also see below). When a national programme for developing research, treatment and rehabilitation of people with schizophrenia was carried out in Finland in the 1980s (State Medical Board in Finland, 1988; Alanen *et al*, 1990*a,b*), we had a chance to gather wider geographical experiences of our approach. One of the two main sub-projects of the national programme was the New Schizophrenic Patients Project (NSP), accomplished in six districts representing different parts of the country. The follow-up results of this project were promising even if the realisation of the therapeutic approach varied from one district to another (Salokangas *et al,* 1991; Salokangas, 1994; Alanen, 1997*a*). Maybe the most important result of the national programme was a wide interest in the integrated, psychodynamically oriented treatment of schizophrenic psychoses. Based on the experiences of the national programme, a detailed model for treatment and rehabilitation of schizophrenic psychoses was published in Finnish in 1987 and in English in 1990 (Alanen *et al,* 1990*a*).

New projects based on different applications of the original Turku project are continuing in Finland. In this chapter, the experiences and results of the main projects are described. The Finnish integrated model has inspired development of treatment practices in centres abroad, especially in Scandinavian countries (Chapters 9, 11 and 13 show evidence of this influence).

Turku Schizophrenia Project

This is an action research project initiated 30 years ago by the investigators and the clinical staff of a university hospital, the Turku Clinic of Psychiatry. Its aim is to develop the treatment of new patients with psychoses in the schizophrenia group in the community psychiatric setting of the town of Turku (population 160 000).

In a context marked by a basic psychotherapeutic attitude and supported with training and supervision activities open to all mental health professional groups, hospital wards were developed into psychotherapeutic communities (Alanen, 1975, 1997*a*; Salonen, 1979). Individual therapeutic relationships, family therapy and other family-centred activities were developed. Pharmacotherapy was regarded as a mode of treatment supporting psychosocial therapies. The aim was to develop and implement therapeutic tools in the general treatment setting in the catchment area of the Turku mental health district.

Since service development was our priority, it was decided to evaluate a natural service setting, which has the advantage of better generalis-ability. Our main principle, adaptation of the treatment to the patients and their networks' therapeutic needs, excluded randomised patient cohorts based on strictly pre-defined kinds of treatment. Randomisation would have inhibited the service development process. A naturalistic follow-through cohort design with open (non-randomised) treatment allocation was chosen (Alanen *et al,* 1980). We studied the efficacy of different treatment methods in different developmental stages through prospective follow-up studies of cohorts including all patients first diagnosed with schizophrenia spectrum disorders from specific periods of time (see Table 12.3). The advantages and limitations of this approach are considered later. The cohorts as well as the general frames and the development of the Turku project are described in Alanen (1997*a*). The Turku project also formed the Finnish part of the Inter-Scandinavian Early Treatment for Patients with Schizophrenia Project (NIPS) Project (Lehtinen *et al*, 1994).

At first, the focus was in developing psychodynamically oriented long-term individual therapies, carried out by the medical and nursing staff members under supervision (Aaku *et al*, 1980; Alanen *et al*, 1986). Family therapies were seen as a more secondary treatment mode and rehabilitative activities were poorly developed. However, a three-year multi-professional training in systemic-oriented family therapy, established in Turku in 1979, had a revolutionary impact on the Turku treatment model. Three main principles that formed the practical focus of the new development were introduced in 1983 (Lehtinen & Räkköläinen, 1986; Alanen *et al*, 1990*a*).

(a) The patient should be present in the situations that concern him or her and his or her treatment. The patient is needed as an expert on his or her life situation. The patient's presence also helps him or her regain lost reality-testing. It is the task of the staff to conduct the discussion in such a way that this is made possible.

(b) Regular conjoint meetings are arranged with staff members, the patient and his or her family members and/or other important network persons all present. This starts at the intensive initial evaluation when the patient is admitted to treatment. Because these meetings turned out to have a significant therapeutic effect on many of the patients, relieving their psychotic regression and shortening their need for hospital treatment, we began to call them 'therapy meetings' (Räkköläinen *et al*, 1991).

(c) A systemic general orientation is put into practice as follows: the chain of shared experiences, hypotheses and observations generated in the multi-professional therapy meetings and other common situations with the patient creates a shared understanding within the therapeutic system (Alanen *et al*, 1989, 1991). We have called the outcome of this process the 'shared image guiding the treatment process' (Aaltonen & Räkköläinen, 1994).

The onset of psychosis is understood as an interactional phenomenon and the focus was transferred to family-centred interventions and family therapy, while long-term individual therapies were continued with some of the patients. The family and crisis orientation focused the attention on present difficulties in the patients' life situation. Short treatment times were favoured in order to avoid interference with normal development after an interactional reformulation had been achieved.

In comparison with the earlier follow-ups, the outcome results of patients treated with the new interactional approach clearly proved to be favourable (Lehtinen, 1993*b*, 1994) (see Outcome data section). However, the follow-up results also indicated that with many seriously ill patients the relatively limited intervention appeared too optimistic. The need of many patients for continuing family or individual therapy and for rehabilitative activities appeared to be insufficiently met. Because of this, and because of the adverse consequences of breaks in therapeutic relationships, the need for a fourth principle became evident.

(d) Continuity of treatment has to be maintained (Lehtinen, 1993*a*). It is essential to maintain therapeutic relationships. Ideally, the team that initially started the work with the family should continue as long as they are needed. In some cases this means continuous family work, in others less frequent contact but, for instance, being available at times of particular difficulty or potential crisis.

Principles

The general principles of the integrated need-adapted treatment based on the experiences of the Turku project have been expressed as follows (Alanen *et al*, 1991; Alanen, 1997*a*).

(a) Therapeutic activities are planned and carried out flexibly and individually in each case so that they meet the real, changing needs of the patients as well as of the persons in their interactional networks (most often, the family). This is principally carried out by means of the intensive initial therapy meetings referred to above. The interactional approach is of the utmost importance in the planning of treatment because of the possibility to assess the family situation, including the mutual (and sometimes very concrete) symbiotic relationships prevailing in the family environment of many patients. The orientation of treatment as either an individual-therapeutic or family-therapeutic direction is largely determined during these meetings. An empathic contact established with the people closest to the patient may also stimulate their positive resources, increase their confidence in the treatment (even if it turns into individual-centred treatment) and may motivate them to attend family-focused treatment at later stages, whenever such treatment is indicated.

(b) Examination and treatment are dominated by a psychotherapeutic attitude. This refers to the process of understanding
   what has happened and is happening to patients and the
   people in their interpersonal network and how we can use this
   understanding as a basis for approaching and helping them.
   An attitude of this kind also involves observation of one's own
   emotional reactions.

(c) The different therapeutic activities should complement each
   other rather than constitute an 'either/or' approach. There
   should be a general plan to integrate various activities (different
   psychotherapeutic modalities, psychopharmacological treatment and rehabilitative activities) with one another. One of the
   prerequisites for integration is also cooperation between
   different persons and units responsible for the treatment of a
   patient.

(d) The treatment should attain and maintain the quality of a
   continuing process, instead of being allowed to decline into a

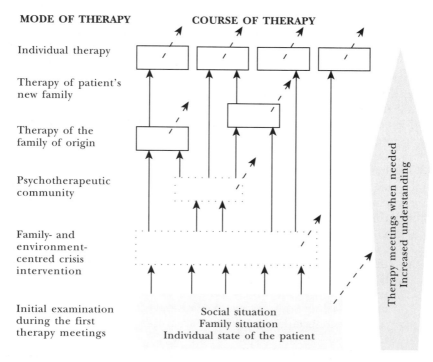

Fig. 12.1. The treatment process and different modes of therapy

routine sequence of sessions. This aspect may be best illustrated by Fig. 12.1.

(e) Follow-up is important of both individual patients and of the treating units and the treatment system as a whole, supporting the development of each in the light of experience. (Lehtinen, 1993*a*).

Different components of the integrated psychotherapeutic treatment

The relative weighting of psychotherapeutic treatment modes during the course of the need-adapted treatment of schizophrenic psychoses is illustrated in Fig. 12.1.

The bottom of the diagram represents the starting point, the initial intervention that is mainly constituted by usually repeated therapy meetings involving the team, the patient and the family and/or other important network members. Individual contact with the patient is also established at the initial stage – necessarily so, if the patient is admitted into a hospital ward or in other situations if this is indicated or wished for by the patient. The social situation refers to the larger network, possible adaptation problems and immediate rehabilitation needs.

The vertical arrows show how the focus of treatment subsequently shifts, differently for different patients, from one mode of treatment to another, while the diagonal arrows indicate the discontinuation of treatment, which, as can be seen, is possible at all stages. The large grey arrow symbolises the development of the shared image guiding the treatment process.

Fig. 12.1 should not be interpreted too literally. Single cases may require exceptions to the order presented in the diagram. It is extremely important to notice that the therapeutic mode in the diagram always means the 'primary therapeutic concern', the dynamic focus of the treatment at a certain stage, which does not exclude other treatment modes being used at the same time. For example, it is common that the patient has an individual therapeutic relationship besides family therapy. In psychotherapeutic communities he or she always has a personal nurse, but the focus of treatment may only move over to individual therapy when preconditions for it have been strengthened by family therapy.

Therapy meetings

The initial therapy meetings have, all at the same time, informative, diagnostic and therapeutic functions. They often lead to an alleviation or even the disappearance of the patient's psychotic regression, especially if the outbreak of the psychosis has been acute. In our experience, most families are quite well motivated for teamwork at the time of the first admission of a family member with psychosis. If therapy meetings are continued as an effective crisis intervention, it may be possible to avoid hospital admission. With regard to patients admitted to the psychotherapeutic community of the hospital ward, therapy meetings are continued there, forming a crucial part of the milieu therapeutic process and in developing the shared image. Therapy meetings are also apt to diminish experiences of rejection felt by the patients and to lessen the tendency to label them as ill with its likely consequent psychological isolation by family members (cf. 'closure', as described by Scott & Ashworth (1967)). However, the team may also arrange therapy meetings with the patient alone if the family members are not willing to participate in them or if otherwise indicated.

Therapy meetings are usually continued during later stages of the treatment. This is especially important for maintaining the integration and continuity of treatment when there are changes of therapists, therapy modes or therapeutic units.

Conjoint family therapy

Our family therapeutic orientation may be described as systemic–psychodynamic (Lehtinen, 1994; Alanen, 1997*a*), even if different developments have occurred in different centres. The therapists form a team and may use an observation room provided with audio-visual and telephone connection between the team members. Conjoint therapies of families of origin are most urgently needed by young patients whose contacts outside the home are quite limited, and whose differentiation from parents is inadequate. With severely autistic patients, this may be the only way to stimulate a therapeutic process. But conjoint therapy is also indicated for less severely ill, acutely distressed young patients of the schizophrenia group, whenever the core of their problems appears to lie in ambivalence about growing independent of their families. The goals of therapy include helping family members gain better understanding of their thoughts, feelings and intentions towards each other, as well as providing support for establishing boundaries between each other and assisting individuation.

Those patients who have established a new family or a couple relationship before the manifestation of their psychosis form another indication for family therapy. Therapy of the family of origin or couple therapy for the patient and his or her spouse or partner is often indicated. According to our clinical experience, psychosis in these cases is usually a regressive decompensation and the chances of recovery are better in family or couple therapy than individual therapy, even if dependent on the attitudes of the partner (Alanen *et al*, 1986). However, individual therapy following the initial intervention may sometimes be the therapy of choice.

Psychodynamic individual therapy

Psychodynamic individual therapy from the beginning is best suited to patients whose personality development is more differentiated than that of the average person with schizophrenia. Many of them have also moved out from their primary families. For many others, a conjoint family therapy or a therapeutic process in the psychotherapeutic community may be an important requisite for successful individual therapy. The well conducted family therapy and/or therapeutic community provides patients with curiosity and motivation to study their problems.

Alanen (1997*a*) has emphasised the importance of the therapist's empathic personality and the 'fit' between the therapist and patient. This is more significant in the therapy of patients with psychosis than in more technically structured neurosis psychotherapy. The process of development is rooted in the patient's transference relationship with the therapist, as well as identifications with the therapist and his or her attitudes and a release of the patient's previously constrained resources for personality growth. Following Kohut's (1971) concept the therapist thus becomes an increasingly important self-object for the patient, correcting the deficiencies of earlier self-object relationships.

During the assessment phase of first-admission patients, if possible, no neuroleptic medication will be administered. Benzodiazepines may be used to control the patient's anxiety. The main effort is on approaching and establishing a psychological contact with the patient as well as with the participants in the first therapy meetings. Thus, we are better able to examine his or her life situation *in vivo,* and the definition of the patient's condition as an illness in the medical sense is postponed. Furthermore, the psychological approach is often just as effective in calming down the patient as neuroleptics are. Later, neuroleptics in small or moderate doses are used, when necessary, to support the psychotherapeutically oriented treatment. As the patient's condition improves, the dosage should be lowered gradually, preferably aiming at discontinuation. According to the experiences of the Inter-Scandinavian NIPS Project (Alanen *et al*, 1994), long-term psychotherapeutic treatment clearly diminishes the patients' need for neuroleptics. Our projects in Finland have indicated that many acutely ill patients of the schizophrenia group can be effectively treated without neuroleptics if the psychotherapeutic resources are developed vigorously and in a comprehensive way.

As pointed out by Ugelstad (1979), the number of individuals who annually become severely schizophrenic is so small – and the financial losses incurred by society due to their illness so large – that it should be possible to provide much more active and intensive treatment for these patients than is available currently. However, the resources of public health care remain limited, even when strengthened by cooperation with private services. Supportive therapeutic relationships with relatively infrequent sessions are useful for many patients, but the prospects of intensive, psychoanalytically oriented long-term therapies are not good for all of them. Therapy of the latter kind is best suited when:

(a) the schizophrenic disorder does not belong to the most serious clinical category;
(b) insightful motivation for long-term work is being or has been aroused in both the patient and the therapist;
(c) the requisites for sufficient continuity of the therapeutic relationship exist.

However, indications often arise during the ongoing process and certain flexibility is warranted even here.

Development of training programmes

The developmental process in Turku was begun without any formal training of staff members. Many therapists, mostly nurses, displayed a good natural inclination and enthusiasm for this approach. When supported by supervision activities they attained promising results with patients. However, difficulties were encountered and the need for a more formal training became evident.

We have already referred to the revolutionary impact of the systemic psychodynamically oriented family therapy training. Beginning in 1986, the initial three-year training courses (a 'special level training' later accepted as the basis for state registration of psychotherapists) were completed in Turku by a further deeper two-year course (an 'advanced specialist level training').

In 1986, a three-year special level training programme in 'psycho-dynamic individual psychotherapy' also began, with the last year being dedicated to psychosis psychotherapy. Personal psychodynamic psychotherapy of the trainees was one of the preconditions for the training. In 1994, a complementary three-year advanced special level training in psychodynamic individual therapy for patients who were severely disturbed (with psychosis or a borderline personality disorder) was established. The purpose of this training programme was to close the gap in most psychotherapy training programmes by offering systematic training in the treatment of the most serious psychic disorders and to integrate some of the special demands of public and private psychiatric health care. The trainers were psychoanalysts especially familiar in the psychotherapy of patients with psychosis the trainees – psychiatrists, psychologists and nurses specialised in psychiatry – had had a personal psychoanalysis. A special emphasis was put on the handling of the countertransference problems met by the trainees.

The comprehensive training programme designed to change the whole treatment culture in Western Lapland is described in the next chapter.

Implementations of the need-adapted model

In the 10-year follow-up of the NSP, in 1992, 50 psychosis teams were found to operate in different parts of the country (Tuori, 1994; Tuori *et al*, 1998). These teams and the routine inclusion of patients and family members in the treatment through therapy meetings have been the most widespread tools of the need-adapted model.

Creation of a working new treatment system is a relatively slow process where the local needs and resources meet the new ideas in a co-evolutionary process. There has been local psychotherapy training courses arranged that have greatly raised the competence of the staff. Inclusion of all levels of staff is important. At its best an individual staff member is involved in a long-term, need-adapted process to develop his or her clinical skills. This helps to avoid the typical paradox in psychiatry where those with least training tend to work with the patients with the most challenging problems.

The adaptive quality of the model led to local variations resembling the need-adapted process of the individual patient's treatment. Psychosis teams that originally operated from hospitals are now most often out-patient based. Some function mainly as psychosis teams, others work also with other crisis situations. The sizes of the teams vary, being usually 2–5 members, and they have maintained their multi-professional quality. Due to the abundant availability of family therapy training most teams have members with a formal three-year family therapy training.

Therapy meetings have a central role in establishing the initial shared image or understanding of the patients and his or her network situation. Our understanding is that an image of this kind is always created and guides the interaction in the network (Lehtinen & Räkköläinen, 1986, 1993; Aaltonen & Räkköläinen, 1994). In therapy meetings it becomes a conscious shared construction of the therapeutic process that guides the interaction and actions. A common failure is that therapy meetings are used as reporting sessions where family members and staff discuss the problem of the patient's illness. When this happens the shared image is simplified to that of a medical illness and the potential available in the systemic and psychodynamic understanding is lost. For therapy meetings to function the staff involved need enough experience and training. Therapy meetings require sensitivity, therefore good cooperation between the staff members is needed. This is true of any teamwork in the need-adapted model.

Local developments

In some areas with poor organisation and little previous training in different forms of psychotherapy the development has been quite rapid with intense investments. The strategies have varied between the two extremes of providing a variety of training programmes to different staff members to giving most staff members a similar basic training. The latter approach has been chosen in Western Lapland and Tampere.

Western Lapland

The Western Lapland Health District (WLHD) is situated to the north of the Gulf of Bothnia and on the border with Sweden. The southern part of the district is industrialised, including two towns. The total population of the catchment area is 72 000 inhabitants. Rapid development started and concrete goals were set through the Western Lapland Project in 1987 (Seikkula *et al*, 1995). It aimed to develop a comprehensive family and network-centred psychiatric treatment model on the boundary between the out-patient and in-patient treatment systems. It was to acheive this by giving all the municipal psychiatric staff involved in out-patient and in-patient care three years of on-the-job training in systemic and network-oriented family therapy. The district staff are 8 psychiatrists, 11 psychologists, 5 social workers, 41 registered psychiatric nurses and 43 mental health nurses – a total of 108 staff members. The systemic three-year family therapy training programmes were started in 1989.

The main theoretical background was systemic family therapy influenced by the integrating principles of the need-adapted approach of the Turku project (Alanen *et al*, 1991), and the reflective approach

(Andersen, 1990; Seikkula *et al*, 1995). In addition to the family therapy programmes, a two-year psychodynamically oriented individual therapy training programme was started in 1992.

The training has been carried out according to the following principles:

(a) Training is a continuing process and all staff members receive it.
(b) The training is wholly conducted as on-the-job training. All the supervised patients and families are from the staff members' normal case load and the supervised training forms a part of the patients' treatment programme. As a result there is no decrease in the number of patients treated by the staff during the programme.
(c) A special focus of the training has been to tailor it as an integral part of the special features of the culture by emphasising home visits as an essential part of the training. The aim is a culture syntonic method of treatment, based on flexible interaction between patient, family and the social network in every phase of the process.
(d) The principal trainers are members of the municipal psychiatric staff of the mental health district (psychologists, psychiatrists, social workers – a total of eight trainers). They have first received training of their own in the family therapy training programme arranged by the Finnish Association for Mental Health or in an individual therapy training programme arranged by the University of Jyväskylä. Training others is part of their everyday clinical work as members of the municipal staff. Consequently the costs of the training are minor.

By 1995, 90% of the out-patient and in-patient psychiatric staff had received at least two years of formal training in some form of psychotherapy and over 70% of the staff had received at least three years of formal training in family therapy. The municipal psychiatric system of treatment became saturated with family-therapeutic skills. This resulted in a development where the specific psychosis teams became unnecessary and most staff members were competent enough to work in case-specific teams. This development hopefully solves a major drawback of the psychosis team approach. Ideally, the team that initially is in contact with the patient and the network should continue with the treatment throughout. The case load of psychosis teams often makes this impossible and they tend to be involved only in the acute phases.

Another development is the modification of the need-adapted approach called the 'open-dialogue approach' (ODA) (Seikkula *et al*,

1995). In ODA the focus is not only on illness. The team has to generate open dialogue between all participants (patient, family members, professionals). The aim of dialogue is to construct a new language for the difficult experiences of the patient and of those nearest to him or her in connection with the patient's psychotic behaviour. The question of the schizophrenia-specificity of the symptoms is left totally open, and in consequence the aim of the system of treatment is to facilitate an alternative, not problem-saturated story (White & Epston, 1990). Discussions in treatment meetings are arranged according to principles applied from the reflective approach (Andersen, 1990).

Tampere

In Tampere, as in Western Lapland, home visits are strongly favoured. The Tampere project is an example of an attempt to apply the need-adapted model in an area with plenty of pre-existing structures. The experience has been that introducing the model in more established settings is difficult and the development tends to be slower. Tampere is the largest city except for Helsinki in Finland; local in-patient and out-patient psychiatry is organised by Tampere University hospital. The hierarchy is complex and the model applied in the treatment of psychoses is mostly medical. Independent staff members may have extensive training in some forms of psychotherapy or other special skills, though the general level of psychotherapeutic competence is low. A psychosis team was established in 1991. This was quite late compared with most other parts of Finland. Therapy meetings were not a routine.

The approach chosen was to combine the psychoeducational (Falloon & Fadden, 1993) and the need-adapted models. The psychoeducational model was more acceptable and more 'in tune' with the medical approach. Working to combine the two models has been highly beneficial. The practicality of the psychoeducational approach has made it easier to comprehend the general frame of the need-adapted model. The emphasis on early intervention and extensive work with the families at home visits has rapidly changed the experience of a large portion of the staff members. The one-year training that has been designed has been given to over 120 staff members since 1994. New developments incorporated into the need-adapted model include better understanding of how to give information to the patient and the family – a previously neglected area in the model. Instead of rigid psychoeducation the aim is to provide the patient, and other involved persons, with pertinent information that supports the treatment process, to create an atmosphere of 'it is good to know and understand, and questions are important'.

On *diagnosis*

The systemic and psychodynamic orientations of the need-adapted model make diagnosis problematic. The present non-aetiological and phenomenological diagnoses of the DSM and ICD classifications are of limited use. Especially in the initial phases of treatment, where the aim is to tolerate the uncertainty before enough understanding is gained, a premature diagnosis limits and may misguide the treatment process. With the introduction of systemic ideas into the need-adapted model the need for simultaneous understanding of different levels became evident. There was also concern about the effects that a diagnostic definition on one level might have on the other. The diagnosis of schizophrenia or a symbiotic relationship serves as an example: they both imply a multitude of conscious and unconscious material that has effects on the experience and behaviour of the patient, his or her network members and the staff (Lehtinen & Räkköläinen, 1993).

The integrated and need-adapted approach is founded on being problem-oriented. The diagnostic categories introduced below are based on different perspectives, the first being more individual-interactional and the other family-interactional. They are overlapping; both have specific implications for treatment and should be evaluated separately. The individual-interactional diagnostic grouping developed in the Kupittaa project has been inspired by Pao (1979). (see Tables 12.1 and 12.2).

Malignant isolation syndrome is a term chosen to describe an interactional pattern where the patient has been seen by the family as weak and a patient for years before treatment is sought. Quite often this weakness has resulted in close involvement with one of the parents, most often the mother. This has left the other spouse alone more, and the family as isolated, having a very closed network mostly consisting of relatives. Typically, the patient has slowly isolated him- or herself socially and has missed the normal psychosexual developments in adolescence, which is highly dangerous and malignantly undermines his or her possibilities for independent adult life. The family and the patient are in a vicious circle of isolation, worry, shame and increasing isolation.

In treatment it is important to recognise the chronicity and hopelessness in the situation. Treatment easily becomes a partner in maintaining the status quo. Rapid and effective interventions focusing on the vicious circle of isolation are necessary. It is important to gain some often small and practical improvement and open a window of hope. Linking the illness to daily life must happen in small practical steps. Keeping the patients as much as possible connected to a normal network as opposed to hospitalisation has seemed beneficial. It is most

TABLE 12.1.
*The individual-interactional diagnostic grouping developed in the Kupittaa
project for planning of the treatment and follow-up*

Group	Properties	Specific implications for treatment
1 Identity crisis	While there may have been cumulative traumata in the patient's psychological and social development, the patient's history reveals nearly phase-adequate development, functioning and identity. The interactional atmosphere of the family is open; the parents do not include the patient in their struggles. Constituents for good prognosis.	Need for safety, extensive first aid and holding that gives space for spontaneous remission and the further maturation process of identity. If psychotherapy is needed, individual therapy supported by family therapy is indicated. No neuroleptics are needed.
2 Separation crisis	Prolonged and tortuous separation process, appears as stormy and unrealistic attempts at individuation. Developmental lag in each phase of psychological and social development. Underlying borderline personality organisation (Kernberg, 1981). The interactional atmosphere of the family is not open; the parents tend to include the patient in their struggles. Constituents for good *or* poor prognosis.	Intensive family- and individual psychotherapy from the beginning, in many cases for years. Neuroleptics are indicated with good response.
3 Double-blind crisis	Prolonged symbiosis appears as flattened affect, autistic thinking, psychosocial regression and isolation. The psychosocial development and identity forming is diffuse and the onset of symptoms insidious. Chronic psychotic personality organisation. The interactional atmosphere of the family is a mystified, double-bind situation (Bateson *et al*, 1956) leading to unbreakable psychological ties. Constituents for poor prognosis.	Extensive rehabilitative interventions. Neuroleptics: need evaluation on an individual basis.

important to call forth and support the patients' own initiatives and
activity. Here the team must work at home with a flexible method,
extending the work to the larger network. This can be done more

TABLE 12.2

The family-interactional diagnostic grouping for planning of the treatment and follow-up (Lehtinen, 1993a, 1994)

Group	Family interaction	Social state	Specific implications for treatment
Acute crisis	The psychosis is clearly and easily linked to the intensification of long-term problems in the family, sometimes involving also other important relations. It is often seen that several family members have symptoms and they may have sought help individually.	The patient and the family function relatively normally in connection to the larger network.	Immediate family crisis intervention focused on recognising the problem areas in family interaction. Rapid symptom relief of all burdened by the crisis is usual when the proper target has been located.
Stagnated crisis	Family interaction is locked; an unsatisfactory and burdening arrangement has become chronic. From a systemic viewpoint the patient's psychosis appears to be a solution to an impossible situation, an attempt to get something to move. The stagnation in the interaction has a timeless quality (Lehtinen *et al*, 1985) and this balance is threatened by children growing.	The family is relatively closed. The "rubber fence" phenomenon (Singer & Wynne, 1963) limits integration with the larger network.	Immediate family crisis intervention. Though rapid changes are not to be expected it is important to analyse the problem areas. Due to the long history of interactional problems this group needs long-term work with a suitable form of therapy. Good continuity and follow-up essential.
Malignant isolation syndrome	The patient has been treated as if a patient by the family for years before treatment is sought. The family and the patient are in a vicious circle of isolation, worry, shame and increased isolation. The situation is chronic from the very beginning of treatment.	Family is extremely closed and isolated. The network consists of close relatives.	The patient has missed age-specific developments thus ties to normal life need to be rapidly built and any existing ties strengthened. Good continuity and follow-up essential. Risk that hopelessness seduces unrealistic attempts to cure.

easily when observations on practical problems lead the way.

In the larger network there is a tendency to leave the patients isolated because of fear and of not knowing how to approach and behave. A practical reformulation can be used in these situations:

> V has for some reason isolated himself from his age group and has not gained the experience of how to be in contact with other people as a grown-up, especially this is a problem in relation to women. The task is so difficult that he has created an imaginary world, which he enters when the difficulties seem too big or when the isolation becomes unbearable. Our task is to repeatedly shake him out of his imaginary world to our common reality and thus pull him into this reality. These experiences are essential for him because they are the primary means for gaining enough relational skills to feel secure enough to slowly loosen himself more and more from his imaginary world.

It has appeared to be important that the therapists continually focus on the worst that has happened and unearth it into the discussion. Otherwise, the unspoken undermines the entire work and treatment alliance. It has also been our repeated experience that when the worst is focused on by the therapists, others bring up the good and healthy in the patient's behaviour. In some families, when enough improvement over the years is achieved, the problems in the marriage, which we had prematurely focused an intervention on initially, start to appear and may be worked with.

Evidence of efficacy

The crucial question is: does the model work in everyday clinical practice? In this section the scientific evidence of the efficacy of the model is presented briefly.

Repeated follow-up studies in Turku

The efficacy of the core model has been assessed by several follow-up studies of cohorts of consecutive first-admission patients in the schizophrenia group from the Turku Mental Health District from the 1960s to the 1990s (see Table 12.3). Because of the priority of developmental goals, methods usually applied in controlled psycho-therapy trials were not used into these prospective follow-up studies. If we had divided the patients in randomised groups, and predefined the kinds of treatments to be given to each group, this would have prevented the development of a treatment model based on an analysis of each patient's and his or her network's idiographic, unique and changing needs (Alanen *et al*, 1980).

Finnish integrated model 253

TABLE 12.3.
The different cohorts of first-time patients in the Turku Schizophrenia Project. Study
design and outcome (Alanen, 1997a)

Cohort	Year of admission	n	Development of psycho-therapeutic approaches	Follow-up studies
I	1965–67 (24 months)	100	Single patients in individual therapy, hospital-centred. A retrospective 8-year follow-up study	1973–74
II	1969 (12 month)	75 (39)	Single patients in individual or family therapy, psychotherapeutic communities initiated	1971 1977
III	1976–77 (19 months)	100 (56)	Individual therapy and psychotherapeutic communities well developed, open care included	1979 1981 1983
IV	1983–84 (12 months)	30	Need-adapted approach with initial family-centred therapy meetings, family therapy well developed (Cohort is part of the NSP sample)	1985 1987
V	1989 onwards		Kupittaa project. Follow-up becomes a routine. Better integration of individual and family therapy. Indications for neuroleptics under closer scrutiny. Biological research is integrated. (A sub-cohort is part of the API sample)	1994 1997

The numbers in parentheses (Cohorts I–III) refer to patients diagnosed with 'typical schizophrenia'. In Cohorts IV and V the DSM–III–R classification was applied. This classification was retrospectively applied to Cohort III (cf. Table 12.4.). Cohort V differs from the previous in that the patient collection and periodic follow-up has become a routine. NSP, National Schizophrenia Project. API, Acute Psychosis – Integrated Treatment Project

We would like to add that, despite their ostensible objectivity, the controlled psychotherapy trials involve significant limitations, which have not been generally recognised (Alanen, 1997a). Due to the clinical heterogeneity of schizophrenia and the differences in both the motivation to treatment and the therapeutic needs of the patients, a single mode of treatment may be successful only in a portion of the patients, being unsuitable for the others. However, in the statistical analysis of an unselected population, these kinds of differences do not appear. Furthermore, the treatment of most patients with schizophrenia requires an integrated approach where several modes of therapy are optimally combined. The investigation of a single treatment mode, as is usual in a controlled trial, cannot evaluate the multiple possibilities of a compre-hensive psychotherapeutic treatment of schizophrenia. Furthermore, it would also be very difficult to study over time such combinations of

Alanen et al

treatment elements using a controlled method because this would require too great a number of treatment cells and patients.

Instead, our strategy allowed comparison of the outcomes between different stages of the development of the model. The cohorts as well as the general frames and development of the Turku project are described in more detail by Alanen (1997a).

The interpretation of these follow-up data (Salokangas, 1986; Alanen *et al*, 1991; Lehtinen, 1993b; Lehtinen & Räkköläinen, 1993; Alanen, 1997a) is difficult because of the research design. As the out-patient care of the Turku Mental Health District and Kupittaa hospital did not participate in the development work at the beginning, but became involved later, the data do not only represent the effects of the therapeutic orientation centred in the activities of the Turku University Clinic of Psychiatry. The latter provided most of the hospital care. Another factor that made outcome comparison between cohorts difficult was the difference in the diagnostic criteria. The classification initially used was in accordance with the Scandinavian tradition initiated by Langfeldt (1956). Extensive records from the previous studies made re-diagnosing of the older series possible. This was done using DSM–III–R diagnostic criteria applied in the later series. These diagnoses have been used in the comparison of the five-year follow-up findings of Cohorts III and IV (see Table 12.4).

Comparing the five-year follow-up outcomes of Cohorts III and IV favours the systemic family therapy-based approach introduced between Cohorts III and IV. It is important to keep in mind the limitations of using historical controls, although the findings are also supported by clinical experiences.

The patients in Cohort IV utilised hospital for a total of less than half the number of days of the earlier cohort. They also needed less

TABLE 12.4
Detailed comparison of five-year outcomes in Cohorts III and IV of the Turku Schizophrenia Project, DSM–III–R classification (Lehtinen, 1993b)

Cohort	Year of admission	n	No. of psychotic symptoms*	On disability pension (%)**	Hospital days during 5 years, per patient
III	1976–77 (19 months)	56	38	51	272
IV	1983–84 (12 months)	30	61	18	132

Patients with the diagnoses schizophrenic disorder, schizophreniform disorder and schizoaffective disorder are included. the percentages are calculated for the patients who attended the follow-up examination (53 earlier, 28 later cohort). There were 2 suicides in the earlier, 1 in the later cohort. *Difference between cohorts P<0.05, Pearson's X^2-test. **Difference between cohorts P<0.0005, Pearson's X^2-test.

out-patient care. Yet they were functioning much better with less psychotic symptoms and fewer were registered for a disability pension. The difference in hospital days was highly significant (non-parametric Mann–Whitney test $P=0.002$). However, this is partly an unfair comparison because the aim for Cohort III was to encourage 'long-enough' admissions to allow full engagement in treatment. Only 18% in the 1983–84 series were on disability pension compared with 51% in the 1976–77 series. The sum of the Strauss–Carpenter (Strauss & Carpenter, 1974, 1977) sub-scales (range 0–16) at the five-year follow-up was compared using the noN-parametric Mann–Whitney test; the later series managed significantly better ($P=0.008$). The Strauss–Carpenter scale includes hospitalisation during the last year, the analysis was conducted also without the hospitalisation variable and the difference remained significant ($P=0.020$) (Lehtinen, 1993*b*).

The results were most impressive in the acute crisis group (see Table 12.2); these patients could most often be treated in one to three family sessions within community care or with short hospitalisations; neuroleptics could be avoided or were used for a limited period. In the group of stagnated crisis the benefits were less clear: the patients seemed to need longer treatment – whether it was family or individual therapy. In the third group, consisting of more patients with chronic illnesses with malignant isolation syndrome, rehabilitative activities focused on everyday life problems and inclusion of the larger network when needed seemed to give a better result than systemic family interventions. Some of these practices developed resemble those of the psychoeducational approach in the Buckingham Project (Falloon & Fadden, 1993). The family approach seemed to improve the outcome especially for male patients, a finding that is congruent with our clinical experiences.

Preliminary follow-up data from the Kupittaa study

A specific aim in the Kupittaa Project in Turku has been to find relevant indications for neuroleptic use in 'drug-naive' cases within the frames of psychotherapeutically oriented integrated treatment (Vuorio *et al*, 1993). For this purpose neuroleptics have been initially avoided in a study cohort that now numbers 85 cases. The use of neuroleptics followed the diagnostic principles presented earlier in Table 12.1. It consists of all treatment naïve cases from both in-patient and out-patient services during years 1989 to 1998. The 4–8-year outcome of the first 37 patients in the schizophrenia group is shown in Table 12.5.

The most intensive psychotherapeutic work was done with Group 2 patients; therapies in Group 1 were clearly shorter. All six cases in Group 3 had been in rehabilitation programmes. During the follow-up, 17 of the total 37 cases had not used neuroleptics at all. In addition, following the first episode, none of the 17 had a psychotic relapse.

TABLE 12.5.

The 4–8-year outcome of the 37 cases in the Kupittaa project (Räkköläinen, 1997)

Group (see Table 12.1)	n	No psychotic symptoms	Still in treatment	No disability pension	No neuroleptics during follow-up[1]
Identity crisis	10	10	1	9	9
Separation crisis	21	15	10	13	7
Double-bind crisis	6	2	5	0	1
Total	37	27	16	22	17

1. The period from the beginning of treatment to the follow-up 4-8 years later.

TABLE 12.6.

The two-year outcome of the API cohort by study site; figures are percentages

Outcome measure	Experimental group (%)	Control group (%)	Total (%)	χ^2	P
Less than 2 weeks in hospital during 2 years	51	26	42	6.40	0.01
No psychotic symptoms during last year	58	41	52	2.92	0.09
Employed at follow-up	33	31	32	0.05	0.83
GAS score 7 or more	49	25	40	5.51	0.02
Retained grip on life[1]	66	55	62	1.11	0.29

1. With retained grip on life we mean that the patient continues, at least in his or her thoughts pertaining to the future, to maintain his or her efforts to achieve the goals and modes of satisfaction associated normally with the interpersonal relationships and social life of an adult human being (Salokangas *et al*, 1989).

Two-year outcome in the Acute Psychosis – Integrated Treatment Project

As a spin-off from the Turku Project and the NSP and especially because of the experiences from earlier phases of the Kupittaa Project a new project was started in Finland in 1992. The project, which was called API (Acute Psychosis – Integrated treatment), was conducted as a multi-centre endeavour in six psychiatric catchment areas from different parts of the country (Lehtinen *et al*, 1996).

One of the main aims of the API Project was to assess the role of neuroleptic drug treatment when patients were treated according to the principles of the model described above in a semi-controlled study design. The subjects in the project consisted of consecutive first-time patients with non-affective psychosis collected from the six study centres during years 1992–93. Three of the centres (experimental) agreed to implement a scheme of minimal neuroleptic use while the other three centres (control) used neuroleptics as usual. The minimal neuroleptics use scheme included a three-week neuroleptic-free initial period whenever possible and initiation of neuroleptics with particular restraint (only when considered as definitely necessary).

The total sample of the project was 135 patients of whom 106 (67 in the experimental group and 39 in the control group) participated in the two-year follow-up study. In the experimental group 43% of the patients did not receive neuroleptics at all during the total two-year follow-up period including the initial phase of treatment while the corresponding figure in the control group was 6%. On the other hand,

TABLE 12.7

Predictors of psychotic symptoms at two-year follow-up; step-wise logistic regression analysis using gender, age, diagnosis, time since first psychiatric symptoms, time since first psychotic symptoms and site as independent variables

Variable	Relative risk	95% CI		P
		Low	High	
DSM–IV diagnosis				0.029
Schizophreniform psychosis	1.0			
Schizophrenia	5.88	1.82	19.61	
Delusional psychosis	1.79	0.27	11.76	
Atypical psychosis	1.45	0.43	4.76	
Site				0.009
Experimental	1.0			
Control	3.33	1.28	9.09	

all patients had therapy meetings and almost all received some form of other psychological treatment.

Generally, the situation of the patients at the two-year follow-up was relatively good but the outcome was somewhat better in the experimental group than in the control group (Table 12.6).

To control for possible confounding factors (e.g. differences in the diagnostic distribution) a stepwise logistic regression analysis of the outcome measures were conducted using age, gender, diagnosis, time from first psychiatric symptom, time from first psychotic symptom and site (experimental or control) as explanatory variables. The clearest difference in outcome between the experimental and control group (in favour of the experimental group) appeared in the length of hospital treatment and occurrence of psychotic symptoms. The analysis of the last-mentioned outcome measure is shown in Table 12.7. As can be seen, only the diagnosis and the site came into the model as significant explanatory variables. The most remarkable finding from this analysis is the difference between the sites: the odds ratio of showing psychotic symptoms during the last follow-up year was more than three-fold for the control group in comparison to the experimental group.

The routine use of neuroleptics in the treatment of patients diagnosed with first-episode schizophrenia-type psychosis seems not to be as essential as it usually has been considered. The two-year outcome of a group of unselected patients, treated according to the Finnish model but avoiding neuroleptics in almost half of the patients, was even somewhat better than that of the control group receiving neuroleptics as usual.

In interpreting the results of this study one has, however, to consider its weaknesses. Among them is the lack of information on the reliability of diagnostics, the heterogeneity of diagnosis and the possible bias caused by the fact that the project teams who also participated in the treatment of the patients made all the outcome assessments. The fact that there were drop-outs both in the initial recruiting phase and in the follow-up may also have some effect on the results. We believe, however, that these factors do not invalidate the main result of this study.

It should be mentioned that in the two-year follow-up of Cohort III of the Turku Schizophrenia Project, that an independent psychiatrist made a parallel clinical assessment of the patients. The correlation between her assessments and those of our team members was of the order of 0.6–0.7. It was noteworthy that the assessments of the independent examiner were consistently more optimistic prognostically than those of the team, probably because of the team's more comprehensive knowledge of the patients (Alanen *et al*, 1986).

Preliminary results of the Western Lapland Project

Decline in the number of long-term hospital patients with schizophrenia

In spite of scarcer resources in the out-patient sectors than is average in Finland, the number of new long-term (hospitalised for the first time for more than one year but less than two) hospital patients with schizophrenia fell to zero in the early 1990s. This has only ever occurred in this single psychiatric catchment area in Finland and has remained so ever since. The national average in 1992 was 3.5 per 100 000 inhabitants (Tuori, 1994).

Decline in the indications for hospital treatment

In a sub-project by Keränen (1992) it was found that 40% of the patients referred by general practitioners and the psychiatric out-patient clinics to the hospital could be successfully treated in out-patient care if family, and network, centred treatment meetings were arranged by the multi-disciplinary team as the first alternative instead of admitting the patient to the hospital. Previously, all these patients were hospitalised.

Changes in the incidences of schizophrenia

According to a retrospective survey the incidence of treated schizophrenia has clearly decreased during the years that the new treatment system has been used in all severe psychiatric crises. The annual incidence of the schizophrenia group psychoses (DSM–III–R) decreased from an average of 24.6 per 100 000 during the years 1985–89, when the comprehensive family and social network-centred system of treatment was not in use, to 10.4 (*P*<0.001) during the years when the system of treatment was well established (1990–94).

Summary of outcome data

Our treatment model has evolved greatly during the years of research and development. Follow-up cohorts have been collected to study the effects of changes in the treatment approach by comparing results in the new cohort with its changes or additions to the treatment model with the previous cohort and model. Our findings support the conclusion that early family and network interventions and an inter-actional general orientation should be the basis for the treatment of schizophrenic psychoses in community psychiatry. Promising family-centred preventive activities have also been achieved.

In recent years, the widespread use of this approach in Finland has made open multi-centre studies possible, as is the case in the API

Project. Its results support our clinical observations that, in contrast to current beliefs, neuroleptics are not always needed in the treatment of the schizophrenia group of psychotic conditions and the indications for use of neuroleptics should be more closely defined.

Some conclusions, observations and recommendations

The general trends in psychiatry during the last two decades have had a narrow focus. Increasing complexity of the phenomenological diagnostic systems and the development of new drugs have drawn psychiatry away from the psychosocial approach. Most of the research published today is either biological or epidemiological. Though there should be no doubt of the benefits of integrated approaches combining different treatment modes with each other in order to produce the best possible results in each case, such approaches are rarely seen in the psychiatric research and literature. There is an urgent need to develop further the theory, training and research into integrated approaches.

The development of the need-adapted approach is a process that has been going on for several decades. It is the result of a complex endeavour where in the background the main principles are guiding the continuation of the developmental process. New additions to the model are evaluated in general psychiatric settings where there is responsibility for the whole of the local population; all new cases of psychoses leave the·model always incomplete and developing. We emphasise that this developmental quality is an essential part of our approach, as of any psychotherapeutic work. The experiences from the separate sub-projects clearly show that new implementations of the model are context sensitive and not straightforward replications of the original. This feature has been observed not only in the examples presented here but also in other implementations.

Our choice of research methodology is deliberately based on problem-oriented (or need-oriented) action research principles, aimed at the development of a real life range of therapeutic activities within community psychiatry, rather than being separate treatment trials studying the efficacy of single treatment modes. Each developmental project is different and tailored to local circumstances where flexible and integrated use of different psychotherapeutic modalities becomes both practical and necessary. The treatment results of the comprehensive approach are also good compared with those of other first-episode follow-up studies where the treatment has been mainly medication-oriented (Biehl *et al*, 1986; Shepherd *et al*, 1989). The integrated approach has a humanising effect on psychiatric treatment; in the medical approach the patient easily becomes a treatment object.

It is important to note that the amount of staff resources in the project centres has been similar to those in other parts of the country. The changes have been qualitative and have involved all levels of staff. This development and research context makes our approach more applicable to general mental health care than those derived from more isolated research settings.

Successful projects have been characterised by the involvement of all levels of staff and by the general aim to develop the project according to the integrated guidelines of the need-adapted model. Our experience has been that those who work most closely with patients are enthusiastic with the approach. Working as part of a well-functioning team is helpful for both the patient and the staff. Therapy meetings, when successful, are in themselves a learning experience for those involved. A major developmental goal is to improve the general atmosphere and create a milieu of enthusiasm and realistic optimism in the units involved. In our experience it is important that the work is enjoyable. This can be achieved by involving all levels of staff in a need-adapted development process where the units and the individual member of staff's needs and skills are met with training, supervision and possibly personal therapies in the long run. While awareness among staff increases it is important that the new needs are met with further training and supervision options. Systemic curiosity, where different observations are seen as additions to the understanding, support the deeper involvement of staff members in the work. It is most important that development is supported and nourished by those in charge of the organisation. This vital ingredient of the milieu helps staff, patients and relatives maintain or regain their optimism.

Training gives staff members new tools to master and tolerate the burdens they are involved in. With regard to long-term individual therapies, training helps avoid the danger of burn-out leading to stagnation of the therapeutic processes. Nevertheless, we like to encourage staff members without formal training in psychotherapy to begin psychotherapeutic relationships with their patients, with the help of supervision. This often leads to an increasing interest in the problems of psychosis psychotherapy, possibly followed by one's own therapy and a motivation to acquire further training in therapeutic work. An established training system is also one of the factors having a positive effect on the likely continuation of the psychotherapeutic orientation.

Accepting the approach has been slower in units that are hierarchical and/or have a long history of commitment to some particular treatment approach. This can be viewed as resistance or as an indication of unobserved positive capacities in the system. Larger units also tend to be hierarchical and this makes the staff members cautious. Psychosis teams are in an unusual strategic and observatory position. Their role as coordinators of treatments may be experienced as problematic and threatening to the existing practices. The work needs special support from those in charge. The psychosis teams also need to analyse carefully their position in the system they operate in.

An increasingly difficult problem is the lack of psychotherapeutic knowledge and skills of psychiatrists. The new training programmes do not properly prepare psychiatrists in psychodynamic and systemic understanding. At worst, this leads to a split between the doctors and other staff. It is important to analyse carefully the situation in this respect before attempting to start a development project. There is often a temptation to raise the barricades against the medical establishment, but in such cases the potential development is at risk of dissolving into futile and endless struggles.

There are several important developmental trends in the present projects. Some are directed to more specific therapeutic techniques and their indications. These include better understanding of the indications for neuroleptics, separate therapies and new approaches to informing the patient and his or her network. Others are focusing more on the overall working context of the approach.

Our findings indicate that the use of neuroleptic medication is not as mandatory in the treatment of psychoses as has been suggested and that there are cases where neuroleptics should be avoided. This is especially true for the acute identity crises type of psychoses. The other group where the use of neuroleptics needs caution is the malignant isolation group. These patients often tend to withdraw from interaction and neuroleptics may intensify this behaviour. When really needed in this patient group, it might be better to try drugs that have been shown to lessen this isolation tendency, for example, clozapine.

A major development in the general setting has been inclusion of the wider network than just the family. Home visits and an increased out-patient orientation help to keep the patient better connected with his or her normal life context. Attempts to develop means for helping the patients in prodromal phases are highly important and need close follow-up to analyse their effectiveness. In the future, the preventive activities of the acute psychosis teams should be extended. It is important, however, not to forget those patients who have a less favourable prognosis and still need long and continuous care.

According to our experiences, the establishment of acute psychosis or case-specific teams and the systemic-oriented initial investigation carried out by the teams are the key positions in the development of the treatment of the new schizophrenia group of patients in the

SHEPHERD, M., WATT, D., FALLOON, I., *ET AL* (1989) *The Natural History of Schizophrenia: A Five-Year Follow-Up Study of Outcome and Prediction in a Representative Sample of Schizophrenics.* Cambridge: Cambridge University Press.

SINGER, M. T. & WYNNE, L. C. (1963) Differentation charasteristics of parents of childhood schizophrenics, childhood neurotics and young adult schizophrenics. *American Journal of Psychiatry,* **120,** 234–243.

STATE MEDICAL BOARD IN FINLAND (1988) *Handbooks: The Schizophrenia Project 1981–1988. Final Report of the National Programme of the Study, Treatment and Rehabilitation of Schizophrenia Patients in Finland,* No. 4. Helsinki: Valtion Painatuskeskus.

STRAUSS, J. (1977) Prediction of outcome in schizophrenia. Five-year outcome and its predictors. *Archives of General Psychiatry,* **34,** 159–163.

—— & CARPENTER, W. (1974) The prediction of outcome in schizophrenia: ll. Relationships between predictor and outcome variables. *Archives of General Psychiatry,* **31,** 37–42.

TUORI, T. (1994) *Stakes Raportteja, 143: Skitsofrenian hoito kannattaa. Raportti skitsofrenian tutkimuksen, hoidon ja kuntoutuksen valtakunnallisen kehittämisohjelman 10-vuotisarvioinnista.* Helsinki: Gummerus.

——, LEHTINEN, V., HAKKARAINEN, A., *ET AL* (1998) The Finnish National Schizophrenia Project 1981–1987: 10-year evaluation of its results. *Acta Psychiatrica Scandinavica,* **97,** 10–17.

UGELSTAD, E. (1979) Possibilities of organizing psychotherapeutically oriented treatment programs for schizophrenia within sectorized psychiatric service. In *Psychotherapy of Schizophrenia* (ed. C. Müller), pp. 118–125. Amsterdam: Excerpta Medica.

VUORIO, K. A., RÄKKÖLÄINEN, V., SYVÄLAHTI, E., *ET AL* (1993) Akuutin psykoosin integroitu hoito I. *Suomen Lääkärilehti,* **48,** 466.

WHITE, M. & EPSTON, D. (1990) *Narrative Means and Therapeutic Ends.* New York: Norton.

13 Psychotherapy and recovery in early psychosis: a core clinical and research challenge

PATRICK McGORRY

Prior to the 1960s, psychotherapy was seen as an optimal form of treatment for schizophrenia and related psychoses (Arieti, 1974). Since that time, for a variety of reasons, it has virtually disappeared from the landscape of care for people with psychosis in most parts of the world and is in retreat elsewhere.

Although older forms of psychotherapy may not have been demonstrably effective (Davidson *et al*, 1998), the consequences of this change have been serious in human terms. While the potential quality of psychopharmacological treatment of psychosis has improved substantially over the past decade, and the systems for providing treatment and care have also been enhanced in many countries, the loss of a psychological and personal perspective has meant that mental health professionals have become deskilled and ill-equipped to properly understand their patients and to respond with skill to their human and developmental needs.

Conversely, there is accumulating evidence supporting a revival of interest in psychotherapeutic interventions (e.g. Hogarty *et al*, 1997*a,b*; Kuipers *et al*, 1997; 1998; Shergill *et al*, 1998). While this is encouraging, there is a need to ensure that a range of interventions can be developed and offered. What would be optimal is a spectrum of therapies ranging from simple interventions to the more complex. These would inevitably have to be offered in stages depending on the needs and desires of individual patients, as well as their progress with their recovery. The accessibility and motivation of the patient and their clinical and personal needs differ according to phase of illness, diagnostic subtype, response to drug treatment, personal resources, degree of personal therapeutic alliance and global experience of care. The value of a dynamic and developmental perspective, as well as a set of related therapeutic techniques, is likely to be critical and can be conceived as a complementary paradigm to the illness model and its corresponding treatment strategies.

Such a blended approach has been difficult to engineer in an integrative way in frontline services (Ugelstad, 1979). This is partly because advocates of the psychological approach have often found it difficult to accept the need to integrate psychological therapies with biological treatments. The crudeness of biological reductionism in full flight only reinforces the fears that underpin this resistance, and it is genuinely difficult to achieve comfortable integration at the theoretical level. Other factors, notably the culture and belief systems within the therapeutic environments in which patients with psychosis have been treated (Barrett, 1996), and economic considerations, particularly in the era of managed care, conspire to retard a balanced integration.

Ugelstad (1979) did illustrate how this task might be tackled on a more systematic basis. Nevertheless, in the current era, one of the most powerful influences on broader practice is the establishment in the 'real world' of models of practice that successfully overcome difficult obstacles and provide innovative care. Demonstrating that something previously thought to be unrealistic or impossible can, in fact, be done provides motivation, a boost in morale and a working model for others with similar ideas and goals.

It could, therefore, be seen as a priority to try to create such flagship programmes that comfortably integrate individual psychotherapeutic interventions with biological treatments within a strong community-oriented case management framework. Programmes of this kind, if they are of sufficient size and scope and operate in a frontline or 'real world' manner, can go beyond pure research studies and demonstration projects and play a role not only in directly treating individuals but in influencing, often profoundly and extensively, the treatment and quality of life of a much broader range of people. They do this by acting as a creative space or 'clinical laboratory' in which new skills can be developed, integrated and evaluated, and by showing in a substantive way what is possible under everyday conditions. In this chapter an attempt will be made to identify some of the elements of a psychotherapeutic model for early psychosis in the modern era.

Brief historical overview of psychotherapy in psychosis

The 20th century witnessed the creation of sophisticated forms of psychotherapeutic intervention based on various psychoanalytical theories, originating with the Freudian approach. Freud's original view was that people with schizophrenia and other psychoses were unable to benefit from psychotherapy because they were felt to be unable to form an adequate therapeutic relationship. According to Federn (1952), Freud regarded patients with psychosis as "a nuisance to psychoanalysis". Freud's dismissive comments were rapidly questioned by other psychoanalysts in the first two decades of the 20th century (Nagel, 1991) and later in a substantive way by Sullivan (1931) and Fromm-Reichmann (1948), who showed that, even in the pre-neuro-leptic era, when unchecked and florid psychosis clearly impaired the patient's capacity to relate, it was possible to develop therapeutic relationships with patients with psychosis and, furthermore, a modified form of psychotherapy that appeared to help them recover from their illness.

While much of the care at this time was highly custodial and laden with pessimism, the only hope for recovery was vested in psychoanalytical psychotherapy, and it was the interpersonal school, culminating in the work of Arieti (1974), that provided this humanising influence. Later Arieti was able to partially integrate the biological perspective and to introduce a cognitive dimension to the understanding and treatment of patients.

Unfortunately, at this earlier stage in history, causal models were relatively primitive and reductionistic, so that when apparently more specific and effective forms of drug therapy were serendipitously discovered in the early 1950s, the value of psychotherapy in the treatment of schizophrenia and related psychoses was increasingly called into question. This culminated in research studies (May, 1968) that, based on this reductionistic or 'either/or' model, showed that in the absence of antipsychotic medication, psychotherapy was of little therapeutic benefit. The way these findings and those of later researchers (Gunderson *et al*, 1984) were construed led to catastrophic results for patients and for balance in the treatment of psychosis. The confidence of professionals was seriously undermined in continuing to work in a psychotherapeutic way with patients with psychosis. Biological reductionism took over in most places and the task of studying and refining the integration of treatment strategies was not addressed.

An important exception has been Scandinavia, where a pragmatic form of long-term supportive psychodynamic psychotherapy has survived and remained integrated with other aspects of the care of the patient, at least for the more 'resourceful' patient (Gilbert & Ugelstad, 1994; Alanen *et al*, 1994). Elsewhere, the personal care of patients suffered and professionals virtually stopped talking with their patients. The demise of the psychoanalytical model meant that clinicians lost any blueprint to guide psychotherapeutic work, since no serious alternative was immediately available. For nearly two decades there has been a process of 'die-back', so that it became conventional wisdom that any form of psychotherapy was contraindicated for patients with psychotic disorders.

Custody of the psychological paradigm reverted initially to radical behaviourists, who developed crude interventions, such as the token economy, based on conditioning principles. These were as ineffective as they were dehumanising. Gradually, a third paradigm began to gather strength, as a cognitive perspective emerged, almost as a form of compromise, from the confluence of the two great tributaries of psychoanalysis and behaviourism. Initially and for some time it remained focused upon the neurotic disorders, particularly depression and anxiety. More recently, its influence has lapped on the shores of serious mental illness and even psychosis, a development that was originally foreshadowed in the work of the interpersonal analyst Arieti. Interestingly, this was the same pattern of evolution that occurred with psychoanalysis, which was applied to psychotic disorders only by the second generation of analytical thinkers. In each case a revision of technique was required, particularly in relation to the process of engagement, as well as the specific needs of the patient. This development has begun to restore the psychological perspective and approach in the treatment of patients, and there is accumulating evidence of its effectiveness (Davidson *et al*, 1998; also see Chapter 2).

However, a purely cognitive approach has limitations. While it will have relatively wide potential applicability and utility, one size will not fit all. There is a need for a wider theoretical base and set of therapeutic techniques on one the hand, and for the capacity for greater depth and duration of therapy on the other. Different subsets of patients will need different approaches within a broad psychotherapeutic model. The current situation is one in which we are witnessing a revival of interest arising from the extension of pragmatic if correspondingly limited forms of psychotherapy to the task of promoting recovery from psychotic illness. The challenge then is to ensure that a psychological understanding and formulation, as well as some psychological intervention, forms part of the treatment of all patients, and that more sophisticated approaches with greater depth and scope are available to those who might benefit from them, usually the more 'resourceful' patients described by Gilbert & Ugelstad (1994). The latter component needs further developmental work in the context of emergence from acute psychosis, but clearly needs to draw upon psychodynamic understanding and a modified supportive as well as expressive–investigative technique (Gabbard, 1994; Davidson *et al*, 1998), or a conscious blend of cognitive and analytical approaches something along the lines of the modified cognitive–analytical therapy developed by Ryle for the more serious non-psychotic disorders (Ryle,1995, 1997). This array of psychotherapeutic treatment will need to be much more adequately integrated with modern drug therapies – a difficult, but essential and overdue, task. This will require the development and refinement of new and existing expertise within a facilitating environment. Such environments are difficult to construct and to maintain but not impossible.

Current context for the treatment of psychosis

Within Australia and other developed countries that have been involved in reform of mental health services, the concept of serious mental illness has become popular, partly as a device for containing mental health budgets and targeting finite and often shrinking resources (derived from the stand-alone psychiatric hospitals or asylums), so that as the services move to the community they will not be overwhelmed by an influx of the high prevalence or common mental disorders. This has functioned in some of these countries as a constructive mechanism to prevent the dissipation of funding released from the dissolution of the old state psychiatric hospital system, acting as an organising principle for the allocation of resources in a community-based system. People suffering from schizophrenia and other psychoses fall within the serious mental illness rubric, and not only have a profile of severe morbidity and mortality, but have traditionally been the most neglected when it came to the quality of their psychiatric care. The essence of the serious mental illness profile is that a disorder of this type typically has its onset during adolescence or early adult life (Mrazek & Haggerty, 1994) and is associated with a pervasive disturbance of mental functioning that puts at risk the normal life trajectory and quality of life for the person. The early course is one of several years of relapsing illness with background disability, suffering and distress, punctuated by illness episodes or crises, a significant risk of suicide (a lifetime risk of at least 10%) and ultimately, in most cases, an amelioration of the disorder over time as the person matures or the vulnerability lessens. The latter is qualified by the degree of irreversible damage done while the disorder is at its peak, and by the risk of not surviving the onslaught of the early years of illness. Clearly several disorders, not only schizophrenia, can be characterised by such a profile. Despite the targeting of people with these illness as recipients of scarce mental health resources, there is a lot of catching up to be done to enhance the quality of care and recovery for people who experience the more severe and pervasive psychotic disorders. However, in Australia at least, there is increasing competition for these scarce mental health resources from those advocating a broadening of the diagnostic focus of specialist mental health care (Andrews, 1997; Australian Health Ministers, 1998). Unless there is an increase in overall spending on mental health, clearly justifiable by the data contained in the recent report on the Global Burden of Disease from the World Bank and Harvard University (Murray & Lopez, 1996), this is likely to compromise the advances made in the care of people with psychosis in recent years (McGorry, 1997; Singh & McGorry, 1998). Different threats with perhaps similar or even more severe consequences exist in other countries, particularly the USA.

The facilities and environments in which treatment has been offered have been extremely neglected and underfunded in the past, and this is beginning to be addressed in some countries with more sophisticated deinstitutionalisation programmes, though in others serious new errors have been made so that funding and facilities were dissipated. In Australia, there has been a significant reform process in recent years that has established, particularly in Victoria, a service model that is better integrated with health care generally. Within this structure, however, skill levels, particularly in the psychotherapeutic area are lacking, and there is an urgent need to enhance them. While the funders, applying business-oriented models to mental health care, acknowledge the need for 'quality' and for higher skill levels and even superficially require these as part of their rhetoric and planning, they do not necessarily see psychotherapy at present as a means of achieving these goals. Nevertheless, within a model of integrated hospital and community services and good continuity of care through case management and medical care, the framework is in place to introduce psychotherapeutic interventions. How should we go about this challenging task? One approach is outlined below.

A stitch in time … the case for an early psychosis focus

"The psychiatrist sees too many end states and deals professionally with too few of the pre-psychotic." Sullivan (1927)

" … we should lay great stress on the prompt investigation of failing adjustment, rather than, as is so often the case, wait and see what happens." Sullivan (1927)

At what phase of disorder should this initiative commence? We have argued extensively elsewhere (McGorry, 1992; McGorry & Singh, 1995; McGorry *et al*, 1996), in conjunction with others (Wyatt, 1991;

Birchwood & MacMillan, 1993; McGlashan & Johannessen, 1996; Birchwood *et al,* 1997), that early detection and optimal treatment of psychotic disorders is a logical strategy to reduce morbidity and mortality and to enhance quality of life. There is an equally powerful argument that a psychotherapeutic perspective should be influencing care, and be available at some level from the very beginning of the disorder (shown below). The onset of illness generally occurs in young people in adolescence or early adult life. We know that there is a strong link between delays in treatment and poorer outcome (Wyatt, 1991; Loebel *et al,* 1992). This may derive partly from the impact of the untreated biological disturbance, that may rapidly become treatment resistant (Wyatt, 1991, 1995), but the psychosocial damage wrought by unchecked psychosis, superimposed upon its more subtle yet disabling prodrome during the exquisitely sensitive developmental period of adolescence and early adulthood, is considerable in its own right and may be difficult to repair.

The young people affected are attempting to negotiate major developmental tasks, such as separation–individuation and the establishment of a secure identity. There may be unresolved issues from earlier stages that resurface at this time to complicate the process (e.g. childhood physical or sexual abuse; gross or subtle neglect) and of course the emerging psychosis is not the only evidence of failure to adapt, often apparently linked to a key developmental stressor – such as leaving home. There may be a psychological contribution to vulnerability to, as well as precipitation of, psychotic disorder. We know from the seminal work of Tienari *et al* (1994) that the presence of a disturbed family environment during childhood and adolescence is a critical additive factor increasing the risk of translation of underlying genetic vulnerability into manifest disorder. Conversely, psychotherapeutic attention to the effects of such environmental influences, ideally in the pre-psychotic high-risk phase, or even following the first psychotic episode, may help to reduce initial and subsequent vulnerability to psychotic symptoms.

Furthermore, the impact of the psychosis itself adds serious additional burdens and twists to the task. Serious damage can be done to the person's emerging and fragile sense of identity through the effects of stigma, peer and family relationships suffer and the vocational trajectory is compromised and often truncated. Increased risks of substance misuse, offending behaviour and self-harm occur (Hambrecht & Haefner, 1996). The total experience is one of potential personal disaster (McGorry, 1992; McGorry *et al,* 1996).

There is an urgent need for skilled medical care, but equally for skilled psychotherapeutic treatment, usually beginning with crisis intervention, emotional support, active needs-based intervention, psychoeducation and subsequently individual psychotherapy at some level, provided, that engagement has been possible through the turmoil of the experience and its consequences.

If there is no psychotherapeutic influence on the treatment from the beginning, the task will be correspondingly much more difficult at a later stage, since much more developmental damage and derailment will be manifest, and the malignant erosion of hope and self-esteem resulting from repeated relapse or persistent symptoms and disability may be too advanced. Furthermore, there will be greater access to earlier developmental material during early psychosis than later on, and it will be easier to gain a clearer understanding of the young person independently of the illness and thus develop a better formulation. In the early psychosis, one can begin to engage with and consider with him or her the psychological issues of the person and the greater the preventive opportunities – not only in relation to the psychosis itself, but also to other problematic issues for the young person. This becomes a 'second chance' to tackle earlier developmental failures, this time with skilled help, and comorbid problems of various kinds, which otherwise would have eluded attention. These issues can now be identified and assistance offered.

We know that psychosocial problems and disorders in young people have increased dramatically in prevalence in recent times (Rutter & Smith, 1995), and while these may be even more likely in the context of psychosis (Hambrecht & Haefner, 1996), there is also a greater likelihood of getting some help. It may even be the case, especially for the subgroup of people who can be identified as having an 'ultra-high risk' of developing psychosis even prior to an initial florid episode (McGorry & Singh, 1995; Yung *et al*, 1996, 1998), that a purely psychological intervention may be sufficient and optimal treatment, at least in a proportion of cases. It certainly should be a central element of such preventive intervention (McGorry *et al*, 1998*a*).

Has progress been made in developing preventive strategies?

Although there were early pioneers with very similar ideas and objectives (e.g. Sullivan, 1927), it is only within the past decade that the potential for early intervention has begun to receive widespread international attention (Wyatt, 1991; McGorry, 1992; Birchwood & MacMillan, 1993; McGlashan & Johannessen, 1996). Consequently, a more optimistic attitude to prevention in psychosis has re-emerged. A critical stepping stone for these positive developments has been the focus in Scandinavian countries during the 1970s and 1980s on preventive strategies in early psychosis, which preceded and inspired many of the current generation of clinical researchers (Alanen *et al*, 1994). Interestingly, the Scandinavian projects have been characterised by a commitment to an integrative model that values psychological and biological interventions in a very similar manner to our own programme. The Early Psychosis Prevention and Intervention Centre (EPPIC) programme has sought to play a role in contributing to this international momentum for a more optimistic and holistic approach to psychotic disorders, particularly in young people (Edwards & McGorry, 1998). Within Australia, this momentum has seen the establishment of a state-wide early psychosis service in Victoria, and a National Early Psychosis Project, funded through the National Mental Health Strategy. The fruits of these initiatives across the nation were seen at the recent Second National Early Psychosis Conference held in Hobart in September 1998, where it was clear that all Australian States had developed significant early psychosis strategies and programmes. In addition, there is now an International Early Psychosis Association with over 1500 members from all continents and a very wide range of projects and services focusing on early psychosis (Edwards *et al*, 2000). Substantial amounts of published resource material are becoming available (e.g. McGlashan, 1996; McGorry, 1998; McGorry & Jackson, 1999). We are, therefore, on the threshold of creating a facilitating international environment for preventive interventions in psychosis.

Creating facilitating environments

EPPIC: synergy of clinical developments and outcome research

There has been some progress in Melbourne in establishing a preventively oriented clinical environment for young people, within which efforts have been made to revive and modernise psycho-therapeutic interventions in psychosis (Edwards *et al*, 1994; McGorry, 1996; McGorry *et al*, 1996; McGorry & Jackson, 1999). This process will be described briefly below and illustrates the importance of the integration and synergy of clinical and research endeavours.

The EPPIC programme is a frontline regional mental health service for young people from the Northern and Western suburbs of Melbourne funded by the Department of Human Services, currently through the North-Western Health Care Network (Edwards *et al*, 1994; McGorry *et al*, 1996). Each year EPPIC provides treatment and care for 250 young people receiving treatment for the first time for a psychotic illness, and offers follow-up care for up to 18 months. During this time a range of individual and group-based services are available to the young person and their family, including home-based crisis care, inpatient care, day care and a range of specific treatments including drug therapy and psychological therapies, all within a community-oriented case management context. The initial outcome studies, albeit of quasi-experimental design (i.e. controlled but not randomised), have shown a significant and clinically important improvement in outcome at 12 months for patients treated in this programme compared with those treated in the specialised first-episode programme that immediately preceded it. The latter had been in operation for eight years prior to the advent of the EPPIC model, and was a period of germination of clinical research ideas, as described in Edwards *et al* (1994) and McGorry *et al* (1996), which required a community-oriented model for their full flowering to occur. The 23% improvement in psychosocial functioning and quality of life was achieved with a substantial reduction in dosages of neuroleptics and a shift of the locus and intensity of care to community settings. Completed suicides were reduced over the time frame 1991–1998 from 4% per annum to 0.4% through, we believe, an optimistic clinical stance combined with greater intensity and psychological focus of the community-based programme (McGorry *et al*, 1998*b*). The programme was also highly cost effective, even within this short time-frame, and so soon after the programme began operating (Mihalopoulos *et al*, 1999). It is not yet known whether the longer term outcomes will be enhanced, and clearly this may also depend upon the quality of care provided over the subsequent period. It is likely that if an initial gap or 'cushion' of improved outcome can be established in the first year, it should be possible to sustain or even widen this, provided that optimal care continues where it is required.

Research issues

Randomised controlled studies would be ideal to definitively answer these questions, however, it has been conceded by even the most rigorous of researchers that this may be difficult to achieve at the programme level in early psychosis for a variety of reasons (McGlashan, 1996). Randomised controlled trials are perhaps more practicable in developing and evaluating the specific building blocks and individual components of intervention programmes. Even here they should follow the development of appropriately conceived and piloted interventions derived from an evaluation of the clinical and personal needs of the patients at particular phases of illness, followed by open trials of treatment. Integration with drug therapies in more complex designs is a feasible and important goal. The ultimate objective is large-scale multi-site randomised trials of well-developed patterns of intervention.

We have made an effort to move in this direction over time since 1992, through a clinical research programme originally funded by the Victorian Health Promotion Foundation. There has been a specific emphasis on the development and evaluation of recovery-oriented psychotherapy (Cognitively Oriented Psychotherapy for Early Psychosis, COPE; Jackson *et al*, 1996, 1998), as well as other forms of psychological intervention (Edwards *et al*, 1998; McGorry *et al*, 1998a,b). The programme has tried to provide a venue for the ongoing development of psychotherapeutic interventions that are pragmatic and tailored to the particular needs of the young person recovering from psychosis.

Development and evaluation of cognitively oriented psychotherapeutic interventions

From 1992 to 1998, our group employed a 'task force' approach to develop two novel and related psychotherapeutic strategies for the recovery phase of first-episode psychosis. The first, COPE, was intended to promote adaptation to the experience of the illness and its treatment and to identify and reduce secondary morbidity. This was designed as a brief or focal psychotherapy with a key focus upon the process of recovery from the first episode, hence it was time-limited and aimed to avoid tackling long-term or premorbid issues to a great extent. These could be focused on later . The second intervention, the Systematic Treatment of Persistent Positive Symptoms (STOPP), was developed as an adjunct to COPE, and intended for the small minority of people (approximately 10%) whose positive psychotic symptoms, mainly hallucinations and delusions, failed to remit with low-dose antipsychosis medication. COPE was based on a range of theoretical ideas and traditions, particularly constructivism and cognitive theory (Jackson *et al*, 1996). The therapy was a blend of crisis intervention, psychoeducation and cognitive therapy offered within a brief psychotherapy model. The goals were to promote engagement with treatment generally without a negative impact on self-esteem and identity, to promote psychological recovery from the upheaval of the acute phase of illness and to tackle the ubiquitous comorbidity seen in first-episode psychosis using modified cognitive–behavioural therapy (CBT) strategies. STOPP drew on the ideas and expertise of several groups working in the UK, Scandinavia and the USA, who were working with older patients with long-standing persistent symptoms. Hence, modifications were required for STOPP and expectations were correspondingly higher because of the relative recency of the treatment resistance (Edwards *et al*, 1998).

The initial results of a series of projects evaluating the impact of COPE will be briefly summarised in the following paragraphs. (A more complete account is available in Jackson *et al* (1998).) A fully randomised controlled trial of COPE versus EPPIC case management alone has also recently been completed, and the results will be published in due course. Similarly, a more complex randomised controlled trial, known as the 'Recovery Plus' study, which examines the relative influence of clozapine and STOPP individually and combined in early treatment resistance, is currently in progress (Edwards *et al*, 1998). A large-scale UK study, known as the SOCRATES trial, that focuses in similar ways on the role of CBT in recent-onset psychosis was completed in 1999.

In a non-randomised study, 80 patients aged between 16 and 30 years, recovering from their first psychotic episode and meeting other predefined criteria, were recruited and formed three groups. The first group (n=44) were offered and accepted COPE therapy (mean number of sessions=18.00, s.d.=0.27); the second group were those who refused COPE but were provided with access to all other EPPIC services (n=19); and the third group were those who were neither offered COPE nor other EPPIC services, but were essentially treated during the recovery phase in other services, after a brief initial period of acute treatment with EPPIC. These cases were from or rapidly moved to other catchment areas and hence could not be offered COPE. For the purposes of this study they acted as a purer control group than the refusers who received in an informal way some of the therapeutic interventions structured within the COPE programme. The study was, however, non-randomised, and the COPE acceptors may clearly have had some characteristics, for example, more dysphoria, more psychological-mindedness or more capacity to form a relationship, which increased the likelihood of accepting COPE and having a better outcome. We were interested in: defining the acceptability and optimal duration and intensity of COPE; when was the best time to offer it and how long to keep it on offer; to specify its content and technical aspects; and to determine its initial efficacy, both on proximal (intrapsychic and cognitive) and distal (outcome) variables.

Assessments were carried out prior to being offered COPE and after 12 months using a range of diagnostic, symptomatic, cognitive and functional measures. These included a measure of integration/sealing over (McGlashan *et al*, 1977), a measure of explanatory models (Kleinman, 1980) for the current problem, the Brief Psychiatric Rating Scale (BPRS; Overall & Gorham, 1962), the Scale for the Assessment of Negative Symptoms (SANS; Andreason, 1984), the revised Symptom

Check-List–90 (SCL–90–R; Derogatis, 1983), the short-form Beck Depression Inventory (BDI–SF) (Beck & Beck, 1972) and the Quality of Life Scale (Heinrichs *et al*, 1984). The results provided significant encouragement for the further development of COPE. The therapy was acceptable to a substantial proportion of patients, although the length of therapy that seemed necessary varied, and some patients who initially refused or were ineligible would later have accepted the offer and may have benefited from such a second chance option. The full outcome data are reported in Jackson *et al* (1998). In summary, COPE was clearly superior on most measures of outcome when the COPE group was compared with the control group who received no EPPIC treatment and had not had an opportunity to accept or refuse COPE. These advantages were of at least moderate effect size, and extended to all areas: cognitive changes in level of integration, acceptance of the illness and symptoms. Most importantly negative symptoms responded well, as did measures of psychosocial functioning, which were particularly good in the COPE group. This improvement may have been at the expense of a lesser degree of resolution of mild levels of dysphoria in the COPE group, however, this was not at clinically important levels. The advantages for COPE when compared with the refusers who were also treated within EPPIC were less clear cut, and only the cognitive variable of integration was significantly better. However, trends for other variables were in a direction favourable to COPE. It may be that the refusers were different in important ways that did not favour COPE, for example, COPE acceptors were more dysphoric at baseline and remained relatively more so. Also, some of the elements of the COPE intervention may have been delivered to the COPE refusers via their EPPIC case managers in this relatively flexible and developmental study. Overall, the study was a valuable and encouraging learning experience that provided a solid foundation for a second-generation study, which has been recently completed.

Future clinical and research challenges

There is a further challenge ahead, however, namely to develop a more complete range of psychotherapeutic options in an environment that supports and values a psychological perspective in conjunction with a biological one. The soil remains fertile and receptive for a second period of growth that can build upon the experience of our first generation of work. The existence of the EPPIC state-wide team (a training and consultation unit) within the programme, as well as educational programmes, such as the Graduate Diploma in Youth Mental Health, which is offered by distance education through the Centre in conjunction with the University of Melbourne, enables new psychotherapeutic knowledge and skills to be effectively translated and sustained in other parts of the service system.

Towards a modern approach: timing, depth, breadth and peaceful co-existence

"If there is any good reason for a policy of delay, it must reside in our lack of certainty as to what is to be done." Sullivan (1927)

"Interpersonal factors seem to be the effective elements in the psychiatry of schizophrenia." Sullivan (1927)

"Now that the biological revolution is in ascendancy, we need to step back and reflect on what a biologically based distortion of the human spirit means for the person who suffers it, and for the intervention required. In our rush to discover the basic biology of schizophrenia, we have ignored the human experience of schizophrenia ... I would suggest that we now need to rebuild a biologically sound, problem-specific approach to psychotherapy with schizophrenia that is grounded in the human experience of the disorder." (Coursey, 1989)

Case for a biopsychosocial model

As Coursey (1989) recognised, the recent wave of biological determinism has served patients as poorly as psychological reductionism. He stressed appropriately that the current revival of interest in psychotherapeutic interventions must be soundly based on a biopsychosocial model of disorder. This revival is gaining momentum, yet it is based purely on the evidence accumulating from a series of randomised controlled trials of cognitive and related forms of psychotherapy in psychosis (e.g. Kuipers *et al*, 1997, 1998; Hogarty *et al*, 1997*a,b*). There is a need to identify the evidence and the key gaps in relation to other approaches to psychotherapy.

The theory that informs the approach described below regards psychotic disorders as a collection of illnesses in which there is a biological disturbance of central nervous system function resulting in a variable mix of symptomatology, cognitive–emotional disorder and disrupted psychosocial functioning. This biological disturbance derives from an interaction of biological vulnerability, which may arise on genetic or environmental grounds such as perinatal birth complications, with environmental and psychological factors. Biological vulnerability alone, however, is usually not sufficient for the expression of the disorder (Miller, 1997). One or a series of additional contributory causes are required for onset, and a similar model influences the course of illness. It is also likely (indeed assumed by many psychological theorists, such as Sullivan (1962), Fromm-Reichmann (1948), Arieti (1974) and Perris (1989)), that psychological and social influences can contribute to the level of vulnerability. Good candidates are childhood trauma and other consequences of adverse family and social conditions. Tienari *et al* (1994) give convincing evidence for the importance of family functioning of both parents in determining the extent of the expression of genetic vulnerability.

In summary, a psychosomatic approach to this group of central nervous system disorders based on the general biopsychosocial model for disorders of all kinds (Engel, 1980) seems appropriate, and such a model was originally pioneered by Arieti (1974) (see also Margison & Mace, 1997). This allows for a revival and realignment of psychological interventions as powerful components in the treatment of patients with psychosis particularly so given that the biological disturbance affects the central nervous system and subjective experience in a fundamental and usually pervasive way. The effect on the person and their environment is often profound.

"None of the findings of biological research attenuates the impact of one irreducible fact – schizophrenia is an illness that happens to a person with a unique psychological makeup." Gabbard (1994)

"... dynamically informed therapeutic relationships can fundamentally improve the quality of life of schizophrenic patients. In a study of fully recovered schizophrenic patients (Rund, 1990), 80% had been in long-term psychotherapy and had attached great importance to it. Even when full recovery is not achieved, the therapeutic relationship may be of extraordinary value in the patient's overall adaptation to life." Gabbard (1994)

"The schizophrenic patient's accessibility to all other forms of therapeutic intervention is greatly enhanced by the judicious use of neuroleptics ... For the patient whose positive symptoms remit as a result of antipsychotic medication, treatment has just begun." Gabbard (1994)

Case for an optimal range of psychotherapeutic approaches

Psychological interventions can be:

(a) based on clinically testable theories in individuals and groups of patients;
(b) highly compatible with biological models of vulnerability and disorder;

(c) pragmatic in terms of length and depth of intervention;
(d) offered as part of a multi-modal treatment approach;
(e) within the general psychotherapeutic approach, there can be a range of interventions specific to the individual patient.

All of these have in common with each other, and with many other forms of psychological treatment, an optimistic and humane approach to the patient and their disorder. The foundation for all improvement and progress is a healthy and stable relationship with the patient, which is actively nurtured. An understanding of each individual as a unique person with idiosyncratic sets of schemas and constructions of the world is the next building block, and this is combined with a knowledge of similar patterns in others with these disorders. Psychotic disorders and those who experience them are diverse and heterogeneous, hence the strategy of developing an individual formulation for each patient and using this as the basis for psychotherapeutic work is a valuable principle (Fowler *et al*, 1995). This differentiates the therapeutic method from superficial forms of CBT. The acknowledgement of an internal world, some aspects of which are outside awareness, is another key feature that adds depth to a more restricted or formulaic cognitive approach and puts it more in harmony with psychodynamic and hybrid approaches (Ryle, 1995).

In developing psychological interventions for the seriously mentally ill, it is an undoubted advantage to incorporate a range of theoretical ideas to broaden and deepen the approach: examples include psychoanalytical theories and techniques, cognitive psychology, constructivism, attribution theory and attachment theory. A corresponding pluralism also allows the psychological approach to coexist with and catalyse biological and social elements within the treatment programme. When used as part of the treatment for complex disorders with multifactorial aetiology, such integrative pluralism is essential (Margison & Mace, 1997), particularly since the needs of individual patients and their personal qualities and resources are so diverse. At the 'coalface' with the patient then, the therapy must remain flexible and pragmatic without being superficial. This is a difficult balancing act. In the real world, many patients are young, immature, not introspective or particularly insightful or necessarily especially intelligent. Their disorders have often further impaired their capacity to reflect and to contain disturbing emotions, as well as, in many cases, their cognitive capacity. If we are serious about developing a blueprint for personal psychotherapy with people with serious mental illness, we need to develop a therapeutic approach that can engage and help a broad spectrum of people, not just a select minority. A staged approach with a series of levels to be mastered, as pioneered by Hogarty and colleagues (Hogarty *et al*, 1997*a,b*), is one solution to this practical problem. This ensures a place both for longer term work and a more psychodynamic dimension to emerge for some patients.

In my opinion, this is the essential issue. The work of Hogarty *et al* shows that psychological intervention must be linked to a hierarchical appreciation of the needs and capacities of the patient. The most urgent, such as finding food, shelter, emotional support and a stable and secure environment, must be dealt with first. Helping the person with these imperatives, even if they are not so urgent or stark, demonstrating a commitment to the person beyond the arcane and (to the therapy-naïve young person) opaque niceties of 'therapeutic neutrality', is critical in developing trust and a workable relationship. This sort of trust is vital if there is to be a chance of overcoming the powerful forces like stigma, denial, temptations to use substances or act out destructively, which undermine the global therapeutic task of recovery. This can be done without risking 'over-involvement' if the therapist is professional and experienced, and has access to supportive supervision if necessary. The capacity for psychodynamic understanding is helpful for all patients; it is even essential for a good proportion, however, much of the traditional mythology regarding technique and timing must be unlearned for working with more complex comorbidities and mixtures of aetiological factors. Ryle (1995, 1997) has shown an impressive ability to blend and modify psychoanalytical and cognitive theory in the service of the humane yet efficient treatment of people with serious and complex disorders. This task could now be extrapolated to the psychotic disorders and would be an undertaking of large scope.

Summary of the general principles of psychotherapeutic approaches

Gabbard (1994) has summarised the principles of technique in the psychotherapy of schizophrenia. Though based upon psychodynamic perspectives, they do not require any particular emphasis on either exploratory or supportive therapy, a distinction he regards as less rigid in psychosis than in other patients. These principles are probably valid for all forms of psychological intervention in psychosis:

(a) the main focus should be on building a relationship;
(b) the therapist must maintain a flexible stance regarding the mode and content of therapy;
(c) for psychotherapy to proceed, therapists and patients must find and maintain an optimal distance;
(d) the therapist must create a holding environment;
(e) the therapist must serve as a 'container' for the patient;
(f) the therapist must serve as an auxiliary ego for the patient;

(g) the therapist must be genuine and open with the patient;
(h) the therapist should postpone interpretation until the thera-
    peutic alliance is solid;
(i) the therapist must maintain respect for the patient's need to be
    ill.

All of these points are consistent with what I have already stated,
however some require clarification; for example, the person with early
psychosis does not really need to be ill. They simply are ill for a period
at least and the pace and extent of their recovery is a constraint on the
scope of the psychotherapy offered. I assume what Gabbard means is
that the direct effects of the illness need to be respected while they
are operating and that reductionism should be avoided, both in theory
and, more especially, in technique.

Margison & Mace (1997) pay tribute to Arieti's contribution in
developing an integrative model of treatment. He distinguished four
aspects of the therapeutic task, which broadly correspond to four
different approaches:

(a) establishing relatedness;
(b) treatment of the overt symptoms (some of which is cognitive–
    behavioural, some psychopharmacological);
(c) understanding and analysis (psychodynamic);
(d) general participation in the patient's life (systemic).

Arieti paved the way for an integration of drug and psychosocial
treatments, and also for an integration of cognitive and dynamic
concepts and techniques. His approach exemplifies pragmatism,
idealism and the integration of traditions (Margison & Mace, 1997).
This is an excellent foundation upon which to build a model of
psychotherapy provision in the real world of modern mental health
services.

Offering a spectrum of psychological interventions

A range of psychotherapeutic interventions will need to be available
to young people with early psychosis and these will need to be
tailored to the stage of illness, range of clinical problems (diagnostic
group, level of comorbidity, other premorbid issues), personal
resources and desire for psychotherapeutic intervention (McGorry
et al, 1998*a*). The concept of stages of complexity of therapy already
mentioned, developed by Hogarty *et al* in their personal therapy
model for schizophrenia, is a useful one, and can be adapted to
develop a layered model with criteria for progression to more
intensive and longer term work.

Three levels of intervention

Level 1

Level 1 comprises the simpler forms of therapy with a supportive and educational focus combined with needs-based case management attending to practical real world problems.

Level 2

Interventions could be available concurrently with Level 1 for some people, or offered later for others when engagement is secure and lifestyles have stabilised. This level would involve a cognitively oriented intervention of relatively short duration aimed at promoting symptomatic recovery and optimal adaptation to the onset of the illness. Identity and developmental issues are a central part of such an intervention and the impact of self-stigmatisation is an important focus (Jackson *et al*, 1996; 1998; Edwards *et al*, 1998; McGorry *et al*, 1998*a*). Early evaluations of this approach, as described above, have proved promising (Jackson *et al*, 1998).

Level 3

Level 3 intervention involves a longer term approach that has the scope to incorporate premorbid issues as well as identity and developmental issues from an increasingly psychodynamic perspective. Dynamic techniques can be introduced progressively, however, a pragmatic and active therapeutic stance is most important, taking account of the developmental stage of the young person and their personal resources. Like Gabbard, we have found that a sound working alliance and high levels of trust, with significant activity and emotional support and encouragement on the part of the therapist, are key elements in a successful psychodynamically informed approach to the patient.

Treatment resistance (Fowler *et al*, 1995; Edwards *et al*, 1998) requires sophistication and intrinsic understanding of the person at multiple levels. This is therefore rated as a Level 3 intervention because of the skill level required and also because of the scope and duration of the intervention.

The spectrum of psychological approaches for individuals, groups and families is summarised in Table 13.1 and linked to approximate phase of illness, as well as therapeutic targets and desired outcomes. In the pre-psychotic phase, a flexible approach will need to be adopted in the absence of extensive research or clinical experience. Again, a range of interventions, flexibly offered, from the simple and brief to the more complex and extended, would seem to be appropriate, given the degree of individual variation in needs and resources (McGorry *et al*, 1998*a*). Measures of outcome can be linked both to clinical foci and phase of illness.

Individual therapy and group therapy can be provided for a variety of subgroups within the early psychosis population. These would include the pre-psychotic or high risk population (Yung *et al*, 1996; 1998), young people with affective psychoses who have some specific educational and coping needs, and other clinically relevant subgroups, such as people with substance abuse problems, especially cannabis, and those identified as at particular risk of early suicide. The clinical foci can be selected and tailored for each patient. For example, all patients will need supportive psychotherapy and some kind of intervention to develop a shared model of the problem or disorder on which to base the therapeutic contact. On the other hand, only some will need or accept more specific help for particular issues such as substance abuse or longer standing premorbid issues. This is where staging of the therapeutic foci and goals can be critical. If the goals of each stage of therapy can be kept in mind and integrated with biological therapies, then appropriate outcome measures can be selected on this basis. Each focus gives rise to a more proximal outcome measure (impact evaluation) such as level of cannabis usage or suicidal ideation. These measures can be seen as intervening variables in relation to global outcome (e.g. knowledge about illness and treatment) and in some cases as an end in themselves (reduction in suicidal ideation). More distal and global outcome measures (outcome evaluation) such as quality of life and psychosocial functioning reflect the influence of longer term interventions as well as the effects of integrated biopsychosocial management. These issues have been discussed elsewhere (e.g. Jackson *et al*, 1998; McGorry *et al*, 1996).

An optimal clinical environment is likely to be one in which a broad range of psychotherapeutic endeavours for young people recovering from a psychotic disorder can be developed, sustained and offered to patients directly, tailored carefully to their needs and according to their personal resources at a particular point in time, and furthermore from which the skills and technical expertise can be exchanged with the wider service system and the various professional audiences.

Conclusion

While there is growing optimism about the prospects for recovery for young people affected by psychosis, it is clear that optimal recovery will not occur or will be made much more difficult to achieve in the

TABLE 13.1
The spectrum of psychological interventions in early psychosis

Phase	Level	Modality
Pre-psychotic	1–3	Psychoeducation Supportive dynamic psychotherapy Cognitive–behavioural therapy Expressive dynamic psychotherapy 'Family work' Family therapy
First-episode psychosis Acute 0–2 months approximately	1	Crisis support and intervention Psychoeducation
Early recovery 2–6 months approximately	1	Needs-based case management Supportive dynamic psychotherapy Psychoeducation 'Family work' education and support Needs-based group interventions
	2	Recovery interventions (cognitive–behavioural)
	2	Cognitively oriented psychotherapy for early psychosis (COPE)
	2	Suicide prevention intervention
	2	Cannabis reduction intervention (Cognitive/educational/motivational)
Late recovery 6–24 months + (beyond 24 months if indicated)	2	COPE
	2	Supportive dynamic psychotherapy
	2	Relapse prevention (+psychoedu-cation+compliance therapy; see Chapter 3)
	3	STOPP (Systematic Treatment of Persistent Positive Symptoms) for treatment resistance
	3	Expressive dynamic psychotherapy especially for premorbid and comorbid issues
	2–3	Intensive support and education for families with treatment-resistant or frequently relapsing relative
	2–3	Vocational, relationship and psycho-therapeutic group interventions

TABLE 13.1
(continued)

Focus	Therapeutic goals
Individual	Reduction in symptoms and disability generally
Individual	Reduction in risk of psychosis
Individual	Improved quality of life
Individual	
Family	Improvement in family functioning
Family	
Individual and family	Reduced emotional distress
	Improved knowledge and understanding of psychotic illness
	Adaptive coping strategies
	Return to normal functioning
	Reduced maladaptive coping strategies
Individual	Optimal adaptation to onset of psychotic disorder and its
Individual	implications
Individual	Reduction of emotional distress
Family	Optimal family adjustment and minimal emotional distress in family members
Group	Reintegration, relationships, knowledge, leisure
Group	Vocational rehabilitation. Interpersonal skills
Individual	Good knowledge of illness-related issues,
	Good adaptation and illness management
	Reduction in comorbid problems
	Optimal psychosocial functioning
Individual (high risk for suicide)	Reduction in suicidal ideation, behaviour and risk
Individual (cannabis users)	Reduction of harmful cannabis usage
Individual	Optimal adaptation and functioning minimal emotional distress
Individual	Developmental trajectory largely or completely restored
	Better quality of life
Individual	Good knowledge: a working "explanatory model"
	Minimal relapse rate reasonable – good adherence to prescribed medication
Individual	Reduction in persistent positive symptoms
	Reduced emotional distress
	Improved psychosocial functioning and quality of life
Individual	Improvements in psychological well-being, resolution of specific premorbid and developmental problems, enhancement of developmental trajectory, reduced comorbidity
	Improved self-esteem and completion of key developmental tasks of adolescence/young adult life
	Individual growth. Better quality of life
Family	Reduction of distress and impact on family
	Better coping responses from family members
	Family growth and improved quality of life
Group	Vocational progress and positive outcomes. Improved psychosocial functioning. Better peer and family relationships

absence of skilled psychotherapeutic support and intervention. It is equally clear that the resources to create, disseminate and mandate this component of treatment have not yet been mobilised in a sufficiently substantial way to fully meet the challenge. To appreciate this we merely need to reflect on the huge research and development resources allocated in support of the second generation of antipsychosis medications, an investment that has clearly benefited patients greatly. While not being critical of this investment, we do need to obtain more substantial funding support for the range of activities involved in developing and implementing new treatments, and modifying and field testing older ones. There is a sense, however (Johannessen, personal communication, 1998), that the synergies that exist between the growing early psychosis movement and the re-emergent field of psychological interventions in psychosis, if harnessed effectively, could help to overcome some of the obstacles. This idea has influenced the arguments advanced in this chapter. Both areas are characterised by a holistic and humanistic approach to the patient who is respected, as Sullivan originally emphasised, as first and foremost a human being with unique potential. In other words, whatever the symptoms and altered subjective experience and behaviour, the patient is more like us than different, and has similar needs, aspirations and dreams. This view is completely at odds with the alienist and alienating models of Jaspers and Kraepelin, which emphasised the differences between people with psychosis and others, and reinforced and perpetuated corrosive stigma for patients, relatives and those who worked with them (McGorry, 1995). The latter view was congruent with the design of mental health services at the end of the 19th century, when virtually no effective treatments were available, and the response was essentially one of social policy. It sits very poorly with the way reformed mental health services are being provided, at last 'mainstreamed' with other health services and integrated within the community, at the end of the 20th century. The modern view also supports a preventive and optimistic stance to the prospects of the patient for recovery and a good quality of life, something the pharmaceutical industry too is beginning to champion for more complex reasons. To maximise the benefit from the advances in psychopharmacology, the reforms in the mode of provision of mental health care, the rise of consumerism and the recognition of the potential of early intervention, we need to recognise the central place of the person and the therapeutic relationship in the treatment process. This in turn means that the place of psychotherapy and psychological treatments should be made absolutely secure. This is not a short-term task, since much of the skill and expertise remains to be created, developed, honed and widely disseminated and applied. There will be significant cultural and subcultural differences in the way this task is approached and completed, and we will all have to be prepared for and celebrate the opportunity to learn from each other. This should not be a case of the blind leading the blind, but one of planned research and development, with a timetable that includes widespread and systematic real world implementation as the final objective. This strategy should be modelled in design, if not scope, on pharmaceutical industry principles. This means substantial intellectual and financial investment in the discovery and development phase of new forms of psychological interventions, followed by open studies to determine the optimal intensity or 'dose', the subgroups for whom the therapy is most helpful, and to discover the common adverse effects. When these issues have been clarified, randomised controlled trials, both single centre and multi-centre, would be the next phase, followed by 'Phase 4' real world effectiveness studies. Finally, a large-scale marketing and implementation strategy is essential, so that treatments of proven effectiveness are actually taken up and properly used at the coalface. Psychosocial treatments have the capacity to add substantial quanta of improvements in symptoms, outcome and quality of life. Since there is not the same profitability factor as with pharmaceutical products, the financing of the development and implementation phases for psychosocial interventions is more problematic. Who will pay for and drive these processes? A coalition of forces could be mobilised, since the ultimate outcomes will not only be beneficial in human terms, but there will be commercial and societal benefits as well, since the synergy with drug therapies and early intervention is likely to prove cost effective (Mihalopoulos *et al*, 1999). Governments and societies may come to realise this. If this massive task can be effectively tackled, we will also have taken a critical step to create a more balanced therapeutic approach and a more humane and effective recovery environment for our patients and their families.

References

ANDREASON, N. C. (1984) *Scale for the Assessment of Negative Symptoms (SANS)*. Iowa: University of Iowa.
ANDREWS, G. (1997) Managing scarcity: a worked example using burden and efficacy. *Australasian Psychiatry*, **5**, 225–227.
ALANEN, Y. O., UGELSTAD, E., ARMELIUS, B. A., ET AL (1994) *Early Treatment for Schizophrenic Patients. Scandinavian Therapeutic Approaches*. Oslo: Scandinavian University Press.
ARIETI, S. (1974) *Interpretation of Schizophrenia*. New York: Basic Books.
AUSTRALIAN HEALTH MINISTERS (1998) *Second National Mental Health Plan*. Canberra: Mental Health Branch, Commonwealth Department of Health and Family Services.
BARRETT, R. (1996) *The Psychiatric Team and the Social Definition of Schizophrenia: an Anthropological Study of Person and Illness*. Cambridge: Cambridge University Press.

BECK, A. T. & BECK, R. W. (1972) Screening depressed patients in family practice: a rapid technique. *Postgraduate Medicine*, **52**, 81–85.

BIRCHWOOD, M. J. & MACMILLAN, F. (1993) Early intervention in schizophrenia. *Australian and New Zealand Journal of Psychiatry*, **27**, 374–378.

———, MCGORRY, P. & JACKSON, H. (1997) Early intervention in schizophrenia. *British Journal of Psychiatry*, **170**, 2–5.

COURSEY, R. D. (1989) Psychotherapy with persons suffering from schizophrenia: the need for a new agenda. *Schizophrenia Bulletin*, **15**, 349–353.

DAVIDSON, L., LAMBERT, S. & MCGLASHAN, T. H. (1998) Psychotherapeutic and cognitive-behavioural treatments for schizophrenia: developing a disorder-specific form of psychotherapy for persons with psychosis. In *Cognitive Psychotherapy of Psychotic and Personality Disorders: Handbook of Theory and Practice* (eds C. Perris & P. D. McGorry), pp. 1–20. Chichester: John Wiley and Sons.

DEROGATIS, L. R. (1983) *SCL–90–R; Administration, Scoring and Procedures Manual – II for the Revised Version*. Towson, MD: Clinical Psychometric Research.

EDWARDS, J., FRANCEY, S. M., MCGORRY, P. D., *ET AL* (1994) Early psychosis prevention and intervention: evolution of a comprehensive community-based specialised service. *Behaviour Change*, **11**, 223–233.

———, MAUDE. D., MCGORRY, P. D., *ET AL* (1998) Prolonged recovery in first-episode psychosis. *British Journal of Psychiatry*, **172** (suppl. 33), 107–116.

——— & MCGORRY, P. D. (1998) Early intervention in psychotic disorders: a critical step in the prevention of psychological morbidity. In *Cognitive Psychotherapy of Psychotic and Personality Disorders: Handbook of Theory and Practice* (eds C. Perris & P. D. McGorry), pp. 167–196. Chichester: John Wiley.

———, COCKS, J. & BOTT, J. (2000) Preventive case management in first-episode psychosis. In *Recognition and Management of Early Psychosis: a Preventive Approach* (eds P. D. McGorry & H. J. Jackson), pp. 308–337. New York: Cambridge University Press.

ENGEL, G. L. (1980) The clinical application of the biopsychosocial model. *American Journal of Psychiatry*, **137**, 535–544.

FEDERN, P. (1952) *Ego Psychology and the Psychoses*. New York: Basic Books.

FOWLER, D., GARETY, P. & KUIPERS, E . (1995) *Cognitive Behaviour Therapy for Psychosis. Theory and Practice*. Chichester: John Wiley.

FROMM-REICHMANN, F. (1948) Notes on the development of treatment of schizophrenia by psychoanalytic psychotherapy. *Psychiatry*, **11**, 263–273.

GABBARD, G. O. (1994) *Psychodynamic Psychiatry in Clinical Practice*. Washington, DC: American Psychiatric Press.

GILBERT, S. & UGELSTAD, E. (1994) Patients' own contributions to long-term supportive psychotherapy in psychotic disorders. *British Journal of Psychiatry*, **164** (suppl. 23), 84–88.

GUNDERSON, J. G., FRANK, A. F., KATZ, H. M., *ET AL* (1984) Effects of psychotherapy in schizophrenia: II Comparative outcome of two forms of treatment. *Schizophrenia Bulletin*, **10**, 564–598.

HAMBRECHT, M. & HAEFNER, H. (1996) Substance abuse and the onset of schizophrenia. *Biological Psychiatry*, **39**, 1–9.

HEINRICHS, D. W., HANLON, T. E. & CARPENTER, W. T. (1984) The Quality of Life Scale: an instrument for rating the schizophrenic deficit syndrome. *Schizophrenia Bulletin*, **10**, 338–398.

HOGARTY, G. E., KORNBLITH, S. J., GREENWALD, D., *ET AL* (1997*a*) Three-year trials of personal therapy among schizophrenic patients living with or independent of family, I: Description of study and effects on relapse rates. *American Journal of Psychiatry*, **154**, 1504–1513.

———, GREENWALD, D., ULRICH, R. F., *ET AL* (1997*b*) Three-year trials of personal therapy among schizophrenic patients living with or independent of family, II: Effects on adjustment of patients. *American Journal of Psychiatry*, **154**, 1514–1524.

Psychotherapy and early psychosis 291

JACKSON, H., McGORRY, P. D., EDWARDS, J., ET AL (1996) Cognitively-oriented psychotherapy for early psychosis – COPE. In Early Intervention and Prevention in Mental Health (eds P. J. Cotton & H. J. Jackson), pp. 131–154. Melbourne: Australian Psychological Society.

——, McGORRY, P. D., EDWARDS, J., ET AL (1998) Cognitively-oriented psychotherapy for early psychosis (COPE). Preliminary results. British Journal of Psychiatry, 172 (suppl. 33), 93–100.

KLEINMAN, A. (1980) Patients and Healers in the the Context of Culture. An Exploration of the Borderline between Anthropology, Medicine and Psychiatry. Berkley, CA: University of California Press.

KUIPERS, E., GARETY, P., FOWLER, D., ET AL (1997) London–East Anglia randomised controlled trial of cognitive–behavioural therapy for psychosis: I. Effects of the treatment phase. British Journal of Psychiatry, 171, 319–327.

——, FOWLER, D., GARETY, P., ET AL (1998) London–East Anglia randomised controlled trial of cognitive–behavioural therapy for psychosis: III. Follow-up and economic evaluation at 18 months. British Journal of Psychiatry, 173, 61-68.

LOEBEL, A. D., LIEBERMAN, J. A., ALVIR, J. M. J., ET AL (1992) Duration of psychosis and outcome in first episode schizophrenia. American Journal of Psychiatry, 149, 1183–1188.

MARGISON, F. & MACE, C. (1997) Psychotherapy of Psychosis. London: Gaskell.

MAY, P. R. A. (1968) Treatment of Schizophrenia: a Comparative Study of Five Treatment Methods. New York: Science House.

McGLASHAN, T. H. (1996) Early detection and intervention in schizophrenia: Research. Schizophrenia Bulletin, 22, 327–345.

——, WADESON, H. S., CARPENTER, W. T., ET AL (1977) Art and recovery style from psychosis. Journal of Nervous and Mental Disease, 164, 182–190.

—— & JOHANNESSEN, J. O. (1996) Early detection and intervention with schizophrenia: rationale. Schizophrenia Bulletin, 22, 201–222.

McGORRY, P. D. (1992) The concept of recovery and secondary prevention in psychotic disorders. Australian and New Zealand Journal of Psychiatry, 26, 3–17.

—— (1995) Psychoeducation in first-episode psychosis: a therapeutic process. Psychiatry, 58, 313–328.

—— (1996) The Centre for Young People's Mental Health: blending epidemiology and developmental psychiatry. Australasian Psychiatry, 4, 243–247.

—— (1997) THEMHS Debate: Who should be treated? Burden versus health gain. Australasian Psychiatry, 5, 275–276.

—— (1998) Preventive strategies in early psychosis: verging on reality. British Journal of Psychiatry, 172 (suppl. 33), 1–2.

—— & SINGH, B. S. (1995) Schizophrenia: risk and possibility. In Handbook of Studies on Preventive Psychiatry (eds B. Raphael & G. D. Burrows), pp.491–514. Amsterdam: Elsevier.

——, EDWARDS, J., MIHALOPOULOS, C., ET AL (1996) The Early Psychosis Prevention and Intervention Centre (EPPIC): an evolving system of early detection and optimal management. Schizophrenia Bulletin, 22, 305–326.

——, HENRY, L., MAUDE, D., ET AL (1998a) Preventively-orientated psychological interventions in early psychosis. In Cognitive Psychotherapy of Psychotic and Personality Disorders: Handbook of Theory and Practice (eds C. Perris & P. D. McGorry), pp. 213–236. Chichester: John Wiley.

——, HENRY, L. & POWER, P. (1998b) Suicide in early psychosis: Could early intervention work? In Suicide Prevention – The Global Context (eds J. Kosky, H. S. Eshkevan, R. Hassan, et al), pp. 103–110. New York: Plenum.

—— & JACKSON, H. J. (eds) (1999) Recognition and Management of Early Psychosis: a Preventive Approach. New York: Cambridge University Press.

MIHALOPOULOS, C., MCGORRY, P. D. & CARTER, R. C. (1999) Is early intervention in first episode psychosis an economically viable method of improving outcome? *Acta Psychiatrica Scandinavica*, **54**, 1–9.

MILLER, R. (1997) Schizophrenia: a tameable tiger? *New Zealand Medical Journal*, **110**, 283–285.

MRAZEK, P. J. & HAGGERTY, R. J. (eds) (1994) *Reducing Risks for Mental Disorders: Frontiers for Preventive Intervention Research*. Washington, DC: National Academy Press.

MURRAY, C. J. L. & LOPEZ, A. D. (1996) *The Global Burden of Disease*. Boston: Harvard University Press.

NAGEL, D. B. (1991) Psychotherapy of schizophrenia: 1900–1920. In *The Concept of Schizophrenia: Historical Perspectives* (ed J.G. Howells). Washington, DC: American Psychiatric Press.

OVERALL, J. E. & GORHAM, D. R. (1962) The brief psychiatric rating scale. *Psychological Reports* **10**, 799–812.

PERRIS, C. (1989) *Cognitive Therapy with Schizophrenic Patients*. London: Guilford Press.

RUND, B. R. (1990) Fully recovered schizophrenics: a retrospective study of some premorbid and treatment factors. *Psychiatry*, **53**, 127–139.

RUTTER, M. & SMITH, D. J. (eds) (1995) *Psychosocial Disorders in Young People: Time Trends and Their Causes*. Chichester: John Wiley.

RYLE, A. (1995) *Cognitive Analytic Therapy: Developments in Theory and Practice*. Chichester: John Wiley.

—— (1997) *Cognitive Analytic Therapy and Borderline Personality Disorder: the Model and the Method*. Chichester: John Wiley.

SHERGILL, S. S., MURRAY, R. M. & MCGUIRE, P. K. (1998) Auditory hallucinations: a review of psychological treatments. *Schizophrenia Research*, **32**, 137–150.

SINGH, B. S. & MCGORRY, P. D. (1998) The Second National Mental Health Plan: an opportunity to take stock and move forward. *Medical Journal of Australia*, **169**, 435–437.

SULLIVAN, H. S. (1927) The onset of schizophrenia. *American Journal of Psychiatry*, **105**, 135–139.

—— (1931) The modified psychoanalytic treatment of schizophrenia. *American Journal of Psychiatry*, **11**, 519–540.

—— (1962) *Schizophrenia as a Human Process*. New York: Norton.

TIENARI, P., WYNNE, L. C., MORING, J., ET AL (1994) The Finnish adoptive family study of schizophrenia: implications for family research. *British Journal of Psychiatry*, **164** (suppl. 23), 20–26.

UGELSTAD, E. (1979) Possibilities of organizing psychotherapeutically oriented treatment programs for schizophrenia within sectorized psychiatric services. In *Psychotherapy of Schizophrenia: Proceedings of the 6th International Symposium on the Psychotherapy of Schizophrenia* (ed C. Mueller), pp. 221–228. Amsterdam: Excerpta Medica.

WYATT, R. J. (1991) Neuroleptics and the natural course of schizophrenia. *Schizophrenia Bulletin*, **17**, 325–331.

—— (1995) Early intervention for schizophrenia: can the course of the illness be altered? *Biological Psychiatry*, **38**, 1–3.

YUNG, A. R., MCGORRY, P. D., MCFARLANE, C. A., ET AL (1996) Monitoring and care of young people at incipient risk of psychosis. *Schizophrenia Bulletin*, **22**, 283–303.

——, PHILLIPS, L. J., MCGORRY, P. D., ET AL (1998) Prediction of psychosis. A step towards indicated prevention of schizophrenia? *British Journal of Psychiatry*, **172** (suppl. 33), 14–20.

Index

Compiled by NINA BOYD